HOOSIER SPORTS HEROES
An Introduction to Indiana Sports

By
DALE OGDEN
CURATOR OF HISTORY AT THE INDIANA STATE MUSEUM

Contributing Editor
BOB COLLINS
SPORTS EDITOR EMERITUS, *INDIANAPOLIS STAR*

GUILD PRESS OF INDIANA
6000 Sunset Lane
Indianapolis, Indiana 46208

Copyright 1990 by Guild Press of Indiana

Library of Congress Catalogue Card Number 90-084308

ISBN 1-878208-01-2

Book design by Steven D. Armour, Alexander Graphics, Indianapolis

All rights reserved, including the right to reproduce this book or portions thereof in any form whatsoever. Rights reserved for photographs by individual sports agencies supplying them.

How Else Would You Dedicate a Sports Book?

Hi Mom!
We're #1!

And to the Two I Love Above All Others

Kaitlyn Dale and Dotsie Ann

Author's Preface and Acknowledgments

When Terry Witzky and I used to stand under his mother's kitchen exhaust fan smoking Kools and pretending to be Kurt Vonnegut, it was agreed that being an author was about the highest calling to which a human being could aspire. Well, it's far from the Great American Novel. And it wasn't a very romantic experience. But it's a book, Blue. It is a book.

We began this project as a children's volume—a modest project, one hundred twenty pages with lots of photos. The deeper we got into it, though, the more compelling (obsessive?) the material became. Why does this Everyman of a state have such an unparalleled athletic tradition? The answer is . . . I don't know. Anybody who tells you they do know probably has one more Ph.D. than they really need.

The obvious question is, does Indiana truly have an extraordinary sports heritage? Surely all states have their heroic figures. Is this book just an exercise in Hoosier chauvinism? Perhaps. But it seems that a very strong case can be made for Indiana's preeminent athletic position.

The Indianapolis "500" is the largest single-day sporting event in the world. That's not a subjective judgment. It's simply a statistical fact. John Wooden developed the most dominant program in any major sport at the collegiate or professional level in the history of American athletics. (Yankee and/or Celtic fans relax. Neither of your teams ever came near the realm of a four-season, 88-game winning streak).

The University of Notre Dame football program is the most omnipresent athletic program in the world. OK, this assertion is somewhat more argumentative. And yet, what other sports team has its own world-wide broadcasting network? How many Crimson Tide games can you pick up on Guam? Quick, hum a few bars of the Nebraska fight song. How many ex-presidents have starred in the role of a former USC punter? How many coaches have their unlisted numbers on the Almighty's Rolodex?

Hoosier Hysteria—Indiana High School Basketball—has a mythology that is unique in American prep circles. Maybe this is an even more controversial proposition. But when Hollywood recently set out to make a movie—an Academy Award nominated movie—about the mystical properties of interscholastic competition, they didn't call the film "Tar Heels," or "Buckeyes," or "Cowboys." Fifty years from now "Hoosiers" will still be putting lumps in the throats of many a late-night classic movie buff.

Throw in a few names like Kenesaw Mountain Landis, Charley Finley, Don Mattingly, Weeb Ewbank, Bob Griese, Oscar Robertson, Larry Bird, Bob Knight, Doc Counsilman, Jerry Yeagley, Tony Zale, Kid McCoy and Major Taylor—you're talking about more than your average dime-a-dozen superstars here, folks. Not that Indiana can't boast a few score of those, too. Over and over, throughout the course of the past century, Hoosier personalities, teams, and events have been at the forefront of revolutions in American sport.

Why? . . . I don't know. Perhaps our conservative parochial ways have nurtured some obsession to excel. Maybe our small, close-knit communities have provided the communal support necessary to dedicate oneself to athletic achievement. Maybe there's never been much to do around here besides play games. It could be a matter of a simple accident of history. Move Notre Dame five miles to the north and take the auto industry out of 1911 Indianapolis, and maybe this book doesn't exist.

Fortunately, this is not a pseudo-psycho/sociological thesis, so we don't need to worry about the WHY too much. What we have here is an introduction to Hoosier athletic achievement. Not every outstanding athlete or all of the memorable teams are included. Some were simply overlooked. Many others are being filed away for some future "Everything You Ever Wanted to Know." We expect to hear "But you forgot . . ." quite a bit. The author's wife has already introduced him to the phrase.

What you have in your hands, however, is a pretty amazing smorgasboard. We hope these pages will stir many fond memories of the greatness profiled herein.

One of the wonderful things about being a sports fan in Indiana is that not only have we been blessed with so many of the epochal figures in American sports history, we've also been fortunate to have some of the best chroniclers in the business to document the adventures.

Bobby Knight has compared Bob Collins to Will Rogers. Who am I to argue with omniscience? What I do know about Bob Collins first-hand is that he has been a constant source of encouragement for me throughout the project. He has been patient and honest. He taught me a few new words, and I can even use a few of them in print. I look forward to the day when my prose flows as effortlessly as Bob Collins'.

Bob Williams at the IHSAA has been a ready source of info and a constant target for "one more small favor" at the other end of the phone line. The IHSAA is the model to which all other state high school athletic associations aspire. People like Bob Williams are the reason.

If you want something more than an introduction to Hoosier Hysteria, pick up anything with Herb Schwomeyer's name on it. If you can't find it in one of Herb's books, it didn't happen.

To my friends the PR honchos at IU, Purdue and Notre Dame—Chuck Crabb, Jim Vruggink and John Hisler—thanks, guys. I know it's real important for you boys to outdo each other, but in the interest of my future career I'll call this one a dead heat. Thanks also to the sports public relations at the universities: Ball State, Butler, Vincennes and Evansville, UCLA, Michigan, and Louisville. And to the Indians, Colts and Pacers.

I should thank, too, the reference librarians at Central Library for pretending I wasn't getting annoying.

Lastly, but most assuredly not leastly, thanks to Lori Vollnogle and to Nancy Baxter at Guild Press and to Steve Armour at Alexander Typesetting. Thanks to Lori for doing all the real work. Thanks to Steve for things that only Steve could fully appreciate. And thanks to Nancy. Whatever the agonies, your irresistible obsessions are the only reason this book exists.

As this is, after all, my first book, I feel entitled to a few personals. For the incomprehensible blind faith they held in me, I thank my mother and my father, my grandmother, my brother and my sisters.

To Bill and Julie—thank you for putting up with my moodiness these past twelve months. I promise to try to do better.

Jill Hanna, Doc Wellman, Ed Johnson-Ott and Dale Martin: thanks for keeping me alive through times I might not otherwise have survived. Thanks for making the survival the fun it's been.

To Ron Newlin—my best friend. I don't believe the deity is malevolent. I don't think He puts that much effort into it. Our best revenge is to just do it 'till it's over. I'm sure it's the visceral gratification, not the monument . . . or not.

Harper's Weekly, 1867.

Prologue

There's an old debate in Indiana about whether participation in sports and athletics is a useful way for healthy men and boys to spend their time.

In 1867 the city of Lafayette boasted three baseball teams: the "Hoosiers," the "Independents" and an Irish squad called the "Fenians." While all three proudly represented their clubs and their fans on the field, not all citizens of Lafayette were impressed by displays of baseball skill. One anonymous letter writer to the Lafayette newspaper suggested that "if the baseballists need physical exercise they had better turn their attention to sawing wood for the poor."

Since the Hoosiers didn't wish to be thought of as lazy boys, engaged only in silly games, they immediately challenged the Independents, the Fenians and the Lafayette YMCA to a wood-sawing tournament. All money and cut wood produced by the tournament was to be donated to the poor for heating during the frigid days of winter.

Newspaper accounts of the contest report that the result was a complete triumph for the Hoosiers, with the muscular YMCA Christians finishing a strong second. Three hundred dollars was collected from admissions and through the sale of saws, and the four teams combined to cut thirty-six cords of wood—enough logs to cover a football field to a depth of over three feet.

But, as is so often the case, the competition created a great deal of bad feeling. The Fenians protested angrily that the judges were prejudiced against them. The Irishmen had been disqualified after their excited fans rushed onto the field to help carry and stack the cut logs. A riot nearly broke out when fans of the Hoosiers and Christians discovered that the Independents were secretly sawing soft pine instead of hardwoods like hickory and walnut. "Seventy-two blistered hands, thirty-six lame backs and thirty-six pairs of sore legs" were also produced.

The Lafayette wood-sawing contest was reported throughout the country, and many similar competitions helped fill the woodboxes of the poor for the winter of 1867. Baseball fans around the United States began shouting at the opposing team, "You guys are so bad, why don't you go home and saw wood?" Sound familiar?

We can't say whether the Hoosiers' wood sawing victory and all the charity it produced for the poor made it easier for Indianans to "play" at their sports. Maybe baseball and basketball and football, track and field, boxing, auto racing, swimming, bicycle racing, bowling, golf, tennis and all the other sports that have produced great Hoosier athletes would have been accepted as useful ways for young men and women to spend their time. Maybe we would still know the names of Knute Rockne, Bob Griese, Mark Spitz, Oscar Robertson, Wilma Rudolph, John Wooden, Wilbur Shaw, Fuzzy Zoeller, Marvin Johnson and all the rest without that beginning in Lafayette.

Then again . . . maybe we wouldn't.

PART ONE
The Pioneer Period
1862-1919

The National Pastime

It's difficult to pinpoint an exact birthdate for organized sports in Indiana, but April 22, 1862, might be as good a date as any. On that day the Summit City Baseball Club was organized in Fort Wayne. In the years that would follow the American Civil War, baseball provided a much healthier outlet for the aggressively competitive tendencies of Hoosier youth than had cavalry charges and artillery duels. Most Indiana cities, towns and villages had at least one team to carry the community's honor onto the Diamond Battlefield. Baseball was just beginning to become "America's Pastime."

When the war ended in 1865, Summit City reorganized as the Fort Wayne Kekiongas Choral, Debating and Baseball Club. Kekionga is the name of the Miami Indian village that had been on the land upon which the white men built Fort Wayne. The Kekiongas traveled to Chicago, Peoria, Ottumwa, Joliet and other Midwestern cities in search of baseball competition.

They found more than they had bargained for. In 1869 the Kekiongas lost to the Cincinnati Red Legs 86-8 and 41-7. Embarrassed by such terrible play, the Kekiongas offered to pay several players from a failed Baltimore team if those players would join the Hoosier club. Baltimore's star pitcher, Bobby Matthews, was expected to lead the Kekiongas to new glories. Indiana had raided Maryland in search of professional ballplayers 114 years before the Colts moved from Baltimore to Indianapolis.

On Saint Patrick's Day in 1871, the first American baseball league was formed in a smoke-filled, gas-lit cafe on the corner of 13th and Broadway in New York City. The National Association of Professional Baseball Players (NA) charged an entry fee of $10 per team. Each club promised to face every other league member in a five-game series. The team with the best record had the right to fly the "Championship Streamer" over its home field for one year. NA teams included the Philadelphia Athletics, Boston Bostons, Chicago White Stockings, Forest City of Cleveland, Troy Haymakers, Washington Olympics, New York Mutuals, Forest City of Rockford and the Fort Wayne Kekiongas. Other professional baseball teams, like the already famous Cincinnati Red Legs, chose to remain independent squads who would schedule games against any team, including members of the NA.

On May 4, 1871, the first professional baseball

"Take Me Out To The Ball Game"
Words by Jack Norworth
Music by Albert Von Tilzer

Katie Casey was baseball mad,
Had the fever and had it bad
Just to root for the home town crew
Ev'ry sou — Katie blew
On a Saturday, her young beau
Called to see if she'd like to go,
To see a show, but Miss Kate said "No,
I'll tell you what you can do":

Chorus:
Take me out to the ball game,
Take me out with the crowd
Buy me some peanuts and cracker jack
I don't care if I never get back
Let me root, root, root for the home team
If they don't win its a shame
For its one! two! three! strikes you're out
at the old ball game.

Katie Casey saw all the games,
Knew the players by their first names;
Told the umpire he was wrong,
All along—good and strong
When the score was just two to two,
Katie Casey knew what to do
Just to cheer up the boys she knew,
She made the gang sing this song:

Chorus:
Take me out to the ball game, etc.

Albert Von Tilzer was born in Indianapolis in 1878. Albert and his brother Harry wrote the words and/or music to many of the great songs of the "Gay 90s" including: "Put Your Arms Around Me Honey, Hold Me Tight," "I Want A Girl Just Like The Girl That Married Dear Old Dad," "Wait Til The Sun Shines Nellie" and "I'll Be With You In Apple Blossom Time."

league game on record pitted Forest City of Cleveland against Fort Wayne on the Kekiongas' home field. Fort Wayne's Bobby Matthews threw the first pitch. "Balllll One!" barked the umpire. Kekionga shortstop Tom Carey fielded the first double play—unassisted—in inning one. The Cleveland right fielder, a Mr. Allison, reached on the first passed ball, which was alowed by Fort Wayne catcher Jim Lennon. In the second inning Lennon made up for his historic faux pas by scoring the first run on a single by Joe McDermott. The Kekiongas, leading 2-0 and batting in the bottom of the ninth, were awarded the victory when the contest became the first professional league baseball game called on account of rain.

By August the Kekiongas were in severe financial trouble. They were forced to drop out of the National Association with a record of 7-21. Several Fort Wayne players went to play for the Brooklyn Echfords who took the Kekiongas' place in the NA. The Brooklyn Echfords would eventually become the Brooklyn Trolly Dodgers, who are better known today as the Los Angeles Dodgers.

The demise of the Kekiongas signaled the beginning of professional baseball in Indiana, not the end.

By 1875 the National Association collapsed under the weight of the vast superiority of the Boston team combined with the negative influence of professional gamblers. A new reform group was founded in 1876. Today we call that group the National League.

Between 1878 and 1889 an Indianapolis team, sometimes called the "Blues" and sometimes called the "Hoosiers," alternated between playing in the National League and playing in the now forgotten Western League. In four full years in the National League, the Indianapolis team compiled a record of 146 wins and 249 losses against teams from Chicago, Cincinnati, Boston, Milwaukee and other great American cities. Indianapolis' best finish in the league was fifth place.

Finally, in 1902 owner John T. Brush entered the team, which had taken the nickname "Indians," in a new league called the American Association. The A.A. quickly became a "minor league" that trained young players for the "big

Indianapolis' Major League Baseball Team, 1889. Courtesy Baseball Hall of Fame, Cooperstown, New York.

"Kickapoo," "Bubbles" and "Fat Freddie"

If the end of the 19th century and the beginning of the 20th century represent the Pioneer Period in American sports history, that era also marked the vintage years of baseball nicknames. Everybody had a nickname, not boring names like "Bo" or "Woody," but real nicknames.

The most famous book about Indiana pioneers was The Hoosier Schoolmaster, *written by Edward Eggleston in 1871. Vic Aldridge was born in Indian Springs in 1893. He became one of the National League's top pitchers and pitched the Pittsburgh Pirates to two World Series victories over the Washington Senators. Since Vic taught school in the off-season, he was known to Lloyd and Paul Waner and to all his other Pirate teammates as* **Vic "The Hoosier Schoolmaster" Aldridge.**

Eugene and William Hargrave were the two roughest, toughest baseball players to ever come out of New Haven. Playing for the Cubs, Reds, Senators and Tigers during the teens and twenties, the brothers were catchers in an era when protective equipment was little more than a figure of speech. The Hargrave boys had to be tough, for even if they hadn't chosen to play baseball's toughest position, **Eugene "Bubbles" and William "Pinky" Hargrave** *would certainly have been given the hardest of hard times by their opponents for their "monikers" alone.*

The origin of most nicknames is easy to imagine. Fredrick Fitzsimmons of Mishawaka was a great pitcher for the Giants and Dodgers. He won 217 games and pitched in three World Series. Fred was one of baseball's best, but at 235 pounds, what could his fans and teammates call him but **"Fat Freddie" Fitzsimmons?**

Ewell Russell was born in Jackson, Mississippi, only twenty-four years after the end of the Civil War. Between 1913 and 1919 he compiled a 2.35 ERA with the White Sox. Then in 1922 he hit .368 as an outfielder with the Pirates. Ewell won the American Association batting crown when he hit .385 with Indianapolis in 1927. Though he spent the last forty-seven years of his life in Indianapolis, this son of the Rebel South would always be known as **"Reb" Russell** *to his Hoosier fans and friends.*

"Hod" Eller *of Muncie and the Reds must have worked for a bricklayer in his youth.* **"Babe" Adams** *of Tipton was firing a blazing fastball for the Pirates before he turned twenty in 1902.* **Al "The Curveless Wonder" Orth** *from Danville couldn't have weighed 150 pounds when he won twenty-seven games for the Senators.*

The most interesting thing about the era of great baseball nicknames is that most sports fans have no idea where many of those names came from. Use your imagination to come up with the origins of **"Bunions" Zeider,** *the Cub infielder from Auburn;* **"Kickapoo" Summers,** *the Tiger pitcher from Ladoga; or* **"Nemo" Leibold,** *the White Sox pitcher from Butler.*

---

leagues." In the eighty-eight years since that time, the Indianapolis Indians has become one of the oldest and most successful professional sports teams in America.

Indiana did take one more shot at the "Major Leagues" during The Pioneer Period of American sports history. Baseball leagues and baseball teams were only loosely organized in the first years of the 20th century. Teams often shifted from league to league, and players shifted from team to team. Sometimes players changed teams on the basis of which owner was paying the most money that day. Gamblers often paid players to switch teams almost on a moment's notice.

In 1914 a group of wealthy American industrialists, headed by coal baron James Gilmore and the founder of the Sinclair Oil Company, Harry Sinclair, invested a great deal of money in a small minor league called the Federal League. The investors intended to compete with the National League and the recently founded American League by offering the best players in those leagues large sums of money to join the Federal League. One of the cities they chose to represent the new league was Indianapolis.

In 1914 the Indianapolis Federals compiled a record of 88 wins and 65 losses. They then defeated a Chicago team in what is now Wrigley Field for the first Federal League pennant. The

Federal League, however, didn't last very long. Owners from the better known National and American Leagues, which were losing many of their best players, threatened that any player who played for a Federal team would be banned from the National and American Leagues for life. The Federal League was branded an "Outlaw League" that succeeded by stealing players from other teams.

The Indianapolis team moved to Newark, New Jersey, after the 1914 season. The Federal League went into decline and eventually folded in 1919. Indiana would not have a Major League Baseball team again—at least not up to the present year.

By 1900 baseball was the unchallenged "American Pastime." As many as twenty-five Indiana cities had outstanding minor league teams that were often led by fine Hoosier ballplayers who would go on to great careers in the Majors. In 1906, Anderson, Fort Wayne, Marion, and Muncie fielded teams in the Interstate League, while South Bend, Evansville and Terre Haute were key franchises in a strong minor league called the Central League.

In 1883 two Terre Haute barnstorming teams—the "Blues" and the "Awkwards" joined forces to form the "Terre Hautes" baseball club. In '84 the Hautes joined the Northwest League and throughout the remainder of the Pioneer Period the Wabash Valley community played host to some of America's foremost baseball talent.

Though the nicknames changed often, from the Hautes to Hottentots (or 'Tots) to Highlanders and back to 'Tots, and league affiliations fluctuated as well from the Northwestern to the Three-I (Illinois-Iowa-Indiana) to the Central and back to the Three-I, the talent level remained constant.

Three-Fingers Brown graced the Sportsman's Park Field in 1901. Branch Rickey played for Terre Haute in 1903, forty-four years before he hired Jackie Robinson to play second base for the Brooklyn Dodgers. Gabby Street caught for the Tots in 1905 before moving on to the Reds and Senators.

Art Nehf graduated from Rose-Polytechnical College in Terre Haute in 1913 and began his baseball career with the Hottentots the following season. Nehf went on to win 184 Major League games for a variety of National League clubs. Art pitched in the 1921, '22, '23, '24, and '29 World Series, compiling a 4-4 Series' record with a 2.16 ERA. Nehf also holds the distinction of pitching a twenty-one-inning complete game against Pittsburgh (8/1/18), yet coming out on the short end of a 2-0 score.

Terre Haute's love affair with professional baseball began early and would last nearly a century. One of the city's fiercest baseball rivals of the Pioneer Period was Evansville. The barnstorming Evansville Riversides joined the Northwestern League for five games in 1884 before establishing themselves as a consistent league team the following season. The powerful Northwestern League soon evolved into the American League, while Evansville moved on to Central and Three-I League affiliations.

Though the "Pocket City" missed out on its shot at the Big Leagues, plenty of baseball glory days would come during the Golden Age and Modern Era of American sports history.

In addition to historic teams, Indiana produced some of the greatest players of baseball's Pioneer Period. Mordecai Peter Centennial "Three-Fingers" Brown may have been the greatest Hoosier baseball player of his time. He may be one of the greatest baseball players ever, period.

Mordecai Peter Centennial "Three Fingers" Brown. Courtesy Baseball Hall of Fame.

Born and raised in Nyesville, Indiana, near Terre Haute, Brown lost his right forefinger, and much of his thumb and middle finger in a childhood argument with a corn shredder. But Three-Fingers didn't let the disfigurement discourage him. He learned to cradle the ball between the stubs of his thumb and index finger. The spin created from firing the ball from this unique launching pad produced one of the meanest curve balls in the history of professional baseball.

Playing most of his games with the Chicago Cubs, Brown dominated the National League from 1903 through 1916. His 2.06 lifetime earned run average ranks third on the all-time list. In 1906 he was practically impossible to hit, as he gave up little more than one run per game.

Three-Fingers won 239 games in his career (excluding five World Series games). His fifty-eight shut-outs are second best in baseball history. In 1949, Brown was inducted into the Baseball Hall of Fame in Cooperstown, New York.

Perhaps the best thing about Three-Fingers Brown is that not only was he one of baseball's greatest players, he was also one of baseball's finest gentlemen as well. Liked and admired by both players and fans, Three-Fingers Brown is one of Indiana's premier contributions to American sports history.

Another great player from the pioneer days of professional baseball is Amos "The Hoosier Thunderbolt" Rusie. Rusie took his dominating fast ball from Moorseville to the Indianapolis Blues of the old National League in 1889, then on to the New York Giants in 1890. Rusie's "heater" was so overpowering that he is generally credited with being the reason for the decision to move the pitcher's mound from its previous fifty foot location from home plate to sixty feet, six inches.

Though Rusie struck out 1,957 batters, his 1,716 walks rank fourth on the all-time list. At fifty feet away, Rusie was just too dangerous to hit against. There simply wasn't time to get out of the way of his blazing, and often wild, fast ball.

Rusie completed 392 of the 462 Major League games he started and posted 243 victories in his career. "The Hoosier Thunderbolt" was elected to the Baseball Hall of Fame in 1977.

"Big Sam" Thompson of Danville was one more Hoosier who achieved a Hall of Fame career during professional baseball's Pioneer Period. Playing for the Philadelphia and Detroit entries in the National League from 1885 through 1905, Big Sam was the terror of the league. He hit over .300 eight times, and posted a .404 batting average in 1894. A clutch hitter, Thompson drove in 166 runs in 1887 and another 165 in 1894. Thompson's career batting average of .331 still ranks as one of the greatest of all time. Big Sam was inducted into the Hall of Fame at Cooperstown in 1974.

Tipton's Charles Adams hasn't made it into the Hall yet, but with Baseball's Old Timers' Committee taking a hard look, "Babe" still stands a chance. Adams was firing a blazing fast ball while still in his teens. During his nineteen-year career with St. Louis and Pittsburgh, Babe won 194 games. Pitching in an era before relief specialists were common, Adams completed 206 of his

Amos Rusie, the "Hoosier Thunderbolt." Courtesy Baseball Hall of Fame.

"Big Sam" Thompson. Courtesy Baseball Hall of Fame.

starts with 47 shutouts and a career 2.76 ERA. Babe had a 1.11 ERA in 1909 and capped that fabulous season by pitching the Pirates to three World Series victories in the Bucs' downing of Ty Cobb's Tigers.

One home-town ballclub that enjoyed a great deal of success was the Wadena "Plowboys." Led by the Crandall brothers, Karl, Arnold, and Doc, the Plowboys had a habit of pounding lumps on teams from the surrounding communities. After absorbing a 63-14 drubbing, the Kentland nine requested a temporary halt to the rivalry.

The Crandall boys eventually tired of such massacres and moved on to greater glories. Karl had a long career with Indianapolis in the American Association and with the Memphis Chicks in the Southern Association. Arnold was a standout with Buffalo in the International League. Brother James—"Doc" to all who knew him—joined the New York Giants in 1908. One of baseball's first relief pitchers, Doc won 101 games during his eleven-year career and pitched in the 1911, '12 and '13 World Series. He also hit for a career .285 average—a pretty good accomplishment for a pitcher.

Late in his career Doc was pitching in the minors for the Los Angeles Angels of the Pacific Coast League. On April 7, 1918 the wily veteran hurled a perfect game at the Salt Lake City club for eight and two-thirds innings. The masterpiece was ruined when brother Karl stepped to the plate with two outs in the bottom of the ninth and promptly lashed a single to center.

The Crandalls weren't the only players to leave Wadena for the big city. Plowboy Fred "Cy" Williams enjoyed a nineteen-year Major League career. Playing for the Chicago Cubs and Philadelphia Phillies, Cy led the National League in home runs four different seasons during the nineteen teens.

Fisticuffs Figured Formidably

One other sport rivaled baseball's popularity during the Pioneer Period of organized athletics in Indiana. Some referred to it as "pugilism." Some called the sport "the manly art of fisticuffs" or "prizefighting." Poets refer to the competition as the "Sweet Science." You probably know it as "boxing."

Fighting for money has always been a hard and dangerous way to earn a living. For poor American farm boys and recent immigrants, boxing has also long been thought of as a way to escape from poverty. Unfortunately, the history of Indiana boxing is filled with more sad stories than happy endings.

Prizefighters often fought under names they thought made them sound more mysterious or more dangerous. Ernest Price of Frankfort took the name Jack Dillon. In the fight game he was known as "The Giant Killer." In 1912 he won the 175-pound World Light Heavyweight Championship when he knocked out Hugo Kelly in Indianapolis. Dillon himself weighed only 158 pounds at the time. Dillon fought over 240 fights in his fifteen year career, but 127 of them were declared a draw, or were stopped when both fighters became too exhausted to continue.

Though he was a champion and was later elected to the Boxing Hall of Fame, Dillon never became a rich man. He died in 1942 at the age of fifty-one. Whether or not all the terrible blows he took from bigger men during fifteen years of fighting contributed to his early death is a question to be argued.

In 1927 Charles "Bud" Taylor, "The Blond Terror of Terre Haute," defeated Tony Canzoneri for the World's Bantamweight Championship. Unfortunately, if Taylor is remembered at all, it is for the fact that he had earlier killed a fighter by the name of Clever Sencio in the ring. Boxing deaths weren't uncommon in those days, because there were few rules to protect the fighters. Many matches were allowed to continue until one fighter was unable to box. But Sencio was actually Taylor's second victim. Frankie Jerome had met the same end after a particularly brutal beating at Taylor's hands. "The Blond Terror of Terre Haute" retired in 1931 and eventually drifted out to Los Angeles, California. He died an unknown in 1962.

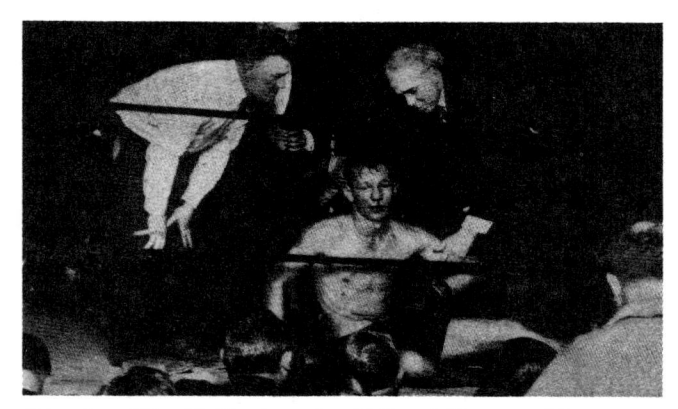

Charles "Bud" Taylor, the "Blond Terror of Terre Haute," in a fight Taylor lost. Taylor claimed he had been low-blowed by Tony Canzoneri. Police Gazette from Indiana State Museum collection.

The Real McCoy had a Brief, Brilliant Moment In the Spotlight

Kid McCoy in his heyday. Bettman Archives.

Norman Selby, also known as "Kid McCoy," enjoyed the most brilliant, and in the end the saddest career of all the early Indiana prizefighters. Born in Moscow, Indiana, in 1870, he was the World Welterweight and World Middleweight Champion at the turn-of-the-century. The Kid was the busiest fighter of his time, and he entered the ring with every stud of the period. Great battles with legendary fighters like Tom Sharkey, Gentleman Jim Corbett and Peter Maher captured the public imagination.

Adopted by newspaper sportswriters and gossip columnists as the original "Real McCoy," the simple Hoosier farmboy plunged into the fast life with a vengeance. Selby married ten times and starred in silent films for great Hollywood directors like Mack Sennett and D.W. Griffith. America's greatest actor of the time, Lionel Barrymore, became Selby's close friend and starred in a fictional movie that was allegedly based on Selby's life. Selby's tavern in New York City was one of the most popular hangouts for showbusiness people from the Broadway theaters.

But Norman Selby was never able to live up to the myth of Kid McCoy. On December 31, 1924, financially bankrupt, physically exhausted and usually drunk, he was sentenced to forty-eight years in San Quentin prison for killing one of his lovers, a Mrs. Thelma Mors.

The "Roaring Twenties" was a decade famous for a string of sensational trials, and the destruction of the legend of Kid McCoy ranked near the top in the excitement it created in the press and with the public.

Paroled from prison in 1932, Selby attempted to live out his life quietly as a gardener for the automobile inventor, Henry Ford, and as a sometime lecturer on the evils of strong drink and wild women. But he was never able to accept the fact that his glory days had ended before most of his life had begun. On April 17, 1940, Kid McCoy—the real Real McCoy—swallowed a bottle of sleeping pills in the Hotel Tuller in Detroit, Michigan. He died alone.

The Kid brought to justice in Los Angeles, 1924. Bettman Archives.

Major Taylor: The Fastest Bicycle Rider In The World

While baseball and boxing dominated the loyalties of American sports fans at the turn of the 20th century, another sport enjoyed brief but immense popularity. Unheard of speeds reaching thirty-five to forty miles per hour could be achieved by racing a new-fangled contraption called a bicycle. And, a young boy from Indianapolis was the fastest bicycle racer of them all.

In 1893 fifteen-year-old Marshall Taylor broke Indianapolis' Capital City Track record for the mile by over seven seconds. It was a great record for the youngster everyone called "Major" Taylor, but many people in Indiana were not proud of him. Many people didn't want him to race at all, for Major Taylor was a black man.

In the United States between 1890 and 1900, 1,217 people were hung, burnt, shot or beaten to death by mobs. Almost all of the victims were black. Some were suspected of terrible acts, but many were killed for such "crimes" as "using offensive language" and "trying to act like a white man." Though nearly all of these "lynchings" occured in the South, Indiana was not without prejudice. Major Taylor's record resulted in many death threats, and the Capital City Track was soon restricted to white riders only.

Unable to compete in Indiana, Taylor moved to Worcester, Massachusetts, in 1896 in search of new records to conquer. Over the next fourteen years, "The Ebony Streak" became one of the greatest athletes in history. He set World Records for seven different distances, was American Champion in 1899 and became World Champion in 1900.

Major Taylor faced bigotry every day. Gangs of white riders tried to wreck him on the track and white officials cheated him. Taylor wasn't allowed on many American tracks, and he often had difficulty finding food and a place to stay in those cities where he was allowed to ride.

Even the few racers who admired Taylor's Christian beliefs and good sportsmanship showed their prejudice. One rider was quoted as saying, "The boys willingly acknowledge that Taylor is the fastest man on the track, and also that he is a 'good fellow,' but on account of his color they cannot bear to see him win. If it were possible to make him white, all the boys would gladly assist in the job."

Major Taylor finally decided to leave America to race elsewhere in the world. In 1901 he toured Europe, where bicycle racing is still extremely popular today. His 42 wins in 57 races against the greatest European champions made him one of the most famous men in Europe. He received fan

Major Taylor at the starting line for his first European race, Berlin, 1901. Indiana State Museum collection.

mail addressed simply, "Major Taylor, Paris France." The kings and queens of Europe came to see him race and waited eagerly for the chance to meet him. He stayed in the finest hotels, ate in the best restaurants, and traveled on the most luxurious ocean liners. A 1902 world tour drew crowds of over 20,000 from Chicago, Illinois to Sydney, Australia. A 1903 tour netted the Champion over $35,000 in winnings—over a quarter million in 1990 dollars.

Major Taylor with his wife Daisy and daughter Sydney in Paris 1907. Indiana State Museum collection.

Unfortunately, the story of Major Taylor does not have a happy ending. He vanished from the public eye nearly as fast as he had appeared. Hounded by prejudiced racing officials, involved in terrible financial investments and physically exhausted by the years of racing, Taylor was the champion of a dying sport. The great racer Barney Oldfield had abandoned his interest in Indianapolis's Newby Oval bike track to invest in an exciting new venture called the Indianapolis Motor Speedway. Taylor faded from view. His 1928 autobiography *The Fastest Bicycle Rider in the World* was a financial disaster. Taylor died in 1932 and was buried in an unmarked pauper's grave in Chicago. Years later, Frank Schwinn of Schwinn Bicycle fame provided a tombstone for the forgotten hero.

But, perhaps the story of Major Taylor's life has not yet ended. In 1983, with bicycle racing again increasing in popularity, Taylor's hometown of Indianapolis built one of America's best race tracks—the Major Taylor Velodrome. In 1988 a fine biography was published on his life, and some of Hollywood's biggest stars were at this writing rumored to be negotiating for the right to star in a movie based on Major Taylor's career. Maybe Hoosiers and all Americans are finally ready to recognize the accomplishments of this fine gentleman and great champion.

Carl Fisher: Father of the "500"

Carl Fisher, automobile mogul and dreamer of the "500" dream. Indy "500" Photos.

Carl G. Fisher of Greensburg was one of America's principal land developers. In 1930 he began work on a remote wilderness swamp in Florida that soon came to be called Miami Beach. The legendary humorist Will Rogers called Fisher, "The man that took Miami Beach away from the alligators and gave it to the Indianians."

But, if Carl Fisher had never gone to Miami, even if he had never heard of Florida, he would still be one of Indiana's most important men. Carl Fisher was the "father" of the Indianapolis "500."

In 1904, Fisher founded the Prest-O-Lite Storage Battery Company in Indianapolis. The fortune he made with this company allowed him to join with A.C. Newby, the owner of the Newby Oval bicycle track, Indianapolis restauranteur Frank Wheeler and James A. Allison in a risky investment called the Indianapolis Motor Speedway. Fisher had done a little auto racing himself, including setting a world record by covering two miles in two minutes, two seconds on a dirt track. His then incredible speed of nearly sixty miles per hour, combined with the fact that countless automobile companies were springing up all over Indiana, convinced Fisher that a testing track in Indianapolis could improve the automobile and draw thousands of fans to exciting races at the same time.

Early auto races at the Speedway were exciting; unfortunately they were also deadly. The first series of five-mile races, which were held on August 19, 1909, were halted after a few contests when the crushed stone and tar track began falling apart. Two drivers, a mechanic and two spectators were killed in the resulting mess.

By Memorial Day in 1911, the track had been paved with 3,200,000 bricks, and Carl Fisher roared down the straightaway in the first Indianapolis "500" pace car, a 1911 Stoddard-Dayton. Hoosier Ray Harroun drove his Indianapolis manufactured, yellow and black Marmon "Wasp" to victory by covering the 500 miles in six hours, forty-two minutes and eight seconds—a breathtaking 74.59 mile per hour average speed.

Starting in twenty-eighth place, Harroun and his single-seater defeated thirty-nine other two-man teams consisting in each case of a driver and a riding mechanic. Since simple breakdowns

GENTLEMEN, START YOUR BALLOONS!

It was a great race. 3,500 fans paid for grandstand seats, while another 40,000 lined the fences and picnicked in the surrounding cornfields. It was June 5, 1909, and the Indianapolis Motor Speedway was open for racing. The spectators were filled with excitement as the daredevils climbed aboard their racers. All awaited with eager anticipation to see which bal-

were common in the early days of auto racing, riding mechanics were nearly always along to repair problems as they occurred. Harroun not only raced without a mechanic, he also designed the "Wasp" himself—complete with several revolutionary innovations like a rear view mirror.

Unfortunately, auto racing safety had not improved dramatically in the two years since the first races at Indy. The headline in the May 31, 1911, Indianapolis Star read: "Smoking Monsters Thrill From Start! Queen of Tragedy Hovers Over Race!" A front page "List of Dead and Injured" included one mechanic killed and seven drivers or mechanics injured. Many casualties occurred when a riding mechanic would jump from a stalled car to repair a breakdown, only to be struck by one of the other race cars. The prospect of spectacular crashes never seemed to hurt ticket sales.

Finishing in a relatively anonymous eleventh place in that first Indianapolis "500" was a twenty-one-year-old daredevil by the name of Edward V. Rickenbacker. Eddie Rickenbacker would drive in four more Indy "500s," racing Duesenbergs, Peugeots and even a kerosene-burning Maxwell designed by Ray Harroun. Rickenbacker's first love, though, was piloting airplanes, and it was in the field of flying that he would eventually make his mark.

When America entered World War I in April of 1917, "Captain Eddie" joined the United States Army Air Corp where he formed the "Hat-in-the-Ring" 94th Aero Squadron. Rickenbacker displayed the same courage and skill in aerial dogfights that he had shown in automobile racing. He downed twenty-one German fighters and five observation dirigibles to become the American "Ace of Aces."

At war's end, Captain Rickenbacker returned to America and his love affair with fast cars. His continued fascination with the speed, danger and excitement of automobile racing hinted that a new era in Indianapolis "500" history was about to begin.

loon would prove the fastest. Which balloon? Well, race car drivers were ready for the Speedway in the spring of '09, but the Speedway wasn't quite ready for race cars. The first contest at the Indianapolis Motor Speedway, home of the world's most famous automobile race, was a balloon race.

"500" Facts

The 3,200,000 bricks that were used to pave the Indianapolis Motor Speedway in 1910 were laid in sixty-three days—an average of nearly 51,000 bricks a day.

In 1912 Indianapolis' **Joe Dawson** swept past "500" legend **Ralph DePalma**'s crippled Mercedes on the 199th lap to win the second Indy "500." DePalma and mechanic Ruppert Jeffkins shoved their vehicle across the finish line to an eleventh place finish. DePalma returned to capture the checkered flag in 1915.

Frenchman **Jules Goux** won the 1913 Indianapolis "500" in spite of the fact that he consumed seven bottles of champagne during the race.

In addition to the Packard and the Rickenbacker, early "500" pace cars included the Indiana-manufactured Duesenberg, Studebaker, Stutz, Premier and Cord.

In 1914 the top four finishers were Frenchmen. **Barney Oldfield**, who finished fifth in an Indianapolis-manufactured Stutz was the highest American finisher.

In 1916 **Dario Resta** won the only Indianapolis "500" scheduled to run only 300 miles. The twenty-one cars in the 1916 field also represented the smallest field in "500" history. All future "500s" would be scheduled for a full 500 miles.

In 1917 and 1918 **Carl Fisher** voluntarily shut down the Speedway due to World War I. For two years, the track was used as a landing field and airplane repair depot by the U.S. Army.

In the first race since war's end, Frenchman **Rene Thomas**, took the 1919 pole position with the first 100MPH qualifying lap in "500" history; 104.78MPH.

Crawfordsville brothers Maurice (1844-1922) and Will (1848-1931) Thompson are considered the "grandfathers" of American sport archery. Better known for his classic work *Alice of Old Vincennes* (1900), Maurice is also the author of *Witchery of Archery* (1879) and several other books on outdoor sports.

In 1878 Will Thompson was elected the first president of the National Archery Association (NAA). Between 1879 and 1908 he was a five-time NAA National Champion. Also recognized for his work *High Tide at Gettysburg* (1898), Will was elected to the US Archery Hall of Fame in 1979.

In the field of literature, the Thompson brothers followed closely in the footsteps of their famous uncle, General Lew Wallace of Crawfordsville. In addition to his Civil War exploits, his governorship of New Mexico Territory and his service as Minister to Turkey, General Wallace is remembered for his authorship of *Ben Hur: A Tale of the Christ*.

Hoosiers aren't used to settling for second best, not even in horse racing. And to be sure they haven't done so in the sport of harness racing. They've turned out some of the greatest names in the sport's history—Adios, Good Time, Star's Pride, Worthy Boy, Rambling Willie. All these were marvels of their time.

No horse, however, in the heyday of harness racing could have measured up to the appealing Dan Patch. Dan Patch? Why, this swift, free legged pacer must go down as not only the finest harness horse in Indiana history, but perhaps the greatest in all of American history. He was so far ahead of his time that sports historians wonder at his feats.

The bay stallion with the tremendous stride averaged 2:02 3/4 for 122 race or exhibition miles on almost every surface imaginable and with all kinds of race equipment. It took thirty-three years for another horse to break his record, and then that record fell to the great contender Billy Direct.

Foaled in 1896 at Oxford, Indiana, out of Zelica and by the noted speedster Joe Patchen, he was owned by Dan A. Messner, who almost put him down when he saw his crooked back leg. Eventually a special training cart and racing sulky were constructed to accommodate the crooked leg, and Patch was on his way.

In 1901 Dan Patch won twelve races under the guidance of Myron McHenry and was sold to M.E. Sturgis for $20,000 at the end of the racing season. In 1902 Marion Willis Savage took a liking to Dan Patch and finally bought him before the season closed—for the then shocking price of $60,000.

Under Savage's loving guidance the great stallion became the most famous and most publicized horse in history, for thirty-three years wearing the crown and being called "World's Fastest Harness Horse." His record 1:55 mile became a byword, even though horse trainers complained Patch had had another horse in front of him to break the wind, and thus obtained unfair advantage when making the record.

Dan liked people and people loved him. His name was added to all kinds of feed, tobacco, equipment, and linaments. He travelled in his own private railroad car and at home had a large paddock enclosed in glass. He was the first horse to pace a mile in two minutes at the famed Red Mile in Lexington, Kentucky, and he continued to break records as he aged. At ten he opened the year with a 1:57 3/4 trip, came back with a 1:58, a 1:56 and then unleased his famed 1:55 circuit.

All this time his beloved owner and trainer Marion Savage was guiding him. And, when Dan Patch died, Savage followed him the next day. Few partnerships in sports have been so enduring or brought so much satisfaction to so many people.

The Great Dan Patch

While boxing, racing and baseball were popular sports in the Pioneer Days of professional athletics in America, not everyone approved of such competitions, sometimes with good reason. One cause was that these early "games" tended to be more than a little violent. Boxing deaths, as we have shown, were not uncommon. Major Taylor lamented that many people who came to view long-distance bicycle races came for the crashes or to witness the agony of the exhausted riders. He expressed his regret that so many bike fans also enjoyed dog fights and prizefighting.

Even baseball had its share of violence. Throwing at a batter's head was an accepted part of pitching. On-field brawls were common. The great Ty Cobb filed his spikes to a razor's edge, so that when he attempted to steal a base the opposing fielder would be afraid to come near him to make a play. Cobb put a few stitches in many a fine infielder.

As is the case today, one-hundred years ago professional sports provided a potential escape from poverty. Irish immigrants, big city slum dwellers, small-town boys and poor farmers could earn a living, if they were willing to live dangerously. The money wasn't really very good, and black men were generally unwelcome, but a young, strong, fast, uneducated, white man could earn his keep, if he was tough enough.

But in this Pioneer Period of American sports history, many of the greatest athletes weren't professionals. Athletic contests were viewed as a part-time hobby for young men and boys—something serious adults outgrew. Testing one's physical skills against others was acceptable, as long as such tests didn't interfere with educations or occupations.

From Olympus to Greencastle: The Beginnings of Modern Track & Field

Track and field events were favored forums for such tests. By 1900 most Indiana colleges and many Hoosier high schools fielded at least part-time track teams. The best of these sportsmen went on to national, and even international, competitions.

One reason that running, jumping and throwing were considered legitimate endeavors was that such competitions were enjoyed by the ancients. It was felt that if the sophisticated Greeks and Romans had found such games acceptable, they must have merit.

In 1896 the world gathered to compete at the capital of the ancient games, Athens, Greece. Located at the very foot of Mount Olympus itself, this first modern Olympics gave hope that such peaceful competitions, conducted at regular intervals, would replace the impulse for military competition. Unfortunately, this proved to be a false hope.

Two of America's top Olympic competitors during the Pioneer Period were Ray C. "Jumping Deak" Ewry of Lafayette and Purdue and James "Deerfoot" Lightbody from Muncie and DePauw. At the Paris Olympics of 1900, Ewry captured the standing high jump, the standing broad jump and the standing hop, step and jump. He repeated the sweep at the 1904 Olympics in St. Louis. Though the standing hop, step and jump was abandoned after the '04 Olympics, Ewry went on to win Gold Medals in the standing high and standing broad jumps at the semi-official Olympics held in Athens in 1906 and at the 1908 London Olympics. As the winner of ten Gold Medals, Ewry is easily the most dominant jumping athlete in Olympic history.

Jumping Deak was also the World Record holder in all three of his events. Even though he was restrained by rules that allowed no running starts, Erwy was able to leap 5'5 1/4" in the standing high jump, 11' 4 7/8" in the standing broad jump and 34' 8 1/2" in the standing hop, step and jump. If those distances don't sound particularly impressive in this age of eight-foot high jumps, twenty-eight foot broad jumps, and fifty-seven foot triple jumps, give it a try yourself. See how high or how far you can jump standing flat-footed. It's safe to say that Jumping Deak Ewry would have been the favorite in any slam-dunk contest.

While Ewry dominated the standing jumps, his Olympic teammate, J.D. Lightbody, controlled the middle-distance races. Lightbody had left DePauw University before graduating, in order to train at the University of Chicago under one of the fathers of American football, Amos Alonzo Stagg. At St. Louis in 1904, Deerfoot won the 800-meters in 1:56, the 1,500-meters in 4:05.4, and the 2,500 meter steeplechase in 7:56.9. He was also a member of the Silver-Medal-winning, four-mile cross-country relay team. Lightbody returned to Olympic competition in 1906 with a Silver Medal in the 800-meters and victory in the 1,500. Lightbody's four Gold and two Silver Medals made him formidable competition for Ewry in the race to be Indiana's premier Pioneer Olympian.

Wabash college football team, the collegiate champions of Indiana, 1886. Back row, Shull, Earle, Stover. Middle row, Magner, Lloyd, Essick, Kieff, Harding, Hughes. Front row, Stockbarger, Martin, and Garrigus. Courtesy Indiana State Library.

Having thus demonstrated their superiority over all foes, Ewry and Lightbody left athletic competition and returned to the serious world of American business. They had, however, set a pace for future Hoosier athletes who would contribute to the great Olympic tradition.

'Boot-the-ball' Was a Part of Every Fall

In the late 19th century playing football, like participating in track and field, was becoming an acceptable method for college men to work off the excess energy of youth. It wasn't exactly football that any of us today would recognize. The main object appeared to be simply kicking a rubber ball about. Some attempt was made to advance the ball by kicking or batting it forward with the hands. Early football must have resembled a combination of soccer and rugby, with a game of back yard "smear 'em" thrown in.

The Hoosier State's first intercollegiate football game took place in Indianapolis in the spring of 1884. Butler University defeated DePauw by the score of four goals to none. In the fall of '84, a group from Wabash College challenged Butler to defend its honor.

Several years after the battle, Butler Captain Henry T. Mann recalled the Wabash team's suggestion that the game be played according to a recent rules' change. It seems that Wabash had become aware of an Eastern innovation—carrying the ball—that expanded the traditional method of advancing the ball by kicking or batting it forward with the hands.

"The Wabash team, through Capt. Martin, proposed that the men should be allowed, when they should wish, to carry the ball in their hands or arms." Main said "In as much as this had been our hard part in the rules to comply with, that is, to so refrain from carrying the ball, we thought we should readily be able to 'get on' to it; and, further, as we had never seen any such playing, we thought it couldn't be any great advantage, even if we couldn't do it. With those thoughts, we agreed to the Wabash proposition."

Wabash went on to defeat Butler, six goals to four. Football had come to Indiana.

In the fall of 1885 most colleges in the state were fielding football clubs. That year, Butler claimed the first unofficial "State Championship" by defeating Hanover. By '86, a group of Eastern graduate students who were residing in Indianapolis, had formed the Indianapolis Athletic Association. This association supervised the creation of the Indiana Intercollegiate Athletic Association which included Hanover, Butler, Wabash, Franklin and Indiana University. Clubs at Purdue and Notre Dame were in the process of forming.

All Indiana Intercollegiate Association games were played in Indianapolis during these early years. The first semi-official Indiana State Championship went to Wabash College, which had defeated Hanover, which in its own turn defeated Butler.

There was no such thing as the National Football League in 1886. Professional football of any kind was still thirty years in the future. Unless they could find an informal club team, even the very best Indiana football players of the time were forced to give up football at the end of their college years and move on to less glamorous professions like medicine, law and business.

THE PURDUE FOOTBALL TEAM OF '92

Reprinted with permission of the Purdue University Libraries, Special Collections, West Lafayette, Indiana.

Football's First Touchdown Pass

While running with the football had become the preferred method for advancing the pigskin as early as the 1880s, throwing the ball was generally considered to be too risky a tactic. The quarterback would often lateral the ball to his halfback, who would run behind a "wedge" of linemen. But no one thought to throw the ball downfield. It was believed holding onto the ball was the object, not putting it up for grabs.

Then, in the fall of 1913, Notre Dame quarterback Gus Dorias took the ball from Irish center Al Feeney and backed up toward his own goal line. The confused defensemen from Army, unable to understand why Dorias seemed to be heading the wrong direction, stopped in their tracks. Meanwhile, Notre Dame end Knute Rockne sprinted forty yards downfield, where Dorias hit him with a perfect spiral for college football's first touchdown pass.

The Irish went on to destroy the Black Knights from West Point 35-13. The stunned Cadets were so impressed they asked Dorias and Rockne to hang around for a few days to teach this revolutionary tactic to their arch rivals. The basic nature of the game of football was thus changed forever.

In 1913 Dorias became the first of over one hundred Notre Dame All-Americans. Rockne became Irish head coach in 1919, and is probably the most famous football coach of all time. After a short pro basketball career, Feeney went into politics. He became the sheriff of Marion County and eventually mayor of Indianapolis.

"Ode to a Football Player"

Monarch of this *fin de siecle*,
   How your breast must fill with pride
When you come upon the "gridiron,"
   Look around on every side.

Low you bow before the plaudits;
   Autumn winds bear to your ears
Yells of wonderful construction
   Mingled with hoarsest cheers.

Thing of Beauty! Joy forever!
   Hair that floats out on the breeze,
Face all covered with a muzzle,
   Enormous bumps upon the knees.

Shoes with spikes that look ferocious,
   Ears both tied up with a rag;
Eyes that glare with wild endeavor,
   Showing nerve that will not flag.

After punts and lovely tackles,
   touchdowns, fumbles, runs and goals,
All is finished and your victory
   Brings delight unto our souls.

Covered then with mud and glory,
   you retire from mortal view;
Be assured, O football player,
   Our best wishes go with you.

J.L.C., in the Butler Collegian, *1894.*

Hoosier Hysteria: A 19th Century Beginning

Of all the sports we've come to refer to as "major" sports, ironically, basketball was the last to take root in Indiana. But once Indianans got a handle on the game, it was only a matter of time before "Hoosier Hysteria" became an affliction that is famous worldwide.

Legend has it that the first basketball contest played outside of Massachusetts was played in Indiana. The game had been invented in 1891 by Dr. James Naismith of the Springfield, Mass. YMCA as a means for keeping football players in shape during the off-season. In 1893 two coffee sacks were hung on either end of the Crawfordsville YMCA calisthenics gymnasium to act as baskets. A group of fellows from the "Y" then staged a pick-up game. After every basket, the ball would be dug out of the sack for a center jump to restart the game. Center jumps after every score would continue until the out of bounds play was adopted in 1937.

In March of 1894 the first scheduled game in Indiana pitted the Crawfordsville YMCA against the Lafayette "Y." Crawfordsville came out the victor, 45-21. As the ball could only be advanced by passing or shooting it, scores of the first games were generally very low. After dribbling the ball was legalized in 1898, most games became much more exciting and basketball's Hoosier popularity skyrocketed. Soon, even tiny rural high schools with barely enough boys to field a team were competing on the hardwood.

"The Cradle of Indiana Basketball"

*While other regions of the state may have passed by west-central Indiana as the hotbed of Hoosier hoops, there can be no debate that this area is where it all began. Schools within thirty miles of Crawfordsville won the first eight State Championships, (Crawfordsville, 1911; Lebanon, 1912, '17 and '18; Wingate, 1913 and '14; Thorntown, 1915 and Lafayette, 1916). The Wingate teams may have been the most popular champions ever. The tiny Montgomery County school had no gym and less than two dozen students. Led by 6'4" All-State center, **Homer Stonebraker**, the "Wingaters" were the state's first repeat champions.*

In an era of 5'10" centers, Stonebraker dominated his era. He later won All-America honors with the Wabash College "Wonder Five" and starred for several of pro basketball's pioneer teams.

In 1911, the first official Indiana Boys Basketball Tournament was held at Indiana University in Bloomington. Twelve teams from around the state were invited based on their season records. Crawfordsville High School became the champion of the two-day tourney when it defeated Lebanon High School 24-17. "Hoosier Hysteria" was tightening its grip on Indiana.

High school basketball provided one of the few, limited outlets for women who wished to participate in Indiana sports at the beginning of the 20th century. The recorded history of women's basketball at this time is minimal at best. Most of the American public felt that women weren't physically suited for athletic activity, and even if it could be argued that they were, it wasn't believed to be proper behavior for a lady, at any rate.

It appears that Indianapolis High School (Shortridge) formed the first Indiana high school girls basketball team in 1898. Games were probably limited to intramurals. It's not suprising that in a state consisting mainly of conservative small-towns and farming communities, a radical idea like females in sports would germinate in Indiana's largest city.

The first recorded Indiana girls basketball game between two schools took place in Indianapolis on December 15, 1900. The final score was Indianapolis High School (Shortridge) 18, Indianapolis Girls Classical School 9.

By 1900 at least the cities of Indianapolis, Wabash and Covington had organized girls intramural teams. Though many Indiana high schools would begin fielding female squads during the 1920s, records of players, teams and games would remain extremely limited for several more decades. Though occassional "State Tournaments" were held, and several schools claimed "State Championships," an officially sanctioned regularly scheduled Indiana high school basketball tournament for girls would not be founded until 1976.

Crawfordsville High School—Hoosier Hysteria's first champs. Back row, Coach D. A. Glascock, Grady Chadwick. Middle row, Carol Stevenson, Orville Taylor, Olio Shaw, Benny Meyers, Newton Hill. Front row, Hugh Miller. Courtesy of Indiana High School Athletic Association.

(original caption typed by photo's owner)

GIRL'S BASKETBALL TEAM OF ATTICA HIGH SCHOOL----1902

The player's costume consisted of very full bloomers coming almost to the shoe tops, blouse waists with a small v shaped opening at the neck, three quarter length sleeves, and were made of heavy woolen material.

THESE COSTUMES WERE CONSIDERED TO BE SO DARING THAT MEN WERE NOT ADMITTED TO THE GAMES.

Attica had no gym at that time and the games were played on the second floor of the city hall. Those not yet initiated into sports looked upon the young women who played basketball with stern disaproval.

Miss Allen was their coach and Miss Petit the business manager. Blanch McConahey (Mrs. Don Minnick) was the captain. Miss Petit (Mrs. Frances Macoughtery) was the German teacher in the school. Through the influence of Miss Allen and Miss Petit the team was organized.

THE TEAM - 1902

Top: Blanch McConahey Minnick - Captain

Back row: Coral Hunter Odle, Christine McConahey Robinson, Nellie Shackleton Robinson, Rae Parnell ; Leah Beasley, Lelia Brant Eckhart.

Front row:'

Jean Rupert Corlett, Bessie Clark Heiner, Sarah Clark Allen, Vera Hay, Bertha Johnson, Ruth Whitelsey.

Courtesy Indiana Basketball Hall of Fame.

Bring on The Celtics

As college basketball, and particularly high school basketball, began to catch on in Indiana, it didn't take very long to figure out that a little money could be made playing the game. In 1912 Indianapolis' Em-Roe Sporting Goods began sponsoring one of America's pioneer professional basketball teams. Like many professional and semi-pro sports teams of the period, the Em-Roes were a "barnstorming" team. Games would be set up with any team that could be scheduled. Spectators were charged a nickel, and the Em-Roe players would split the take after the game.

Between 1912 and 1924, the Em-Roes won over 400 of the 425 games they contested. Victims included the Original Celtics, the Buffalo Germans, the New York Rens, IU, Notre Dame, Purdue, DePauw, various YMCA and high school teams and most of the national club and barnstorming squads of the period.

Players on the Em-Roes changed frequently from season to season and often within a single

The Indianapolis Em-Roes. Indiana State Museum collection.

season. Some legendary names in Indiana sports history put in stints with the Em-Roes. Al Feeney, the center who hiked the ball to Gus Dorias, who threw the first touchdown pass to Knute Rockne, played for the team, as did the great Wingate High School center Homer Stonebraker. Ward "Piggy" Lambert of Crawfordsville played briefly with the Em-Roes before taking the head coaching position with the Purdue Boilermakers. (Lambert won 364 games and eleven Big 10 titles with the Boilers and is a member of the Naismith Basketball Hall of Fame. Lambert was the all-time winningest coach in Big 10 history until Bob Knight surpassed his record with a victory over Northwestern in 1990.)

World War I hampered the Em-Roes' ability to find players and competition, but the great days of the barnstormers would finally come to an end during the 1920s. In the course of this exciting decade, professional teams in baseball, football and basketball would begin forming stable leagues with dependable rules and schedules. Sports was begining to be seen as a legitimate means of earning a living, and the American appetite for athletic competition was growing rapidly. Indiana, like the rest of the country, was about to enter the Golden Age of American Sports.

Homer Stonebraker   Ward "Piggy" Lambert
Indiana State Museum Collection.

PART TWO
The Golden Age
1920-1959

When World War I ended in 1918, Americans longed for a return to the quiet, prosperous days they had enjoyed before the war. The Republicans elected two presidents who promised "A Return to Normalcy." As part of this desire to escape the horrible memories of war, Americans turned out in increasing numbers to view high school, college and professional sports competition. Huge sports arenas like Yankee Stadium, Soldier Field, Michigan Stadium, and Butler Fieldhouse were constructed to accommodate the growing crowds. America was entering the Golden Age of Sports.

Human beings have a natural tendency to remember great events and great people as even more magnificent than they might truly have been. The Golden Age is remembered as a time When Giants Walked the Earth. Legends and myths surround the great players and teams of the era. Babe Ruth pointed to the exact spot where he hit a home run on the next pitch (off Terre Haute's Charlie Root, no less). Red Grange, "The Galloping Ghost" from the University of Illinois, carried an entire opposing football team across the goal line. Heavyweight Champion Jack Dempsey could kill a horse with one punch; Olympic hero Jesse Owens could out-run one. Are these stories exaggerated? Probably. But who cares? What wonderful stories they are.

The Roaring '20s gave way to the tragedy of the Great Depression in the 1930s, which in turn faded into the horrors of World War II. All through these years, great and terrible, the popularity of athletic competition continued to grow. At the end of World War II in 1945, another great desire for a return to better days swept the country. Sports contests provided the perfect escape from the hard days so recently passed.

The years 1920 to 1959 represent the Golden Age of American Sports. Athletic teams and their players became a central focus of American society. Nowhere in the country were greater teams, greater players and greater legends born than in The Great State of Indiana.

The Baseball Czars Rule

As the 1920s began, baseball remained the unquestioned king of the American sports world. The game, however, was also facing the biggest crisis in its history. While Indiana's Major League teams disappeared from the baseball scene, several of the era's greatest players claimed Hoosier roots. The most important man in baseball during this time hailed from Indiana, but he wasn't a ballplayer. He was the first commissioner of Major League Baseball, Kenesaw Mountain Landis.

The story begins in the sordid backrooms and pool halls of the betting world. As had been the case since baseball's earliest days, professional gamblers continued to exert a large influence on the baseball season. In 1919 several top players from the great Chicago White Sox team, including "Shoeless Joe" Jackson, who was the best player in baseball at that time, had been accused of throwing World Series games. The scandal that came to be known as the Black Sox World Series severely shook the confidence of many fans who came to believe that their teams couldn't be trusted. Team owners saw they needed a strong leader who could reestablish honest baseball if the professional game was to survive. They turned to a Hoosier.

Judge Kenesaw Mountain Landis had grown up in Logansport, worked as a reporter for the *Logansport Journal* and had served as clerk of the court in South Bend. Walter Q. Gresham of Lanesville had commanded Landis' father at the Civil War battle of Kennesaw Mountain (for which the young man was named). When Gresham was appointed Secretary of State in the Cleveland Administration, he chose the younger Landis as his personal secretary. Landis' blunt manner allegedly irritated the President and shocked his dignified colleagues. In 1905 Teddy Roosevelt appointed Kenesaw Federal Judge for the Northern Illinois District. In this position Landis levied the largest legal fine to that time, penalizing Standard Oil of Indiana $29,240,000. Any man tough enough to stare down John D. Rockefeller was tough enough for a few gamblers. Judge Landis was just the man baseball owners were looking for.

As a federal judge Landis was earning about $5,200 a year. The owners offered him $50,000 a year to serve as the first Commissioner of Baseball. Further, they agreed to waive all legal rights and be bound to any decision he made regarding the rules, regulations and practices of professional baseball.

As his first act, Judge Landis expelled for life most of the players suspected in the Black Sox scandal even though they had been acquitted by a Chicago jury. Included were several players who were probably innocent, or at worst, foolish. Landis decreed that any players implicated in any future gambling scandals would also be suspended for life. This ruling affects baseball even

Judge Kenesaw Mountain Landis preparing to throw out the first ball of the 1930 Major League Season. Courtesy Baseball Hall of Fame.

today; Pete Rose's suspension and the 1990 ruling on George Steinbrenner, for example, are based on Judge Landis' decree. After the Black Sox players were banned, the influence of gamblers on baseball declined dramatically.

From 1920 until 1944, Judge Landis ruled baseball with an iron hand. He has been called the only successful dictator in American history. A strong-willed man given to shouting obsenities and chewing tobacco, he was feared and respected by owners, players and fans alike.

Over the years many came to admire him greatly. Others held a less favorable opinion. Future commissioner Ford Frick described Landis as "intolerant of opposition, suspicious of reform and skeptical of compromise. He ruled the game of baseball as if it were a courtroom and the players and officials were culprits awaiting sentence for their misdoing."

In any event, Judge Landis changed baseball forever. In addition to attacking gambling, he banned the formation of "outlaw leagues" and oversaw the growth and stability of the National and American Leagues. In 1938 and again in 1940 Judge Landis struck down the common practice of stockpiling players on minor league teams when he voided a total of 163 players' contracts. For a quarter of a century he ruled on all baseball questions, great and small. He even decreed that it was unsportsmanlike conduct for fans to pelt umpires with pop bottles.

Judge Kenesaw Mountain Landis was the "father" of modern professional baseball, and Judge Kenesaw Mountain Landis was a Hoosier.

Though Judge Landis was unquestionably the most influential Hoosier executive in professional baseball, he was not alone in his efforts. Two other Hoosiers helped solidify the game as the National Pastime during the Golden Age of Sports.

Ford C. Frick of Wawaka graduated from DePauw University in 1915. After a brief stint as an English professor at Colorado College, Frick embarked on a long and distinguished career as a journalist. Newspapers he worked for included the prestigious *Rocky Mountain News* and the *New York Journal*. While at the *Journal*, he became president of the influential New York Chapter of the Baseball Writers of America.

In 1934 Major League owners elected Frick president of the National League. He would hold that position until 1951. For most of that period,

---

"Eight Men Out"

Oakland City Hall of Famer Eddie Rousch. Courtesy Baseball Hall of Fame.

The Black Sox of Orion Picture's Eight Men Out. Courtesy Orion Pictures.

In addition to **Kenesaw Mountain Landis**, Indiana exerted other important influences on the Black Sox story.

Muncie's **"Hod" Eller** pitched the Reds to a victory in game five of the Series, shutting out the Sox 5-0 on three hits. Eller also won the eighth and deciding game in the nine game Series, 10-5. It was never determined which, if any, games were actually fixed.

"Nemo" Leibold from Butler was an outfielder for the Sox. He was not implicated in the scandal. Leibold played for several more years and participated in the 1925 Series with the Washington Senators.

The best Indiana player to play in the Black Sox Series was Oakland City's **Eddie Roush**. A great outfielder, Roush had three hits and four RBIs in the deciding eighth game. Eddie compiled a career .323 batting average playing for the Reds, Indianapolis Federals and other teams between 1913 and 1931. He was the top National League batter in 1917 and 1919, and he hit .352 in 1922. Though Roush was elected to the Baseball Hall of Fame in 1962, he complained bitterly until his death that the '19 Series had not been fixed. He maintained that his Reds had simply been the better team.

In 1987 Hollywood produced a major motion picture on the Black Sox scandal called "Eight Men Out." Most of the game film was shot in Bush Stadium, home to the Indianapolis Indians. The courtroom scenes were filmed in the old Federal Building in downtown Indianapolis. Most of the "extras" in the ballpark and courtroom scenes were average citizens from throughout central Indiana.

Frick was responsible for seeing that Judge Landis' rulings were followed throughout the National League.

In 1951 Ford Frick was elevated to the position of Commissioner of Baseball, with most of the powers and responsibilities that Judge Landis had exercised. In the fourteen years he occupied the Commissioner's office, Frick oversaw the evolution of professional baseball into the Modern Era. He negotiated the first national television contracts and supervised the first serious moves to expand the number of teams playing in the Major Leagues. The New York Mets, Houston Astros, Minnesota Twins and California Angels, who all joined the Big Show during Frick's tenure, were the first new clubs added to the National and American Leagues since the birth of those leagues.

In honor of his contributions to the growth of professional baseball in America, the National League Most Valuable Player Award is justly called the Ford C. Frick Award.

Commissioner Ford Frick. Courtesy Baseball Hall of Fame.

The other Hoosier executive who had a great impact on professional baseball during the Golden Age was Owen J. "Ownie" Bush.

Unlike Landis and Frick, Bush had been a great player before moving into management. Born in the "Irish Hill" section of Indianapolis in 1888, Ownie came up through the ranks, playing for teams like Waverly Electric and Fairbanks-Morse in the Indianapolis sandlot leagues. In 1904 he hooked up with a semi-professional team from Shelbyville where he played for $3 a game. By '07 he was playing for South Bend in the Central League for nearly $100 a month. Bush made it to the Major Leagues in 1908 when the Detroit Tigers purchased his contract from the Indianapolis Indians.

Owen J. Bush, Mr. Baseball in the Hoosier State. Indiana State Museum collection.

Bush hit second in the Tiger lineup for the next thirteen years—batting in front of the fabled Ty Cobb. Known principally for a great glove at shortstop, Bush stole over 400 bases in his career and led the American League in runs scored in 1917 with 112.

Outstanding as he was on a ball diamond, the most important times in Ownie Bush's baseball career would come after his playing days were over. From 1923 until 1933, he managed several different Major League teams. His best club was the 1927 Pittsburgh Pirates, a team that included Paul and Lloyd Waner, Pie Traynor and Vic "The Hoosier Schoolmaster" Aldridge. That team lost the '27 Series to the Babe Ruth, Lou Gehrig-led Yankees—probably the greatest baseball team of all time.

In 1934 as the manager of a minor league team in Minneapolis, Bush helped develop the talents of one of baseball's best hitters, Ted Williams. In later years, Williams was quoted as saying of Bush, "He was some guy to play for... I've been in the game thirty-six years and nobody has any closer affection to my heart than Ownie."

Bush's most important contributions to Indiana baseball were still to come. After two brief stints as manager of the Indianapolis Indians, Bush joined with Indianapolis banker Frank E. McKinney, Sr. and purchased the struggling franchise in 1941. By '46 the Indians were drawing over 300,000 fans a year and had become perennial American Association pennant contenders. In 1956 the club became community owned when shares were sold to over 6,000 individual Hoosier investors. Ownie Bush became president of the new corporation and served in that capacity until 1969.

Today, the Indianapolis Indians is one of the oldest and most successful professional sports teams in America. In honor of his many contributions to the game of baseball, the Indians play all of their home games in Owen J. Bush Stadium.

These Too Played Upon The Field of Dreams

Hoosier contributions to professional baseball during the Golden Age were not limited to the efforts of baseball executives. Judge Landis and Ford Frick have been elected to the Baseball Hall of Fame, and six Indiana ballplayers from the era can also claim that honor. In addition to Eddie Roush, those players are Max Carey, Sam Rice, Chuck Klein, Billy Herman, and Oscar Charleston.

Max Carey was born Maximillian Carnarius in Terre Haute in 1890. Carey had an uncommon background for a baseball player in his era: he had a college education. After graduating from Fort Wayne's Concordia College, he spent twenty years as an outfielder for the Pittsburgh Pirates and Brooklyn Dodgers. Carey set National League records for most games played by an outfielder (2,421) and career put-outs by an outfielder (6,702). He also set Major League records for career stolen bases (738), including an amazing 51 in 53 attempts in 1922, and for most years leading the majors in stolen bases (10). Between 1910 and 1930, Carey compiled a .285 career batting average.

Three for the Price of One

"Funny thing. I played in the Big Leagues thirteen years (1914-1926) and the only thing anybody seems to remember is that I made a triple play in the World Series."

"Many don't even remember the team I was on or the position I played or anything... you'd think I was born the day I made that play and died the day after." Those words were spoken by Bill Wambsganss many years after he performed a feat so stunning and dramatic that it mattered not if he had only played in that one game. The feat, the only unassisted triple play in World Series history, won him a permanent place in baseball legend.

The son of a Lutheran minister, Wambsganss was born in Cleveland. His family moved to Fort Wayne when he was four. Wambsganss completed grade and high school at Fort Wayne and attended Concordia College there for two years.

Eventually his talent sent him to the Big Leagues, and he played second base ten seasons for Cleveland, two with the Boston Red Sox and one with the Philadelphia Athletics. He finished with a lifetime batting average of .259.

Wambsganss made his unassisted triple play playing for Cleveland against Brooklyn in the fifth game of the 1920 Series. Here is the way he described it: "Pete Kilduff was on second and Otto Miller on first. Pitcher Clarence Mitchell hit a rising liner toward centerfield. I jumped and just caught the ball in my glove. My momentum carried me towards second, and I stepped on the bag. Miller, who had run almost to second, was just standing there. So I ran over and tagged him. There was a dead silence in the crowd for a second. They started cheering when we ran off the field."

Since Cleveland was leading 7-0, the play had no effect on the outcome of the game. But it will be recalled as long as fans talk baseball; the magic moment when a man was in the right place at the right time and wrote his name in the record book forever.

Bob Collins Sports Profile

Morocco's Sam Rice gathered 2,987 career hits during nineteen years as an outfielder for Washington and Cleveland. In compiling a .322 career average, Rice led the American League in hits in 1924 (216) and '26 (216). He hit .349 in 1930 and led the league with 63 stolen bases in 1920. Rice played in the 1924, '25 and '33 World Series, and his most famous moment may have come in one of those games. In 1925, one of the great Washington Senator teams of that decade was playing an equally talented Pittsburgh squad. In game three Pirate Earl Smith drilled a shot deep to the center field bleachers. Rice leaped high, crashed over the railing and vanished into the stands. He reappeared moments later holding the ball aloft. "Yer Out!" shouted the umpire and one of the biggest rhubarbs in baseball history erupted as the Pirates went berserk. The call stood. The Senators won the game. The Pirates won the Series and Sam Rice took his place in baseball legend.

Chuck Klein graduated from Southport High School in 1922. Over the next several years he played for a number of Indianapolis' top amateur teams including Silver Nook, the Keystones and city amateur champs, Indianapolis Power and Light. In 1926 Klein tried out for the Indianapolis Indians, but was told he was too old to start a baseball career. Unwilling to take that as a final answer he persisted. Eventually he caught on with Evansville of the 3-I League, which turned around and sold his contract to Fort Wayne for $200.

Klein finally made the Big Show when he signed with the Philadelphia Phillies in 1928. In '29 he hit .356 and socked 43 homers. Klein was National League MVP in 1931 and 1932. When his contract was eventually sold to the Cubs, it had become worth $65,000 and three players.

Chuck retired after the '44 season with 300 career home runs, 1,201 RBIs and a lifetime .320 batting average.

Born and raised on a small farm near New Albany, William Jennings "Billy" Herman may have been the best Hoosier baseball player of his time. Billy had a great bat. Playing mostly for the Cubs and Brooklyn Dodgers between 1931 and 1947, he compiled a .304 lifetime average and hit .341 in 1935. Herman hit over .300 eight times and scored more than 100 runs five times. He played in the World Series with Chicago in 1932, '35 and '38 and with Brooklyn in 1941.

As good as Billy Herman's bat was, he is more famous for his glove. When Rogers Hornsby left

Chuck Klein, the pride of Southport High. Courtesy Baseball Hall of Fame.

to go to the Cardinals, Cub fans believed they would never see another second baseman who could field like "the Rajah." Herman took Hornsby's position at second. By the time his career ended in 1947, Billy ranked ninth on the all-time assist list. He led the National League in put-outs seven times and in double-plays four times. Though he was quick enough to get to most balls hit near him, Herman was so sure handed that he led the league in fielding average three different years.

Another Hoosier who might have made it to Cooperstown if not for a bad set of wheels is Tommie Thevenow of Madison. A protege of Cardinal manager Rogers Hornsby, the Indiana shortstop played fourteen seasons with a variety of National League clubs.

A glove wizard, Thevenow led all NL shortstops in fielding in 1926 and again in '30 while compiling a .247 career batting average. In the Cards' '26 Series victory over the Babe's Yanks the Madisonian hit .417 with one homer, five runs scored and four RBI.

Paul Trout of Sandcut isn't likely to get his ticket to Cooperstown under any circumstances, but he was a fine hurler, in addition to being one of baseball's colorful characters. "Dizzy" Trout won 170 games for Detroit, Boston and Baltimore between 1939 and 1952. He led the AL in wins in '43 (20), losses in '50 (14), ERA in '44 (2.12), complete games in '44 (33) and shut outs in '43 & '44 (5 and 7). In 1945 Dizzy pitched six games in nine days—winning four—in the Tigers' successful drive to the pennant.

A compulsive practical joker, Dizzy was the director of the Chicago White Sox Speakers Bureau from 1959-1972. Younger baseball fanatics are probably more familiar with Dizzy's son Steve Trout, late of the Cubs and White Sox.

Baseball's Invisible Heroes....

The Golden Age of sports was barely gilded for many of the finest athletes in America. As early as 1888 the Central Interstate League claimed five black players among its numbers. Bud Fowler was the best of this group and he played all nine positions for Crawfordsville's CIL entry. When the Crawfordsville club folded in July, Fowler joined the newest team in the CIL the "Terre Hautes."

By the turn of the century, however, all players "of color" had been banned from white professional baseball. During the '20s, '30s and '40s Major League Baseball was most definitely a "Whites Only" game. Blacks, most Cubans and other Hispanics were relegated to the Negro National and American Leagues. It was here that many of the nation's top ball players labored.

Two of the more important franchises in Negro League baseball were C.I. Taylor's Indianapolis ABCs and Syd Pollock's Indianapolis Clowns. Taylor founded the ABCs about 1914 as a barnstorming outfit. In 1920 he joined with Rube Foster to spearhead the formation of the first negro league. Charter members of the Negro National League in addition to the ABCs & Foster's Chicago American Giants included the St. Louis Giants, Detroit Stars and Kansas City Monarchs. The Birmingham Black Barons, Memphis Red Sox, Cuban Stars and numerous others soon joined in.

As had been the case in the early days of white Major League Baseball, teams changed leagues often and players frequently jumped from team to team. Though formal records are extremely scarce, it appears that the ABCs or some form thereof fielded competitive Negro Major League teams from 1920 through 1946.

The '22 team that finished 46-33 and second to Foster's American Giants was the cream of the Indy crop. Led by Hall of Fame center fielder Oscar Charleston, the '22 team also featured Negro All-Stars Ben Taylor (C.I.'s brother) at first, Connie Day at second & Crush Holloway in right.

The Indianapolis Clowns provide a different kind of story. The Clowns were essentially a barnstorming squad loosely based in Indy and occasionally flitting in and out of the Negro National and American Leagues. Founded in 1929 the Clowns eventually evolved into "Baseball's Number One Show Team" or "The Globetrotters of Baseball."

Employing midgets, lady umps and "Nub" Anderson, the one-armed shortstop, the Clowns toured the country taking on all comers for transportation, lodging and $5.00 a day meal money. Though the Clowns did possess a great deal of genuine athletic talent—Goose Tatum was a Clown, and the Milwaukee Braves actually purchased the contract of a young Henry Aaron from the Indy club—the Clowns' antics gave the white baseball establishment an excuse for not taking negro players seriously.

When Branch Rickey hired Jackie Robinson in 1947, he opened the doors for Don Newcombe, Roy Campanella, Hank Aaron and all the legions of outstanding black players to come, but these names are only part of the legacy—the legacy of Oscar Charleston, Cool Papa Bell, Josh Gibson, Judy Johnson, Satchel Paige and all the rest of baseball's invisible heroes.

Bill Owens Tells His Own Story: Negro League Baseball in the 1920s

I was born in Indianapolis—in the Haughville neighborhood—in 1901. I went to grade school at #52 and #63. When I was an adult, I went to Attucks night school to finish elementary. That's all the further I went.

I practiced some with C.I. Taylor's Indianapolis ABCs. C.I. had great teams in the Negro American League and he was a great man. He was a role model for blacks, and he insisted on a few things from his players. They always had to wear collars and ties, and they had to make sure their shoes were shined. C.I. was trying to bring up his community, but a lot of black people resented his success. It was said that when he died he had $8,000 and that was a lot of money in those days.

I played for lots of teams and our crowds were almost always all negroes, but at some ABC games I'll bet the crowd was nearly 70% white. The team played in Washington Park where the Indians played, but they had to wait until the Indians finished. After 1933 the ABCs had the same arrangement with the Indians at Victory Field—before it became Bush Stadium. Capacity was 13,000 and the ABC's often filled the place—especially if Chicago was coming to town.

In 1921 Jim Taylor—C.I.'s brother took me and John Barnes and Moody Allison to Cleveland to play for the Tate Stars. It didn't last long. The Stars were supposed to get into a league but they didn't.

In 1922 I went to Dayton with a boy from the Indianapolis Gas Company team and did some barnstorming. I came home in the fall to practice with the ABCs, but C.I. died and I never did get the chance to play for him.

In '24 I went with another of C.I.'s brothers, Ben Taylor, to play for the Washington DC Potomacs. The Potomacs were a Negro American League team and we played in a Major League ballpark. I was paid $1.50 per day and then a $37.50 a week salary. This was at a time when people with regular jobs made $18.00 a week.

In my eleven years of baseball I was only on salary one and one half seasons and I almost never got what I was due. I was lucky 'cause I could shoot pool. We'd go into a town and I'd get the lowdown on the locals. I could support myself shooting pool.

In 1925 I joined Rube Foster's Chicago American Giants in the Negro Western League. The Giants were good and Rube Foster was first class. We travelled by train—segregated—but it was first class.

I'd been playin' shortstop for awhile now. I was a scratch hitter—singles. Never hit home runs much at all. But I could really field—had a good arm and could knock down anything. Jumped up and grabbed a line drive with my bare hand once. Some of the fellows said it was as good a play as they ever saw.

In 1926 I came home to play with Warner Jones' ABCs. The team hadn't been the same since C.I. died and it folded up for awhile in mid season. Rube Page and John Overton owned Marmons and we'd all pack into those two automobiles. It wasn't too bad—a little tire trouble held us up now and again.

I didn't play baseball in 1927. I never looked for a fight, but I never backed away from one either. A shell-shocked guy from the war came up behind me on a cable car in Indianapolis and we had words. He stabbed me in the ear and it hit my jugular. I was out of baseball for awhile.

I managed George Ray's Indianapolis semi-pro team in 1928, but I really got back to it in '29 with the Memphis Red Sox. Memphis was in the Negro Western League with Chicago, St. Louis, Detroit, Kansas City and Birmingham. Rube Foster's Chicago Stars usually fought it out with the Kansas City Monarchs. Satchel Paige pitched for the Monarchs, and he was the fastest pitcher around.

I only faced him twice, but I never hit him—too fast.

Oscar Charleston was the best I saw. I got to practice with him with C.I.'s ABCs, and we played together for a couple weeks in Harrisburg. Oscar was strong. He could hit anybody and hit 'em hard. And he was fast. He'd run down anything hit to center field. He was the best.

I played against Josh Gibson and Oscar's brother Benny Charleston played for me in '28. There were some great ballplayers.

In 1931 I went back to Dayton to play for the Christian Mens' Association—barnstormers. My career was winding down. In the winter of '33 Jim Taylor took some Indianapolis boys south, but he said I should stay home and practice. The winter was awful and I didn't get to play hardly at all.

When the season started I booted a ball or two and Jim took me out. The crowd gave it to me some, and I was a prideful man, so I quit baseball.

Baseball was good. We never had too much trouble with nasty fans or with white folks—we never got around too many white people in the south.

One time I was outside a pool hall in Memphis when here comes this white policeman waddling from side to side. The boy with me said "Turn around, turn around!" I said "What for?" and he said "If you act like you don't notice him he'll bust you across the head with that billy club." I could see that all the blacks were taking off their hats and saying, "How do you do sergeant" so I did, too.

Bill Clair was County Chairman. He lived in the neighborhood and was favorable to blacks. He cleared it for me to open a black joint about 1935—pool hall, beer and crap games. Sometimes took $1,500 a week on crap games. Pool hall cost me $17 a month to buy. Clair would get me Indians' tickets and I'd sell them and make some money on pool.

It didn't last long. The Republicans came into power and closed down all the joints and opened others for their friends. Bill bought a brewery after WW II and set me up in a tavern on Ray and Kenwood. It was a good business, but I did alot of carpentry work, too. I'm a good carpenter—helped build a lot of these houses around here.

Bill Owens is one of the last survivors of the Negro Leagues. He lives in a house he built himself, within sight of the Hoosier Dome. Lively and active in his eighties, he remembers with pride and a little wistfulness the barnstorming days before baseball was fully opened to Afro-Americans.

The Indianapolis ABCs circa 1916. Courtesy Baseball Hall of Fame.

One of the Lost Legends

You can't yank a record book off the shelf and read about the baseball exploits of Oscar Charleston. The known facts are that he was six feet tall, had a barrel chest and spindly legs and competed with the best of his circuit for close to thirty years.

How good was he at the game of baseball? Opinions vary. He grows or diminishes with the years. Old-timers say he ran like the wind, possessed a rifle arm and hit for distance and average. Some will lean all the way out and say that he was the best outfielder—black or white— who ever played the game.

It has been recorded that John McGraw, the legendary manager of the New York Giants, was so impressed by Charleston that he conducted a one-man crusade to bring him into the National League more than twenty-five years before Jackie Robinson broke the color line. When all other avenues were blocked, McGraw, for whom talent apparently had no color, tried to sneak Charleston in as a Cuban. The barons of baseball wouldn't buy that either.

The facts on Charleston's life are skimpy. He was born in Indianapolis in 1896. At fifteen he ran away from home and joined the Army. While in World War I, he was timed at 23 seconds in the 220-yard dash.

Charleston joined the Indianapolis ABCs in 1915. By 1923 he was earning $325 a month and was one of the highest paid players in black baseball. As he grew older, he lost his speed and moved to first base. But he maintained his batting eye. In 1929 Charleston, age thirty-three, hit .396.

Other stories reveal that even when he was fat and forty—long past his prime—he would play on barnstorming tours against Major League all-star teams and awe white players who were fifteen years younger and fit.

In recent years baseball has taken many steps towards righting a terrible injustice by enshrining stars from the Negro League in the Hall of Fame. Charleston, who died in 1954, was added to the list of immortals in 1976.

The few survivors of those days of baseball before the color line broke, these interpid men who played two to three hundred games a season then opened a second season in Mexico, are old men. Their memories at best are tricky. But all agree that Charleston was as proficient as anybody, white or black, who ever roamed an outfield.

Oscar Charleston
Courtesy Baseball Hall of Fame.

Bob Collins Sports Profile

The Daisies and the Blue Sox

The South Bend Blue Sox (back row, l to r) Chet Grant, Manager, Daisy Junor, Pinky Pirok, Phyllis Koehn, Theda Marshall, Lib Mahon, Jaynne Bittner, Betsy Jochum, Jackie Kelley, Delores Brumfield, Liz Nahtyk, Lucille Moore, Chaperone. (front row, l to r) Evelyn Keppel, Fredda Acker, Viola Thompson, Marie Mahoney, Jean Faut, Ruby Stephens, Shoo-Shoo Wirth, Marge Stefani, Bonnie Baker. Courtesy Indiana State Library.

When many of America's best athletes joined the armed services during World War II, the sports world suffered greatly. Alternatives had to be found to satisfy the fans' craving for athletic competition.

In 1943 the All-American Girl's Baseball League (AAGBL) was formed, with Hoosier Hall of Famer Max Carey as its president. The league consisted of eight teams: the South Bend Blue Sox, Fort Wayne Daisies, Rockford Peaches, Peoria Redwings, Grand Rapids Chicks, Kenosha Comets, Muskegon (later Kalamazoo) Lassies and Racine (later Battle Creek) Belles. Players were recruited nationwide by professional scouts who signed the top prospects to pro contracts. The league reached its zenith in 1946 when over 750,000 fans attended AAGBL games.

The South Bend Blue Sox were one of the more successful franchises. One season they drew over 120,000 spectators for a 112 game schedule, and a league record 7,800 for a single contest. Led by **Mary Baker, Elizabeth Mahon and Betsy Jochum**, the Sox were usually in the running for the Shaughnessy Trophy, which went to the league's champs. Olympic swimmer and movie star Esther Williams personally presented the trophy to South Bend's '46 league champions. **Chet Grant**, a former quarterback for Knute Rockne's "Fighting Irish," served as the Blue Sox manager.

The Fort Wayne Daisies. (back row, l to r) William (Daddy) Rohrer, Manager, Irene Kotowicz, Betty Tucker, Mary Rountree, Dottie Collins, Lilian Faralla, Marian Stancevic, Chaperone. (middle row, l to r) Ruby Heafner, Faye Dancer, Helen Machado, Betty Whiting, Mavis Dabbs. (front row, l to r) Marge Pieper, Velma Abbott, Marge Callaghan, Vivian Kellogg, Marie Kruckel, Alice DeCambra. Courtesy Indiana State Library.

The **Fort Wayne Daisies** were not quite as successful on their Memorial Park field, but they did enjoy healthy fan and community support. **Max Carey** joined the club as team manager in 1950.

At war's end, the best male players returned to their teams. A new invention, television, soon began bringing top-flight professional competition into most American homes. The AAGBL wasn't able to maintain the enthusiasm of the early days. The league went into decline and disbanded in the mid 1950s.

At this writing, Hollywood director Penny Marshall of "Laverne & Shirley" fame, is working on a feature-length movie highlighting the history of the All-American Girls Baseball League.

The Hoosier Hotshots

With the coming of V-J Day in August of 1945 hordes of Major Leaguers left the service and returned to their former teams. Baseball fanatics resumed their obsession with the National Pastime, and a new generation of Indiana ball players took up the Hoosier legacy.

Brooklyn, where the language sounded like it was filtered through rocks and the word "Bums" was screamed with pride, must have seemed like Mars at first to two young men from small-town Indiana.

Yet, Gil Hodges of Princeton and Carl Erskine ("Oiskin" to the faithful) of Anderson came, played, and conquered the hearts of the denizens of a strange place called Ebbets Field.

Hodges played seventeen years with the Dodgers, twelve while they kept their official residence in Brooklyn. Once, when the big (6'2", 200) slugger was in a prolonged batting slump, hundreds of Dodger fans went to church and lit candles for him.

Hodges hit 370 home runs, drove in 1,274 and closed his playing career with a lifetime batting average of .273. He once hit four home runs in a game, but his greatest moment as a Dodger arrived on October 4, 1955.

Gil drove in both runs as Johnny Podres blanked the Yankees, 2-0 in the seventh game of the World Series, and the Dodgers finally won the Fall classic on their eighth try.

Hodges later managed the Washington Senators and the New York Mets. In 1969 he took the "Amazin' Mets" to the National League title and a World Series triumph over Baltimore. Until that season, the Mets never had finished higher than ninth in the NL. Gil Hodges died of a heart attack on Easter Sunday, 1972, after a round of golf with his coaches at West Palm Beach, Fla.

The slightly built Erskine had good control and what baseball people call a "sneaky fastball." His best season with Da Bums was 1953, when he compiled a 20-6 mark. His overall Dodger record was 122-75. Eskine was bothered by arm trouble his last several seasons and retired in 1959, saying "I'm thirty-two, but my arm is one hundred and ten."

Erskine's most memororable accomplishments with the Dodgers were in the World Series. Carl set a record by striking out fourteen batters, including Mickey Mantle four times, as he whipped the Yankees 3-2 in the third game of the 1953 Series.

In 1952 the Yankees got to Erskine for five runs in the fifth inning of the fifth game, but Carl retired the next nineteen batters and Brooklyn won, 6-5 in eleven innings.

Oisk also pitched two no-hitters. He beat Chicago 5-0, June 19, 1952 and achieved his second triumph 3-0, over the Giants in 1956. Erskine went home to Anderson after his retirement from baseball to build one of the Nation's premier small college baseball programs at Anderson College. A long way from Flatbush, he is currently president of his hometown Madison County National Bank.

The Boys of Summer. (l to r) PeeWee Reese, Carl Furillo, Jackie Robinson, Carl Erskine, Gil Hodges, Don Newcombe, Duke Snyder, Roy Campanella. Courtesy Baseball Hall of Fame.

The Instant Hero

Don Larsen was a baseball vagabond. The Michigan City native played for eight different teams in his thirteen-year Major League career. His record, 81 victories, 91 defeats, is neither the stuff of legends, nor a passport to the Hall of Fame. The announcement that Don was to pitch did not draw huge crowds. Not one of his many employers considered doing anything with his number other than cleaning it and assigning to to the next man.

He probably would be best remembered as an amiable fellow who liked the bright lights and had a taste for the grape, had it not been for that one, magic afternoon.

It was Monday, October 8, 1956. The fifth game of the World Series: New York Yankees VS Brooklyn Dodgers. The Series was tied 2-2. Larsen was coming off his best year in the Major Leagues—an 11-5 records. But the Dodgers had made short work of Don in the second game, sending him to the showers after one and two-thirds innings.

Brooklyn had one of the most feared batting orders in modern baseball. This was well documented by the fact that Carl Furillo, the number eight man in the lineup hit 21 homers and drove in 83 runs during the National League season. But the Dodgers were the next thing to helpless as big Don put it all together and pitched the only perfect game in World Series history.

Larsen needed only 97 pitches to retire 27 batters in a row, as the Yankes won, 2-0. Larsen's only shaky inning was the fifth. After Jackie Robinson flied out, powerful Gil Hodges boomed a drive deep to right-center. But Mickey Mantle made a spectacular running catch. Sandy Amoros, the next batter, smacked a pitch into the right field stands that just barely was foul. He grounded out on the next pitch.

After the final pitch—a called strike to pinch-hitter Dave Mitchell—millions watched on television as catcher Yogi Berra raced to the mound and leaped on the big pitcher.

The money came fast. It was estimated that Don Larsen collected over $25,000 for appearances, endorsements and testimonials in the first month after his perfect game.

The new celebrity was unsettling to a man who liked to float free and down a few with old friends. He finally said that enough was enough and went home to San Diego, thereby turning his back on a small fortune.

Bob Collins Sports Profile

The Franklin High School "Wonder Five", champions in 1920, '21, and '22. (left to right) Burl Friddle, Ralph Hicks, Paul White, Fuzzy Vandivier, S. Comer, John Gant, Harold Borden, Harvey Keeling and Coach Ernest "Grizz" Wagner. Courtesy Indiana Basketball Hall of Fame.

B-ball Roars Through the 1920s

While baseball remained the National Pastime during the Golden Age of American sports history, another younger sport came to dominate Hoosier loyalties—basketball.

By the end of the 1920s, the myth and legend of Hoosier Hysteria was firmly established. Each year a new player or a new coach would take his place among the giants of American basketball.

As captain of the Franklin High School "Wonder Five," Robert P. "Fuzzy" Vandivier led his team to State Championships in 1920, '21, and '22. He became one of two players in Indiana history to be selected All-State three consecutive years. Upon graduation from Franklin High School, Fuzzy and his "Wonder Five" teammates entered Franklin College, where they proceeded to dominate college basketball in the Midwest. Fuzzy earned All-America honors in 1925. Vandivier was such a superior high school and college player that he was selected to the Naismith Basketball Hall of Fame in 1974.

Vandivier's greatness was hardly unique in Indiana during the '20s. Charles "Stretch" Murphy led Marion High School to the '26 title before moving on to Purdue. One of basketball's first great big men, the 6'7" Murphy became an unstoppable offensive weapon for the Boilermakers. In 1929 he set Big 10 records for points in a game (26) and points in a season (143). In 1930, he led the Boilers to an undefeated Big 10 title. Murphy was selected as an All-American in 1928, '29 and '30, and was elected to the Naismith Hall of Fame in 1960.

Stretch Murphy might have been remembered as the best player in Purdue basketball history if he hadn't been on the same team with one of the most famous players in the history of the sport—John Wooden.

Wooden led Martinsville High School to three straight championship game appearances in 1926, '27 and '28. The Artesians lost to Murphy's Marion Giants in 1926. Martinsville defeated Muncie Central for the title in '27 and in '28; Central returned the favor by beating Wooden's squad. That championship was the first of a record eight for Central's Bearcats.

Wooden joined Murphy at Purdue in 1929 and quickly became one of college basketball's greatest players. Wooden was named All-Big 10 and All-America in 1930, '31 and '32. He was college Player of the Year in 1932—the year he led the Boilers to a 17-1 record and the Big 10 title.

If Wooden's basketball career had ended in 1932, he still would have been elected to the Hall of Fame. His greatest glories, however, were still more than thirty years into the future. We'll be spending a lot more time with John Wooden when we get to the story of college basketball during the 1960s and '70s.

The Boilers had plenty of competition in their efforts to recruit Indiana's high school basketball heroes during the Golden Age.

Branch McCracken led Monrovia High School to Tri-State titles in 1925 and '26. Playing at IU under coach Everett Dean, McCracken led the Big 10 in scoring in 1928 and '30. In 1930, he broke Stretch Murphy's Big 10 record by scoring 147 points in one season. Though he was a unanimous All-American in '30, McCracken, like Wooden, would experience his greatest achievements many years later.

Vandivier, Murphy, Wooden and McCracken were the top Indiana high school basketball players of their era; the Frankfort "Hotdogs", however, were most often the team to beat. In 1925, 1929, 1936 and 1939 coach Everett Case's squads returned the State Championship to west-central Indiana, the Cradle of Indiana High School Basketball. Case's four championship teams compiled a combined record of 111-11-1. Over a twenty-two year period, Case coached Columbus, Smithfield, Anderson and Frankfort to records of 626 victories and 75 defeats.

During the 1940s, '50s and '60s, Everett Case

John Wooden of Martinsville, 1932 Collegiate Player of the Year. Courtesy Naismith Basketball Hall of Fame.

would again meet up with Branch McCracken and John Wooden—this time in the hardwood battles of big time college basketball.

From 1947 through 1964 the "Old Grey Fox" went 376-133 at North Carolina State University. Case developed seven All-Americans, won ten conference titles (six in the Southern and four in the Atlantic Coast) and helped establish the ACC as one of the nation's premier college basketball powerhouses. The Anderson native was voted into the Naismith Hall of Fame in 1981.

For those who think that basketball coaches pulling shenanigans to gain a competitive advantage is a recent phenomenon—think again. Coach Case was known to have extra coats of wax placed on visiting locker room floors to make it more difficult and distracting for opposing teams to get about. Case also had a habit of seeing that

Ward "Piggy" Lambert and the Purdue Boilermakers of 1934, Big Ten Champs: (l to r) All American Emmett Lowery, Ed Shaver, Ray Eddy, All-American Norm Cottom, "Dutch" Fehring. Courtesy Purdue University Athletic Department.

windows above the visitor's bench were left open—particularly on exceptionally bad winter nights.

Lambert Fuels the Firewagon

Murphy and Wooden at Purdue and McCracken at IU had the significant luxury of playing for coaches who would also be elected to the Naismith Hall of Fame.

Purdue's Ward "Piggy" Lambert from Crawfordsville High School and Wabash College began coaching when it was customary to take thirty and forty-foot shots. Actually, teams didn't shoot the ball very much at all in these salad days of basketball. Lambert devised a new strategy. As the "father of the fast break," Lambert's Purdue Boilermakers took to running opposing teams right out of Memorial Gymnasium. When the Boilers crushed Ohio State 61-25 in 1920, coaches all over the Midwest took notice. Sixty-one points was more than some teams scored in a month. Lambert did not introduce the era of skywalking slam-bam-jam basketball. The game remained essentially a slow-down contest for many years. Lambert's "firewagon" tactics did make the game more exciting for Boiler fans and provided a preview of things to come.

Between 1917 and 1945 Piggy Lambert's teams won 364 games while losing only 145. The Boilermakers also won eleven Big 10 titles. Lambert's record as the Big 10's all-time winningest coach stood for forty-five years, until it was broken by IU's Bob Knight in 1990.

In addition to Murphy, Wooden, Emmett Lowery and Norm Cottom, Ward Lambert coached Boiler Consensus All-Americans Bob Kessler (1936), Jewell Young of Lafayette Jefferson (1937 and 1938) and Fred Beretta (1940). The Purdues were 49-11 in Young's three varsity seasons and took the 1938 Big 10 Crown with an 18-2 mark. Following graduation Jewell spent five seasons with Indianapolis, Toledo and Oshkosh of the National Basketball league—averaging 9.1 PPG.

Who knows how many games Piggy Lambert would have won if he hadn't resigned to become the first commissioner of the fledgling National Basketball League in 1946? Lambert was honored with an induction into the Hall of Fame in 1960. His All-Americans Stretch Murphy and John Wooden received the same recognition soon thereafter.

Following Lambert's departure for the professional ranks, the Boilermaker basketball program lapsed into a period of mediocrity. Records of 9-

11, 9-13, 8-14, 4-18, 9-13 and 10-11 dot the 1940s and 50s. An occasional Joe Sexson, Carl McNulty, Lamar Lundy or Willie Merriweather appeared on the scene, but no Big 10 titles or Consensus All-Americans were produced between Lambert and the end of the Golden Age. The Modern Era would witness a dramatic reversal of this trend.

Hoosiers Take to Hurryin'

Branch McCracken's mentor at IU, Everett Dean, could match Piggy Lambert honor for honor. After graduating from Salem High School in 1917, Dean was named to the All-America team as a center for IU's 1921 squad. Four years later he took over the Hoosiers' head coaching position at the tender age of twenty-seven. Dean steered IU to Big 10 titles in 1926, '28 and '36. In 1942, Dean coached the Stanford University Indians to the NCAA Championship. During his thirty-four-year coaching career, Dean won 374 games. He was elected to the Hall of Fame in 1966. More important than his coaching success was Dean's reputation as one of basketball's finest gentlemen. His graciousness helped establish college basketball as a model for good sportsmanship during the 1920s, '30s and '40s.

Everett Dean's star pupil Branch McCracken beat his mentor to the National Championship when he coached the 1940 Indiana Hoosiers to the prize.

McCracken was all Hoosier. He was a big bear of a man with a booming Hoosier twanged voice. He was high-spirited, friendly, folksy—and competitive. He'd learned the game of basketball in a barnyard, using an inflated pig's bladder for a ball.

Coach McCracken's teams won 457 games over thirty-two seasons—eight at Ball State (93-41), twenty-four at IU (364-174). His Hurryin' Hoosiers placed either first or second in the Big 10 fourteen times. Only three of his teams failed to finish in the first division.

Led by Herm Schaefer and Curly Armstrong of Fort Wayne, Marv Huffman of New Castle, Jay McCreary of Frankfort, Bill and Bob Menke of Huntingburg and Bob Dro of Berne, the Hoosiers went 20-3 in 1940, but finished runners-up to Piggy Lambert's Boilermakers in the Big 10. Lambert didn't believe in post-season play, so McCracken's Hoosiers filled the NCAA void.

Coach McCracken had taken a liking to Coach Lambert's "firewagon" basketball, and according

IU All-American Branch McCracken. Courtesy Indiana University Sports.

to a Kansas City newspaper, his newly designated "Hurryin' Hoosiers" stormed through the NCAA Tourney like a tornado. "That tornado was us," Marv Huffman said. "We just blew 'em out of the stadium."

The Cream and Crimson drilled Phog Allen's Kansas Jayhawks 60-42 in the title game. The sixty points would stand for a decade as an NCAA Championship Game record. The Hoosiers' 34.7% field goal average astounded college basketball mavens.

Huffman and Bill Menke were named Consensus All-Americans. Marv—little brother of IU All-American and former NFL running-back Vern Huffman—played one season of pro basketball as did Bob Dro. Curly Armstrong spent eight seasons as a mainstay of the Ft. Wayne Pistons, while Herm Schaefer put in seven NBL/BAA/NBA campaigns, primarily with Ft. Wayne and Indianapolis. Schaefer was a starting guard on the 1949 and 1950 George Mikan led Minneapolis Lakers who captured the last BAA and the first NBA titles respectively. Jay McCreary coached Muncie Central to the 1952 Indiana High School Basketball Championship.

The 1940 Indiana Hoosiers were a great Branch McCracken team. The 1953 Cream and Crimson were the greatest Branch McCracken team. Consensus All-Americans Don Schlundt of South Bend Washington and Bobby "Slick" Leonard of Terre Haute Gerstmeyer teamed with Indiana High School All-Star Dick Farley of Winslow to lead IU to a 23-3 record and a Big 10 Title. Included in this awesome Hurryin' Hoosier season were 113-78 and 105-70 victories over Purdue and Butler respectively.

In the NCAA Tourney IU nipped Coach Ray Meyer's DePaul Blue Demons 82-80 before crushing Notre Dame and LSU by thirteen points apiece. In the ND game IU not only atoned for a last-second loss in South Bend earlier in the season, Don Schlundt also set a Chicago Stadium record with 40 points.

In the championship game Bobby Leonard's charity toss with twenty-seven ticks remaining provided the 69-68 difference as Phog Allen's Jayhawks misfired at the buzzer. Slick's heroics came as no surprise to Coach McCracken who observed that "the kid's got icewater in his veins." Indiana hoop fans would have plenty of opportunities to witness future proof of that statement.

Slick Leonard was voted a Consensus All-American in 1954. He played seven seasons with Minneapolis/LA and Chicago in the NBA, scoring 4,204 points for a 9.9PPG average. In the 1960s Slick would forever endear himself to the hearts of Hoosier basketball junkies through his adventures as head coach of the ABA Indiana Pacers. Some folks around central Indiana still refer to those teams as the "Real Indiana Pacers." We'll be remembering those guys shortly.

Don Schlundt was a Consensus All-American in 1953, '54 and '55. He was Big 10 MVP in 1953. The 6'9" center scored 2,192 points in 94 games for IU. The point total and his 23.3 PPG career average both established Big 10 standards. His IU career point total mark would stand for over thirty years—until Steve Alford finished his work in Bloomington. Schlundt's game (30), season (249) and career (1,076) free throw attempts remain school standards.

Dick Farley spent three seasons in the NBA. He was a guard on the 1954-'55 Syracuse Nationals team that defeated the Ft. Wayne Pistons for the NBA title. Farley's professional career would have been more extensive save for the two years of military service, an obligation that often interrupted sporting careers during the Golden Age.

Coach McCracken's final All-American of the Golden Age was 6'8" center Archie Dees. Dees was voted to several All-America teams in 1957 and was Consensus choice in '58. He carried the Hoosiers to Big 10 Titles in both campaigns, and was named conference MVP both seasons. Dees' 22.7 PPG IU average ranks second to Don Schlundt while his 13.4 rebound average trails only Walt Bellamy in the IU annals. As a professional Archie averaged 7.7 points and 4.5 boards per game over four seasons with Cincinnati, Detroit and St. Louis.

ND Joins in the Hoosier Madness

Like IU and Purdue, the Irish of Notre Dame were an intercollegiate basketball powerhouse during the Golden Age. Between 1923 and 1943, George Keogan coached the Irish to 327 victories in 423 games. If Piggy Lambert was the father of the fast break, George Keogan was the father of the shifting man-to-man defense. This stifling defense was used to smother teams and force them to rely on long bombs.

Keogan's best player at Notre Dame was Edward W. "Moose" Krause. Enrolling at Notre Dame in 1930, Krause holds the unique distinction of being a three-time All-American for the Irish football team and a three time All-American for the Notre Dame basketballers.

At 6'3" and 215 lbs., Krause is considered to be college basketball's first agile pivot man. "Moose" set all-time collegiate scoring records for one game, one season (213) and three seasons (547) while leading Notre Dame to a three-year 54-12 record. Moose also coached the Fighting Irish to a 98-48 record between 1943-1951. In 1949 Krause became the athletic director at Notre Dame, a position he held for over

All-American Edward "Moose" Krause, "Mr. Notre Dame." Courtesy Notre Dame Sports.

thirty years. Keogan was elected to the Hall of Fame in 1961. Krause followed his coach into the shrine in 1975.

Ed Krause was George Keogan's best athlete, but there were plenty more on the court in South Bend during the Golden Age. John Moir and Paul Nowak were teammates in 1936, '37 and '38. They were also Consensus All-Americans in 1936, '37 and '38. The 6'2" forward Moir and the 6'6" center Nowak led the Fighting Irish to a 62-8-1 record over those three seasons, and ND was voted the 1936 Helms Foundation National Champion. If the NCAA Tournament had begun in 1938 instead of 1939, it's likely that Notre Dame rather than the University of Oregon Ducks would have been crowned the first NCAA Basketball Champion.

In 1939 Moir and Nowak led the Akron Firestones to victory over Leroy "Cowboy" Edwards and his Oshkosh All-Stars for the National Basketball League Championship. The former Notre Damers spent two more seasons in Akron before moving on to other pursuits.

The captain of the 1937 and '38 Irish squads never made it to All-America status, but he did pretty well for himself. As a 5'10" forward Raymond J. Meyer never averaged above 4.5 PPG while at ND. As the head coach of the DePaul Blue Demons, Ray Meyer won 724 games and a spot in the Hall of Fame. Meyer "discovered" George Mikan, lived and died with Mark Aguirre, lost the battle for Isiah Thomas to Bob Knight and unleashed the awesome talents of Terry Cummings.

The Grand Old Man of college basketball, Coach Meyer is one of only five coaches in Division I history to reach the 700-victory plateau. He was elected to the Naismith Hall in 1979 while still an active coach.

Coach Keogan's untimely death in 1943 robbed him of the opportunity of coaching a fine young player from East Chicago—Vince Boryla. As a freshman in 1945, Boryla led ND with a 16.1 point per game average. A two-year hitch in the US Army temporarily interrupted his roundball career. In 1948 Boryla came back to the hardwood as a member of America's Gold-Medal-winning Olympic Basketball Team. From 1950 to '54, Vince pursued an outstanding career with the New York Knickerbockers of the NBA. He won All-Pro honors in 1951 and played for the Knicks Eastern Division champs in '51 and '53.

Three additional Notre Dame All-Americans from the Golden Age are Vince Boryla's teammate Leo Klier of Washington, Indiana (1944 and 1946), Kevin O'Shea (1947, '48 and '50) and Tom Hawkins (1958 and '59).

Klier returned from military service to lead the '45-'46 Irish to a 17-4 mark. His 16.9 PPG average stood as a Notre Dame record until Richard Rosenthal's 20.2 led the Irish to the 1954 NCAA Mideast Regional Final. (The Irish got to the Final by upsetting Don Schlundt, Bobby Leonard and the defending National Champion Indiana Hoosiers.)

"Crystal" Klier went on to average 8.6 PPG over four seasons with Ft. Wayne and Indianapolis of the NBL/NBA. Dick Rosenthal is currently athletic director at the University of Notre Dame.

Kevin O'Shea scored 1,065 career points in four seasons to set the ND standard. O'Shea teamed with Leo Barnhorst to lead the Irish to a 69-27 record between 1947-1950. O'Shea went on to average 5.2 PPG in three seasons with Minneapolis and Baltimore of the NBA.

The most familiar basketball name to matriculate at Notre Dame during the 1950s belongs to 6'5" forward Tom Hawkins. Hawkins' 499 single-season rebounds and 1,318 career boards remain Fighting Irish records. His 1,820 points over three seasons trails only Austin Carr and Adrian Dantly on the Irish all-time chart. Hawkins carried ND to a 44-13 record and NCAA appearances in 1957 and '58.

Throughout the 1960s Hawkins was one of the premier "sixth men" in the NBA. During his ten-year professional career he scored 6,672 points and nabbed 4,607 rebounds for Coach Fred Schaus' LA Lakers and the Cincinnati Royals of Oscar Robertson and Jerry Lucas. Hawkins' teams made the playoffs every year of his career—most often falling to the Celtics in the Semis or in the Finals.

Notre Dame's contributions to the growth and stability of collegiate and professional basketball during the Golden Age extend beyond the provision of a long line of outstanding players and coaches. J. Walter Kennedy was a graduate student at the University of Notre Dame in 1934 and served as the Irish sports information director during the 1940s.

In 1950 Kennedy was appointed the first public relations director of the fledgling National Basketball Association. Following two terms as the mayor of Stamford, Connecticut, and a 1962 run as the campaign manager of US Senator Abe Ribicoff, Walter Kennedy began a twelve-year tenure as Commissioner of the NBA.

Kennedy's term witnessed the largest expansion in number of franchises, and the greatest growth in media coverage in NBA history. The league grew from nine to eighteen teams, and the first national television contract—with ABC—was inked in 1964.

Following his retirement from the NBA in 1975 Kennedy served as president of the Naismith Hall of Fame from 1975-1977. The former commissioner was inducted into the shrine in 1980.

We'll Sing the Butler Warsong

IU, Purdue and Notre Dame were among the nation's top collegiate basketball programs during the 1920s but none of those schools had the best college program in Indiana. That distinction would go to the Bulldogs of Butler University.

It was Harlan O. "Pat" Page who established Butler University as an intercollegiate powerhouse. Page lettered in football and basketball for the University of Chicago. His 1907, '09 and '10 basketball teams captured Western Conference champions hips. (Today the Western Conference is known as the Big 10.) His 1907 and '08 teams won national AAU titles.

Between 1920 and 1926, Page's Butler Bulldogs compiled a record of 94 wins and only 29 losses. His 1924-'25 team captured the National AAU Championship with a 20-4 slate. Of those four losses, one was to Wabash College and two

Hall of Famer Harlan "Pat" Page, who was instrumental in establishing the Bulldog athletic program. Courtesy Butler University.

others were to Fuzzy Vandivier's Franklin College Grizzlies.

Page also coached the Bulldog football team, and in 1926 he left Butler to become head football coach at Indiana University. In 1962, Pat Page was elected to the Naismith Basketball Hall of Fame for his accomplishments as a collegiate player.

A decision made by Page in 1921 is more important to the history of Indiana and American sports than all the games he won as a coach. In '21, Page hired Logansport's Paul D. "Tony" Hinkle as his assistant basketball coach.

"Hink" had been a three-sport star at the University of Chicago in the years immediately after the end of World War I. He was named to the All-Western Conference (Big 10) team in 1919 and 1920 and was an All-American in '20. When Page left for IU in 1926, Tony was the obvious choice to fill the vacant Bulldog head coaching position. Hinkle put in terms as head football coach, head track coach and Butler athletic director, but it was as the Bulldog basketball mentor that he would leave his most lasting mark.

Between 1926 and 1970, Hinkle's " 'Dogs" won 560 games and lost 392. In 1929, Butler posted a 17-2 record and captured its second AAU National Collegiate Championship in four years.

Bridgeport's Oral Hildebrand started for the '29 team and captained the '30 Bulldogs. Following graduation Hildebrand spent ten seasons pitching in the American League. He posted 83 victories—including nine shutouts—and 13 saves for the Indians, Browns and Yankees. Hildebrand contributed four scoreless innings of relief to the Yankees' 1939 World Series victory.

Butler All-Americans during the Golden Age include Frank Baird ('34), Jerry Steiner ('40) and Bob Dietz ('41). Baird went on to spend four seasons with the Indianapolis Kautskys in the NBL while Steiner split two years between the Kautskys and the Ft. Wayne Pistons. After three years of military service during World War II Bob Dietz returned to Indianapolis where he labored as player-coach of the Kautskys for portions of four seasons.

In 1948-'49 Jimmy Doyle and Indianapolis Washington's Ralph "Buckshot" O'Brien teamed with future "Milan Miracle" coach Marvin Wood to lead the 'Dogs to an 18-5 mark. Doyle and O'Brien were voted *Look Magazine* All-Americans the following season, and Buckshot went on to one season each with the NBA's Indianapolis Olympians and Baltimore Bullets.

Tony Hinkle of Butler University defined modern college basketball in over forty years of great coaching. Courtesy Butler University.

During the 1950s Butler made two appearances in the National Invitational Tournament at a time when the NIT was considered to be equal to the NCAA tourney in prestige.

In 1958 Milan alumni Ray Craft and Bobby Plump teamed with Helms Foundation All-American Ted Guzek to lead the Bulldogs to a 16-10 record and a berth in the NIT. The Dogs fell in the First Round to Eastern powerhouse St. Johns.

The '58-'59 team fared even better. Led by former Indianapolis Crispus Attucks "Tiger" Bill Scott, Butler finished the regular season 18-8. A second consecutive NIT bid produced a First Round thrashing of Fordam and a Quarter-Final loss to Bradley.

Tony Hinkle served a two-year term as President of the National Association of Basketball Coaches, and in 1965 he was elected to the Naismith Basketball Hall of Fame. It is doubtful that anyone did more to establish Indiana as the heart of college basketball than did Tony Hinkle.

(far right) Oscar Robertson's consummate basketball artistry led Indianapolis Crispus Attucks High School in the '50s. Courtesy IHSAA.

When you walk into Hinkle Fieldhouse you can sense the presence of the ghosts. They're only shadows now, but you can feel them. **Tony Hinkle, John Wooden, Bobby Plump, Oscar Robertson,** the **VanArsdale twins, George McGinnis, Billy Shepherd, Austin Carr, Judi Warren, Lataunya Pollard, Eric Montross, Damon Bailey** . . . whether as high school standouts, or as part of the great heritage of Indiana's intercollegiate wars, most of the legendary names in Hoosier basketball history have had their memorable moments in Hinkle Fieldhouse.

Butler Fieldhouse was built in 1928. It wasn't a gymnasium. It wasn't a basketball arena. It was a Basketball Palace. Most gyms of the era seated a few thousand spectators at best. The Fieldhouse could comfortably accommodate 15,000 rabid fanatics. It remained the largest basketball hall in America for over twenty years.

The Bulldogs played their first game in Butler Fieldhouse on March 7, 1928—defeating Notre Dame 21-13 in overtime. The Dogs defeated Purdue's Boilermakers 28-27 in the dedication game on December 29, 1928. **Paul D. "Tony" Hinkle** was the Butler coach for both of those games. By the time Butler Fieldhouse was renamed Hinkle Fieldhouse in 1966, Tony had coached over 400 games in the building.

The Fieldhouse became the site of the annual Indiana High School Boys Basketball Tournament Finals in 1928, and remained the Tourney's home until 1972. The first IHSAA Girls Basketball Finals were held at Hinkle in 1976. The Fieldhouse has become so identified with Indiana basketball that it was used as the site for the Championship Game in the Academy Award-nominated motion picture "Hoosiers."

In addition to great college and high school basketball, Hinkle Fieldhouse has hosted speeches by Presidents Eisenhower, Nixon and Ford; the Billy Graham Crusade; four professional basketball teams (including the Indiana Pacers); a three-ring circus; the US Olympic basketball trials; the very first US-USSR basketball game and ABA and NBL All-Star games.

But it is as the site of many of the greatest moments in Indiana basketball history that Hinkle Fieldhouse will always be remembered. Drop by some afternoon when there's no one around. Close your eyes. Listen to the echoes. Feel the presence of the ghosts.

Hey! That's A Double-Dribble

The Fort Wayne Hoosiers were led by Notre Dame All-American Benny Borgman in the late '20s and early '30s. Courtesy Naismith Basketball Hall of Fame.

While high school and college hoops were capturing the hearts of Hoosier sports fans during the 1920s, professional basketball was taking its first tentative steps toward the major sport status it enjoys today. As you would expect, Indiana managed to find a place right in the middle of things.

Like most pro football teams of the 'teens and twenties, the earliest professional basketball squads were barnstormers who took on all comers including high school, college, club and professional opposition. Games were scheduled whenever and wherever an opponent could be found. Players, teams and rules changed constantly.

In 1925 teams from Brooklyn, Washington, DC; Cleveland, Boston, Chicago, Detroit, Rochester, New York; Buffalo and Fort Wayne joined to form the first national professional basketball league—the American Basketball League.

The league had a strong foundation with team owners like Chicago Bear founder George Halas and Cleveland department store mogul Max Rosenblume. They instituted many innovations that revolutionized and standardized the American game. Learning from baseball's problems, all ABL players were required to sign contracts that prevented them from jumping from team to team. Backboards became mandatory for the first time. The five-foul disqualification and the three-second rule were soon implemented. The ABL was the first professional organization to adopt the college prohibition against dribbling with two hands.

For the seven years of the ABL's existence, the Fort Wayne Hoosiers were one of the league's top contenders. Led by **Homer Stonebraker**, and Notre Dame All-American **Bernhardt "Benny" Borgman**, the Hoosiers finished second to the Original Celtics in 1928 and '31 and second to the Cleveland Rosenblooms in 1929. Borgman led the league in scoring in 1926, '27, '29, '30 and '31. His awesome 11.2 points per game average in 1927 thrilled ABL crowds. **Branch McCracken** added additional firepower when he joined the team in 1931.

The onset of the Great Depression in 1929 and the resulting lack of available money for fans to purchase tickets led to the league's demise following the 1930-'31 season. Teams and players returned to regional and barnstorming schedules. Borgman went to play for the Original Celtics. He was elected to the Naismith Hall of Fame in 1961.

The Hoosiers broke up as a team, but Fort Wayne's reputation as a basketball hotbed was assured. That reputation would soon result in far greater glories.

Indiana State Sycamores Flew Before the Bird

Many Hoosier roundball fans are under the impression that the Indiana State University basketball program was born the day Larry Bird moved to Terre Haute and died the day he moved to Boston. The fact of the matter is that Indiana State had a proud hardwood tradition established long before the most recent Pride of the Celtics was born.

In 1946 Indiana State Teachers College finished runner-up to Southern Illinois in the battle for the NAIB (NAIA) National Championship. In '48 Johnny Wooden, in his second year as a collegiate coach, took the Sycamores back to the NAIB Championship Game, where they fell to the University of Louisville 82-70.

ISTC wouldn't have made the final, if not for Duane Klueh. With two seconds remaining in the Semi-final against Hamline, the 6' 3" forward sank a pair of charities to send the game into overtime. With eleven seconds remaining in OT, a double foul resulted in a center court jump ball. Klueh grabbed the tip, drove to the bucket and pulled up to can a jumper as the gun sounded—final score, Indiana State 66, Hamline 65.

Coach Wooden's success with the Sycamores won him an offer to coach a team which had never particularly distinguished itself on the hardwood—the Bruins of UCLA.

After that memorable '48 tournament, Duane Klueh was named Tourney MVP and NAIB All-American. He would spend the following two years with the NBA's Ft. Wayne Pistons. Klueh returned to his alma mater in 1955 for a twelve-year stint as Indiana State University's head basketball coach. His 184-120 record was enhanced by his being named Indiana Collegiate Conference Coach-of-the Year in 1959, '63, '66, and '67. Coach Klueh was president of the NAIA Basketball Coaches Association in 1961-'62. He is a member of the NAIA Basketball Hall of Fame and a member of the All-Time NAIB Basketball Team.

Duane Klueh's Sycamore teammate Bob Royer was also named a 1948 NAIB All-American. The 5'10" guard played for the NBA's Denver Nuggets in 1949-'50, the only season the

Coach John Wooden instructs his Indiana State team during halftime of the 1948 NAIB Championship Game. Courtesy Indiana State University Archives.

original Denver franchise competed in the league.

The departure of Wooden, Klueh and Royer had little effect on the Sycamore juggernaut. Coach John Longfellow had established a friendly rivalry with Coach Wooden when the former was at Elkhart High School and the latter was at South Bend Central. When Wooden departed for UCLA, he recommended his friend for the Indiana State position. Coach Longfellow brought a good portion of his Elkhart Sectional Championship team with him.

In 1950 ISTC copped the NAIB National Championship with a 61-57 victory over Central Oklahoma. Sycamore guard "Leaping Lenny" Rzeszewski led the way with a 15.8 average. Rzeszewski was voted the tournament's MVP and an NAIB All-American.

Indiana State's reputation as a basketball powerhouse won the school a unique distinction. Coach Longfellow was invited to co-coach a team that was to represent the United States in a new international competition to be inaugurated in Buenos Aires in 1951. In addition to Coach Longfellow, seven Sycamores joined this first US Pan American Basketball Team. ISTC players who teamed with AAU National Runners-up Oakland, California, to win the inaugural Pan Am Gold include Bob Gilbert, Ed Longfellow, Dick Atha, Cliff Murray, Roger Adkins and Jim Kern.

As the Latins hadn't quite learned this Hoosier game in 1951, it really wasn't much of a tournament. The US swamped six foes, including Brazil, 74-42, Panama 90-55 and, in the Championship Game, Ecuador 74-52.

According to the United States 1952 Olympic Book Quadrennial Report, "Indiana State players showing well were Bob Gilbert, six foot five inch center; Dick Atha, a sophomore All-American prospect and Ed Longfellow, who caught the fancy of the crowds with his clever ball-handling and speedy floor work."

Coach Longfellow went on to compile a 120-59 career record at Indiana State. The coach's son Ed Longfellow, and Ed's teammate Cliff Murray, both enjoyed long and successful careers in the ranks of Indiana high school basketball coaches. Yet another Longfellow, John, Jr, holds the distinction of teaching one Ron Bonham—"The Muncie Mortar"—the ways of the Hoosier hardwood while they were coach and pupil at Muncie Central. Dick Atha is Athletic Director at Benton Central High School.

Larry Joe Bird would be along some two decades hence sure enough. But it was a long and proud tradition he chose to carry on, not a new

Coach John Longfellow with members of the ISTC National Champions, who formed the core of the first Pan-Am Basketball Team. Private collection.

and untested one he was forced to start.

Off Court Contributions Also Led to the Hall of Fame

Two additional Hoosier basketball figures made critical contributions to the development of the game during the Golden Age.

Arthur L. Trester was born in Pecksburg in 1878. He graduated from Plainfield Academy, Earlham College and Columbia University. Trester was an Indiana teacher, coach, principal and superintendent. In 1913 he became secretary of the struggling Indiana High School Athletic Association (IHSAA). In that position he led the Association to a growth of over 800 schools and developed the Indiana High School Basketball Tournament into a model for the nation.

In 1945 the IHSAA established the Arthur L. Trester Award given annually for excellence in mental attitude. In 1961 the Naismith Hall of Fame recognized Arthur Trester's impact on Indiana high school basketball, and Indiana's impact on the national game when Trester was inducted into the shrine as a contributing member.

Clifford Wells of Indianapolis coached Indiana high school basketball for twenty-nine seasons. Included in his accomplishments were coaching the 1919 Bloomington and 1934 Logansport teams to State Championships. From 1945-1963 Cliff Wells was the head basketball coach at Tulane University. He was a member of the National Rules Committee (1952-1956), president of the National Association of Basketball Coaches (1960) and director of the Naismith Hall of Fame. Clifford Wells was inducted into the Naismith Hall as a contributor in 1971.

Hoosier Teams Dominate Professional Basketball

The history of professional basketball is a story of turmoil, conflict and ultimate success. During the 1930's, '40's and '50's, the game was coming of age, and Hoosier players, teams and fans were there to experience all the growing pains.

Indianapolis grocer Frank Kautsky had sponsored a number of exceptionally successful AAU teams in the early 1930s. These squads evolved into a barnstorming team that played semi-regularly at the Dearborn Gym until 1937. In that year Lonnie Darling coach and general manager of the Oshkosh All-Stars (a team that included Branch McCracken among its alumni), spearheaded the creation of the National Basketball League (NBL). The Indianapolis Kautskys joined as a charter member.

In addition to teams from Akron, Pittsburgh, Buffalo, Columbus (Ohio), Cincinnati, Kankakee and Dayton, the Whiting Ciesar All Americans (starring Johnny Wooden) and Fred Zollner's Ft. Wayne Pistons were along for the inaugural ride. Teams from Sheboygan, Chicago, Detroit and Toledo would soon come aboard, along with Ike Duffy's Anderson Duffy Packers. The Ciesar All-Americans became the Hammond All-Americans in 1938.

With such an amalgam of franchises in such radically different cities, the NBL found some difficulty in establishing itself as a genuine Major League. Nevertheless, the NBL was the genesis of the National Basketball Association, and Hoosier teams formed the league's bedrock throughout its thirteen-year existence. The Pistons won the title in 1943, '44 and '45 and finished runner-up in '47, with the talents of Bobby McDermott and Buddy Jeannette leading the way.

In the fall of '45, Ft. Wayne downed a team of College All Stars 63-52 before 23,912 fans in the Chicago Stadium.

While Indianapolis, Anderson and Hammond couldn't boast equal success, all three franchises enjoyed their moments. In addition to John Wooden, Hammond fans cheered the talents of future Major League Baseball Hall of Famer Lou Boudreau, who played one season of basketball under Coach Bobby McDermott.

In 1940 the Kautskys signed IU All-American Ernie Andres, who immediately became this mar-

The Ft. Wayne Zollner Pistons pay a visit to Coach Doxie Moore's Sheboygan Redskins circa 1940. Indiana State Museum collection.

ginal team's leading scorer with a 10.8 PPG average. Andres' basketball career was interrupted first by military service and then by a season as a third baseman for the Boston Red Sox. In 1947 Andres coached the Indianapolis basketball club to its best finish. A 27-17 record placed the Kautskys in second, behind the Oshkosh All-Stars.

The Anderson Packers got a late start, but quickly made up for lost time. Murray Mendenhall coached the '47 team to a 24-20 record in the club's inaugural season. Indianapolis Cathedral High School's Charley Shipp came over from the Pistons in mid-season to start at guard and chip in 6.7 PPG. Shipp went on to a fifteen season NBL/NBA career. In '48 the Packers blossomed to 42-18 and extended the Rochester Royals (Sacramento Kings) before falling in the NBL Championship Semi-final.

In 1949 Mendenhall coached Anderson to a 49-15 record and the NBL Eastern Division Title. Behind the dominant pivot play of Fort Wayne Central's Catholic High School's Ed "Moose" Stanczak, and the shooting of future Warsaw High School coach Boag Johnson, the Packers downed the Syracuse Nationals (Philadelphia '76er's) of Dolph Schayes and then the Oshkosh All-Stars for the final NBL Championship.

Birth of the NBA

Though the NBL folded following the '49 season, the Anderson Duffy Packers were well positioned for the revolution in professional basketball that was about to occur.

While the Anderson Packers were selling out the old Wigwam and the Pistons and Kautskys were experiencing similar success at the Allen County Coliseum and Butler Fieldhouse respectively, many other NBL teams were not so fortunate. Teams like the Akron Goodyear Wingfoots, Toldeo Jim White Chevrolets and Flint Dow AC's came and went by the year.

The end of World War II had seen an influx of strapping young basketball players looking for employment in the hometowns of America. Professional basketball men had begun searching for larger markets in which they could profitably ply their trade. Piggy Lambert left Purdue University in 1946 to become the commissioner of the NBL. One of Lambert's first moves was to sign the giant (6'9") DePaul All-American George Mikan to an NBL contract with the Minneapolis (LA) Lakers.

Doxie Moore had been a starting guard on the

The Syracuse Nationals found Anderson's Wigwam, home of the Packers, a most inhospitable place, long before their descendants—the Philadelphia '76ers discovered that Boston Garden was equally unpleasant. Courtesy Indiana State Museum collection.

John Wooden/Stretch Murphy Boilermaker roundball team of 1930, and a bruising blocking back for Duane Purvis. In 1948 he was the combative head of the Sheboygan Redskins. The NBL selected him in 1949 as their new commissioner. His vinegar-like strength was needed, for a basketball war had begun.

The Basketball Association of America (BAA), formed in 1948, was ready to challenge the Andersons and the Sheboygans with teams like the Boston Celtics, New York Knickerbockers and Philadelphia Warriors. The BAA absorbed much of the talent of the now Eastern regional American Basketball League and began making serious overtures to the George Mikans of the NBL.

Not needing a crystal ball to see the future clearly, the Minneapolis Lakers, Rochester Royals, Ft. Wayne Zollner Pistons and Indianapolis Kautskys abandoned the NBL for the BAA at the beginning of the '48-'49 seasons. Anderson captured the final NBL Championship, and the old league collapsed.

Both the Pistons and the re-named Indianapolis Jets struggled in their inaugural BAA seasons. Coach Curley Armstrong's Pistons finished 22-38, while the Jets floundered to a last place 18-42. Those positions would change as rapidly as they changed dramatically.

In the fall of 1949, NBL clubs from Syracuse, Sheboygan and Anderson, among others, joined the BAA to form the re-named National Basketball Association (NBA). NBL teams from Oshkosh, Dayton and Hammond disappeared forever while the Indianapolis Jets (Kautskys) were replaced by a brand new franchise—the Indianapolis Olympians.

The 1949-'50 maiden voyage of the NBA was the grandest of all seasons for Hoosier fans of professional basketball. Coach Murray Mendenhall moved to Fort Wayne from Anderson and led the Zollner Pistons to an eighteen-game improvement over the previous season. Hoosiers and future Hoosiers Fred Schaus, Curley Armstrong, Boag Johnson and Duane Kleuh were all instrumental components of the dramatic turnaround. The Pistons downed the Royals before falling to Mikan's Minneapolis Lakers in the first NBA Quarter-final Playoffs.

LSU's Frankie Brian led the Ike Duffy/Doxie Moore-coached Anderson Packers to a 37-27 mark and a Western Division runner-up finish behind Indianapolis. The Packers downed the Olympians in the Quarter-finals before falling to Minneapolis in the Semis. The Lakers eventually defeated Syracuse for the historic title.

The Indianapolis Olympians are in the many ways the most intriguing and most ultimately tragic story in the history of Indiana's professional sports teams. The team actually began south of the Ohio River. Behind the unstoppable offensive machinery of Alex Groza, Ralph Beard, "Wah Wah" Jones, and Yorktown's Cliff Barker, the Kentucky Wildcats of Coach Adolph Rupp claimed the 1948 and 1949 NCAA Championships. As a reward for such success, the core of the Big Blue team was selected to represent the US at the 1948 Olympics. Prior to the 1949-50 NBA season the Indianapolis Jets had fallen into receivership. Groza, Beard, Jones and Cliff Barker, along with UK substitute Joe Holland and Babe Kimbrough—sports editor of the Lexington Herald—purchased the franchise and renamed it the Olympians in honor of their recent accomplishments.

The Olympians packed Butler Fieldhouse for game after game. A 39-25 record claimed the first NBA Western Division crown—prior to the fall against Anderson. Beard finished ninth in league scoring (14.9) while Groza's 23.4 trailed only George Mikan. From all outward appearances, Indianapolis' place in the NBA was secured. Outward appearances hide cruel truths.

In January of 1950, a major point-shaving scandal rocked college basketball. Players from the New York collegiate powerhouses, Manhattan, CCNY, NYU, Long Island and St. John's, were implicated. Adolph Rupp sniffed that investigators "Couldn't touch my boys with a ten-foot pole." They could, and they did. New York District Attorney Frank Hogan's advice was to "tell Mr. Rupp to shorten his pole." Groza and Beard were banned from the NBA for life following the '50-'51 season for shaving points while playing for UK. A knee injury severely limited the effectiveness of Wah Wah Jones. Former Notre Damer Leo Barnhorst did his best to keep the Olympians afloat by averaging 13.6 PPG, but the heart had gone out of the team. The franchise collapsed following the '53 season.

The Anderson Packers had been unable to capitalize on their success, and that club folded after one glorious NBA campaign. Only one club was left to carry the Hoosier torch throughout the NBA wars. And the Ft. Wayne Zollner Pistons made quite a show of it. Led by the Hoosier Pistons mentoned above and NBA All-Stars like LaSalle's Larry Foust, Stanford's George Yardley and Leo Barnhorst, Ft. Wayne enjoyed eight largely successful NBA seasons.

In 1954-'55 the Pistons won the Western Divisions crown and extended Syracuse to the final game of the Championship Series before falling to Dolph Schayes' Nationals. The Pistons repeated as '56 Western Division kings behind Yardley's 17.4 average. Ft. Wayne finished that season falling to the Philadelphia Warriors (Golden State) in the Championship Series.

In 1956-'57 Yardley finished fifth in NBA scoring with a 21.5 average, and though the Pistons slipped to 34-38, the franchise was a healthy one. But the nature of professional sports in America was changing. "Media" and "Money" were conspiring to create the Modern Age of Sports. Professional basketball was eager to shed its small-time skin. The Rochester Royals moved to Cincinnati for the '57-'58 campaign, and Fred Zollner moved his Pistons to Detroit. An era of professional basketball in Indiana had come to an end. It would be a full decade before another began.

The Lowest-Scoring Game in NBA History
November 22, 1950 at Minneapolis

Ft. Wayne Pistons (19)

Player	Pos	FGA	FGM	FTA	FTM	AST	PF	PTS
Fred Schaus	F	1	0	3	3	1	0	3
Jack Kerris	F	1	0	4	2	0	5	2
Larry Foust	C	2	1	1	1	0	3	3
Bob Harris		0	0	1	0	0	1	0
John Hargis	G	1	1	0	0	1	0	2
Ralph Johnson		1	0	0	0	1	1	0
John Oldham	G	5	1	4	3	0	2	5
Paul "Curley" Armstrong		2	1	2	2	0	1	4
Total		13	4	15	11	3	13	19

Minneapolis Lakers (18)

Player	Pos	FGA	FGM	FTA	FTM	Reb	AST	PF	PTS
Jim Pollard	F	1	0	1	1	1	1	2	1
Bud Grant		0	0	0	0	0	1	1	0
Vern Mikkelsen	F	2	0	0	0	3	0	2	0
Joe Hutton		0	0	0	0	0	0	0	0
George Mikan	C	11	4	11	7	4	0	1	15
Slater Martin	G	2	0	3	0	1	2	2	0
Bob Harrison	G	2	0	2	2	0	0	3	2
Arnie Ferrin		0	0	0	0	0	0	0	0
Total		18	4	17	10	9	4	11	18

Score by Periods:	1st	2nd	3rd	4th	Totals
Ft. Wayne	8	3	5	3	19
Minneapolis	7	6	4	1	18

Referees: Jocko Collins and Stan Stutz. Attendance: 7,021.

Coincidentally, the highest scoring game in NBA history occured on December 3, 1983 when the Detroit Pistons defeated the Denver Nuggets 186-184 in triple overtime. For the Pistons, Isiah Thomas scored 47, former Pacer John Long 41, Kelly Tripucka 35, and Bill Laimbeer 17. Ray Tolbert scored 3, while Kent Benson played but did not score. Former Pacer Alex English scored 47 for the Nuggets. Bill Hanzlik had 2 points with 7 boards, 7 assists, and 6 fouls.

Hoosier Hysteria: From the Barnyards to the Playgrounds

So Indiana colleges spent the better part of the Golden Age bullying their neighbors, and Hoosier cities provided the incubators for professional basketball. That would seem to pretty much sum up the story. But this is Indiana, and in Indiana The Game is the story—and The Game is high school basketball.

Indiana is one of the few remaining states to conduct a "one-class" boys basketball tournament. Since private, parochial, black and institutional high schools were admitted to the tourney in 1943 all Hoosier high schools have played for the same trophy. All Indiana boys basketball players dream of the same prize their fathers dreamt of, and their fathers before them and their fathers before them. Kids growing up next to Gary steel mills or next door to Crawford County turkey farms fantasize about sinking the same shot, in the same game, in the same building, under the same circumstances.

Whether you're fast-breaking down the court at Indianapolis' Butler-Tarkington Park, practicing your head-fakes in a driveway in Richmond or stirring dust on a dirt court in Owen County you want the same thing. You want to be the one and only Indiana High School Boys Basketball Champion.

For sociological reasons too complex to explore in this volume, the Indiana educational system was slow to consolidate. Even the smallest communities were likely to maintain their own high schools well into the 1960s—and even the most miniscule of those schools were likely to field a boys basketball team. Whereas in 1990 there were fewer than 400 schools in the State Tourney, 787 schools participated in 1938, and as late as 1959 710 Indiana high schools battled for the same prize.

Many communities and even neighborhoods identified themselves through the local high school—and the basketball team was the most visible representative of the high school. That such a scenario would produce the high drama achieved throughout the 1940s and '50s seems almost inevitable upon reflection. Hammond vs. Mitchell, Fort Wayne vs. Lebanon, Shelbyville vs. Terre Haute, Milan vs. Muncie, Attucks vs. Shortridge—throw in the Lapels, Batesvilles and Springs Valleys and John Steinbeck himself couldn't have created a better stage for playing out the American Dream.

Hoosier moviemakers Dave Anspaugh and Angelo Pizo were so inspired with the legend of the Milan Miracle that they created the Academy Award-nominated movie Hoosiers *in 1986. (l to r) Steve Hollar, Kent Poole, Gene Hackman, Scott Summers, Brad Boyle, and Wade Schenck. Courtesy Orion Pictures.*

Cinderella Keeps the Slipper

The sound engulfed Butler Fieldhouse in wave after unremitting wave. Hoosiers were shouting, screaming, crying. Veterans of the Indiana basketball wars stared at each other in disbelief, shrugged and smiled meekly. The officials stood poised for action, but wearing the looks of two men who had walked in the wrong door and were trying to make up their minds whether or not to back out. The sounds grew and bounded off the ceiling and walls until it seemed the venerable old basketball palace would blow away.

And what was happening on the field of combat? Nothing. Absolutely nothing. A slender youngster with a crew-cut was standing at the center of the floor with the basketball cradled against his stomach. The clock ticked; still he stood.

It was the fourth quarter of the State Championship Game matching two improbable opponents. Lined on the side of the court were the five players representing mighty Muncie Central, the perennial title contender in pursuit of a record fifth championship. With them were four players from Milan, the unlikely opponent from Hicksville, USA.

Muncie Central was one of the largest high schools in the state. Milan, population 1,150 had an enrollment of 162—73 boys. The David-Goliath motif was even followed on the floor. Muncie Central's front line averaged 6-5. The tallest player for Milan was just under 6-2, and he saw limited action due to a back injury.

Although it was Milan's second straight trip to the Final Four, the Indians were not considered in the same league with the other three participants. Muncie Central, Elkhart and Terre Haute Gerstmeyer had ranked at the top of the state polls throughout the 1953-54 season.

In 1953 Milan had reached the finals after winning a controversial overtime game in the Regionals, then was bombed by South Bend Central 56-37.

Milan coach Marvin Wood got the most out of his talent by employing a deliberate offense that utilized picks and screens. To the surprise—and elation—of most of the fans, Milan led most of the way. But Muncie finally moved ahead, 28-26, at the beginning of the fourth quarter.

Then came the shocker. With Milan trailing by two, Bobby Plump dribbled to the center of the floor, stopped and pulled the ball up against his stomach. He held it for four minutes and fourteen seconds as pandemonium became the order of the evening. With 3:38 to play, he called time,

Bob Collins Sports Profile

then held the ball for forty-three seconds before shooting and missing.

Muncie Central was a fast-breaking team, and its rhythm was destroyed by the inactivity. The Bearcats lost the ball, and Ray Craft scored for Milan. Plump was fouled and hit both free throws, but Muncie scored with just forty-eight seconds remaining, 30-30.

With people just flat out going out of their minds, Plump held the ball until only eighteen seconds were left on the clock and again called time. Returning to the floor, Plump began a slow, drag dribble. With eight seconds left, he cut to his right and headed for the basket. A Muncie defender moved out to meet him. Plump stopped at the back of the keyhole, faked, jumped, and sent the ball toward the basket. It swished gently through the hoop with three seconds showing on the clock.

Bobby Plump, who went on to an outstanding career at Butler and now is a succesful Indianapolis insurance executive, said his only conscious thought was, "Boy, if you miss this, you are going to be the biggest goat in history."

Frosting was added to the cake when it was announced after the game that Plump had won the Trester Award for Mental Attitude. He was the first member of a Championship Team to achieve the honor.

The team began the eighty-mile journey home to Milan the following morning with a four-car motorcade. Fans from all over Indiana joined them enroute. The team was met by police cars and fire trucks at the outskirts of two cities and escorted through town with sirens screaming.

By the time the champions reached home, the caravan stretched for thirteen miles and state police estimated that 30,000 were waiting in the area around the high school to pay tribute to the small-town heroes who had beaten the odds.

Bob Collins Sports Profile

If the "Milan Miracle" represents the American Dream—the belief that anyone can overcome great odds to achieve the highest success—the exploits of Indianapolis Crispus Attucks High School stake a mighty claim to the same representation.

Attucks had been constructed in 1927 for the purpose of segregating all black students in Marion County. Indianapolis and Indiana in general were under the heavy influence of the Ku Klux Klan at the time. It had been a scant two years since a murder conviction had removed KKK Grand Dragon D.C. Stephenson from a position of immense political influence. Stephenson's fall had taken Indianapolis Mayor John L. Duvall and Indiana Governor Ed Jackson with him in a wave of corruption-related scandals.

By 1951 Crispus Attucks High School had become the touchstone of Indianapolis' near-Northwest side. In spite of inadequate funding and inadequate attention from the movers and shakers the school prided itself in educating the black community.

Attucks hadn't been allowed to participate in the Indiana High School Basketball Tournament until 1943. When the school made the Final Four in 1951 it amounted to a vindication of the entire black community. Black teams could be as disciplined, organized, creative and successful as any white team, and Attucks' Final Four appearance proved it. CAHS's Bob Jewell was named the first black recipient of the Trester Award for Mental Attitude. Oscar Robertson hadn't arrived on the scene quite yet, but big brother Bailey Robertson contributed significantly to the '51 squad. "Flap" Robertson would go on to establish nearly every offensive record on the Indiana Central University (University of Indianapolis) books and eventually sign a contract with the Harlem Globetrotters.

6'8" "Wee Willie" Gardner and 6'3" Hallie Bryant were the mainstays of the '51 Attucks "Tigers." Bryant scored 10 points in the Semi-Final loss to Evansville Reitz. In 1953 he was voted the state's Mr. Basketball. Following three varsity seasons with Coach McCracken at Indiana University that included the 1957 Big 10 Crown, Bry-

58

The 1951 Attucks Semi-State Champs. Among identifiable people in this photo are (far right), Ray Crowe with Hallie Bryant, Bailey Robertson, (third from left, bottom row), and (third from left, top row), Willie Gardner. Bob Jewell, winner of the 1951 Trester Award for Mental Attitude is obscured by #15.

ant signed with Abe Saperstien's Harlem Globetrotters. The former Attucks star enjoyed a twelve-year playing career with the 'Trotters before moving up to the front office.

William Gardner scored 22 points in the Reitz game and signed with the 'Trotters directly out of high school. In an era when the 'Trotters played a great deal of serious basketball as well as putting on their performances of trick shots, ball-handling and passing, Wee Willie won team MVP accolades in 1954 and '57.

In 1957 the Globetrotters sold Gardner's contract to the New York Knickerbockers in the biggest deal in NBA history to that time. Health problems, unfortunately, spelled a quick and premature end to Willie Gardner's fabulous career.

A still imposing 6'8", 270 pounds, Wee Willie Gardner has been a corrections officer with the Marion County Sheriff's Department for some time. His place in Indiana basketball lore is secure as he holds a coveted position on Hall of Famer Tony Hinkle's All-Time Indiana Hardwood Dream Team.

The 1955 and 1956 Tigers were the definition of Awesome. The '55 team entered the Championship Finals against Gary Roosevelt 30-1. Willie Merriweather scored 21, Sheddrick Mitchell 18 and Oscar Robertson chipped in 30 as Attucks annihilated Roosevelt 97-74. Three Bills—Brown, Scott and Hampton all contributed their efforts to the destruction. Willie Merriweather was named to the Indiana All-Star Team and went on to a fine career at Purdue. Mitchell and Scott were two stalwarts of fine Butler Bulldog teams of the latter 1950s.

Oscar Robertson returned to the Attucks hardwood to lead the '56 Tigers, and this edition was able to one-up its predecessor. The '56 Tigers went 31-0 and demolished Lafayette Jeff 79-57 in the Championship Game. The "Big O" dropped eighteen field goals and three free throws for a Final Game record 39 points. Robertson's 106 "Sweet Sixteen" points also established a new mark. Voting for Mr. Basketball was a mere formality. Stanford Patton scored 33 Final Four points and joined Oscar on the Indiana All-Star Team.

The Instant Dynasty

In 1950 when, at the age of thirty-three, he became head basketball coach at Crispus Attucks, he never had coached an organized team. When he stepped up to the athletic director's position just seven years later, he was recognized as one of the greatest coaches in Indiana basketball history.

Ray Crowe built an instant dynasty. His teams won 193 games and lost only twenty. In one dazzling, two-season period, they put together a 60-1 record, including an all-time high of forty-five games in a row. Crowe won two state titles and was runnerup once. And only one of his seven teams failed to advance as far as the Semi-State in the IHSAA Tournament.

In many ways Crowe was an unlikely candidate for a basketball coach. He always was impeccably dressed—even during practice. He rarely raised his voice, seldom spoke in anger. He sat quietly on the bench during some of the most exciting moments in Indiana high school basketball history. Only his friends knew the turmoil; the battles that raged within.

Ray Crowe met prejudice head on and won a unanimous decision. Many good and dedicated people worked for years to crack the racial barrier in Indianapolis. But if you want to go back to the time when the walls began crumbling, circle the era of Ray Crowe and his Attucks Tigers.

Crowe knew what he was up against; he knew there would be times when his teams would get something less than an even break. But he insisted that his players never complain and concentrate only on the job of winning.

Though soft spoken, Crowe was a strict disciplinarian. He could impale a player on a stare or frighten him half to death by snapping his fingers. He was the absolute boss from the time the players put on their uniforms until they showered.

After that, he was friend and surrogate father; trying to help with problems, trying to keep them in school; trying to keep them in clothes, following after they left school and trying to help them find jobs. In 1950 few Indianapolis teams would schedule Attucks. The Tigers would build impressive records against small schools, then collapse when they ran into good competition in the tourneys. Under Crowe they became the Number One drawing card in the state, playing to crowds as great as 12,000 in Butler Fieldhouse.

Their schedule and performance were awesome. In 1955-56 when they went all the way undefeated, they were ranked Number One all season and beat nine teams in the AP high school poll.

Crowe's coaching philosophy was simple: storm the boards, get the ball and go. His teams would score over 90 points several times each season.

Ray Crowe is far more than a successful basketball coach. He is a man concerned with his community, his home town and his state. Since leaving the game he coached so brilliantly, Mr. Crowe has served on the Indianapolis City-County Council and in the Indiana State Legislature. His contributions to civic responsibilities, charitable causes and commercial endeavors merit a chapter in their own right.

Today Ray Crowe lives in comfortable retirement in the city of Indianapolis, secure in the legacy of an important, well-lived life.

Bob Collins Sports Profile

The Big O: Wizard of "Ahs"

"I would pay money to watch Oscar Robertson play basketball alone"—Alex Hannum

"There's nothing Oscar can't do. He's so great he scares me."—Red Auerbach

"How can you call that traveling? You never saw that move before."—Oscar Robertson

One can imagine Dr. James Naismith sitting among his gymnasts and peach baskets in the Springfield, Mass. YMCA trying to visualize the perfect player for the simple-appearing, but complex game he had invented. The player, ideally, would be well over six feet tall and strong. He would have big hands and quick feet. He would be able to play inside or facing the basket, have the ability to drive or shoot outside. He would have lightning reflexes and a quick mind. He would have an almost supernatural ability to find and hit the open man. And with his own sheer talent and will power, he would be able to control the tempo of the game.

No such human existed during the lifetime of Dr. Naismith. There has been but one real contender since the first game of basketball was played in 1891. Oscar Robertson was basketball's Renaissance Man.

The game has had giants who dominated their era. It has seen spectacular shooters, superb defensive players and flashy, accurate passers. But Oscar was the only one who took all the weapons of the game into combat. After watching Oscar turn the Finals of the 1956 Indiana High School Basketball Tournament into a personal triumph, a writer summed it up with "Robertson doesn't play this game, he conducts a free clinic."

The Big O led Attucks to consecutive state titles in 1955-56. During his last two seasons, Attucks won an all-time record forty-five straight games and compiled a 60-1 mark.

At Cincinnati, the college he chose for his higher education, Oscar led the nation in scoring in 1958, '59 and '60 and was named the outstanding collegiate player in each of his three seasons. His 1,011 points and 33.7 PPG average in 1960 both established NCAA marks. The Big O took the Bearcats to the 1959 Final Four, but his 19 points and 19 rebounds couldn't overcome Coach Pete Newell's California Golden Bears in the Semi-final Game. Robertson and Cincinnati returned to the Final Four in 1960, but an Ohio State team featuring Havlicek, Lucas, Siegfried and a combative sub named Bobby Knight carried the day.

Advance ticket sales soared to $110,000 when Oscar signed to play professionally with the Cincinnati Royals in 1963. And though he never could take the Royals to an NBA title, he was the franchise—and one of the league's—best drawing cards.

Robertson was traded to Milwaukee, where the combination of the Big O and Kareem Abdul Jabbar was awe-inspiring. The Bucks put together a startling 66-16 regular season record, then raced to the NBA Championship, losing only two of fourteen playoff games.

Robertson retired after the 1973-74 season, leaving behind a record which placed him among the all-time NBA leaders in nearly every offensive category. His total of 9,887 assists stood as an NBA record until 1980.*

A proud and sensitive man, he endured racial slurs with dignity but fought tenaciously for his rights and the rights of other players.

He would have made Naismith supremely proud.

*The Big O was 1961 NBA Rookie of the Year when he averaged 30.5 PPG. He was First Team All-Pro 1961-'69 and an NBA All-Star 1961-'71. He was All-Star Game MVP in 1961, '64 and '69 and NBA MVP in 1964. Oscar finished his career number six on the NBA assist list, number five in field goals made, number four in minutes played (43,886), first in free throws made (7,694) and fourth in points scored (26,710). The Big O was elected to the Naismith Hall of Fame in 1979.

Bob Collins Sports Profile

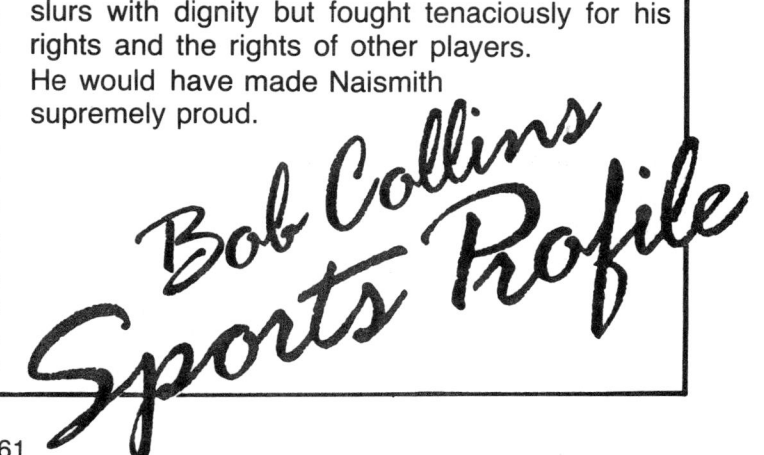

The end of the Crowe-Robertson era at Indianapolis Crispus Attucks didn't signal the end of the era of great Tiger basketball. In 1947 Bill Garrett had scored 46 Final Four points to lead Shelbyville over East Chicago Washington and Terre Haute Garfield for the State Title. The 6'3" center had played Garfield's 6'9" Clyde Lovellette to a 21-25 standoff in the Championship Game. Garrett became the third black man to be designated Mr. Basketball for his efforts.

In 1948 Bill Garrett became the first black player to start for a Big 10 school as he manned the center position for Indiana University. Using speed and deception against Lovellette-sized centers in the Big 10, Garrett seldom was outscored. He was named to the All-America Team and voted IU's MVP following the 1950-'51 season.

An outstanding leader and role model, Bill Garrett was the perfect heir to Ray Crowe. In 1959 Coach Garrett took the Tigers—led by All-Star Larry McIntyre—to a Final Game showdown with Trester Award winner Jimmy Rayl's Kokomo Wildcats. Rayl fired in 26 of Kokomo's 54, but it wasn't anywhere near enough to offset Attucks' balanced attack. The Tigers split 92 eleven ways.

The course of history rolls on. Housing patterns and society's thoughts evolve. Crispus Attucks has been a Jr. High for some years now. Bill Garrett passed away in 1974 at the too-young age of forty-five. Ray Crowe is long retired and the Big O doesn't come around as much as his fans would wish. But the Attucks Tigers will be there forever. They changed Indianapolis as surely as they changed Indiana. Nothing about Hoosier Hysteria will ever be the same—and we're all the better for it.

The Ones That Got Away

It would be nice to report that all of the greatest Indiana high school basketball players of the Golden Age went on to greater glories with Indiana colleges and greater glories still with Hoosier professional teams. But a few did wander, and we must pay a couple of special ones their due.

Leroy "Cowboy" Edwards graduated from Indianapolis Tech in 1933. He is a member of the Consensus Indiana High School All-Star Team, 1926-1940. In 1934 the 6'4" center achieved the distinction of becoming Coach Adolph Rupp's first All-American at the University of Kentucky.

From 1937 through 1949 Cowboy Edwards was one of the NBL's most feared offensive weapons. Shooting a deadly hook-shot with either hand, he scored a record 30 points in one rookie game. Edwards led the league with an unfathomable 16.2 average as his Oshkosh All-Stars finished runners-up to Akron in the NBL's inaugural campaign. Cowboy went on to score 3,221 points for a career 10.0 PPG average. The All-Stars captured three professional titles during his tenure.

Johnny "Jake" Townsend followed closely on the heels of Cowboy Edwards at Indianapolis Tech. Townsend led Tech to the 1934 Indiana High School Final Game where the Titans fell to Logansport 26-19. The 6'4" center went on to earn All-America honors at the University of Michigan in 1936, '37 and '38. An outstanding all-around athlete, Jake Townsend would have been a shot-putter on the 1940 US Olympic Team if Adolph Hitler had restrained his Panzers.

During the 1940s Johnny "The Houdini of the Hardwood" Townsend played sporadically with Hammond, Indianapolis and Oshkosh of the NBL. Like most professional athletes of the 1940s, Townsend's athletic career was dramatically affected by the necessity of military service.

In 1939 Ray Crowe's little brother George led Franklin High School to the Indiana High School Championship Game against Frankfort. George Crowe scored 13 of the 22 points Coach Fuzzy Vandivier's Grizzlies tallied. But Coach Everett Case's Hotdogs prevailed by fourteen. George Crowe—a black man—was named Indiana's first official Mr. Basketball.

Crowe might have found a place in the fledgling/floundering ranks of professional basketball, but he chose to pursue a career in Negro League Baseball instead. By 1952 times had changed, and George Crowe became the first baseman of the Boston Braves. During his nine-year stint with the Braves, Reds and Cardinals Crowe hit .270 with 81 homers and 299 RBI. A deadly clutch hitter, the former Mr. Basketball led the National League with 17 pinch hits in 63 at bats (.270) in 1959.

Following his retirement from baseball, George Crowe spent a number of years working for the Baseball Commissioner's office in New York City.

Ten years elapsed between Cliff Barker's freshman and senior seasons at the University of Kentucky. After one year with the Wildcats the Yorktown product joined the Army Air Corp. His B17 was shot down over Germany in 1943, and Barker spent sixteen months in a Nazi prison camp. One method of whiling away the tedium of incarceration was to obtain a ball from camp guards and spend endless hours working on ball-handling and trick passing.

Barker returned to Lexington following his liberation to team with Alex Groza, Ralph Beard and Wah Wah Jones. UK went 102-8 between 1947-49 and captured two NCAA Titles. Untouched by the point-shaving scandal that brought down Groza and Beard, Cliff Barker was also a member of the 1948 US Olympic Gold Medal Basketball Team. His career was capped by a two-year stint as player/coach of the NBA's Indianapolis Olympians. Included in those two seasons was the 1950 NBA Western Division Championship.

Following the 1948 Indiana high school basketball season, the somewhat clumsy 6'9" center from Terre Haute Garfield didn't have Hoosier collegiate recruiters banging down his door. But Kansas University's Phog Allen saw something he liked in the 250 pounder, so the Hoosier took off for Jayhawk country.

As a collegian "Man Mountain" Lovellette revolutionized the game of basketball. Prior to Lovellette—and George Mikan at DePaul—huge centers were primarily used to rebound and get in the way on defense. Phog Allen changed that thinking. "He's closer to the basket than anyone else on the floor," said Allen of Lovellette, "so I'd rather see him go for it than anyone else."

While he was in high school Lovellette's mother encouraged him to skip rope incessantly in an effort to improve his coordination. But the big kid remained slow and awkward. At Kansas, Coach Allen intensified the rope-skipping regimen, and he gave his aircraft carrier the ball—early and often.

Lovellette was voted a consensus All-American in 1951. As a senior in 1952 the husky Hoosier led the nation in field goals (315), points (795) and average (28.4). As the NCAA Player of the Year he carried the Jayhawks to the '52 National Championship. Lovellette's 1,886 career points, 28.4 single-season average and 33-point NCAA Final Game outburst all established NCAA standards.

Lovellette's greatest impact on the college game was that his success encouraged coaches to seek out behemoths to patrol the lane. One Wilt Chamberlain arrived on the Jayhawk campus soon after Lovellette's departure.

Clyde Lovellette anchored the 1952 US Olympic Gold Medal Basketball Team before embarking on a superb eleven-year NBA career with the Lakers, Royals, Hawks and Celtics. He was voted to the 1956, '60 and '61 All-Star Teams and played for the 1954, '63 and '64 World Champions. Lovellette scored 11,949 points in 704 NBA games for a 17.0 point career average. The Hoosier was elected to the Naismith Hall of Fame in 1987.

Following his retirement from the National Basketball Association in 1964, folks around Terre Haute referred to Clyde Lovellette as Sheriff Clyde Lovellette for eight years. We imagine he wasn't the object of a great deal of abuse from would-be felons during his term. Over the past several seasons Lovellette has worked to help establish a competitive basketball program at White's Institute in Wabash County.

Hoosier Football Fever Declines Between '20 and '60

The history of Indiana football during the Golden Age of American Sports, between 1920 and 1960 is not a story of unbridled success and glory. With one huge exception, football in the Hoosier state entered a period of relative decline.

Perhaps the decline was due to the overwhelming popularity of Hoosier Hysteria. Maybe Indiana's hundreds of small rural schools simply couldn't afford to consistently field quality football programs. There may have been other reasons, but compared to nearby states like Ohio, Michigan and Pennsylvania, Indiana high schools of the era produced few great players and fewer great teams. The state was one of the last to introduce a championship tournament, and official state champions were not even recognized until the 1970s.

The situation with Indiana intercollegiate football was similar, if not quite so dramatic. While early powers like Wabash College and DePauw and Butler Universities continued to be competitive at a lower level, they simply found big-time college football too expensive to justify. By the end of the '30s, most of the state's smaller or private colleges had stopped scheduling the major football schools. The era at IU and Purdue was marked more by the occasional brilliant star than by any record of consistent excellence.

East Chicago's Joe Zeller captained the 1931 Hoosier basketball team and was named MVP of the Cream and Crimson squad. The "two way end" played the '32 season with Curley Lambeau's Packers before signing with the Bears in '33. During Zellers's stay in Chicago, George Hala's Bears defeated the Giants 23-21 for the

1933 NFL title and fell 30-13 to N.Y. in the '34 Championship. The Hoosier retired in 1937 following the Bears' 28-21 setback at the hands of Washington in the NFL title game.

Zora Clevenger had been an outstanding running-back at Indiana University at the turn of the century. He went on to coach football, baseball and basketball at Tennessee, Kansas State, Missouri and Indiana University. He is a member of the National Football Foundation Hall of Fame (NFFHF). Clevenger made his greatest contribution to Indiana sports history when, as the IU athletic director, he hired Alvin "Bo" McMillin as head football coach in 1934.

McMillin had already achieved some degree of fame. In 1921 his thirty-two-yard run had been the only score in the Centre College (KY) "Praying Colonels'" stunning 6-0 upset of the powerful Harvard Crimson. Kentucky's Governor Edwin P. Morrow was quoted after the game as saying, "I'd rather be Bo McMillin at this moment than the governor of Kentucky."

McMillin specialized in perfecting the reverse and throwing from the reverse. A stern, tough taskmaster, Bo coached IU to a 63-48-11 record between 1934 and 1947. In 1945 he put together a team that averaged 235 pounds—a huge team by that day's standards. These "Po' Little Fellas" took IU to an undefeated season, a Number Four national ranking and the Hoosiers' only outright Big 10 championship.

McMillin left IU in 1948 to take the head coaching position with the Detroit Lions of the fledgling National Football League. Though he experienced limited success on the field with the Lions, Bo's election into the NFFHF recognizes his contribution in helping to establish the popularity of American professional football.

McMillin's first great player at IU was New Castle's Vern Huffman. Though he was named to the All-Western Conference (Big 10) Basketball Team in 1936, Huffman's greatest talents were as a running-back/defensive-back. While playing for the Detroit Lions in 1938, Huffman set an NFL record by running back an interception 100 yards against the Brooklyn Dodgers football team.

East Chicago's Eddie Rucinski was an All-Big 10 end/running back for the Hoosiers in 1940. During six seasons with the Brooklyn Dodgers football team and the Chicago Cardinals Rucinski caught 99 passes for 1,408 yards and 8 TDs. He is also credited with intercepting four passes.

Many of McMillin's best players came together at the same time to form his best team. Between 1942 and 1946, Pete "Big Dog" Pihos broke all of IU's pass-receiving, touchdowns and total points records. As captain of the Hoosier's '45 Conference Champions, Pihos called plays and signals from his position at fullback.

Pihos' most important collegiate catch came two plays after a critical pass from a great baseball player. Big Dog's touchdown catch against the Northwestern Wildcats in 1945 salvaged a 7-7 tie, an undefeated season and IU's conference title. The play was set up when Hoosier end Ted Kluszewski faked an end-around and tossed a twenty-one yarder to All-American Bob Ravensburg. ("Big Klu" went on to slug over 300 homers for the Cincinnati Reds and Chicago White Sox. In 1959, Klu set a World Series record by driving in ten runs for the Sox in a six-game Series.)

Another great player on the '45 team was sophomore tailback George Taliaferro. Following his graduation, "Scoop" became one of the top black players in the professional All-American Football Conference. Between 1950 and 1955, Taliaferro enjoyed some success with the New York Yanks, Dallas Texans, Baltimore Colts and Philadelphia Eagles of the NFL.

Unfortunately, after McMillin's departure, IU's football program went into a steep and rapid decline that lasted for twenty years.

IU All-American Pete Pihos hauls in a long bomb as an all-pro for the Philadelphia Eagles. Courtesy Pro Football Hall of Fame.

The Boilermakers Struggle for Consistent Excellence

The football fortunes of Purdue's Boilermakers were in a somewhat better state than IU's fortunes during this era, but the period is marked more by the occasional superstar than by consistent greatness.

The Boilers had enjoyed some success during the Pioneer Period. After joining Butler, DePauw, Wabash, Franklin and IU in the Indiana Intercollegiate Athletic Association in 1890, Purdue had captured the league title four years running. However, in 1895 Purdue joined the Universities of Michigan, Minnesota, Illinois, Wisconsin, Northwestern and Chicago to form the conference that would eventually become the Big 10. This new level of competition drastically limited Boilermaker success on the gridiron for some time.

In 1911 a tough kid from the coal mines of southern Indiana showed up on the campus at West Lafayette. Elmer Oliphant was so tough he kicked a field goal against Illinois in spite of a broken ankle. But Elmer was a lot more than tough. In 1912 he scored five touchdowns and kicked thirteen extra points in a 91-0 rout of Rose Poly (Rose-Hulman). Oliphant also set a world record in the low hurdles while at Purdue and was captain of the basketball team.

In 1914 Oliphant graduated from Purdue and entered the Academy at West Point, where he lettered in football, basketball, baseball and swimming. He also captained the hockey team and captured the Academy's heavyweight boxing title. Unfortunately, the Black Knights' gain was the Boilermakers' loss. Purdue's football program sank back into the doldrums.

Former Notre Damer Jimmy Phelan took over the sagging Boilermaker program in 1922 and struggled to a 1-5-1 record in his first year. By '29 Phelan had taken the Black and Gold to the top of the Big 10. Behind the running, passing and kicking of All-American Ralph "Pest" Welch, the Boilers finished 8-0 and won the undisputed Big 10 Championship. In the season's highlight game, The Pest scored two fourth-quarter touchdowns to rally the Boilers from a 16-6 hole against the Wolverines of Michigan. The Purdue victory was the first against the Wolves in thirty-seven years.

Opening holes for Pest Welch was the job of Elmer "Red" Sleight (pronounced 'Slate"). At 6'3" and 225 pounds, Red was a giant for his time. Sleight became Purdue's first All-American lineman in 1929 before moving on to play for Curley Lambeau's Green Bay Packers.

Following the Championship season, Jimmy Phelan left Purdue to accept the top job at the University of Washington. He took Pest Welch with him as an assistant. Before they left, Jimmy and Pest had laid the foundation for one of the more successful periods in Purdue football history.

Noble Kizer, a Fighting Irish line coach under Knute Rockne, took over the Boilers upon Phelan's departure. Led by All-Americans like end Paul Moss, center Charles Miller and tailback Duane Purvis, the Boilers captured the '31 Big 10 title with a 9-1 record. The Black & Gold followed this success by compiling 7-0-1 and 6-1-1 records in 1932 and '33. Purvis added to his fame by capturing the javelin throw in the 1934 National Collegiate Track and Field Championships.

In 1935 Cecil Isbell joined the Boilers and became one of football's most feared offensive weapons. As a runner and passer from his halfback position, Isbell achieved greatness in spite of a serious handicap. Against Northwestern in his first collegiate game, he dislocated his shoulder. For the next three seasons, Cecil played with his arm strapped so that he could not raise it over his head. Despite this limitation, Isbell went on to star for the Green Bay Packers before returning to coach at his alma mater in 1944, '45 and '46.

In 1936 Purdue's Boilermakers appeared ready to take their place among the top collegiate football programs in America. Unfortunately, the fates can deal cruel blows. In those days, gasoline and naptha were often used as softeners for removing tape. On September 12, 1936, a coal-fired locker room water heater ignited fumes from the gasoline. The resultant fire severely burned four players and killed guard Carl Dahlback and star running back Tom McGannon.

(The fire was the second great tragedy in Purdue football history. In 1903 sixteen people, including thirteen players, had been killed when a train carrying them to Indianapolis for a game against IU slammed into a parked coal train.)

The deaths of McGannon and Dahlback took something out of Coach Kizer. Universally recognized as a kind and humane man, he may have blamed himself for the accident. In addition to the tragedy, Kizer contracted a serious kidney ailment in 1937. He retired prior to the '37 season and eventually moved to New Mexico, where he died in 1940 at the age of forty. Purdue president E.C. Elliott delivered this eulogy: "Noble Kizer was rightly named. He was indeed a nobleman."

At .764%, Kizer's 42-13-3 record over seven seasons remains the top Boilermaker standard.

Following Kizer's departure, the Purdue football program entered a period of extended mediocrity. There were, however, a number of fine players and an occasional outstanding team.

In 1943, at the height of World War II, Purdue's Marine training program produced the likes of guard Alex Agase, halfback Babe Dimancheff and fullback Tony Butkovich. The Marines led

Noble Kizer instructs his Boilermakers. Courtesy Purdue University Athletic Department.

All-American Duane Purvis (far right) takes a break with his 1932 Boilermaker teammates, including NBA pioneer #98 Doxie Moore. Courtesy Indiana State Museum collection.

Purdue to a 9-0 record and the Big 10 title. After the season, their Marine training complete, many of the top players returned to their former schools like the Universities of Michigan and Illinois. Tony Butkovich was killed on the beach at Okinawa in 1945.

Dave Rankin was a superb end on the '39 and '40 teams, and Bob DeMoss became the first in a long series of great Purdue quarterbacks when he came to West Lafayette from Kentucky in 1945. Unfortunately, neither Rankin's nor DeMoss' teams met with much success. The same can be said for the mid-'50s team of future NFL greats Lamar Lundy and Lenny Dawson. Purdue fans would have to wait until the 1960s for Coach Jack Mollenkopf to lead the Boilermakers back to the pinnacle of intercollegiate football.

Bob DeMoss, the first of the great Purdue All-American quarterbacks. Courtesy Purdue University Athletic Department.

Shake Down the Thunder

One Indiana football program did maintain a high level of excellence throughout the Golden Age of Sports, in fact, the legends that surround this team helped create the Golden Age. While the sports exploits of Ruth, Grange, Dempsey, Gehrig, Owens and Louis captured America's imagination, fans also idolized Rockne, Gipp, Leahy, Lujack and Lattner. There has never been a team anywhere, in any sport, at any time that has achieved more glory than the Fighting Irish of Notre Dame.

Notre Dame's football program probably would have attained greatness with or without Knute Rockne, but The Rock took *A* great team and made it *The* great team.

Born in Voss, Norway, in 1888, Rockne emigrated to Chicago with his family in 1893. Between 1911 and 1913 he played offensive and defensive end for three straight undefeated Notre Dame football teams.

Rock took over the Irish head coaching position in 1918. Between 1919 and 1921, his teams won twenty games in a row and outscored the opposition 626 to 68.

In 1924 ND's legendary "Four Horsemen," Harry Stuhldreher, Don Miller, Jimmy Crowley and Elmer Layden (famine, pestilence, destruction and death) rampaged behind a line Rockne dubbed "The 7 Mules." The Irish swept to an undefeated season, crushed Stanford 27-10 in the Rose Bowl, and claimed an undisputed National Championship.

Elmer Layden went on to serve as both ND football coach and athletic director during the 1930s. In 1941 he became the first Commissioner of the National Football League. Layden's NFL reign lasted until he was replaced by Bert Bell in 1946.

Knute Rockne's greatest contribution to American sports history lies in what he gave back to the game of football. Rockne was as famous for his big heart and inspired leadership as he was for his ability as a football coach. The manner in which he conducted himself did as much to popularize American football as any single factor. Rockne defined sportsmanship.

"Football teaches a boy responsibility," he said. "Responsibility as a representative of his college; responsibility to his teammates and responsibility in the control of his passions, fear, hatred, jealousy and rashness. Football brings out the best there is in one."

Rockne's teams played fair and they played exciting. Rock's game was colorful and dashing. "People don't want to see a tug of war . . . they want action and entertainment. The wide open game gives 'em a better show." In 1919 Notre Dame went to West Point and played before 6,000 non-paying customers. Rockne's '29 Fighting Irish were packing them in nationwide. Nearly 100,000 fanatics sold out Soldier Field in Chicago and an even larger crowd packed the unfinished Los Angeles Coliseum for a battle with the Trojans of Southern Cal. It was truly the Golden Age of college football.

Who knows what glory Knute Rockne might have achieved in a long life? During the off-season in '31, Rock was touring the country promoting the Studebaker Automobile Company's new model—"The Rockne." It promised to be a big seller for the South Bend auto manufacturer. On March 31 Rockne was aboard the Transcontinental & Western flight out of Kansas City bound for California. The plane went down shortly after take-off, killing all passengers and crew. Knute Rockne was only forty-three years old. Jimmy Walker, the popular mayor of New York City, delivered this eulogy:

> My words would be worthless if I were not speaking for 60,000 families whose wage earners, out of work, had not been materially aided by the charity game last winter. Knute Rockne came clear from California, and at the risk of his personal health gathered a team that battled for charity on a cold and forbidding day. New York recognizes the contributions his life made to the training of manhood, but it realizes with an unforgetting memory the service this man gave us in a time of need.

If the greatness of Notre Dame had died with Knute Rockne, it would remain a glorious story. But, the legend of the Fighting Irish was just beginning.

The classic Knute Rockne. Courtesy Notre Dame Sports.

Notre Dame's legendary Four Horseman of the Apocalypse. Stuhldreher, Miller, Crowley, Leyden. Courtesy Notre Dame Sports.

CHORUS:

*Cheer! Cheer for old Notre Dame
Wake up the echoes cheering her name
Send the volley cheer on high
Shake down the thunder from the sky
What tho' the odds be great or small
Old Notre Dame will win over all
While her loyal Sons are marching onward to Victory.*

"Win One for the Gipper"

George Gipp was **Knute Rockne's** greatest ballplayer. As a freshman he drop-kicked a sixty-two yard field goal. Against IU he dislocated his shoulder—then—carried seven straight times for sixty yards and a game-saving touchdown. Against Army in 1920 he ran a punt back fifty-five yards, threw a forty-yard touchdown pass, kicked a sixty-yard punt, gained 236 yards rushing, kicked an extra point and played safety. Rock called him the best player, next to Jim Thorpe, who ever lived.

George Gipp was also a "free spirit." He was suspended from Notre Dame for a semester for spending too much time in South Bend's Hullie and Mike's pool hall. He was known to bet as much as $500 on Notre Dame games, then insist the Irish quarterback give him the ball until the point spread was covered. Gipp missed practices regularly and was known to pause for an occasional smoke during practice.

Everyone, including The Rock, was inclined to overlook these lapses when "The Gipper" took the field. George was a natural born leader on the gridiron. He loved the excitement of the game, and crowds thrilled to his flashy play. His lighthearted "no problems today" attitude eased the tensions of the big games for his teammates. More than anything else, football was FUN for George Gipp. He was the heart and soul of a squad that won eighteen in a row in 1919 and '20.

George Gipp would be remembered as a great football player under any circumstances. But he has passed beyond legend and into American mythology. In Rockne's words, "Gipp was nature's pet and, as with many of her pets, nature also punished him." In December of 1920, Gipp contracted strep throat, the infection quickly spread and developed into pneumonia. On December 14, 1920, George Gipp died at South Bend's St. Joseph's Hospital. He was twenty-five.

In death George Gipp gained immortality. Rockne was at his side and quoted one of the player's last statements,

> I've got to go, Rock. It's all right. Sometime, Rock, when the team is up against it, when things are going wrong and the breaks are beating the boys—tell them to go in there with all they've got and win just one for the Gipper. I don't know where I'll be then, Rock. But, I'll know about it, and I'll be happy.

Whether or not this speech ever happened is a matter for debate. One cynical sportswriter has suggested that Gipp's last request would more likely have been to ask Rockne to put a bet down for him some day when the Irish were a sure thing. Rockne swore to his dying day that the sentimental speech had really been delivered, and there were witnesses who backed him up.

Perhaps the story is true, maybe it's just a story—it doesn't matter. In 1928 the Irish lost four games—one third of all the games Knute Rockne teams lost. They went into Yankee Stadium to face a great, undefeated Army team. Rock recounted Gipp's request. "This is the game the Gipper asked for," Rockne told his team. Rockne cried. The Fighting Irish cried. The New York policemen in the locker room cried. New York's mayor Jimmie Walker cried. The Irish won 12-6.

Pat O'Brien starred in the title role of the motion picture, "The Knute Rockne Story." A young actor named Ronald Reagan played George Gipp. Many years later, during his most difficult days as President, Ronald Reagan would urge his supporters and staff to "win one more for the Gipper." That nearly every American understood what the President meant is proof of the influence Indiana sports exerts on American society.

George Gipp. Courtesy Notre Dame Sports.

Frank Leahy had been a tackle on Rockne's '29 and '30 Irish teams. Though a severe knee injury ended his playing days during the '30 season, Leahy wasn't out of football for long. He was born to coach. As the line coach at Fordham, Leahy put together the "Seven Blocks of Granite." Toughest of the Seven Blocks was a young Vince Lombardi.

Coach Leahy moved into the top spot at Notre Dame in 1941 and led the Irish to an undefeated season in his first campaign. Unlike Rockne, Leahy had little use for inspiring speeches. He was a strict disciplinarian who demanded and received perfection from his players.

In 1960 Leahy became the first general manager of a new team, the Los Angeles Chargers, in a new league—the American Football League. The team and league proved to be a great success. Today, the San Diego Chargers are proud members of the NFL's American Conference.

In the thirteen years he coached Notre Dame, Leahy produced twenty-seven All-Americans. Included in this legion are four Heisman Trophy winners. Angelo Bertelli won the award in 1943 even though he left the Irish after six games to join the Marines during World War II. A pinpoint passer, "Accurate Angelo" was also an excellent defensive back and place-kicker. Bertelli returned from the armed services to play for the Los Angeles Dons and Chicago Rockets in the All-American Football Conference.

When Bertelli left Notre Dame for the war, he was replaced by a young quarterback from Pennsylvania named Johnny Lujack. Lujack left to serve in the military in 1944 and '45 and returned to win the '47 Heisman. In an era when professional football players were lucky to make $10,000 a year, Lujack played briefly for the Chicago Bears before moving on to the business world. He did stay in Chicago long enough to set a Bear record by passing for 468 yards in one game against the Chicago Cardinals in December of '49.

In 1949 Leon Hart became one of only two ends to win the Heisman. Hart was fortunate to be drafted by one of the NFL's most successful teams of the period, the Detroit Lions. He played for Championship Lion teams in 1952, '53 and '57. During his seven year NFL career the 6'5" 257 pound end made 174 receptions for 2,499 yards and 26 TDs.

Leahy's last Heisman winner may have been his best. As an Irish running-back, Johnny Lattner gained 1,724 career yards. As a defensive back, he stole thirteen interceptions. As a kick-returner, he ran a kick-off back ninety-two yards for a touchdown against Pennsylvania. Lattner also served as the Fighting Irish punter. In 1954 he was drafted by the Pittsburgh Steelers and made the Pro Bowl his rookie year.

Even the greatest athletes are human beings, and human beings are fragile machines. Playing in an army reserve game during the off-season, Lattner tore up a knee and was forced to retire from the game after one brilliant professional season.

Fortunately, John Lattner, like all Notre Dame football players, had received an education from one of the world's great universities. It wasn't difficult for him to make his way in a world without football. Lattner would go on to become a successful Chicago businessman, and the glory of Notre Dame football would only continue to grow.

John Lattner, 1953 Heisman Trophy winner. Courtesy Notre Dame Sports.

Fritz and the Pros

If you were to state that the Indianapolis Colts are Indiana's first NFL team, 99.9% of all football fans would agree with you. If you were to state that the Los Angeles Raiders' Art Shell, is the first black head coach in NFL history, 99.9% of all football fans would agree with you. Trouble is, you'd be wrong—not once but twice.

In 1919 the American Professional Football Association (APFA) was founded as the first pro football league. Teams included the Canton Bulldogs, Akron Pros, Cleveland Indians, Columbus (Ohio) Panhandlers, Dayton Triangles, Detroit Heralds, Massillon Tigers, Rochester (NY) Jeffersons, Rock Island Independents, Toledo Maroons, a team from Wheeling and the Hammond Pros.

In 1920 Muncie sent a representative to the league meeting, but the city was never able to field a team. In '21 the Hammond Pros and Evansville Crimson Giants both fielded APFA teams. The Crimson Giants defeated the Green Bay Packers and were actually undefeated and in first place when they folded after only two games. The Pros also struggled financially and temporarily suspended operations.

In 1922 Hammond was back as a full-time member of the re-named National Football League. Unfortunately, they weren't particularly successful. In '22 the Pros finished 0-4-1 and in seventeenth place in the eighteen-team NFL.

*Embarrassed by such ineptitude and determined to improve their lot, the Pros signed Brown University's All-American quarterback **Fredrick Pollard** to serve as the Hammond team's quarterback and head coach. Thus, "Fritz" Pollard became the first black head coach in NFL history.*

By the 1924 season Hammond had moved up to 2-2-0 and eleventh place in the league, but a chance for further improvement never materialized. The NFL was still principally a semi-organized association of professional barnstormers. Games were scheduled wherever and whenever there was a possibility of gate receipts. Planned schedules would not be introduced until 1935. Travel was extremely difficult, and players jumped from team to team for an extra payday.

*In 1926 and '27, nineteen professional clubs succumbed to financial defeat. The Canton Bulldogs, Massillon Tigers and Hammond Pros, among others, gave way to Curley Lambeau's Packers, George Halas' Bears and the Giants of New York City. Hammond players like the great Negro players **"Inky" Williams** and **Sol Butler** signed on with other league teams, took up with barnstorming squads or rejoined the real world. **John Shelbourne** accepted a lifelong teaching position with Evansville's Colored High School.*

Fritz Pollard and the Hammond Pros disappeared from the history of the NFL—not from the official records and histories, but at least from the minds of TV commentators, sportswriters and the average football fan.

The One and Only: Number 98

The world of sport is a place where superlatives bloom from every typewriter. And "great" is the most overused—and misused—word in the sport idiom.

In every generation, however, a few athletes come along whose performances fit the adjectives. Their fame is such that often neither a Christian name nor a surname is needed when fans recall their exploits.

Thus, sports conversations are filled with talk of the "Bambino," the "Big Train," the "Brown Bomber," "Joltin' Joe," "Magic," and "Dr. J."

Fewer still so dominate their sport that they are recognized by the mere mention of their uniform numbers. Real quick, any college football fan could name two: "Number 77," Red Grange of the University of Illinois, and "Number 98," **Tom Harmon** *of Gary, Indiana and the University of Michigan.*

Harmon, a gifted all-around athlete, won four letters in four sports at Gary Mann High School. But it was his sensational running with a football that fired the imagination of college coaches. Harmon was heavily recruited, and Purdue thought it had the inside track since Harmon's three older brothers had attended the West Lafayette school. But Michigan won out and got itself a legend.

The big Irish kid from the steel mill region was a virtuoso. He could run, throw and kick. He also was a fine defensive player. He had few peers as a runner—before or since. Harmon had excellent balance, lightning reflexes and a great runner's unerring instinct for daylight. He was one of the rare athletes who could send electricity surging through a crowd. Nearly every time he got the ball from his wingback position the people in the stands—friend and foe—would leap to their feet.

In three years at Michigan, Harmon averaged nearly five yards a carry from scrimmage. He passed for 2,110 yards and scored 237 points. Additionally, he ran back kicks and averaged nearly forty yards a punt.

Against California in 1940, he scored on runs of 72, 80, 86 and 94 yards. Harmon ran and passed for 320 yards and accounted for 34 points in the final game of his collegiate career in 1940. In that contest against Ohio State he scored three times, passed for two touchdowns and place-kicked four extra points. He also averaged 50 yards on two punts. At season's end he was awarded the Heisman Trophy as the outstanding collegiate player in the nation.

No less authority than Amos Alonzo Stagg said, "Harmon was the greatest runner of his time. I'll take Harmon on my team and you can have all the rest." At University of Michigan at the height of his career some grumbled that he was a publicity hound and had gotten too big for the game and the school. He remembers it differently. "People think it was wall-to-wall glamour for me at Michigan, but I bussed dishes from six to eight every night for $85 a month. Out of that I paid room and tuition. I was not allowed to have a car. When I got to be an All-American, I got the best job on campus, hustling cigarettes in the frat house for ten bucks a week."

His legions of fans followed his exploits as a fighter pilot in World War II, where he survived both a crash in the jungle enroute to North Africa and later a shoot-down of his plane by the Japanese over the Yangtze River in China. Harmon returned to a hero's welcome. He dined at the White House, and Henry Ford personally picked a car off the assembly line for him.

He joined the Los Angeles Rams for the 1946 season and turned in the team's two longest runs of the year—84 and 85 yards. But the magic was gone. He retired after the 1947 season and entered the world of broadcasting where "Tom Harmon Sports" introduced him to an audience who had never seen or even read about his accomplishments on the gridiron as Number 98. Tom Harmon died in 1990, leaving a legacy of achievement and excellence that will be hard to beat.

Bob Collins Sports Profile

Tom Harmon of Gary, Indiana and the University of Michigan.

The Golden Age of Sports saw the emergence of football, basketball and baseball as the most popular American athletic contests. In terms of fan attendance, press coverage, salaries payed to professionals and numbers of participants, the "Big Three" sports dominated the national sporting scene.

Though it remained immensely popular in Europe, competitive bicycle racing had almost completely disappeared from the United States by 1920. Prize-fighting and track and field also were not able to keep up with the exploding popularity of the "Big Three," but both sports maintained a substantial following throughout the country, and Indiana produced more than its share of the top stars of the day.

Hoosiers Continue Their Impact on the "Sweet Science"

Boxing remained an alternative to unskilled labor for many first and second generation immigrants. The Irish neighborhoods of Indianapolis produced battlers like Tracy Cox, who advanced to a Number Three position in the ranks of the world's light heavyweights during the 1930s.

Bud Cottey, another Indianapolis Irishman, won $110 when he defeated Jackie Taylor in Dayton, Ohio for the World Junior Welterweight Championship in 1941. Cottey left the fight game long enough to win the Silver Star for bravery while fighting in Italy during World War II. An attempted comeback after the war was halted by a near fatal auto crash. Bud recovered from his injuries and went on to become a valued member of the Marion County Sheriff's Department.

One who was not so lucky was Chuck "The Hoosier Playboy" Wiggins. After cutting up legendary Heavyweight Champ Gene Tunney in one famous 1920's brawl, Wiggins took a bribe to take a dive against eventual champion Primo Carnera. After the fix, Wiggins' career declined rapidly. He died drunk, broke and friendless in the hallway of a fleabag hotel.

Undoubtedly the greatest Hoosier fighter of the Golden Age was Anthony Florian Zaleski—known to fight fans everywhere as the great Tony Zale. A Gary native, Zale appeared on the boxing scene at a time when the middleweight division dominated the sport. Budding champions Sugar Ray Robinson and "The Raging Bull" Jake LaMotta were just young pups in the pen when Zale outpointed Georgie Abrams for the undisputed World Middleweight Title in 1941.

Indiana State Museum collection.

Zale's climb to the top had been less than meteoric. He fought 95 times as an amateur—KO-ing 50 opponents in three rounds or less. After capturing the 1931 Indiana Golden Gloves Lightweight crown the "Man of Steel" turned pro in 1934.

Tony was a crowd-pleaser—a vicious body puncher with a rock jaw. He fought as often as twice a week while working in the Gary steel mills to supplement his income.

The fights that made Zale a legend were three titanic struggles with the great Rocky Graziano. In 1946 Zale defended his title by knocking Graziano out in six at Yankee Stadium. The fight set a world middleweight purse record, as both combatants were paid nearly $80,000 for their battle.

Graziano gained his revenge by knocking out Zale in six at the Chicago Stadium in 1947. The fight set a record for indoor receipts as fans paid $422,009.18 to witness the struggle. Tony ended the rivalry in 1948 when he pummelled Rocky into submission in three short rounds in Newark, N.J.

Both Rocky Graziano and Tony Zale were more famous for their ability to hit people extremely hard than they were for their ability to get out of the way of people who hit extremely hard. Their epic bouts took a toll on both fighters. In September of '48, Zale went down in twelve at the hands of Marcel Cerdan. For Tony it was time to hang up the gloves for good. His 1958 election to the Boxing Hall of Fame secured his spot among the legends of the fight game.

Tony Zale was one of the lucky ones. For a brief moment he captured the fancy of America's sports fans. The money he earned enabled him to go into private business when his boxing days were over. By all accounts, he has lived a long and prosperous life.

Herman Phillips' Bulldogs Lead The Pack

Indiana's colleges and universities continued to turn out many of the nation's top track and field stars throughout The Golden Age of American Sports. Rushville's Herman Phillips won the Indiana High School Mile run in 1920, '21 and '22. In 1923 Phillips set an American schoolboy record for the mile when he won the National Championship in 4:23.

Phillips enrolled at Butler University in 1924. The following year he became the last non-Big 10 runner to win a Big 10 track and field title when he captured the league's invitational 440-yard dash. He followed that victory with the 1925 NCAA 1/4-Mile crown. His 1926 and 1927 titles established Phillips as the only runner to capture three consecutive NCAA 1/4-Mile Championships. In 148 collegiate races, Phillips compiled an unbelieveable record of 147 victories against one defeat.

As a member of the 1928 Amsterdam Olympic Team, Phillips suffered from sea sickness and other physical ailments on the long boat trip to the Netherlands. He finished a disappointing fourth in the 1/4-mile—missing out on a medal by fractions of a second. A Gold Medal as a member of the 1,600-meter relay team surely offered some consolation. An acquaintanceship with '28 Olympic swimmer Johnny Weismuller was another fringe benefit of the trip for the Hoosier track star. Weismuller soon became known to motion picture fans world-wide as Tarzan the Apeman, Lord of the Jungle, while Phillips returned from the Olympics to resume the track and field head coaching duties at Butler that he had begun while still an undergraduate.

As chief of the Bulldog program, Phillips tutored several of America's top athletes. Butler's Joe Siwak was crowned the 1931 National Collegiate Mile Champion. In 1932 Bert Nelson established a World Record in the high jump with a leap of 6'8 3/4". The great Butler distance runner Ray Sears won national AAU Cross-Country and 10,000 Meter Championships in 1933 and set the American Indoor 2-Mile mark in 1934.

Phillips' greatest contribution to American athletics was his establishment of the Butler Relays. Throughout the 1930s and '40s the annual event, held in Butler (Hinkle) Fieldhouse, was one of the nation's premier collegiate track meets. The Relays' highlight may have come in 1935 when the Bulldogs' Kenneth Sandback clocked a world record 7.4 in the 60-yard high hurdles. In 1937, Phillips moved on to Purdue, where he established the Purdue Relays as a prestigious event in its own right.

During the 1970s Herman Phillips was one of the first stars inducted into the United States Track and Field Hall of Fame. It's doubtful that Indiana ever produced a finer athlete.

1928 Olympian Herman Phillips. Indiana State Museum collection.

Track Stars Shine For IU, ND & Purdue

Herman Phillips might have been the top Hoosier track and field competitor of the Golden Age, but he was hardly the only one.

At IU, E. C. "Billy" Hayes from Madison established the Cream and Crimson as a national powerhouse during the '30s and '40s. While he was also serving as assistant football coach under Bo McMillin and as assistant basketball coach under Everett Dean and Branch McCracken, Hayes led the Hoosiers to thirteen Big 10 indoor, outdoor and cross-country titles. The 1932 NCAA Outdoor Team Championship preceeded NCAA team cross-country titles in 1938 and 1940.

The best of the five Olympians Hayes coached at IU was two-mile man Don Lash. Lash's first important record came in 1936 when his 9:10.6 broke Butler's Ray Sears' American indoor two-mile standard. Later the same year Lash shattered the legendary Paavo Nurmi's world outdoor two-mile mark when he posted an 8:58.3 clocking at the Princeton Relays. The following year Lash broke "The Flying Finn"'s twelve-year-old world indoor two-mile mark with an 8:58 flat. During the summer of '37, he teamed with IU mates Tommy Deckard, Jimmy Smith and Mel Truitt to set the world four-mile relay record of 17:16.1.

In 1936 Lash and Deckard joined Jesse Owens on the US Olympic team that proved to the world that the Germans weren't the master race Adolph Hitler had been proclaiming. Lash's career was capped in '38 when the AAU presented him with the Sullivan Award as America's top amateur athlete. His twelve NCAA and AAU track and cross-country titles guaranteed the award.

Though he was disappointed at not winning a medal at the Berlin Olympics, Lash would undoubtedly have been a Gold Medal favorite at the '40 Olympics. Unfortunately, Hitler was determined to prove a point. The war he started in 1939 enveloped the world and stopped any possibility of holding an Olympics in 1940.

Among Hayes' other great runners was Ivan Fuqua, who won a Gold at the '32 Los Angeles Olympics as a member of the world record 1,600-meter relay team. 1932, '33 and '34 NCAA 1/2-mile champ Charley Hornbostel set the world record for the indoor 600-meters in 1933 and tied the indoor 1/2-mile standard the same year. Hornbostel ran the 800 meters for both the '32 and '36 US Olympic teams.

Billy Hayes' last great champion was Fred Wilt of Anderson. Wilt captured the 1941 NCAA cross-country championship and the '41 NCAA outdoor two-mile title. During the '40s he was crowned National AAU cross-country, one-mile, 5,000-meter or 10,000-meter champion nine times. Wilt was a member of the 1948 London and 1952 Helsinki US Olympic Teams. In 1950 he joined fellow Hoosier alum Don Lash as a recipient of the Sullivan Award. In 1952 Wilt matched another Lash accomplishment when he became the second Indiana native in sixteen years to set the world indoor two-mile record.

When Fred Wilt graduated from IU in 1941, an FBI agent recruited him into the Bureau. The agent's name was Don Lash. Both men served with distinction for over a quarter century. Wilt not only continued to run at a world-class level, he also became one of America's foremost authorities on track and field and coaching. He has published nearly twenty books on those and associated subjects. Not one to rest easy in retirement, Wilt took over the women's track and field and cross-country programs at Purdue upon leaving the FBI in 1977. He held that position until retiring in 1989.

Billy Hayes' death in 1943 didn't end the progression of great track stars at IU during the Golden Age of American sports. Milt Campbell may have been the greatest all-around athlete in IU history. A letterman in football and track, Campbell won the Olympic Decathalon Silver Medal in 1952. After capturing NCAA and AAU high hurdle championships in 1955, Campbell returned to the Olympics in '56 and this time to, the Decathalon's gold. Campbell capped his career in 1957 by tieing the world's 100-meter high-hurdle mark of 13.4.

Campbell's IU teammate, Greg Bell, brought the Hoosiers additional fame when he won the 1956 NCAA broad jump crown. Bell joined Campbell in the Olympic winner's circle in '56 when he leapt 25' 8 1/2" to the Gold Medal.

Though IU and Butler were the dominant Indiana track and field powers throughout this era, the two schools did not have a monopoly on Hoosier track stars.

Future Notre Dame track coach John Nickolson was an Olympic hurdler in 1924 and briefly held the world's high hurdle record. Fellow Fighting Irishman Tom Lieb won the 1922 Big 10 Open Event Discus Championship and threw the platter for the '24 US Olympic team. Notre Damer Paul Harrington set the American indoor pole-vault record in 1926 with a leap of 13' 8 1/2".

Purdue's Boilermakers also chipped into the

Drawn by William Mullin, 1950. Indiana State Museum collection.

track and field talent pool. Orval Martin finished first in all eight Big 10 middle-distance races he contested from 1928 to 1930. In 1929 Martin added the Big 10 Indoor Mile Record (4:21.9) to his Big 10 Indoor 1/2 mile standard (1:55.0). In 1930 Martin crowned his collegiate career when he covered a half-mile at the Chicago Stadium in 1:54.1 to establish the NCAA Indoor Record.

Though Orvall Martin's Black and Gold teammate Duane Purvis was better known as an All-American tailback for the Boilers, Purvis demonstrated his all-around ability by tossing the javelin 216' 6 1/4" to capture the 1933 NCAA title. Purvis' throw travelled nearly 3/4 the length of a football field and fell 1/2" shy of a World's Record.

One great Hoosier track star who somehow got away from the Indiana collegiate recruiters is Warsaw's Max Truex. In 1954 he established the Scholastic Mile Record while at Warsaw High School. Truex chose to run in the sun at the University of Southern California where in 1956 he captured the national AAU 10,000-meter Championship.

Truex was a member of two US Olympic teams—participating in the 1956 5,000-meters and placing sixth in the 10,000 at the '60 games in Rome. His 28:50.2 clocking at Rome established a new American Record for 10,000-meters.

Hoosier Women Swim To International Fame

Another major source of glory for America's international teams of the 1950s resided in an outstanding group of female swimmers and divers who hailed from The Great State of Indiana.

The Indiana State Sycamore basketball team wasn't the only Hoosier contribution to the inaugural US Pan American Games team. Indiana swimmers and divers constituted the heart of the American Womens' Swimming and Diving Team that was sent to Buenos Aires in 1951.

Betty Mullen-Brey won a Gold Medal in the 400 meter medley relay, a Silver in the 200-meter freestyle and finished fourth in the 400-meter free. In 1956, the Boilermaker All-American swam the butterfly leg of an American team that established a World Record in the 400-meter medley relay. Also a member of the 1955 Pan Am Team, Mullen-Brey just missed a spot on the '56 Olympic Team when she finished fourth in the 100 butterfly and fifth in the 100-freestyle at the Olympic Trials.

Three of Betty Mullen-Brey's Lafayette Swim Club teammates also nabbed 1951 Pan Am medals. Sheila Donahue won a Silver in the 100 backstroke, Carol Pence took a Bronze in the 200 breaststroke and swam a leg on the winning 300-meter relay team, and Mary Frances Cunningham captured both the Three-meter and High Board Diving Gold medals.

On July 4th, 5th and 6th of 1952, the US Women's Olympic Swimming and Diving Trials were held at Broad Ripple Park Pool in Indianapolis. Although the Indianapolis Athletic Club's Judy Roberts was the only Hoosier woman to secure a '52 Olympic berth, a number of other young Indiana athletes established themselves in the upper echelon of the nation's aquatic competitors.

Ann Moss missed an Olympic berth by .3 of a second in a five-minute race. Sheila Donahue lost her Olympic spot by .1 of a second. Other Indiana representatives at the '52 Trials include: From the Lafayette Swim Club: Anna Hayes, Betty Mullen-Brey, Sally Bowers, Phyliss Calhoun and Kay Manuel. From the Indianapolis Athletic Club: Linda Barton, Betsy Alexander, Gail Moll, Patricia Moll, Susan Schaefer, Brenda Barton, Sharon Feeney, Mary Ann Marchino and Betsey Turner. Barbara Jungclaus represented the Indianapolis Riviera Club, while Indianapolis' Ann Camp swam unattached.

Judy Roberts went on to finish tenth in the Olympic 100-meter freestyle. Jeanne Stunyo attended the University of Detroit, where she captured National AAU silver medals in the 1953 and '56 springboard competitions. Stunyo also won the Silver at the 1955 Pan American Games. On August 6, 1956, the Hoosier diver became one of the first woman athletes featured on the cover of *Sports Illustrated*. Later that same month, she capped a brilliant career by winning the 3-meter Springboard Silver at the Melbourne Olympics.

Mary Ann Marchino graduated from Indianapolis' Saint Agnes Academy in 1956. During the course of the 1950s, she won seven Silver Medals in various national backstroke events. Marchino competed in the 100-meter backstroke as a member of the 1956 US Olympic Team.

Joan Ann Rosazza was yet another dominant Hoosier swimmer of the 1950s. The Purdue coed was named to the All-American Team in 1955 for establishing an American Record in the 100-yard freestyle and anchoring a World-Record-setting, 400-meter freestyle relay team. Rosazza competed in the 100 freestyle as a member of the 1956 US Olympic Team.

The 1950s was a decade in which American women were entering into big-time athletic competition in increasing numbers. Clearly, Indiana's female swimmers and divers were in the forefront of this new and exciting trend.

Indiana basketball players, track stars and female swimmers weren't the only Hoosier athletes to make significant contributions to America's international sports teams of the 1950s. Charlie Adkins of Gary captured boxing's Light Welterweight Gold Medal at the 1952 Helsinki Olympics.

At the 1956 Olympic Games in Melbourne, Speedway's Sandy Ruddick represented the United States in the uneven parallel bars, the vault and the womens' all-around gymnastics competitions. Her teammate, Muriel Davis-Grossfield of Indianapolis, was the American Champion in freestyle calisthenics and represented her country in the event at the '56 Games.

Verle Wright of Fort Wayne was a member of the Intercollegiate All-American Rifle Team while attending IU in 1952 and '53. He was the American Intercollegiate Pistol Champion in 1953 and competed as a member of the US International Shooting Team in 1952, '53 and '54. Wright was a member of the 1955 US Pan Am Team and competed in the '56 Olympics as America's Small-Bore Rifle Champion.

Indiana's male swimmers were also beginning to establish the state's reputation as a leader in mens' swimming competition. Outstanding athletes like Frank McKinney, Jr., Richard Tanabe and Bill Wolsey will be presented later as members of Doc Counsilman's powerhouse IU swim teams.

Pan Am Swimming Team, 1951 (front row, l to r) Jacqueline C. Lavine, Carol Jane Pence, Carolyn V. Green, Sharon Geary, Margaret Hulton; (back row) Mary F. Cunningham, Patricia K. McCormick, Sheila E. Donahue, Betty E. Mullen, Maureen O'Brien.

*(Top to bottom) Carolyn Green, **Sheila Donahue**, Maureen O'Brien, **Betty Mullen**, Margaret Hulton, **Mary Cunningham**, Sharon Geary, **Carol Pence**, Patricia McCormick, Jacqueline LaVine*

Indiana's Female Finalists at the 1952 Olympic Swimming and Diving Trials:

Indianapolis Athletic Club	**Judy Roberts**	2nd 100 freestyle
	Ann Morrison	6th 400 breaststroke
Lafayette Swim Club	**Ann Moss**	4th 400 freestyle
	Carol Pence	5th 200 breaststroke
	Betty Lynch	6th 200 breaststroke
	Sheila Donahue	4th 100 backstroke
Lafayette Unattached	**Lucy Crocker**	5th 400 freestyle
	Sue Storer	7th 400 freestyle
Gary, Indiana	**Jeanne Stunyo**	5th 3-meter springboard

The Rise, Fall, and Rise of the Indianapolis "500"

What does one do for excitement after spending two years buzzing about the skies of France dueling with the Red Baron? Purchasing the Indianapolis Motor Speedway (IMS) may ease the boredom, which is exactly what Captain Eddie Rickenbacker—America's Ace of Aces—did in 1928.

After returning from his service in WW I, "Captain Eddie" had attempted to found his own automobile company. While the Captain's company produced a number of outstanding vehicles—including the Rickenbacker that served as the 1925 Indy "500" pace car—literally hundreds of American auto companies were also attempting start-up production during the 1920s. Like almost all the others, the Rickenbacker Automobile Company was a very short lived enterprise.

By 1928 IMS founder and owner Carl Fisher had lost interest in running the "500." His development of the Miami Beach area was going full-tilt, and that immense project demanded 100% of his time. The Speedway had begun to show tell-tale signs of years of neglect. Fisher sold the IMS to Rickenbacker for about $700,000 and moved to Florida permanently.

Carl Fisher, unfortunately, would soon become one of the millions of victims of the Crash of '29. Nearly bankrupted by the Great Depression, he died penniless in Miami in 1939.

Captain Rickenbacker's ownership of the IMS left a mixed legacy. The track continued to deteriorate. In addition, the 1930 reinstitution of riding mechanics produced a horrendous casualty rate. In 1931 a driver and a mechanic were killed. That same year, eleven-year-old Wilbur Brink was playing in his front yard on Georgetown Road when he was struck and killed by a flying tire. At least six participants were injured in the race dubbed the "Indianapolis '500' Demolition Derby." In 1935 the carnage reached four killed, while another riding mechanic was fortunate to escape with a broken back.

In 1936 Captain Rickenbacker invested $250,000 to replace most of the brick in "the Old Brickyard" with Kentucky rock asphalt. New wide-paved safety aprons and an improved track signal light system were also added. Riding me-

Indianapolis native Wilbur Shaw and his Maserati. Indy "500" Photos.

chanics were barred once and for all in 1938. The total race purse was raised to $75,000 in order to assure that true professionals would continue to be attracted to the event.

But, like Carl Fisher, Eddie Rickenbacker was a man of many interests and obsessions. In 1935 he became associated with Eastern Airlines. In 1938 he purchased the commercial airline titan and became its Chief Executive Officer and President—positions he held until 1963. When the federal government closed the IMS in 1942 due to the outbreak of World War II, Rickenbacker was already preoccupied with his other interests. Upkeep of the Speedway was neglected, and the facility fell into complete disrepair.

One of the great lights in the comparative darkness of the Rickenbacker era was Shelbyville's Wilbur Shaw. Shaw had dropped out of Indianapolis Tech High School to join the service during World War I. He returned to Indianapolis after the war and took up professional race car driving in 1923. The Hoosier finished runner-up at Indy in 1933, '35 and '38. He captured his first "500" in 1937 with a record 113.58 MPH, and followed with victories in 1939 and '40. Shaw was named National Auto Race Driver of the Year in 1937 and '39; then World War II intervened.

When he surveyed the devastated ruin that was the 1945 Indianapolis Motor Speedway, Wilbur Shaw realized the great racing facility needed a local entrepreneur to buy and efficiently manage it if the track were to survive. Shaw introduced owner Eddie Rickenbacker to Terre Haute businessman Anton "Tony" Hulman, Jr., and a $750,000 purchase price deal was soon struck.

Wilbur Shaw served as President and General Manager of the Speedway from 1945 until he was killed in the crash of a small plane near Bluffton in 1954. Captain Eddie Rickenbacker's last association with the Indianapolis "500" came in 1961 when he drove a 1914 Duesenberg on a ceremonial pace lap to mark the "500"'s Golden Anniversary.

Whether he realized it or not in 1945, Tony Hulman was about to embark on a great adventure. During his stewardship, the Indianapolis "500"—"The Greatest Spectacle in Racing"—would become the largest single-day sporting event in the world. The Motor Speedway's rise to zenith happened during the Golden Age of Sports.

Tony Hulman was no stranger to big time athletic competition. Following his service as a seventeen-year-old Red Cross ambulance driver during WWI, Hulman returned to the state of Massachusetts, where he attended Worcester Academy. In 1919 he was the top US prep hurdler, and in 1920 he was the best US prep pole vaulter. In 1920 Hulman entered Yale University as a classmate and friend of future entertainer Rudy Vallee. While at Yale, Hulman lettered as a member of the Eli rowing team and as an end on the school's undefeated 1923 football team. Later that same year, he won a gold medal in the high hurdles at the International Collegiate Track and Field Championships held in Wembley Stadium, London. Squads from Oxford and Cambridge provided the principle competition.

Upon graduating in 1924 with a degree in engineering, Tony Hulman returned to join the family business in Terre Haute. Hulman and Company grocers—makers of Clabber Girl Baking Powder—had long been a cornerstone of Wabash Valley commerce, and Tony had a natural flair for finance. By the time Wilbur Shaw introduced him to Captain Rickenbacker, Tony Hulman was the head of a financial empire that included newspapers, banks, a brewery and part ownership in the Chicago and Eastern Illinois Railroad. The Hulman Foundation, established in 1936, supported numerous civic projects including Terre Haute's Hulman Airport and one of the nation's finer engineering schools, Rose-Hulman University.

Tony Hulman, the spirit of the "500." Indy "500" Photos.

Not content to lean back comfortably on such a fortune, Hulman attacked the dangerous financial challenge the dilapidated Indianapolis Motor Speedway presented in 1946. Several hundred thousand dollars and a like number of man-hours were poured into the Speedway during the spring of '46. New steel stands replaced the wooden slats. The infield "weed patch" was turned into a comfortable general admission area. The track itself had to be weeded before a new layer of asphalt could be applied. Thousands of gallons of paint were slapped on the wood and metal of the facility. New gates and pedestrian bridges were added, and in mid-May, when the IMS opened for practice, spectators were admitted for fifty cents a head.

Contrary to Hulman's nightmares, the first postwar race was a huge popular success. Fans turned out by the tens of thousands to watch Cliff Bergere claim the pole with a 126.471 MPH average in his Noc-Out Hose Clamp Special. George Robson took the checkered flag in his Thorne Engineering Sparks. His 114.820 MPH was just enough to outduel Indianapolis Tech grad Jimmy Jackson for the right to sit in Victory Lane. The Indianapolis "500" was back for good.

In 1946 the popular Mauri Rose posted the second of his three Indy victories when he piloted his Blue Crown Offy to a 116.338 MPH average. The day before Race Day, spectators' cars began what was to become a tiresomely repeated tradition: they backed traffic up for miles waiting for the Speedway's gates to open. The total Race purse was raised to a record $137,425. That may seem paltry by today's standards, but the sum was nearly twice the traditional figure. The Indianapolis "500" was rapidly becoming more lucrative as the Race's popularity grew.

In 1956 the United States Auto Club (USAC) replaced AAA as the "500's" sanctioning body. Following the race, Hulman spearheaded a one-million dollar Speedway renovation. A new 1,322-foot recessed pit area was constructed, and the main straightaway was finally paved—save for the ceremonial "One Yard of Bricks." The most visible change occurred in the razing of the press pagoda that had served as the Speedway's traditional landmark. A new eight-story control tower and thousands of infield seats were constructed in the Pagoda's place. Sam Hanks took the first checkered flag on the refurbished track as his Belond Offy's 135.601 was tops in '57.

The first "500" Festival Parade was also conducted in 1957. The event added to the Race's aura by drawing hundreds of thousands of spectators to the streets of downtown Indianapolis for razzmatazz marching and celebrity-watching.

By 1959 the Indianapolis "500" had become one of the world's premier sporting events. Nearly 250,000 spectators poured into the IMS to see Indianapolis' own Rodger Ward blaze into Victory Lane. Ward established two important records in '59. His Leader Card Offy's 135.857 MPH average was a new "500" mark, and his $106,850 in winnings also set a new standard. The $338,100 total purse was more than 400% higher than the traditional purses prior to Tony Hulman's ownership. Sid Collins, Jim Shelton, Luke Walton and the other great announcers began to develop the Indianapolis Motor Speedway Network into a broadcasting giant that would eventually beam "500" coverage to over 100,000,000 listeners world-wide.

On the track, a changing of the guard had begun. At forty-six, Brownsburg's Duane Carter was the oldest driver in the '59 race. Though he was able to finish seventh, Carter would soon retire from competitive racing. He would eventually be replaced as a "500" contender by a younger Carter—son, Pancho. Jerry Unser—eldest of the Unser Clan—was fatally burned during the '59 Race and '50 winner Johnnie Parsons finally decided that he had had enough of racing. A twenty-four year old A.J. Foyt was the youngest driver in the '59 race. His tenth place finish provided a glimpse of better things to come.

In 1946 Tony Hulman purchased a dilapidated white elephant. By the end of the Golden Age of Sports, that white elephant had become a triumphant, roaring mastadon—home to the world famous "Greatest Spectacle in Racing." When he shouted his immortal command—"Gentlemen, start your engines"—Tony Hulman took his place among the giants of American sports history. But in 1959 it's doubtful that even Tony Hulman could forsee the further growth of the Indianapolis "500" yet to come. The Modern Era of American—and Hoosier—sports history was dawning.

More 500 Facts

1922: WOH Indianapolis and WLK Indianapolis provide the first radio broadcast of the "500". Eight of the first 10 finishers are Duesenbergs making it a "Doozy" of a race for the Indianapolis based auto manufacturer.

1925: **Peter DePaolo** becomes the first Indy "500" winner to average 100 miles per hour by pushing his Duesenberg "Yellow Banana" to an astounding 100.13 mph average speed.

1936: **Louis Meyer** becomes the "500's" first three-time winner, driving his Miller to a 109.069 mph average.

1938: In an effort to reduce fatalities—twenty drivers, mechanics and spectators had been killed since 1930—riding mechanics are barred from the race. One infield spectator is killed in '38 when he is struck by a flying tire.

1940: **Wilbur Shaw** becomes the first driver to win back-to-back "500s". Shaw pilots his Maserati to a 114.277 mph average speed for his third victory in four years.

1941: A huge fire sweeps the garage area and destroys three race cars. **Mauri Rose** abandons his Maserati when it develops early carburetor trouble. Rose relieves **Floyd Davis** in the Noc-Out Hose Clamps/Offy on the 72nd lap and goes on to win the race. Rose's victory is his first of three and is the last "500" to see co-winners.

1942-1945: No races are run at the Indianapolis Motor Speedway, as the federal government decrees that all fuel consumption and transportation production be dedicated to achieving victory in World War II.

1952: Twenty-two-year-old **Troy Ruttman** becomes the "500s" all-time youngest winner when he drives his Agajanian Offy into "Victory Circle." In '49, Ruttman had become the youngest to drive in the "500"—nineteen years, two months and nineteen days.

1955: After winning the '53 and '54 "500s" racing great **Bill Vukovich** is killed when his Offy strikes another car, flips end over end several times, strikes a utility pole, bounces off two passenger cars outside the track wall and bursts into flames.

1958: In the biggest accident in Indy "500" history to that time, fifteen cars pile up in the third turn of the first lap. Driver **Pat O'Connor** is killed. The crash results in a 1959 ruling mandating roll bars and fire proof uniforms. Rookie **A.J. Foyt** spins out in lap 148 and finishes sixteenth.

Indy "500" Photos.

PART THREE
The Modern Era
1960 - Present

Whether or not a true "Modern Era" in sports history began in 1960 is a subject for academic debate.

Dividing any social history into time periods produces a minefield. The 1920s were a "Golden Age" if you were a white, male athlete. During the 1950s baseball was a "modern" game while professional basketball was barely out of its "pioneer" stage. Subjective generalities aside, the year 1960 does present itself as an epochal turning point.

Part of the radical shift into modern gear was determined by forces outside sports.

On the national political scene, John Kennedy ushered in a new generation of leadership when he defeated Richard Nixon for the Presidency. Kennedy's victory was attributed to his winning performance in a debate carried by a young medium whose potential was not fully appreciated—television. Lunch counter sit-ins throughout the Deep South and the desegregation of the Louisiana Public School System hastened the breakdown of American racial barriers. The resultant increase in educational, social and cultural opportunities for the nation's black and Hispanic population almost immediately revolutionized the racial structure of the country's intercollegiate and professional athletic organizations.

On the international front, the world seemed to be shrinking almost as fast as it was getting more dangerous. The Soviet Union shot down pilot Francis Gary Powers' American U-2 spy plane, and Fidel Castro sequestered all US property in Cuba setting the stage for the Cuban Missile Crisis of 1962.

Sixteen newly independent African nations were admitted to the United Nations, but civil wars in the Congo, Laos, the Dominican Republic and other "Third-World" nations seemed about to drag the Superpowers into a world-wide conflagration. In spite of the uncertainties in the world situation, Americans, flush with the economic success of the post-World War II boom, had more money, more time, and a greater need than ever before to pursue the escape that athletic competition provides.

Regardless of what was going on in the real world, in the sports world of 1960, the times they were a-changin'. The National Football League hired the 33-year-old general manager of the Los Angeles Rams Alvin "Pete" Rozelle as the new league commissioner, agreed to new franchises in Dallas and Minnesota and approved the Cardinals' move to St. Louis after thirty-nine years in Chicago.

Why such radical changes in the ultra-conservative league? In 1960 the infant American Football League dared to challenge the established power structure with new franchises in NFL strongholds New York and LA. Worse yet, the upstart AFL usurped virgin and potentially lucrative territory in Houson, Buffalo, Boston, Dallas, Oakland and Denver—markets the NFL claimed by colonial birthright. The ensuing (pun intended) decade-long football war produced an expansion explosion, many innovations to attract new fans, changes in player salaries and benefits, and a major growth in the utilization of TV coverage. The superstar and Super Bowl followed, causing further alterations in contracts and free agency.

After 1960, Big Time Football would never again be mistaken for a game. The sport had become Big Business. Truly the Modern Age in sports was upon us.

This is not to suggest that professional football dragged us into the Modern Era. The revolution spanned the spectrum. In 1960 Major League Baseball agreed in principle to its first expansion in over half a century. By 1962 four new teams had been added—a 20% growth in the size of the National and American Leagues.

The old sportsman/owner system was giving way to corporate ownership, and the resultant promotional pushes significantly increased television revenues and gate receipts. Spring training expanded from the "Grapefruit League" to the "Cactus League." The popularity of American baseball in Latin America exploded as "winter ball" provided increasing numbers of Latins to the Major Leagues.

Though Curt Flood and the quantum changes in free agency were still several years in the future, the traditional player/slave-owner bonds were loosening. Baseball was also entering the Modern Era of sports as big business, and basketball had to follow.

The player-coach rosters of the 1959-1960 NCAA Basketball Final Four teams include the names of Jerry West, Oscar Robertson, John Havlicek, Jerry Lucas, Bob Knight, Pete Newell, Fred Schaus and Fred Taylor. If that group doesn't provide a nucleus for the evolution of basketball into a major, national sport, then one doesn't exist. West, Robertson and Havlicek completely altered the way the game is played. Knight revolutionized the way the game is coached, and Newell and Taylor were his mentors.

The most significant changes were social. In

1958 Adolph Rupp's Kentucky Wildcats downed Seattle for the National Championship. At one point in his career, someone asked the Baron of the Bluegrass why he didn't recruit blacks. Rupp had offered that he didn't need blacks because "A good white team will beat a good black team every time." If times were a-changin', it certainly wasn't one minute too soon.

The change to integrated basketball excellence was rapid. In the *Sporting News* history of the NCAA Final Four, sixteen players are featured in action photos of the '58 Finals—one of those players is black. Eleven blacks are featured in the four photos documenting the 1960 Final Four.

During the '60-'61 NBA season two new stars electrified professional basketball. Black pros Oscar Robertson and Elgin Baylor quicked the pace and elevated the scoring in the same season the Lakers moved to LA. Professional basketball was entering the Modern Era.

That all sports were opening up socially could be developed at thesis length, and this is an introduction to Indiana sports history. Let us, however, have one more example to prove the point.

The 1960 Rome Olympics were the first international games covered relatively heavily by American television. Though Americans won the decathalon, the basketball Gold, the pole vault, three boxing Golds, a sizeable number of the swimming races and many other glamor events, the unquestioned darling of both fans and media was a lithe, stylish, BLACK WOMAN from rural Tennessee. Twenty years before settling in Indianapolis, Wilma Rudolph captured the 100-meter dash, the 200-meter, the 4X100-meter relay and the respect of her countrymen and women. Wilma Rudolph didn't need to explain what she— a woman—was doing running a race. No longer was she excluded—as a black—from competing with and against whites.

America, fitfully, slowly, but inevitably, was entering the Modern Era of Sports.

And Hoosiers, past, present and future—were leading the way.

Indiana's Game Goes National

While basketball had long been a Hoosier obsession, at the dawn of the Modern Era in American sports history the game lagged far behind baseball and football in national prominence. During the 1960s, '70s, and '80s basketball's popularity skyrocketed and Indiana became universally recognized as the heart of the world's hardwood sport.

Indiana high school hoops entered the '60s with an explosion—a mortar explosion to be exact. Ron "The Muncie Mortar" Bonham led Central's Bearcats to their twelfth Final Four appearance on his way to selection as the decade's first Mr. Basketball. Bonham's forty points in a semifinal victory over Bloomington established a new Final Four record, and his sixty-nine combined points in the final two games set another championship round standard. "The Mortar's" heroics, however, were not enough to prevent coach John Baratto's East Chicago Washington Senators from upsetting the undefeated Bearcats 75-59 in the title game. Senator guard Bob Cantrell topped off East Chicago's perfect day by capturing the 1960 Trester Award for Mental Attitude.

Ron Bonham quickly recovered from his disappointing setback. "The Muncie Mortar" kept the Hoosier pipeline to the University of Cincinnati open by leading UC to an NCAA Championship in 1962 and a runner-up finish in 1963. An All-America selection in '63, Bonham finished his collegiate career as Cincinnati's Number Two all-time scorer—right behind the "Big O."

Current Indianapolis resident Wilma Rudolph briefly lent her expertise to the DePauw University track team. Courtesy DePauw University.

Following a two-year stint with the Boston Celtics, Bonham went with a new team in a strange new league. Launching long bombs from well beyond the new-fangled, three-point line for the American Basketball Association's Indiana Pacers was the perfect way for "The Muncie Mortar" to wind down his career.

It didn't take long for the state to produce another talent as exciting as Ron Bonham. In fact, in 1961 Hoosier Hysteria fanatics were treated to not one, but two great players with identical abilities.

Led by the VanArsdale twins, Tom and Dick, Indianapolis Manual dominated the high school hardwood scene in 1961. For some reason, the boys were usually referred to as Tom and Dick. Perhaps it was because Tom was older—much older—fifteen minutes older. At season's end, the brothers were named the state's first co-Mr. Basketballs. Excellent students as well as outstanding athletes (Tom was president of the National Honor Society, Dick was vice-president), the brothers were also the first co-winners of the Trester Award.

As had been the case in 1960, team effort overcame individual talent in the State Championship Game. Kokomo's Wildkats ambushed the VanArsdales' Redskins 68-66 in the first Championship Game since 1918 to be decided in overtime. Kokomo had trailed by seven with little more than a minute remaining in regulation, but coach Joe Platt's tough 'Kats refused to wither. Victory came when All-Star Ron Hughes calmly sank both free throws with three seconds left in overtime.

The 1961 championship defeat marked only the beginning of fabulous careers for both Tom and Dick VanArsdale. Both twins became Academic All-Americans under Branch McCracken at IU where they were named team co-MVPs in 1964 and 1965. In 1965 Tom and Dick led the Hoosiers to a 19-5 record and both were named second team All-Americans. During their collegiate careers, Tom scored 1,252 points in 72 games for a 17.5 average. Dick tallied 1,240 for a 17.2 clip. Tom grabbed 723 rebounds—Dick, 719.

The VanArsdale twins were split up in 1965 when the NBA draft sent Tom to the Detroit Pistons and Dick to the New York Knicks. The first choice of the expansion Phoenix Suns in 1968, Dick finally finished just ahead of his brother by

IU All-Americans Tom and Dick Van Arsdale. Courtesy Indiana University Sports.

being named an All-Star in 1969, 1970 and 1971. Tom followed close behind with All-Star designation in 1970, 1971 and 1972. After playing for the Pistons, Royals, 76ers and Hawks, Tom rejoined his brother in Phoenix for the 1977 season. Both brothers retired at the end of the year. Tom finished his 929 game pro career with 14,232 points while Dick chalked up 15,079 points in a 921 game career. If they ever make the Hall of Fame, it will probably be with the same number of votes in the same year.

The VanArsdales' fame almost completely overshadowed the accomplishments of another 1961 Indiana High School All-Star. Lewisville's Marion Pierce put together a 32.1 point-per-game average during his 94-game high school career. He scored 64 points against Union Township, topped 50 points six times, 40 points eleven times and 30 points eighteen times. His 3,019 career points set an Indiana high school record that would last three decades.

Though Marion Pierce's record stood the test of time, the athlete himself quickly faded into obscurity. With giant powerhouses like Indianapolis Attucks, Muncie Central and Marion to follow, few Hoosier fans paid much attention to the accomplishments of some kid from Lewisville.

It was twenty-nine years before Pierce re-entered the limelight. Another kid from an even smaller burg made a run at his record, and suddenly everyone wanted to talk to and about Marion Pierce. A kid from Heltonville—some kid named Damon—brought back all the memories. Ask the old-timers over in Henry County, they'll tell you. "Man that kid could shoot. No one ever shot a basketball better than Marion Pierce."

Actually, there is one person in the history of the universe who could probably shoot a basketball better than Marion Pierce. And of course, he is a Hoosier.

Rick "The Rocket" Mount was only nineteen when on February 2, 1966 he became the first high school athlete in history to be featured on the cover of *Sports Illustrated*. (We'll pick up Mount's career at Purdue University in an upcoming section)

All-Time Indiana High School Basketball All-Stars

Everybody has his or her All-Time teams. Hoosier Hysteria historian Herb Schwomeyer calls the All-Time Indiana High School All-Star Team this way:

G. John Wooden, Martinsville All-State 1927, '28

G. Oscar Robertson, Indianapolis Crispus Attucks All-State '55-'56

C. Homer Stonebraker, Wingate All-State 1913, 1914

F. "Fuzzy" Vandivier, Franklin All-State 1920, '21, '22

F. George McGinnis, Indianapolis Washington All-State 1968, '69

I'll take these guys. You get anybody else you want. Let's play! Well . . . we'll make Damon a super-sub for the time being.

As the great Oscar Robertson had followed closely on the heels of Bobby Plump, so too was the small town boy Rick Mount soon to be overshadowed by the immense talent of another kid who had mastered the game of basketball on the streets and playgrounds of Indianapolis.

At 6'8" and 240 pounds George McGinnis was an awesome specimen. A two-time All-State football player for Indianapolis Washington, "Big Mac" might have become one of the great tight ends of all time if he had chosen that path. Rumbling into the open field with the pigskin surrounded by one huge paw, "The Baby Bull" had the size, speed and attitude to end the career of many a free safety. But George McGinnis is a Hoosier, and basketball just seemed to make sense.

After an All-State basketball season in 1968, McGinnis teamed with future IU mate Steve Downing to lead Washington to an undefeated state title in 1969. As probably the most publicized Mr. Basketball since the Big O, Big George scored 23 points in the first Indiana/Kentucky All-Star Game of '69. One long-forgotten Blue Grass All-Star made the mistake of telling the press that 23 points was no big deal, and that he wasn't particularly impressed. It is assumed that McGinnis' 53-point, 31-rebound outburst in the second game corrected that impression. Both standards remain Indiana/Kentucky All-Star records.

Big Mac stopped off at IU long enough to average 29.9 points and 14.5 boards per game in his one varsity season. A kid coach from the east by the name of Knight showed up the next year. And while Steve Downing chose to stay and become Bobby Knight's first All-American, Baby Bull took his game to the pros.

Maybe Mel Daniels made the Indiana Pacers a great team. Maybe it was Slick Leonard, or Roger Brown, or Freddie Lewis. We'll argue that point later. But, at his best, surely none was ever greater than George McGinnis.

Big Mac exploded onto the professional scene as 1972 American Basketball Association (ABA) Rookie of the Year. In '73, '74 and '75 he was a league All-Star and in '75 was voted league MVP. He led the Pacers to ABA titles in '72 and '73 and led all league scorers with a Jordanesque 29.8 per game average in '74-'75.

Some will say, "But it was only the ABA." In '73-'74 Big Mac finished second in league rebounding behind only future NBA All-Star Artis Gilmore. McGinnis also finished second in league scoring that year, trailing one "Dr. J" Julius Er-

Big Mac, courtesy Indiana University Sports

ving. That's Big Time Company in any league, folks.

In '75 McGinnis took his talents to the NBA. At Philadelphia he joined with now teammate Dr. J to lead the '6ers to a 1976-'77 runner-up finish behind Bill Walton's Portland Trailblazers. McGinnis was an NBA All-Star in '76 and '77 before moving on to Denver and eventually winding up where he started by finishing his career with the now NBA Indiana Pacers in 1982. Big George averaged 20.3 points over his 842 game career for a 17,039 point total.

The Best of the Best: East Chicago Washington, '71

In the 1970s basketball finally tooks its place alongside baseball and football as the major American sports. Southern powerhouses like the University of Kentucky began accepting black players into their programs for the first time. More and more great athletes were getting the opportunity to display their abilities in high schools, colleges and in the rapidly growing professional leagues. Outstanding Indiana high school ballplayers were beginning to receive recognition nationwide.

One of the great things about being a sports fan is that you are allowed an opinion on almost everything. All your friends can disagree with you, and tell you about it loudly, but you keep the right to your argument no matter what anyone says.

Some say Fuzzy Vandivier's Franklin teams were the greatest high school basketball teams of all time. Others will say it has to be Attucks '56 or Indianapolis Washington '69 or Jay Edwards' Marion teams. But it's really no contest. The greatest Indiana high school basketball team of all time is the 1971 East Chicago Washington Senators. So says this authority.

Coach John Molodet's Senators entered the '70-'71 season rated Number One, stormed to a 29-0 record and finished the season as State Champs. East Chicago broke the 100-point barrier eight times. Their 102 points in a semi-final bashing of Floyd Central tied a Final Four record. The 344 points Washington scored in their final four games (an 86 point per game average) set a Sweet 16 record no team has come near in the last twenty years.

East Chicago forward Pete Trgovich tied a Final Four record held by Ron Bonham and Dave Shepherd when he scored 40 points in the semi-final game. Trgovich proved his outburst was no fluke by scoring 28 in the Championship Game to establish a Final Four record total of 68 points.

Trgovich continued his basketball career with the UCLA Bruins under the tutelage of Coach John Wooden. Teaming with Bill Walton, Richard Washington and Dave Meyers, Pete collected two NCAA championship rings during his stay in Los Angeles (Freshmen were not eligible until 1973).

Trgovich's All-Star teammate Ulysses "Jr." Bridgeman didn't have an outstanding Final Four in '71, but his greatest basketball glories were to be close at hand. Bridgeman signed with the Uni-

East Chicago 1971 Boys B-Ball Champs: (back row, l to r) Coach John Molodet, Robert Smith, Alex Koutoures, Ulysses Bridgeman, Tim Stoddard, Howard Williams, Pete Trgovich, Marcus Stallings, Milan Grozdanich, manager (front row, l to r) Nick Elish, manager, Franciso (Paco) Sanchez, Ruben Bailey, Darnell Adell, Albert Pollard, Michael Monogan, Miodrag Andric, manager. Courtesy East Chicago Washington High School.

versity of Louisville, and in 1975, his 16.2 PPG average led coach Denny Crum's Cardinals to their first Final Four appearance.

Drafted by the LA Lakers in the first round, Bridgeman became part of NBA trivia lore when he was traded to the Milwaukee Bucks as part of a package deal for Kareem Abdul-Jabbar. While Kareem's exploits are legendary, Bridgeman didn't fare badly himself. During his ten-year career with the Bucks and LA Clippers, he scored over 10,000 points. One of the NBA's steadiest ball players, Jr. Bridgeman was an integral part of the Bucks' perennial contenders throughout the late '70s and early '80s.

A third member of East Chicago's '71 champs was a dominant high school ballplayer. Six-foot seven-inch Tim Stoddard chipped in 30 Final Four points and controlled the boards. In 1974, Stoddard teamed with David Thompson and Oak Hill's Monte Towe to lead North Carolina State to an NCAA championship over—who else—the UCLA Bruins of John Wooden and Pete Trgovich. The Hoosier Connection was completed by the fact that NC State coach Norm Sloan got his start playing for Indianapolis Lawrence Central High School.

Tim Stoddard's greatest fame would come on the diamonds of Major League Baseball. During his ten-year career as a relief specialist with the White Sox, Orioles and Cubs, Stoddard pitched in over 300 games and racked up over seventy saves. He gathered one of the three victories the Orioles managed in a 1979 World Series loss to the Pirates and pitched in two games for the Cubs during the 1984 National League Championship Series.

Pete Trgovich, Jr. Bridgeman, Tim Stoddard—throw in superb basketball talents like Darnell Adell and James Williams—who's the greatest Indiana high school basketball team of all time? East Chicago Washington, 1971. No doubt! Any arguments?

The great East Chicago Washington team of '71 heralded a literal explosion of Hoosier basketball talent. A list of great Indiana high school stars of the 1970's not already mentioned who went on to outstanding college and/or pro careers would include Dave Shepherd, Frank Kendrick, Mike Flynn, Steve Green, John Garrett, Kent Benson, Kyle Macy, Jerry Sichting, Ray Tolbert, Roosevelt Barnes, Tom Abernethy, Bob Wilkerson, Larry Bird, Wayne Radford, Walter Jordan, Mike Woodson, Landon Turner, Ted Kitchel, Randy Wittman, Judi Warren, LaTaunya Pollard ... Judi and LaTaunya? Yep, in 1976 The Great State of Indiana—Basketball Capital of the Universe—finally acknowledged a simple truth: girls can play this game, too.

Wow! Those Girls Can Play

The first IHSAA-sanctioned Girls State Basketball Tournament was held in the only place it could have been held—Hinkle Fieldhouse. The boys had moved on to IU's Assembly Hall in 1972 and then to Indianapolis' Market Square Arena in '75, but as of 1976, the girls retained a sense of tradition with the Grand Old Sports Palace.

Indiana's first Miss Basketball, Judi Warren of the Warsaw Tigers. Indiana State Museum Collection.

Coach Janice Soyez's Warsaw Tigers captured the inaugural title behind Miss Basketball Judi Warren's 31 Final Four points. Warren's infec-

East Chicago Roosevelt's Champions: (back row l to r) Coach Bobbie DeKemper, LaTaunya Pollard, Carolyn Bennett, Normela Upshaw, Dana Cook, Barb Fritzsche, Annette Franklin. (front row, l to r) Lisa Sanchez, Vernell Jackson, Pinky McClain, Vicky Martin, Johnnyece Beard, Bertha Demkowicz. Courtesy East Chicago Roosevelt High School.

tious enthusiam did much to assure the success of Indiana girls basketball. In addition to being named the state's first Miss Basketball, Warren added the state's first female Mental Attitude Award to her collection.

Tiger sophmore Chanda Kline contributed 26 points to Warsaw's semi-final victory over East Chicago Roosevelt and 19 points to the Championship margin against Bloomfield. In 1978 Kline would be named the state's third Miss Basketball—and Warsaw's second—after she fired in 29 points in a 75-60 Championship demolition of Jac-Cen-Del.

In the Championship years of 1976 and '78, Coach Soyez's Tigers compiled an impressive 44-0 record.

Sandwiched around the '78 Tiger title were two Championships won by East Chicago Roosevelt. The Lady Rough Riders were led by perhaps the greatest female basketball player in Indiana history, LaTaunya Pollard.

As a freshman, Pollard scored 22 points which amounted to half her team's total. They weren't sufficient to prevent the Riders from falling to Warren and Kline's '76 champs in the semi-finals. The following year, LaTaunya dominated the Championship Game—outscoring Mount Vernon 36-35—as Roosevelt cruised to a 66-35 victory.

In '78, a 46-45 semi-final loss to the Tigers prevented the Rough Riders from defending their title. A brilliant high school career culminated in a second Championship in 1979. Pollard's 41 Final

Four points nearly equalled the 46 achieved by the combined scores of Championship Round opponents Jasper and Anderson Madison Heights. Roosevelt wasn't overly impressed with Warsaw's 44-0 Championship record. E. C. put together a 47-0 slate during their title years and achieved a 91-2 record during Pollard's four years. Both losses were to eventual State Champions Warsaw.

LaTaunya took her 1979 Miss Basketball recognition, and most of the state's girls' scoring records, to Long Beach State University, where she was named All-American in 1981, '82 and '83. In '83 she also received the Margaret Wade Trophy—presented to the nation's top female collegiate player.

Though an injury forced her to withdraw from the team prior to competition, Pollard crowned her career by winning a spot on the 1984 US Olympic team.

The exciting talents of the Warsaw Tigers and the East Chicago Rough Riders assured that the popularity of Indiana girls' high school basketball would grow rapidly. In 1976 7,362 fans witnessed Warsaw's Championship victory. In 1980, the girls joined the boys at Market Square Arena, and by 1985, 14,197 were on hand for Crown Point's defeat of Wawasee—nearly twice the inaugural attendance.

The 1980s have seen continued steady growth in the quantity as well as quality of girls' talent. Columbus East's Maria Stack broke Pollard's Final Game record when she tallied 42 in a 1980 loss to Southport. Miss Basketball Amy Metheny led the Champion Cardinals with 46 Final Four points. Indianapolis Washington's 1980 All-Star Cheryl Cook became an All-American at South-

LaTaunya Pollard of East Chicago Roosevelt's Rough Riders. Courtesy Jim Platis.

ern Cal. Austin's Jodie Whitaker canned 2,095 career points and was named 1985 Miss Basketball and Mental Attitude Award winner. Indianapolis Warren Central's Lindy Godby led the way to the Warriors' State Championship before taking over at center for perennial NCAA contenders Auburn University. 1986 Miss Basketball Courtney Cox of Noblesville halted Godby's bid for a state title. While Cox has moved on to play for IU her future in athletics appears to be in professional golf. Vicky Hall of Indianapolis Brebeuf was named the 1988 *Parade Magazine* High

---

Hoosier Hysteria's Hoop Heavens

Many high school gymnasiums in Indiana are larger than most collegiate gyms. The state is famous for gyms that can hold the entire population of the towns in which they are located. Indiana's top 10 Largest High School Gymnasiums:

*1	New Castle	9,325	6	Richmond	8,100
2	Anderson	8,998	7	Marion	7,690
3	Elkhart Memorial	8,250	8	Michigan City Rogers	7,304
4	Elkhart Central	8,248	9	Southport	7,248
5	Seymour	8,110	10	Gary West	7,216

* *New Castle's Chrysler Fieldhouse is the world's largest high school gymnasium. In addition to Chrysler, Anderson's "Wigwam" and the gyms at Richmond and Marion, the North Central Conference boasts Lafayette Jefferson's 7,200-seater, Kokomo High School's 6,604, Muncie Central's 6,581 and tiny Logansport's 5,830 for a league seating capacity of 60,328 Hoosier Hysterics.*

School Player of the Year and currently stars with one of America's top women's collegiate programs at the University of Texas.

Most importantly, after getting off to a 3-13 start in the annual All-Star series against the Kentucky High School All-Stars, the Indiana girls have captured eight of the last 16 contests. Clearly the Hoosier ladies are showing the guys that girls can play this game, too.

Meanwhile the international legend of Indiana Boys High School Basketball has continued to grow throughout the 1980s.

In 1982 Scott Skiles' 39 points led Plymouth to a 75-74 double overtime victory over Gary Roosevelt in perhaps the most exciting Championship Game in Tournament history. The Pilgrims had barely survived Argos 55-47 in the Sectional Final, squeaked by Elkhart Memorial 77-74 in the Regional Championship, slid by Marion 56-55 in overtime in the Semi-State and outlasted Indianapolis Cathedral 62-59 in the State Semi-final.

Clearly this was a team that refused to lose—or rather it has a captain that refused to lose. Unrecruited by the State's "Big 3" Scott Skiles returned to haunt Knight and Keady on a regular basis as a Michigan State Spartan. His 27.4 PPG average in 1985-'86 earned the 6'1" guard All-America honors.

Too short, too slow, too rooted to the ground, Scott Skiles has none-the-less orneried his way to nearly 1,500 points during four NBA seasons to date. Playing for the Bucks, Pacers, and Magic Skiles continues to display the "yeah, your mama" competitiveness all Hoosier Hysterics came to know and . . . view with mixed emotions.

The Plymouth Pilgrims' arch nemesis—the Tigers of Warsaw—couldn't let their Northern Lakes Conference (NLC) rivals steal all the glory. In 1984 a Boys Basketball Championship trophy joined the 1976 and 1978 Girls hardware in the Tiger trophy case. Warsaw's Jeff Grose followed his junior championship season with a senior Mr. Basketball year in 1985.

Coach Bill Green's 1985, '86 and '87 Marion Giants yawned their way through three consecutive State Championship seasons. In a fratricidal conference (North Central), in a state infamous for its ferocious competitiveness, the Giants waltzed to an effortless 84-4 three-year record.

1987 Co-Mr. Basketballs Jay Edwards and Lyndon Jones dominated Hoosier high school hardwoods for all three championship seasons before embarking on equally stormy relationships with a certain collegiate mentor residing in Bloomington.

Coach Green has recently taken up the challenge of returning estwhile small-college power the University of Indianapolis (Indiana Central) to former glories of the Angus Nicoson days.

The 1990 edition of Hoosier Hysteria may have been the most intriguing of all. Dean Smith won a brutal battle with IU and Michigan for the services of 7' All-America Eric Montross of '89 State Champs Indianapolis Lawrence North. Montross will some day be a focal point of a chapter on "The Ones That Got Away."

What Montross may have finally gotten away from is the legend of Damon Bailey. Eric couldn't return L-N to the state title because when the universe was created the Diety ordained that Damon would lead Bedford-North Lawrence to the 1990 crown.

The story of Damon Bailey to date is likely well known to any reader who has made it this far in this volume. The subject of intense public and media scrutiny since he was profiled—as an eighth grader—in the John Feinstein best-seller *A Season on the Brink: A Year with Bob Knight and the Indiana Hoosiers*, Bailey had led a mythical childhood.

In spite of the intense pressure, the kid from Heltonville has met every challenge and maintained a disarming perspective as well. Playing in front of sold-out throngs from New Albany to Kokomo, Bailey set the all-time Indiana High School record with 3,134 career points. Most fans said it couldn't be done, even as Bailey was in the process of surpassing Marion Pierce's 30-year old standard.

It's likely that some future Hoosier screenwriter will put a mythologized version on Damon's high school career on the big screen. If that future screenwriter has his hero score the final 11 points in his team's 63-60 championship victory over a superior team in front of 41,046 fans rocking a big city domed stadium, film buffs and movie critics will no doubt question his overdone sense of bathos. Of course that writer will only be remaining true to historical truth—ask the Minutemen of Concord.

Mr. Bailey will join Mr. Knight for the 1990 season. It should be fun. There's a future Oscar Robertson playing on a Hoosier playground today—or he will be tomorrow. There's a Larry Bird or a Damon Bailey practicing his jump-shot on an Indiana dirt court as this is being writtten—or there will be tomorrow. The best is yet to come.

1986 Co-Mr. Basketball Jay Edwards of the Marion Giants. Courtesy IHSAA.

1990 Mr. Basketball Damon Bailey of Bedford-North Lawrence. Photo courtesy of Sanford Gentry.

Hoosier College Basketball Moves Into Prime Time

To begin talking about Indiana's contribution to American Collegiate basketball during the Modern Era of US sports history, we must return to an old familiar name. During the 1960s and early '70s there was only one name in college basketball—John Wooden.

As a high school player at Martinsville, Johnny Wooden was great. As a collegian at Purdue he was greater—great enough to make the Hall of Fame as a player in 1960. As a college coach at Indiana State Teacher's College and UCLA, he was the best basketball coach that ever lived. His UCLA teams won NCAA Championships in 1964, '65, '67, '68, '69, '70 '71, '72, '73 and '75. His ten championships exceed the combined total of his two nearest competitors (the University of Kentucky's Adolph Rupp won four, Bob Knight has three at IU). Wooden won two National Championships after he was elected to the Naismith Hall of Fame as a coach in 1972.

In addition to his championships, Coach Wooden was named National Coach of the Year in 1964, '66, '69, '70, '72 and '73.

John Wooden of the UCLA Bruins

Among the legion of All-Americans who played for Coach Wooden are Walt Hazzard, Gail Goodrich, Lew Alcindor (Kareem Abdul-Jabbar), Lucius Allen, Mike Warren (from South Bend Central and "Hill Street Blues"), Sidney Wicks, Curtis Rowe, Bill Walton, Keith Wilkes, Richard Washington, David Meyers and Marques Johnson.

As an inspirational leader, a determined and dedicated competitor and as a gentleman, John Wooden is and was one of the most respected men in the game.

We can disagree about the greatest high school basketball team of all-time. We can disagree about the best quarterback, or the toughest pitcher, or least deserving Heisman winner. We can argue about almost anything. The greatest college basketball coach of all-time? There may be no argument statistically and perhaps otherwise—John Wooden.

And that allows us to mention the second greatest collegiate basketball coach of all-time—Indiana University's Bob Knight. OK, we can argue about this one.

Bob Knight Inherited the IU Tradition

Contrary to popular thought, Bob Knight did not invent the IU basketball program. In addition to the many legendary names we've already remembered, there are many more. Branch McCracken led the Hoosiers through the 1965 season, and his Modern Era All-Americans included Kokomo's "Splendid Splinter" Jimmy Rayl, the VanArsdale twins and one of the great basketball players of the Modern Era, Walt Bellamy.

Bellamy was an IU All-American in '60 and '61. He still holds all the Cream and Crimson's rebounding records including 33 in one game, 428 in one season (an unbelievable 17.8 average) and 1,088 over a career. Bellamy was also a member of the 1960 US Olympic Gold Medal Basketball Team that many consider the best ever. Among his US teammates were Jerry West, John Lucas, Oscar Robertson and Purdue's Terry Dischinger.

In 1961 the Chicago Zephyrs (Washington Bullets) made Bellamy their number one draft choice, and he rewarded them by scoring 31.6 PPG during his Rookie-of-the-Year season. Walt retired in 1975 following a fourteen-year career with the Zephyrs, Bullets, Knicks, Pistons and Hawks. When he hung up his size seventeen sneakers, Bellamy had scored 20,941 points in 1,043 games. He had been named an NBA All-Star in 1962, '63, '64 and '65. At retirement his career numbers placed him ninth in NBA field goals made, eighth in minutes played, fifth in fouls committed (Walt liked to throw his substantial weight around), sixth in free-throw attempts, sixth in rebounds (14,241) and ninth in points scored.

The last great player at IU during the McCracken era was Franklin's Jon McGlocklin, who captained the '64 and '65 VanArsdale teams. McGlocklin was a third-round draft choice of the 1966 Cincinnati Royals. He proceeded to put together an outstanding, if a bit surprising, ten-year NBA career. In 1969 he became the Milwaukee Bucks' first All-Star. The Bucks drafted Kareem Abdul-Jabbar the following year and traded for McGlocklin's former Royal teammate—none other than Oscar Robertson. The trio led the Bucks to the 1971 NBA Championship. McGlocklin was hardly along for the ride. He contributed 15.8 PPG from his starting guard position.

Jon retired following the '76 season with 9,169 points scored in a 792-game NBA career.

Coach McCracken turned over the Hoosier reins to Lou Watson in 1966. And while the Hoosier program didn't flourish, it didn't collapse ei-

The winningest coach in Big Ten History, Robert Montgomery Knight. Courtesy Indiana University Sports.

ther. Butch Joyner, then George McGinnis saw to that. When the Administration at IU decided to bring in some new blood in 1971—some brash, young new blood from the US Military Academy at West Point—they weren't turning over a (pardon the pun) basket case to Bobby Knight.

It probably doesn't matter what kind of case Coach Knight inherited. He most likely would have built the Hoosiers into a perennial powerhouse under any circumstances.

As a player, Bob Knight would not have been a threat to John Wooden, but he was good enough to be a top sub on one of college basketball's great teams. With starters like John Havlicek, Jerry Lucas and Larry Siegfried, Ohio State University cruised to Big 10 titles in 1960, '61 and '62. The '60 Buckeyes won a National Championship, while Oscar Robertson's last Cincinnati Bearcat team finished third. In '61, OSU lost to UC in the title game, and in '62, Ron Bonham showed up in Cincinnati to again lead the Bearcats over the Bucks for the NCAA title. While Knight was never a central figure in these epic battles, he was known to come off the Buckeye bench for spurts of fiery competitiveness. Everyone knew Bob Knight hated to lose.

In 1964 Knight joined the US Army, where he was assigned to assist Coach Tates Locke at West Point. The following year, Locke left for Miami (Ohio) University and, at age twenty-four, Bob Knight became one of the youngest head coaches in NCAA history. During his six years as head basketball mentor at the Academy, Knight's teams went 102-50 despite Academy restrictions limiting cadets to a maximum 6'6" height. Four Army teams were invited to the National Invitational Tournament (NIT) at a time when only thirty-two college teams qualified for post-season play.

In 1971 Knight brought his motion offense and suffocating man-to-man defense to Bloomington. He wasn't universally well received. The "Hurryin' Hoosiers" played in a fast-paced, high scoring league. Iowa had won the '70-'71 Big 10 crown by scoring over 100 points per game. In 1970, the Hoosiers had scored 99 points against Michigan, and lost! Big 10 fans and spectators in IU's brand new Assembly Hall weren't sure they cared much for some guy who stressed . . . ugh . . . defense.

Bob Knight revolutionized basketball—IU basketball, Big 10 basketball, collegiate basketball, international basketball. Within a decade of his arrival in Bloomington, Big 10 teams were averaging 62 points per game. IU's smothering, swarming, help-out, in-your-face, in-your-uniform defense had produced success, and success breeds imitation.

In 1976 Coach Knight became the youngest coach in NCAA history to win 200 games. In '80, he became the youngest to win 300. He is the youngest to win 400 and 500. In 1992, he will likely become the youngest coach to win 600 collegiate games.

In 1990, Coach Knight passed Purdue's Piggy Lambert as the Big 10's All-Time winningest coach. Knight's IU teams have won nine Big 10 titles, an NIT, a College Commissioners' Tournament (this invitational collapsed after Knight branded it a tourney for losers) and NCAA Championships in 1976, '81 and '87. The Hoosiers have qualified for fifteen NCAA tournament bids in Knight's nineteen years.

There have been nearly twenty All-Americans, over two-dozen All-Big 10 players and nine Big 10 MVPs during Knight's IU tenure. He has been named National Coach of the Year three times.

Bob Knight is a shoe-in for the Hall of Fame. He would have made it years ago if not for his unfortunate penchant for making headlines—negative headlines—real negative headlines. The General has never been obsessed with winning, but he is obsessed none the less. He's developed a reputation as a gracious loser and an obnoxious winner.

Regardless of who was at fault, Knight's shoving match with a Puerto Rican policeman at the '79 Pan American Games nearly created an international incident. It didn't help matters when, after winning the Gold, Knight spent several moments gesturing his satisfaction to the San Juan crowd.

The embarrassing incident almost generated enough outrage in the American basketball community to prevent Knight from coaching the 1984 Olympic Gold Medal Basketball Team.

At the 1981 NCAA Finals at New Orleans, Knight stuffed a boorish Lousiana State fan in a trash can. Now, it can be argued that any fan of LSU coach Dale Brown should be stuffed in a garbage can, but many respected critics pointed out that it's not the sort of behavior one would expect of a John Wooden, or a Dean Smith, Fred Taylor, Henry Iba or Pete Newell.

Knight's chair-throwing incident during the 1985 Purdue game and his phone slamming during the 1987 NCAA Tournament have become part of America's cultural memory.

Coach Knight's commitment to education, his uncompromising adherence to the rules of fair play, his hard work on behalf of worthy causes and his loyalty to his friends are also well-known character traits. Yet, The General's unfortunate inability to control his temper prompted the Naismith Hall of Fame to pass him over as a Hall of Fame inductee. Knight reacted by throwing a temper tantrum—declaring that he would never accept a place in the Hall.

A complex individual, Coach Knight is a brilliant man, a compassionate man, a sometimes silly and insensitive man. He will likely lead IU to more championships. He may someday become the winningest coach in collegiate basketball history. One hundred years from now, they may speak of Bob Knight and John Wooden in the same sentence. Or, they may speak of Bob Knight and Woody Hayes in the same context. History will decide these issues. The statistics and the record, however, presently speak for themselves.

As with Notre Dame football or the Purdue University athletic program, any in-depth treatment of IU basketball under Bob Knight would result in an encyclopedia. Even a quick look will reveal an awesome legacy.

Steve Downing didn't follow high school teammate George McGinnis into the pros in 1971. He stayed to lead IU to a Number Three NCAA finish in 1973. The '73 Big 10 MVP might have changed history if a controversial charging call had gone against UCLA's Bill Walton instead of against IU's All-American center late in the semi-final game.

If nothing else, sportscaster Curt Gowdy learned that it was Indiana University and not the University of Indiana when IU students presented him with a Golden Turkey Award for repeating the mistake not more than 30,000 times. IU basketball was back on the national sports scene.

After a short career with the Boston Celtics, which included a World Championship season in 1974, Steve Downing returned to IU where he has served as an assistant athletic director since 1986.

During the 1974-'75 and '75-'76 seasons, Indiana University fielded two of the great teams in college basketball history. They combined to win 63 games against one bitter defeat, set a Big 10 record with 36 consecutive league victories and won the NCAA Championship in 1976. If not for a broken arm suffered by All-American Scott May, the Hoosiers might have been the only team since John Wooden's Bruins to gain back-to-back national titles. As it was, arch-enemy Kentucky knocked the Cream and Crimson out of the '75

The 1976 Player of the Year IU forward Scott May. Courtesy Indiana University Sports.

"You ain't seen nothing like the mighty Quinn." IU's Quinn Buckner. Courtesy Indiana University Sports.

1973 Mr. Basketball and former NBA standout Kent Benson of New Castle. Courtesy Indiana University Sports.

tourney by a meager two-point margin.

Following the '75 heartbreak, Super-Sub John Lazkowski moved on to the Chicago Bulls and All-American Steve Green took his sweet baseline jumper to the Utah Jazz and later on to the Indiana Pacers.

In 1976, the Hoosiers came back with a vengeance. National Player of the Year Scott May's high-powered scoring was complemented by All-American Quinn Buckner's leadership and ball-handling. New Castle's All-American center Kent Benson contributed rebounding and more scoring. South Bend's Tom Abernethy and Anderson's Bob Wilkerson chipped in with Bob Knight defense and block-out rebounding. Many teams were intimidated right out of their game when they took the floor to find Wilkerson, a 6'7" guard, preparing to win the opening "center-jump."

Buckner and May added a 1976 Olympic Gold Medal to their '76 NCAA Championship rewards. Benson returned to IU for a Big 10 MVP season in 1977. All five '76 starters eventually joined Lazkowski and Green in the NBA.

Scott May's physical problems continued to hamper his effectiveness, but he put in seven years with Chicago, Milwaukee and Detroit nonetheless. Buckner enjoyed a more successful pro career, playing ten years with Milwaukee, Boston and Indiana. Quinn made the NBA All-Defensive Team in 1978, ' '81 and '82. He finished third on the NBA's All-Time steals list and won a World Championship as a starting guard with the 1984 Celtics.

Kent Benson's NBA career got off to a rocky start when Kareem broke Benny's jaw in the Hoosier's very first pro game. Jabbar broke his hand in the discussion, so justice was served. Benson's career smoothed out somewhat after that indoctrination, and he enjoyed an eleven year career, primarily with Milwaukee and Detroit.

Bobby Wilkerson went on to become a starting guard with the Denver Nuggets, and Tom Abernethy enjoyed a surprisingly effective, if relatively short NBA stint with the Lakers and Pacers.

Coach Knight has always maintained that the '76 team was the second best college team ever. He asserts that the '75 team could have taken 'em. Either way, its doubtful that Hurryin' Hoosier fans will ever see better.

Great teams and outstanding players continued in Bloomington as a matter of course. 1980 Big Ten MVP Mike Woodson learned his game on the playgrounds around Indianapolis Broad Ripple. A member of Knight's '79 Pan Am Gold Team, "Woody" finished his IU career with 2,061 points. It's likely that he would have become the Big 10's all-time leading scorer if a back injury had not forced him out of a dozen games during his senior year. Since his graduation, Woodson has enjoyed an excellent ten-year NBA career with the Knicks, Kings, Rockets and other teams. Through the end of the '89-90 season, Woody had scored nearly 11,000 professional points.

In 1981 Woodson's '80 teammates Isiah Thomas, Ray Tolbert, Landon Turner, Randy Wittman and Ted Kitchel returned to take IU to its fourth NCAA Championship. The Hoosiers cruised to the Big 10 Title, then demolished all post-season competition. Tourney victims included Lefty Dreisell's Maryland Terps, 99-64. Dale Brown's LSU Tigers went down 67-49 in a satisfying Semi-final. It was a strictly no-contest Final as Dean Smith's North Carolina Tar Heels were dispatched 63-50. Isiah Thomas was voted All-America for the second year running and was named NCAA Tournament MVP, while Ray Tolbert was voted MVP of the Big 10.

Hoosier joy in the Championship, unfortunately, was short-lived. Isiah Thomas passed up his final two years of collegiate eligibility to join the NBA's Detroit Pistons. Thomas had been a member of Bob Knight's 1979 Pan Am Gold Medal Team and had been named to the 1980 US Olympic Team which fell victim to the American boycott of the Moscow Games.

Cream and Crimson fans had great expectations for Thomas' junior and senior seasons, but Isiah was ready for the NBA. He was an All-Star his rookie year, and by 1984 he was the All-Star Game's MVP. Currently one of professional basketball's top players, Thomas has been an All-Star every year that he's been in the NBA. He has scored over 14,000 points, dished over 6,500 assists, and led the Pistons to back-to-back championships in '89 and '90. Isiah Thomas' reservation in the Hall of Fame has already been secured.

A true tragedy compounded Hoosier disappointment over Thomas' departure. During the summer of 1981, IU's junior forward Landon Turner was severely injured in an automobile accident. The resulting paralysis put an abrupt end to one of the nation's most promising basketball careers. An Indiana All-Star at Indianapolis Tech, Turner had struggled for two and a half years under the rigid discipline of Bob Knight's program. Turner's scoring and rebounding explosion during the '81 NCAAs had as much to do with

IU All-American Isiah Thomas VS Purdue in 1981. Courtesy Indiana University Sports.

IU's championship as any single factor. He was an easy choice for the All-Tourney Team.

Landon Turner's accident put an end to his athletic career, but it didn't end his active participation in the Indiana sporting community. Whether as a speaker on self-motivation, or as a participant in an Indiana wheelchair basketball league, Turner is a sterling example of perseverance over self-pity. In 1988 he was named the NCAA's Courageous Athlete of the Year.

The IU program struggled forward. In 1983 Wittman, Kitchel and company took the Hoosiers to their fourteenth Big 10 title. Lewis Cass High School's Ted Kitchel was a two-time All-Big 10 selection and received All-America mention in 1982 and '83. Indianapolis Ben Davis' Randy Wittman became IU's tenth Big 10 MVP in 1983. The two-time Academic All-American also received substantial support from the '83 All-America selectors. Wittman has been active in the NBA since 1984 and is currently a member of the Indiana Pacers.

The IU basketball steamroller rolls on. In 1988-'89 potential future Oakland A's outfielder Joe Hillman and current LA Clipper Jay Edwards led IU to its fifteenth Big 10 Championship. Many experts believe Edwards was premature in taking his Big 10 MVP game to the NBA following his sophomore season. It's hoped that Jay will be able to get his physical problems—and his head—straight in time to become one of pro ball's top long-range bombers. The jury will be out for some time to come.

The 1989-'90 version of the Hurryin' Hoosiers boasted a lineup that often featured four freshmen and a sophomore. 1989 Big 10 Freshman of the Year Eric Anderson and 1990 Big 10 Freshman of the Year Runner-Up Calbert Chaney of Evansville were able to lead IU to the school's 17th NCAA Tournament appearance nonetheless. Throw in 1989 Indiana Mr. Basketball Pat Graham, 1990 Mr. Basketball Damon Bailey and an outstanding supporting cast . . . Coach Dean and Coach McCracken can rest easy.

The leading scorer in IU history, Steve Alford. Courtesy Indiana University Sports.

Most of the great sports debates are over the "fastest," the "strongest," or "the greatest." Here's a nomination for the "Least Talented NCAA Basketball Champions in History"—the 1987 Indiana Hoosiers. A slow, slight, short, guard as your "go-to" man? A short, not-quick, non-leaping forward as your principle rebounder? A short, skinny, sophomore at small forward? A Jr. College transfer at center, and another JC—a former burger-flipper with three years of basketball experience at point guard? You're kidding, right? Not with Bob Knight at the helm.

Steve Alford needed one basket in the last ten minutes of the NCAA Final Game to become the Big 10's all-time leading scorer. He didn't get it. He did get 33 points in the semi-final to help hold off UNLV. Two less than his 23 in the finals would have sent the Syracuse Orangemen home as Champions.

Forward Daryl Thomas fought and clawed and willed his way to 20 points and seven rebounds against Syracuse. In the Midwest Finals, Rick Calloway grabbed a Thomas airball and put it through at the buzzer to dump the despised LSU Tigers 77-76. The Hoosiers had trailed by nine with four minutes to go. Dean Garrett battled to 28 Final Four points and 18 rebounds. And Keith Smart hit THE SHOT. Smart hit several shots—he scored 12 of IU's final 15 points—but with five seconds remaining he hit THE SHOT. The sixteen foot, floating, baseline jumper made the final tally IU 74-Syracuse 73.

Talent? Three of the Orangemen have gone on to careers in the NBA. Steve Alford has scored 700 or so points in three journeyman seasons with Dallas and Golden State, while Smart and Garrett have hung around the fringes of minor-league basketball. Hard work, dedication, teamwork, intelligence, coaching? The Indiana Hoosiers—1987 NCAA Basketball Champions.

The Trials of Job—Boiler Basketball in the Modern Era

If Purdue University were located in any other state in the Union, the Boilermakers would likely dominate that state's collegiate basketball scene. The Old Gold and Black have won more Big 10 titles (18 won or shared), more Big 10 games (over 600), and have a better winning percentage (over 58%) than any other league team. The Boilers have appeared in nine NCAA Tournaments—finishing second in 1969 and third in 1980—and six National Invitational Tournaments—winning the Championship in 1974 and finishing runner-up in 1979 and 1982. Purdue University has produced over seventy First Team All-Big 10 players, nine Big 10 scoring leaders and over two dozen Consensus All-Americans. The Boilermakers have a winning record against Notre Dame, have defeated IU nearly 100 times and have more than twice as many victories versus Butler than the Bulldogs have been able to post over the Boilers.

And yet . . . ? When IU and Notre Dame get together to stage a "Big Four Classic" in front of 40,000 Hoosier Dome fans and a national TV audience, the Universities of Kentucky and Louisville are invited, while Purdue stays home. Ask an average fan in Montana to name college basketball's powerhouse programs and Kentucky, Indiana, North Carolina and UCLA will inevitably be mentioned. Purdue may or may not come up in the conversation. While a Dick Vitale or an Al McGuire will ramble on endlessly about "The General," Gene Keady is likely to be referred to in the context of "and lets not forget Gene Keady."

Why the absence of recognition? Perhaps it's because Purdue has lacked a big-time telegenic figure, a la Bob Knight or Isiah Thomas, for most of basketball's television age. During Rick Mount's heyday, fans were lucky to get one network game a week—and the game was almost always UCLA against whomever. Maybe the lack of respect comes from the fact that the casual fan doesn't pay close attention until the NCAA Tournament, and the Boilers' Tourney performance has been something short of stellar of late. It could be that Purdue grads disperse to become engineers in California, astronauts in Texas and farmers in myriad rural communities, while IU grads tend to cluster in boisterous and intimidating communities inside several of the Midwest's larger cities. Whatever the pet theory, Boilermakers have had to suffer a long period in the role of homely step-sister. It's time they received their due.

When the Modern Age of American sports history began about 1960, Purdue University basketball gave no hint of being anything other than what it had always been—one of the nation's premier programs.

In 1960 Boiler Terry Dischinger was the youngest member of the fabulous Robertson-West-Lucas-Bellamy Olympic Gold Medal Team. Dischinger was in fast company, but he had no trouble keeping up. An All-State center at Terre Haute Garfield in 1957 and '58, Dischinger became a three-time All-American at Purdue. He led the Big 10 in scoring in 1960, '61 and '62; set the Big 10 single-game scoring mark with 52 against Michigan State; established the Big 10 single-game field goal standard with 20 versus Illinois and set the league single-season free throw record with 179 made. Dischinger finished his three-year career as the Boilermakers' all-time leading scorer. His 1,979 points and 958 rebounds in 70 games work out to a phenomenal 28.3 points and 13.7 rebounds per game career averages.

Upon graduating from Purdue, Dischinger embarked on an outstanding professional career. He was named 1962-'63 NBA Rookie of the Year after averaging a league best 25.5 points per game for the Chicago Zephyrs (Baltimore/Washington Bullets). His Zephyr teammate, Walt Bellamy of IU, had been NBA Rookie of the Year the previous season. Dischinger scored 9,012 points during his nine-year pro career with Chicago/Baltimore, Detroit and Portland. He was named to the NBA All-Star Team in 1963, '64 and '65. Dischinger likely would have scored over 12,000 NBA points had his career not been interrupted at its peak due to the necessity of military service in 1966 and 1967.

Terry Dischinger established several marks of excellence at Purdue University. Many of them would be erased by other Boilermakers within the decade. Indiana High School All-Star Dave Schellhase came out of Evansville North in 1962 as a prototypical Hoosier jump-shooter. Schellhase led the Big 10 in scoring in 1965 and '66 and was a Consensus All-American and an Academic All-American both seasons. His 32.5 PPG average in 1966 led the nation. The Boiler forward bettered Terry Dischinger's Purdue records by scoring 2,074 career points for a 28.8 average.

As a professional, Schellhase had the misfortune of being too short to remain a forward (6'3")

Purdue All-American Terry Dischinger. Courtesy Purdue University Athletic Department.

and being too slow to make the transition to NBA guard. His pro career was limited to a two-year hitch with the Chicago Bulls.

After watching Dischinger and Schellhase for six of seven seasons, Purdue fans may have believed that the era of Boilermaker mega-scorers was over. Of course the best was yet to come.

Rick Mount enrolled at West Lafayette the year after Dave Schellhase graduated. Lebanon, Indiana is less than fifty miles from West Lafayette, and many Boiler fans believe that "The Rocket" could have just stayed home and shot from there. Mount did need to be in town to score. He even preferred to be in the building before he started launching his missiles. But he didn't necessarily need to be in-bounds to be within range. The Rocket could score from anywhere.

In 1967-'68 Rick led the Big 10 in scoring, averaged 28.4 points in all games and was a Consensus All-American as a sophomore. In 1968-'69 he led the Big 10 in scoring, averaged 33.3 points in all games and was a Consensus All-American. The '69 team was undoubtedly the Boilers' best ever. Mount canned 36 in the NCAA Semi-final to help throttle North Carolina, 92-65, but in the Championship Game Coach John Wooden's UCLA Bruins took great satisfaction in "limiting" The Rocket to 28 points. Lew Alcindor's (Kareem Abdul-Jabbar) 37 points more than offset Mount's output, and the Boilers went down, 92-72.

Rick Mount returned to West Lafayette in 1969-'70 for an outstanding senior season. He was named All-American for the third straight year and Boilermaker and Big 10 MVP for the second consecutive season. He set Big 10 single-game records of 61 points and 27 field goals in a game against Iowa, and Big 10 single-season records of 522 league points and 221 league field goals. For his three-year career Mount averaged 32.3 PPG. He is still the leading scorer in Boilermaker basketball history with 2,323 points. Imagine the numbers if freshmen had been eligible, or if there had been a three-point line, or if seasons had included thirty to thirty-five games rather than twenty-five. A 4,000-point college career would have been likely.

As Rick Mount's Boilermaker career came to a close, Hoosier basketball fans were talking about the "Greatest Scorer Ever." They were talking about "Rick and The Big O" or "Rick and Jerry West." And there's the rub.

At 6'4", Rick Mount confronted the same problem that Dave Schellhase had faced—too small for an NBA forward, too slow for an NBA guard. The worst thing that happened to Mount is that he signed with the Indiana Pacers. It's not like The Rocket embarrassed himself at all—far from it. He averaged 14.3 PPG for the Pacers' '71-'72 ABA Champions and 14.9 PPG for the '72-'73 Kentucky Colonels. The problem was he had a difficult time holding the opposition down, and ABA fans expected him to continue scoring at a 32-point-a-game pace.

A private, almost introverted individual, Mount didn't respond well to the sudden criticism from his one-time admiring legions. Four team changes in four seasons and a resulting loss of confidence led to his retirement following the 1974-'75 season. His 3,330 points in five professional campaigns seemed fewer than he had scored in college.

Since leaving the game, Rick "The Rocket" Mount has led a life far from the spotlight. Residing in Lebanon, he has avoided public appearances to the point of not attending his son's games at Lebanon High School and Purdue. It doesn't seem fair. It doesn't seem fair that one who played Indiana's Game with the best of them should be so put off by the experience. It doesn't seem fair that some Hoosier basketball fans recall his name with a faint sense of disappointment. There are still lots of Indianans around who remember Rick Mount fondly. Good Lord, could that kid shoot a basketball . . . .

The Rocket's heroics overshadowed the accomplishments of a Boiler teammate who built an outstanding basketball career in his own right. Billy Keller established Indianapolis Washington High School as a powerhouse when he led the Continentals to the 1965 State Championship. Named Mr. Basketball four years before Washington's George McGinnis gained the same honor, Keller scored 22 points in the semi-final game against Princeton and 25 in the Championship victory over Fort Wayne North.

A year older than Mount, Keller was ensconced in the Boilermaker point guard position when the Rocket arrived at Mackey Arena. In tandem, they provided the Boilers with a dynamic backcourt duo. Keller, along with Herm Gilliam, was team co-captain in 1968 and '69. He led all Big 10 free-throw shooters with a 90.9% average in '68 and a 91.8% average in '69. The 1969 NCAA loss to UCLA closed out Billy Keller's college career, but his floor generalship and 1,056 points assured that Boiler fans would remember his contributions to their greatest team for many years.

Surprisingly, Bill Keller's best moments in basketball were yet to come. As a starting point man for the Indiana Pacers, the local favorite played on ABA Championship Teams in 1970, '72 and '73. During his seven-year pro career, Keller scored 6,588 points. Though these are not overwhelming numbers by professional standards, Billy Keller may be remembered as a significant footnote in pro basketball history.

When Keller joined the professional ranks in 1970, the American Basketball Association was a struggling young league attempting to compete with the well-established NBA. The new kids on the block needed something fresh and exciting to draw attention to themselves. A red, white and blue basketball was one means; the three-point shot was a much more important one.

Like any self-respecting Hoosier, Billy Keller was a deadly outside shooter. His 123 three-pointers in 1975-'76 and 506 career three-pointers set ABA records. Keller was as responsible as anyone in the game for demonstrating the potent potential of the three-point weapon. When you talk about the masters of basketball's "home run," you have to mention the Larry Birds and the Reggie Millers—but Billy Keller did it first, and none ever did it better. Boom Baby!

Co-captain Herman Gilliam was the third deadly weapon on the great '69 Boiler basketball team. Like Dave Schellhase before him, Herm played forward for the Boilermakers despite his 6'3" size. Named team MVP in 1967 and '68, Gilliam scored 1,118 career points for Purdue and was voted All-Big 10 in 1969.

Unlike Schellhase, Herm Gilliam was able to make the transition to guard in the NBA. Playing prinicipally for the Atlanta Hawks, he scored 6,225 points for a 10.8 average over the course of his eight-year professional career.

The 1970s was a decade of great success but unfulfilled expectations for Boilermaker basketball. In 1972 George King turned the head coaching position over to Fred Schaus in order to dedicate his energies to the Purdue athletic directorship full time.

Schaus came to West Lafayette with a long and colorful basketball history. In 1950 he had been an NBA All-Star as a rookie forward with the Ft. Wayne Pistons. In 1959 Schaus coached the University of West Virginia to the NCAA runner-up spot behind the talents of the great Jerry West. Throughout the 1960s West continued to play for his old coach as a member of the NBA's LA Lakers. The two combined with Wilt Chamberlain to lead the Lakers to four Western Division Championships. As LA General Manager, Schaus negotiated the trade that brought Kareem Abdul-Jabbar to the Lakers in 1972.

Purdue fans have been less than enthusiastic about Schaus' tenure in West Lafayette, although he had plenty of success to show for six seasons of play. In 1973-74, the Black and Gold finished 22-8 and 11th in the nation. As only league champs were invited to the NCAAs at the time, and as Michigan had won the Big 10, the Boilermakers were invited to the National Invitational Tournament where they became the first Big 10 team to win the prestigious affair. Co-captains Frank Kendrick of Indianapolis Tech and John Garrett of Peru received All-America mention. Kendrick was named first team All-Big 10 and spent one season with the NBA's Golden State Warriors.

With a huge influx of talent in the form of Indiana High School All-Stars Walter Jordan, Wayne Walls and later, Kyle Macy, Boiler backers anticipated a quick return to the NCAA Final Four. When the young Boilermakers came within a point of knocking off the 1974-'75 powerhouse Hoosiers of IU, the future looked grand. When in 1976 guard Kyle Macy established a single-game Big 10 freshman scoring record with 38 points against Minnesota, the horizon seemed painted black and gold.

In 1976-77 center Joe Barry Carroll left his Colorado home for West Lafayette. Purdue went 20-8 and gave eventual NCAA runner-up North Carolina all it could handle before falling 69-66. With four starters returning, plus Martinsville High School All-Star Jerry Sichting subbing for Macy, who had departed for the University of Kentucky, 1977-78 appeared to be the season when future potential would finally become present glory.

And then the wheels came off the wagon. The team had no chemistry. The "enigmatic" Carroll sulked. The budding professional careers of Jordan and Walls evaporated. The team struggled to a 16-11 record and no tournament bid. Despite a 106-58 record at Purdue, Coach Schaus, stung by grumbling audible from Clinton to LaGrange, resigned to take the athletic directorship at the University of West Virginia—his alma mater.

Fred Schaus left a West Lafayette cupboard that was far from bare. During the two years of Lee Rose's headmastership, the Black and Gold gathered 50 victories against 18 defeats. In '78-'79 the Purdues finished in a three-way tie for the Big 10 Championship, and Rose was named District V Coach of the Year. The "enigmatic" Carroll led the Big 10 in scoring, missed the league rebounding title by one board and was named to several All-America teams.

Still, the season ended in frustration. IU's Butch Carter hit a next-to-the-last second shot. Purdue's Jerry Sichting missed a last-second shot. IU 53—Purdue 52. IU, NIT Champions—Purdue NIT Runners-up.

Finally, in 1980 the wait paid off for long-suffering Boiler backers. The Black and Gold, after finishing third in the Big 10 to IU's first, went on to the NCAA Mideast Regional where they defeated the evil Hoosiers led by the eviler Isiah Thomas and the evilest Bobby Knight. A trip to the Final Four held at Indianapolis' Market Square Arena produced a loss to UCLA in the semis and a victory over Iowa in the consolation game. The "enigmatic" Carroll again led the Big 10 in scoring, and with 2,175 points finished second only to Rick Mount in career points scored at Purdue.

Taken by the Golden State Warriors with the first pick in the 1980 NBA draft, Joe Barry Carroll has continued his "enigmatic" career. He has: been named to the NBA All-Rookie Team, averaged 24.1 points in 1982-'83, averaged 12.7 in 1987-'88, made the NBA All-star Team in 1987, dropped out of the league for a year to play in Italy, been traded to Houston for the "enigmatic" Ralph Sampson, experienced "personality conflicts" with numerous basketball people, scored over 12,000 points in his NBA career and yanked down over 3,500 rebounds. For most of the past nine years, Carroll has been one of the better players in the NBA. No telling how great he might have been without all that blasted "enigma."

Two other Boilers from the '70s have enjoyed productive NBA careers. After five years with Phoenix and one with Chicago, Kyle Macy was allowed back into the state to play a season with the Pacers. Considering his defection to the University of Kentucky, Macy was fortunate that the Pacers weren't exactly perennial NBA powerhouses in 1986-'87. Otherwise, some Hoosier Hysteria fanatics might have objected more strenuously.

At ten years and counting, Jerry Sichting has

Purdue University coach Gene Keady demonstrates "The Stare".   *Courtesy Purdue University Athletic Dept.*

Purdue University All-American Joe Barry Carroll

demonstrated a remarkable NBA longevity. A 1980 fourth-round draft pick (82nd overall) Sichting was waived by Golden State before his rookie season began. The Indiana Pacers—looking for warm bodies—picked him up. They found a right-fair guard. Sichting has scored over 4,000 career points and dished out nearly 2,000 assists. In 1986, he was first guard off the bench for the Boston Celtic's World Champions.

Coach Rose departed West Lafayette following the '79-'80 season to accept the challenge of building a Division I program in the fledgling Sunbelt Conference at the University of South Florida. Rose's departure gave the athletic administration at Purdue the opportunity to make one of their smartest moves: they named Gene Keady head basketball coach. As a result, the 1980s witnessed some of the most successful years in Boilermaker basketball history—and of course, they also saw some of the most frustrating years.

Keady's Kids got off to a roaring start when his first edition went 21-11 and finished third in the 1981 NIT. The "enigmatic" Joe Barry Carroll had been replaced by the "enigmatic" Russell Cross. Cross' 16.9 PPG average made the 6'10" center a unanimous choice for Big 10 Rookie of the Year. The '82 team moved up to a second place NIT finish and Keith Edmonson was named an Academic All-American.

The '82-'83 season marked the beginning of renewed Boilermaker frustration. Seven miracle finishes—including the scoring of the game's final 18 points to defeat Illinois 63-62 on Jim Rowinski's buzzer-beating, twenty-foot bank shot—produced a 20-9 record, a Big 10 Runner-Up finish and a Second Round NCAA loss to Arkansas.

The litany of frustration continues. Following the '83 season, Russell Cross became the first Boiler to forego his senior year and enter the NBA's "hardship" draft. Cross joined Joe Barry Carroll when the Golden State Warriors made him the number six pick in the draft. It was a major mistake for all involved. Cross played part of one ineffectual season for the Warriors and vanished from the NBA.

Former Mr. Basketball Dan Palombizio compounded the Boiler loss when at the end of the '83 season he transferred into the program of the Ball State Cardinals.

The Black and Gold regrouped nicely. Picked by nearly everyone to finish at the bottom of the Big 10, the '83-'84 team clawed to a first place tie. Led by league Defensive Player of the Year Ricky Hall, Chicago Tribune Big 10 MVP the "Prince of Pecs" Jim Rowinski and Consensus National Coach of the Year Gene Keady, the Boilermakers went 22-7 . . . and lost a First Round NCAA game to Memphis State 66-48 on the Tigers' home court.

The '84-'85 team over-achieved to a 20-9 record, the first series sweep over IU since '77, an NCAA bid and, characteristically, a First Round 59-58 loss to Auburn in South Bend. The '86 team overachieved to a 22-10 record, victories over six NCAA Tournament teams, an NCAA bid and a First Round loss to LSU on the Tigers' Superdome court.

In 1987 the Boilers went 25-5, captured a

share of their league-leading 17th Big 10 Championship, climbed to a Number Two national ranking and won an NCAA First Round game for the first time in four tries, defeating Northeastern 104-95. Unfortunately, the Boilermakers lost the Second Round game to Florida 85-66.

The '87-'88 edition of Boiler Basketball may have been the second best version ever. Behind All-Big 10 seniors Everette Stephens, Todd Mitchell and former Mr. Basketball Troy Lewis of Anderson, the Black and Gold went 29-4 and took their 18th Big Ten title. The Boilers set school overall, regular season and Big 10 victory records. 1988 saw the university's sixth straight NCAA Tournament bid, tenth straight post-season tourney action, sixth straight 20-plus win campaign, twenty-second straight winning season and twenty-second straight Big 10 upper division finish. Additional team and individual marks would fill this book. Troy Lewis was a John Wooden National Player of the Year Award finalist.

In December of '87 Purdue defeated Kansas State 101-72. In March of '88 Gene Keady's alma mater returned the favor by stunning the nationally third ranked Boilers 73-70 in the NCAA Regional Semi-final. Another Boilermaker dream season slammed to a crashing halt.

Following a disappointing 15-16 season in 1988-'89 that ended the long list of streaks enumerated above, the Boilers returned to the pinnacle of Big 10 competition during the 1989-'90 season. A lightly regarded Purdue squad overachieved to a second place league finish, a Number two NCAA Mideast Regional ranking and . . . a shocking Second Round upset loss.

The decade of promise and frustration culminated with Coach Keady's blasting NCAA officiating in a Tournament post-game press conference. The pressure-valve-releasing-tirade cost the University a $10,000 NCAA fine. Once, when asked why he hadn't accepted a lucrative offer from Arizona State following the 1988 season, Keady cited his love for Purdue, Boilermaker tradition and the fact that as long as he remained in Indiana he could behave like the second biggest SOB in the state and no one would notice. Just so he doesn't start offering his chair to little old ladies in the heat of Boiler-Hoosier battles.

What do we say about Boiler basketball in the Modern Age? Many of the finest players in collegiate history belong to this program. The greatest glories have been tempered by the most crushing defeats. Gene Keady will go 20-8 with outstanding talent or with no talent. IU fans used to grudgingly admit that Coach Keady was the second best coach in the Big 10. Face it folks, there's none better anywhere. Purdue will continue to win Big 10 titles. The litany of All-Big 10 and All-American players will continue. An annual bid to the NCAA will remain a given. And this one's money says there's a Final Four appearance on the near horizon. Get by the sub-regionals and the rest is clear sailing—guaranteed.

You Can't Dribble a Football—Even in South Bend

As the sun rose over the Golden Dome at the dawn of the Modern Age, there was little thunder ringing down on the Notre Dame basketball program. The Fighting Irish had fallen on hard times. A 7-16 record in 1961-'62, followed by a 5-21 mark in '65-'66 contributed to an overall 80-100 slate through the first seven full seasons of the 1960s. There were a few bright spots along the way—Bob Arnzen was a three-time All American before he spent four nondescript years with the Royals and Pacers, and the Irish were NCAA First-Round victims in '63 and '65—but the B-ball landscape in South Bend was generally pretty bleak. The '65 NCAA team was a real high point, despite its mediocre 15-12 record.

The sorry state of things was about to change—abruptly.

Was Rick Mount the greatest collegiate scorer of all time? Was he the finest offensive machine of 1970? Was he the premier scoring weapon in Indiana during his own career? Fighting Irish fans will tell you otherwise—at least those who saw Austin Carr play will tell you otherwise.

A three-year starter from 1969-'71, Carr was the Irish captain during his junior and senior seasons. He achieved a 38.1 scoring average in 1969-'70—second in the nation to LSU's "Pistol" Pete Maravich. In '70-'71 Austin Carr led ND to the school's second consecutive NCAA appearance. He slipped all the way down to a 37.9 PPG average, but his performance was enough to take the Irish back to the Big Dance. The 6'3" guard was a 1970 Consensus All-America, and in '71 he was the easy choice for NCAA Player-of-the-Year.

Some of Austin's Carr's collegiate numbers are difficult for even an avid basketball fan to comprehend. He is Notre Dame's all-time leading scorer, having accumulated 2,560 points during his 84 game career—a 34.6 PPG career average. He

Austin Carr—one of College Basketball's scoring machines. Courtesy Notre Dame Sports.

scored 61 against Ohio University in February of 1970. Two weeks earlier he had established an Athletic and Convocation Center record with 55 in a win over West Virginia. A week prior to that achievement, he had poured in 36 second half points in a 95-93 victory over Detroit. On December 15, 1970, Carr scored 54 points against IU. George McGinnis was having an evening of it, however, and IU prevailed 106-103. The Irish sharpshooter scored 42 or more points 23 times, has 19 of ND's twenty-one top scoring games and holds or shares 29 Notre Dame scoring records.

Austin Carr never proved to be the NBA scoring machine his collegiate rival Pete Maravich became. Still, the Irish star did enjoy an outstanding professional career. During his ten pro seasons, played almost exclusively with the Cleveland Cavaliers, Carr scored 10,473 points for a 15.4 average. He was voted to the NBA-East All-Star squad in 1974—a year in which he averaged 21.9 points per game.

Maravich is one of the greatest collegiate scorers of all time, and his 44.2 career average would be hard to argue with. Rick the Rocket Mount's 32.3 and Austin Carr's 34.6 PPG may pale by comparison, but the Hoosier collegians did outnumber The Pistol two to one.

Austin Carr graduated from the University of Notre Dame in the spring of 1972, and it appeared the Irish basketball program would return to the doldrums from whence it came. A new coach arrived from Fordham to begin the '71-'72 season—an undertaker's son from Beacon, New York named Richard "Digger" (no, really we're serious) Phelps. Digger appeared to be preparing his own shallow grave when his maiden season produced a 6-20 record. Included in the catastrophe was a 29-94 debacle at IU's Assembly Hall. The Irish followed that glorious moment with a 56-114 squeaker at Pauley Pavilion four days later.

Fortunately, Notre Dame got better—a lot better—quickly. Gary Novak, John Shumate, Dwight Clay and Gary Brokaw showed up in the starting lineup in '72-'73. An 18-12 record was something of an improvement, and only a 92-91 overtime loss to Virginia Tech in the final game prevented the Irish from capturing the NIT title.

A chunky 6'5" freshman forward by the name of Adrian Dantley joined the fold in 1973-'74, and the University of Notre Dame climbed back to the heights of NCAA basketball. Two years after the 6-20 embarrassment, the Irish led the nation with a 26-3 mark. A disappointing loss to Michigan in the Mideast Regional ended the season on a sour note. Dantley, however, was scheduled to stick around for two more seasons and the Irish were back for good. Gary Brokaw and Consensus All-American John Shumate—the catalysts in ND's explosive return, later spent four years with Milwaukee and five years with about everybody in the NBA, respectively.

Sophomore All-American Adrian Dantley stayed off the doughnuts and finished second in NCAA scoring in 1975 with a 30.4 PPG average. He nearly matched the feat by finishing fourth at 28.6 in '76. Both Fighting Irish squads were NCAA Regional participants. If not for an 80-76 loss to Michigan in the '76 Regionals, that year's championship could well have been an IU-ND brawl.

Dantley passed up his senior season to enter the NBA's hardship draft. As a professional he has blossomed into an even-money bet for the Hall of Fame. Following his 1977 Rookie of the Year season with the Buffalo Braves (LA Clippers), "A.D." was traded, along with Mike Bantom, to Indiana for the Pacers' all-time leading scorer Billy Knight. The Pacers soon packaged Dantley with Dave Robisch for the Lakers' James Edwards and Earl Tatum. Of course, the Clippers and Pacers ended up with none of the

The Luck O' The Irish: Notre Dame Upsets in the 1970s

Jan. 23, 1971   **ND 89 - UCLA 82**   **at ND**

Austin Carr scored 46 points on 17 of 30 field-goal attempts and 12 of 16 free throws as ND handed the eventual National Champions their only loss of the season. The victory snapped UCLA's 48-game nonconference winning streak.

Jan. 13, 1973   **ND 71 - Marquette 69**   **at Marquette**

Dwight Clay's corner jumper with four seconds remaining downed Al McGuire's 25-4 Warriors. The Irish victory snapped Marquette's 81-game homecourt winning streak. Gary Brokaw led with 28.

Dec. 11, 1973   **ND 73 - IU 67**   **at IU**

In the first visit to Assembly Hall since the 94-29 debacle in '71, the Irish snapped the Hoosier's 19-game homecourt winning streak. John Shumate paced ND with 26 and dominated the paint.

Jan. 19, 1974   **ND 71 - UCLA 70**   **at ND**

A furious 12-0 Irish comeback over the last 3:22 put an end to UCLA's 88-game winning streak, the longest in college basketball history. Another Dwight Clay corner jumper with 29 seconds remaining nailed the coffin. Brokaw and Shumate led again with 25 and 24 respectively.

Dec. 11, 1976   **ND 66 - UCLA 63**   **at UCLA**

The Bruins 115-game non-conference home winning streak came to an end when Donald "Duck" Williams led the Irish with 22 points on 11 of 16 shooting. The non-league loss was the first by the UCLAns in their fifteen years at Pauley Pavilion.

March 1, 1977   **ND 93 - San Francisco 82**   **at ND**

The Number One rated Dons were 29-0 coming into the ACC—29-1 going out. Duck Williams led with 25, but NBC Sports voted the Irish student body the game's MVP Award.

1970's Plus One

Feb. 27, 1980   **ND 76 - DePaul 74**   **at ND**

The Number One rated Blue Demons were 25-0 coming into the ACC—25-1 going out. Orlando Woolridge's pair of free throws with nineteen seconds remaining in double-overtime iced the victory. Kelly Tripucka led the Irish with 28.

above, while Edwards and Dantley both found their way to the Detroit Pistons. The Pistons acquired Dantley plus two second round draft choices in exchange for Kelly Tripucka and Kent Benson in a 1986 deal.

Despite all this moving about, A.D. has managed to make the NBA All-Star team six times, to lead the league in scoring in 1981 (30.7) and 1984 (30.6), to win the '84 Comeback Player-of-the-Year Award following knee surgery, to score over 23,000 career points and to haul down over 5,500 rebounds. Famous for his broad posterior, the 6'5", 210 pound forward is known for his ability in the paint. One result is that he shares the NBA record for most free-throws made in one game—28—-VS Houston, January 4, 1984.

Adrian Dantley is in the twilight of his career. He may have seen his last NBA action, but Hoosier basketball fanatics will always remember him as the man who put Notre Dame basketball back on top.

A hard-nosed, 6'11" freshman center on the '75-'76 Irish team has also achieved substantial basketball fame... or is it infamy. Bill Laimbeer, Jr.,—baddest of the World Champion Detroit Pistons' "Bad Boys"—came to his current lofty status by a circuitous route. After scoring a not exactly Dantley-ish eighty-two points in ten games as a freshman, Laimbeer left South Bend for a year to put his academics in order at Owens Tech Jr. College in Toledo.

Though he returned to Notre Dame for his junior and senior seasons, his 8.1 and 6.4 scoring

"A.D." Adrian Dantley. Courtesy Notre Dame Sports.

Baddest of the Bad Boys—Bill Laimbeer of Notre Dame. Courtesy Notre Dame Sports.

averages were poor predictions of things to come. The Fighting Irish went 23-8 and finished fourth in the '78 NCAA Tourney. In '79 they were 24-5 and fourth in the AP poll before falling to Magic Johnson and the eventual Champion Michigan State Spartans. Laimbeer toiled away on the inside doing all the dirty work for both teams, but it was teammates Kelly Tripucka, Bill Hanzlick and, in '79, Orlando Woolridge for whom big NBA futures were predicted. Those futures materialized, but Bill Laimbeer's future turned out to be the best of all.

Following a year with Brescia in the Italian League and two journeyman seasons with the Cleveland Cavs, Laimbeer was traded to Detroit along with Kenny Carr for Phil Hubbard, Paul Mokeski and 1982 first and second round draft choices. In the eight seasons since the trade, Laimbeer has developed into one of the premier "enforcers" in the NBA. He has scored over 11,000 points to date and has been named to the All-Star Team four times. A 260 pound immovable object with a bad attitude, Laimbeer has claimed over 8,500 rebounds. In 1986 he led the NBA with 1,075 boards—a 13.1 per game average. Along with teammate Isiah Thomas, Laimbeer has established the Pistons as the Rolls Royce of professional basketball with World Championships in 1989 and '90.

An athlete of somewhat limited natural abililty, Bill Laimbeer has carved his place in the NBA by refusing to back down from anyone inside. Love him or hate him—there is no in between, and many choose the latter—you have to admire any human who can take the battering Laimbeer takes and still show up night after night. Bill didn't miss a game for several years and only sat out four nights during his first nine professional seasons.

Laimbeer's Irish teammates Hanzlick, Tripucka and Woolridge haven't done too badly for themselves either. Bill Hanzlick (a 6'7" guard) played for four NCAA Tourney teams at ND from 1977-'80. He truly came to the forefront at the 1980 Olympic Trials, where he won a position on the US team. Though the Olympic boycott prevented any further demonstrations of his talents, he had impressed enough people to become the first round (twentieth pick) choice of the Seattle Supersonics. During his ten-year NBA career with Seattle and Denver, he has scored over 5,000 points, and in 1986 he was named to the League's All-Defensive Team.

Kelly Tripucka came to South Bend the year after Bill Hanzlick arrived and also played on four NCAA Tourney teams. The son of former Irish and NFL quarterback Frank Tripucka, Kelly's 1,719 career points rank fifth on the all-time Notre Dame scoring list. The 92-26 record achieved by the Irish during the younger Tripucka's four-year career mark the most succesful period iin Notre Dame basketball history.

After receiving substantial All-America support during his sophomore, junior and senior seasons, Tripucka was taken by the Pistons with the twelfth pick in the 1981 NBA draft. As a professional he has shown a somewhat suprising proclivity for high scoring. Named to the NBA All-Rookie and All-Star teams in 1982, Tripuka also found a spot on the 1984 All-Star Team. He has scored nearly 12,000 points to date in nine years with the Pistons, Jazz and Hornets.

Orlanda Woolridge is the fourth member of the 1978-'79 Fighting Irish to go on to an outstanding professional career. The 6'9" forward improved dramatically over the course of his collegiate career, and by his senior season the co-captain averaged 14.4 PPG and finished third in the nation with a .605 field goal percentage.

The Chicago Bills tabbed Woolridge with the sixth pick of the '82 draft. During nine seasons with Chicago, New Jersey and the Lakers, he has amassed nearly 9,500 points and snared 2,600 rebounds. In 1989 he scored 122 playoff points for the Western Division champion LA Lakers.

The graduation of Woolridge and Tripucka following the '80-'81 season marked the end of an era in Notre Dame basketball history. And while ND has maintained a generally successful program over the past nine seasons, the Fighting Irish haven't quite been up to the stature they achieved during the 1970s and early '80s.

John MacBeth Paxson was the lone highlight on the '81-'83 Irish teams, which registered a combined 29-27 record. The son of Jim Paxson, Sr, a forward with the Minneapolis Lakers ('56-'57) and Cincinnati Royals (57-'58) and the brother of Boston Celtic guard Jim Paxson, Jr, John fired in 1,366 points for Notre Dame. John was named to several All-America teams in 1981 and was a Consensus choice in 1982. During seven seasons with San Antonio and Chicago, "Pax" has scored over 3,500 points and dished out over 2,000 assists. Though not a native of Indiana, Paxson was a Hoosier long enough to learn how the game is supposed to be played. In the great Hoosier mad bomber tradition, John has canned over 200 NBA three-pointers.

In 1982 Digger Phelps resurrected a long dormant practice at Notre Dame. He began recruiting Indiana High School All-Stars. Joseph Price had scored 14 points in a 1980 State Semi-final loss to eventual Champion Indianapolis Broad Ripple, Ken Barlow had tallied 22 and junior Scott Hicks chipped in 18 in a 1982 Semi-final loss to Scott Skiles and his Champion Plymouth Pil-

Erstwhile mortician Digger Phelps keeps things lively on the Notre Dame Campus. Courtesy Notre Dame Sports.

grims. By the '85 NCAA Tournament Price, Barlow and Hicks had become solid players on the first Irish NCAA qualifier in four years.

While none of these three Hoosiers went on to epic collegiate careers, all contributed considerably to righting the listing Irish ship. The experience seems to have belabored an obvious truth. You don't have to travel from South Bend to Brooklyn to find Fighting Irish talent. Two current ND recruits, 6'9" twins, John and Joe Ross of Northfield High School, should reconfirm that notion in Irish minds.

The most recent hotshot to matriculate in the shadow of the Golden Dome is a slight, 6' guard named David Rivers. Compared to Isiah Thomas by the network talking heads throughout his college career, Rivers relentlessly amassed 2,058 Irish points while at Notre Dame. He trails only Austin Carr and Adrian Dantley on the all-time Notre Dame scoring chart. Whether because he is a real talent, or because Dick Vitale, Al McGuire and Billy Packer incessantly proclaimed him one, Rivers was named to several All-America teams during his four years in South Bend. A 44% collegiate shooting average would seem to leave the issue open for debate—so would two less-than-memorable seasons with the Lakers and Timberwolves. There's no arguing Rivers' quickness and tenacity. The question is, how far can a short, skinny guard with an at best marginal shot go in the NBA?

Will Digger Phelps take the Fighting Irish back to the Final Four? Will ND teams of the future swagger into Assembly Hall, Rupp Arena, Pauley Pavilion and Dean Smith Arena to calmly dispatch seemingly invincible teams? You can probably count on it. The '90 upset of Syracuse in the Carrier Dome and the promising talent of such players as LaPhonso Ellis promise good things to come. Many an echo has been awakened in South Bend in the last thirty years, and a goodly number of them bear the unmistakable music of round ball meeting hard wood.

The Indiana State Bird

Though IU, Purdue and Notre Dame have come to dominate Indiana intercollegiate basketball in the Modern Age, the Big Three don't come anywhere near a monopoly on great moments or great players in recent Hoosier college basketball history.

There had been good seasons and good teams at Indiana State University; the years with John Wooden as coach in the '40s, the perennial NAIB/NAIA contenders in the 50s, the NCAA College Division runners-up in 1968. But, the years 1976 to 1979 weren't merely good years in Terre Haute—they were dream years. They were Larry Bird years.

Though an Indiana All-Star while at Springs Valley High School, Larry Joe Bird had not demonstrated the kind of dominance at the high school level that Oscar Robertson or George McGinnis showed. In fact, he was not as heavily recruited as All-Star teammates Walter Jordan and Wayne Walls. Bird enrolled at IU-Bloomington in the fall of 1974. He stayed only a few weeks. No, it had nothing to do with a Bob Knight rage. Seems the "Hick from French Lick" wasn't ready for a dormitory that housed more citizens than inhabited his hometown. Seems Terre Haute was a more comfortable haunt. IU's loss was ISU's gain.

After not playing in '74-'75 and then sitting out a transfer season in '75-'76, Bird led the Sycamores to their first NCAA Division I post-season invitation with a berth in the 1977 NIT. His 32.8 PPG average established a still existing ISU single-season record. 1977-'78 was even better as State came within a bucket of upending Creighton in the Missouri Valley Conference Tourney. A victory would have put the Sycamores into the NCAA Tourney for the first time. A First Round NIT victory over Illinois State at the Terre Haute Hulman Center provided some consolation.

But 1978-'79 was the season. The kind of season legends—even myths—are made of. The year started badly when Coach Bob King came down with a serious illness and was forced to hand the reins to his assistant, Bill Hodges. There would be no more bad news for over five months. Purdue went down at Mackey 63-53. Evansville, Ball State and Butler fell; so did Bradley, Creighton and, in the MVC Final, New Mexico State. Oklahoma took a 93-72 pounding in the NCAA Mideast Regional. Arkansas went home after the Regional Final. Big, bad DePaul was the favorite in the Championship Semi-final, but Bird's 35 points and 16 rebounds more than offset Mark Aguirre's 19 points. ISU entered the NCAA Championship Game with a record of 33-0. All that stood in the way of a national title was ... Michigan State ... and Magic Johnson.

Sports is about rivalries—titanic rivalries. Johnson VS Cobb, Robinson VS LaMotta, Russell VS Chamberlain, Ali VS Frazier, Schembeckler VS

The Bird lights up the Hulman Center. Courtesy Indiana State University.

Hayes; the names are inseparable. In March of 1979 a rivalry for the ages was born—the Birdman VS the Magicman.

It was the perfect match. They were completely different. Big City Magic VS The Hick, smooth and articulate VS. . . . not so articulate, Big 10 VS MVC, Black VS White. But, they were almost the same— 6'8" VS 6'9", passer VS passer, leader VS leader, winner VS winner. Bird canned 19 and hauled down 13 boards. (Carl Nicks chipped in 17 and Bob Heaton 10 for ISU). Magic dropped in 24 and pulled 10 rebounds, but the Sycamores had no Greg Kelser—no Jay Vincent. Final Score, Michigan State 75, Indiana State 64. ISU finished 33-1 and NCAA Runners-up. Has there ever been a finer season?

Of course '79 was just the beginning for the Johnson-Bird match up. Johnson has been NBA MVP thrice—Bird thrice. Bird has been playoff MVP twice—Johnson thrice. Bird has played for

One can make the statement that Larry Bird has been the most dominant basketball player in the world for the last fifteen years, but exaggeration is the lifeblood of sports dialogue and such an assertion may not be accepted. Let the record speak for itself.

Indiana State University
1976-'77 1st, 2nd or 3rd Team All-America; UPI, AP, Sporting News, USBCA, Sportfolio
Leading Scorer-Missouri Valley Conference
3rd Leading Scorer-NCAA (32.8)
7th Leading Rebounder-NCAA (13.3)
12th Player in NCAA History to Average 30 or More Points as a Soph
1977-'78 Consensus All-America; UPI, AP, USBWA, Sporting News, Basketball Weekly, USBCA
Missouri Valley Conference Player of the Year
NCAA District Four-Player of the Year
Naismith Trophy Runner-Up (UPI Player of the Year Balloting)
Rupp Trophy, 3rd Place (AP Player of the Year Balloting)
Second in NCAA Scoring Average (30.0)
Gold Medalist, US World University Games Team
1978-'79 Consensus Player of the Year and 1st Team All-America; UPI, AP, Sporting News, Basketball Times, Basketball Weekly
Adolph Rupp Trophy
James Naismith Trophy
USBWA Trophy
Eastman Trophy
Joe Lapchick Award
All-Missouri Valley Conference, Player of the Year
Kodak All-America
Most Valuable Player-1979 Pizza Hut All-Star Classic
5th All-Time Leading Scorer in NCAA History (even with only three years of eligibility)
Holder of fourteen ISU Records Including: Career Points (2,850), Points One Season (973), Scoring Average Career (30.3), Points in One Game (49), Career Rebounds (1,247), Rebounds One Season (505), Rebound Average Career (13.3), Steals One Season (85)

AND

NBA Rookie of the Year; 1980
NBA All-Star; 1980, '81, '82, '83, '84, '85, '86, '87, '88 and '90
NBA All-Pro; 1980, '81, '82, '83, '84, '85, '86, '87 and '88
NBA All-Star Game MVP; 1982
NBA All-Defensive 2nd Team; 1982, '83, '84 and '85
NBA MVP; 1984, '85 and '86
Member, NBA Champions; 1981, '84 and '86
NBA Playoff MVP; 1984 and '86
NBA Playoff Record Points in One Year (632, 1984)
NBA All-Time Three-Point Field Goals Made (Over 500 and Counting)
Over 19,500 NBA Points, 8,000 Rebounds and Nearly 5,000 Assists

The numbers would be more impressive, but Bird was forced to sit out the 1988-'89 season with bone-spurs—and he ain't done yet!

three NBA Champs—Johnson five. Johnson has 15,500 points—Bird 19,500. Bird has 5,000 assists—Johnson 9,000. It is a rivalry for the ages.

Watching Larry Bird evolve from the Hick from French Lick into an articulate spokesman for basketball has been almost as much fun as watching him play. Madison Avenue spotted the possibilities right away. The early Magic/Bird TV promos for gasoline and soft drinks were more than a little embarrassing. But Bird has thrived under the dim lights of Boston Garden and the bright lights of the Eastern media. Watching Larry flip a deft left-handed behind-the-back pass to Kevin McHale or just as easily handle a bank of microphones after a big win or a tough loss reminds one of the ISU sign at the NCAA Finals: "The Indiana State Bird is Larry."

Still More Hoosier Roundball Dynasties

Coach Arad McCutchan led Evansville College to 514 victories between 1946-1977. A 1930 graduate of Evansville Bosse High School, McCutchan coached ten College Division All-Americans, won fourteen Indiana Intercollegiate Conference titles and achieved a 40-10 post-season tournament record. The Purple Aces won NCAA College Division (Division II) Championships in 1959, '60, '64, '65 and '71. McCutchan is thus, along with John Wooden, one of only two coaches to win more than four NCAA basketball crowns. He was named College Division Coach of the Year in 1964 and 1965 and served as a coach at the US Olympic Trials in 1960 and 1968. Arad McCutchan was elected to the Naismith Basketball Hall of Fame in 1980. He was the first person associated with College Division basketball to be so honored.

Coach McCutchan's two best players at Evansville could, and did take the floor with anybody . . . anybody! Jerry Sloan was a Consensus College Division All-American in 1963, '64 and '65. The Purple Aces went 76-9 during his collegiate career and captured two NCAA College Division crowns. A bullish forward, the 6'5 1/2" Sloan averaged 12.4 rebounds per game at Evansville. During an eleven-year NBA career with Baltimore and Chicago, Sloan played in the 1969 All-Star Game, scored 10,571 career points and grabbed 5,615 rebounds.

A second outstanding Evansville College player bears a name that recalls many fond memories for Pacer fans everywhere. Don Buse was impressive enough to be named to the 1968 Indiana High School All-Star Team despite the fact that he played for tiny Holland High School. Holland was yet to merge with its Dubois County neighbor, Huntingburg, to form the massive (502 students in four grades) Southridge High School. Buse stayed home to play for Arad McCutchan, and he led the Purple Aces to their fifth, and last, College Division title in 1971. Don scored 1,426 points during his Evansville career and was named MVP of the '71 NCAA College Division Tournament.

Though he was drafted by the NBA's Phoenix Suns, Buse signed with the ABA's Indiana Pacers

1971 NCAA College Divison Tournament MVP Don Buse of the Evansville Purple Aces. Courtesy Evansville University.

after the club purchased his rights from the Virginia Squires. Several years later, the Pacers traded Buse to the long-covetous Suns for Ricky Sobers—one of a long series of grossly unpopular moves that nearly destroyed the Pacer franchise.

During an eleven-year ABA/NBA career with the Pacers, Suns and Trailblazers, Buse scored 6,291 points and dished 3,919 assists. One of the premier defenders of his era, he was named to the ABA All-Defensive Team in 1975 and '76 and to the NBA All-Defensive Team in 1977, '78, '79 and '80. Don was a member of the Pacers 1973 ABA Championship Team, and in 1976 he was voted to the last ABA All-Star Team. In 1977 he was the Pacers first NBA All-Star—an honor he won for leading the league in both assists and steals.

Buse capped his outstanding career when he returned to the Pacers for the 1981-'82 season and—what else—set the NBA record for most three-point field goals in a season (73). Arad McCutchan knew basketball talent when he saw it. He knew that in Indiana it grew up on the big city asphalt playgrounds, and he knew that it grew up on the dirt courts of rural Dubois County.

The end of the McCutchan era came with the coach's retirement at the conclusion of the 1977-'78 season. The new era of Coach Bobby Watson appeared to hold bright promise as the University of Evansville Purple Aces prepared to embark on their first NCAA Division I campaign. On Tuesday, December 13, 1978, the chartered DC-3 took off from Evansville's Dress Regional Airport bound for Middle Tennessee State University at Nashville. Moments later it slammed into a southern Indiana hillside killing all thirty persons aboard, including the thirty-seven year old Coach Watson and his team. Evansville Triplets radio announcer Marv Bates, who achieved a certain acclaim for being the last known American sportscaster to recreate live baseball play-by-play from wire service reports and in-studio sound effects, was also lost in the crash. The American sporting community had suffered one of its greatest human tragedies.

As painful as the calamity was, life and the game of basketball did go on. New coach Dick Walters led the Aces to a 13-16 record one year after the disaster. By 1981-'82 the University of Evansville was able to post a 23-6 record and extend Marquette to the final minute in the Aces' first NCAA Division I Tournament game.

In 1973 Jim Crews was Quinn Buckner's fellow freshman backcourt mate on IU's NCAA Final Four team. Crews' steady contributions off the bench were integral to the Hoosiers 67-1 run from 1974-'76. Since 1985 Coach Crews has led the U of E to two NCAA appearances. Noblesville's Scott Haffner was a member of both Tournament squads. He averaged 24.5 points in 1988-'89 and later labored with the Miami Heat of the NBA. A typical Hoosier, Haffner sank 245 of his 569 collegiate three-point attempts. The legacy of Arad McCutchan, Jerry Sloan and Don Buse is alive and well at the University of Evansville.

Vincennes University, the Smallest Giant in B-Ball

Yet another Indiana collegiate basketball program that has traditionally dominated its competition belongs to Vincennes University. Playing in the National Junior College Athletic Association (NJCAA), the "Trailblazers" of Coach Allen Bradfield were victorious in 608 of the 784 games they contested between 1952 and 1979. Success has continued under Blazer alumnus Coach Dan Sparks. VU has been invited to twenty NJCAA National Tournaments—placing fourth in 1974 and 1982, and winning National Championships in 1965, '70 and '72.

Vincennes University has established a national reputation with major college recruiters in search of that diamond in the rough. Before moving on to play for Dean Smith at the University of North Carolina, Bob McAdoo played 60 games for VU, scored 1,292 points and grabbed 617 boards. The Trailblazers went 51-9 during the NJCAA All-American's Hoosier stay and copped the 1970 NJCAA title. The 6'9" forward went on to NBA Rookie of the Year, and later, NBA MVP honors. McAdoo was a five-time NBA All-Star, and scored nearly 19,000 professional points.

Bob McAdoo teamed with Clarance Walker at VU in 1971. It must have been a fun team to watch, but it would be one more season before "Foots" Walker would lead the Blazers to their third NJCAA title. The 6'1" guard graduated from VU and passed through West Georgia College on his way to the NBA. In ten seasons with Cleveland and New Jersey, Foots scored 4,199 points, pilfered 992 steals and distributed 3,111 assists.

Recent Indiana Pacer guard Ricky Green was a third outstanding NBA player with a Vincennes University diploma. The Blazers went 60-10 during Green's tenure and finished fourth in the 1974 NJCAA Tournament and twelfth in the '75 Tour-

Future NBA scoring leader Bob McAdoo leading the Vincennes Trailblazers. Courtesy Vincennes University.

ney. Green scored 1,295 Junior College points and was named an NJCAA All-American in both '74 and '75.

Because this was the era before Bob Knight discovered that Junior College players weren't poisonous, the cat-quick guard was picked up by the University of Michigan. Green was reintroduced to basketball Indiana style via the 86-68 drubbing Coach Knight's Indiana Hoosiers put on the Wolverines in the 1976 NCAA Championship Game. Rickey led UM with a futile 18 points.

In twelve NBA seasons, Rickey Green scored over 8,000 points, passed out over 4,700 assists and grabbed nearly 1,300 steals. Green led the NBA with 215 steals in 1984—the same season he registered eleven assists in the NBA All-Star Game.

The list of VU players who've gone on to outstanding major college or professional careers is a long one. Oscar Evans, Tony Fuller, Courtney Witte, et al have all done their alma mater proud. Next time you're at a Trailblazer game, say "hello" to the fans in the stands—Johnny Orr, Dean Smith, Bob Knight, Norm Sloan, Don Haskins . . . .

Rickey Green, late of the Indiana Pacers, got his college start with the Vincennes University Trailblazers. Courtesy Vincennes University.

The Bulldogs Falter

An unsettling story of the Modern Age of sports in Indiana involves the disintegration of the basketball program at Butler University. In the early '60s it appeared that the Bulldogs would continue in their powerhouse ways indefinitely. Building on NIT appearances in 1957 and '58, the 'Dogs won their first NCAA Tourney bid in 1962. An 87-86 victory over Western Kentucky was followed by an 81-60 lesson administered by Adolph Rupp's Kentucky Wildcats. All seemed right with the world. In fact, 1962 was the high water mark. Somebody pulled the plug.

As blasphemous as it sounds, Tony Hinkle may have hung around a bit longer than he should have. Hink retired after the '70 season at the age of seventy-one. His last four teams combined for a 47-57 record. Throw out those years and Tony's ledger is 513-335.

Billy Shepherd—he of the "I can make a basket from ten feet further than you can throw the ball" Carmel Shepherds—signed with Butler following his 1968 Mr. Basketball season. Shepherd did score. He holds Butler records for points in a game (49 VS Arizona), season (724), season average (27.8) and career scoring average (24.1). His 1,733 points in three varsity campaigns ranks Number Two on Bulldog charts. Shepherd's supporting cast, unfortunately, won't be mistaken for the Boston Celtics. The Bulldogs slid through a dismal 6-20 slate in his senior season. Shepherd took his jump-shot to the ABA for three journeyman years while his alma mater settled into perpetual 13-14 seasons.

In 1977 Butler hired Mr. Basketball and Trester Award winner of 1952, Indianapolis Tech High School's Joe Sexson to revive the Bulldog hardwood program. From 1954 through 1956 Sexson had set the Boilermaker record for career points (1,095). Sexson still shares a Purdue record he set by playing all seventy minutes of a six-overtime game against Minnesota in 1955. Prior to hiring on at Butler, Joe had labored for seventeen seasons as a Boiler assistant basketball coach, and with 221 wins, he is the all-time winningest baseball coach in Purdue history.

Joe Sexson appeared to be just the tonic Butler basketball needed. His first squad went 15-11—the first Bulldog winner in five seasons. In 1978 the 'Dogs left the Indiana Intercollegiate Conference for the newly formed and more prestigious Midwestern City Conference (MCC). In 1984 Sexson was named MCC Coach of the Year despite a 13-15 record. In 1985 he guided Butler to the school's first post-season competition in twenty-three years. Though the Buldogs fell at IU's Assembly Hall in the First Round of the NIT, Butler basketball appeared to be back in the Big Time.

It was an illusion. It wasn't poor coaching that produced the 5-22 and 7-20 records. With one assistant and a $40,000 recruiting budget, Coach Sexson found attracting Division I talent increasingly difficult. Venerable Hinkle Fieldhouse hadn't seen a good coat of paint in years and a non-existent PR budget produced more birds and bats in the rafters than fans in the rickety stands.

In 1989 Butler University announced a full-fledged campaign to raise the Bulldog basketball program back to its traditional lofty perch. Three million dollars went to dress-up the Fieldhouse, and she sure looks fine. Hire a couple of new assistants. Hike the recruiting budget 100-200%. Put up some eye-catching billboards and bring in a new coach and a new A.D. What becomes of Joe Sexson and Bill Sylvester—two guys who busted their keisters for all those years in the face of benign neglect? They become two more expendable components in the Big Business called American Sports.

All Hoosier basketball fans wish the best for the new roundball regime at Butler. One hopes that people learn from their mistakes

Angus Nicoson—A Winner On and Off the Court

One Hoosier basketball genius almost universally overlooked by the casual fan is Angus J. Nicoson of Clay County. Nicoson took the head coaching position at Indiana Central College (University of Indianapolis) in 1947. He retired in 1977 as the seventh winningest collegiate basketball coach to that time with 483 victories.

With talent like the "Big O's" big brother Bailey "Flap" Robertson, Nicoson was a seven-time Hoosier Collegiate Conference Coach of the Year, and a three-time NAIA District 21 Coach of the Year. Flap could hold his own with little brother on the playground. He scored 35 or better twelve times as a collegian and still holds the U of I mark with 2,280 career points scored.

Angus Nicoson was a member of the US Olympic, Pan-American, AAU and International Basketball Federation Committees. He is a member of the Helms Foundation Hall of Fame, and the University of Indianapolis Greyhounds play all of their home games in Angus J. Nicoson Hall.

In the best tradition of sportsmanship, Nicoson

is best remembered in many Indiana basketball circles for the time and effort he donated to the kids who play the sport. From 1952-1965 and from 1969-1971, Coach Nicoson served as the mentor of the Indiana High School All-Stars in their annual battle with the Kentucky high school hotshots. If you were a great Hoosier high school roundballer between 1952 and 1971 you probably took a lesson from Coach Angus Nicoson.

David Letterman's Favorite College Joins the Ranks of Hoosier B-Ball Titans

In 1988-'89 a fat man, perpetually dressed in flashy ski sweaters, stunned the college basketball world when he directed the historically pedestrian Ball State Cardinals to a 29-3 record and an NCAA First Round upset of the University of Arkansas. After failing at the high-pressure task of replacing Al McGuire at Marquette University, Rick Majerus found the low-expection, low-pressure attitude in Muncie, Indiana to be the perfect environment for rehabilitating his basketball reputation.

Following the '88-'89 season Majerus parlayed his new-found respect, his congenial personality and his consistent quotability into a top-dollar contract with the University of Utah. Hopefully the physical problems that precluded his participation in the '89-'90 roundball wars will not deprive fans of the enjoyment derived from his expected return in '90-91.

Rick Hunsaker took the reins at State following Majerus' departure. Inheriting nine seniors, the former BSU assistant suddenly found himself confronted with a high-expectation, high-pressure attitude in Muncie. Early season returns were not promising.

Purdue crushed the Cards 57-43 in the season opener and BSU dropped three of its first nine contests—one more defeat than had been absorbed throught the '88-'89 regular season.

Coach Hunsaker stood by his veteran team and the ship soon righted itself. BSU captured 15 of its final 18 contests, swept to a 26-7 mark and capped the grandest season in Ball State history with a virtuoso performance in the NCAA Tourney.

Led by the punishing inside play of Paris McCurdy and Curtis Kidd, the floor generalship of Billy Butts, and most memorably by the flashy one-on-one abilities of former Muncie Central forward Chandler Thompson, Cardinal success was a true team effort. Eleven players averaged ten or more minutes per game. And while McCurdy's team-leading 11.8 PPG and a team average of 71.5 PPG wouldn't appear to indicate success, all fifteen Cardinals contributed to State's limiting opponents to a paltry 58.6 PPG average. Shades of early Bobby Knight.

After becoming the first Mid American Conference team in twenty-seven years to repeat as outright Conference Champions, the Cards entered the NCAA Tourney tabbed as one of the perennial early round sacrificial lambs. As Purdue, Notre Dame and IU can attest from firsthand experience, opening round lambs have taken to humiliating their over-hyped foes of late.

PAC-10 Champs Oregon State scored with three seconds remaining to take a 53-51 First Round command. A long inbounds pass knocked out of play preceded Paris McCurdy's six-footer at the buzzer. Fouled on the play, McCurdy tossed in a free throw with no time on the clock, making the final score BSU 54-OSU 53. The Cardinals, in true fashion, won the game by holding OSU guard and AP National Player of the Year Gary Payton to 11 points and five assists below his season average.

In Second Round action, Louisville's 62 points and 45% shooting average both represented team season lows. Ball State's Cards outraced Denny Crum's Cards to lead by 17 and hung on for a thrilling 64-62 victory. "We had respect for Louisville and their post-season success," Hunsaker said. "But we weren't intimidated or awed by their athletes. Their Cardinal is the same as our Cardinal. It's the heart inside the jersey, not the name of the institution that's on the jersey you win with."

The second MAC team in history to reach the "Sweet Sixteen," BSU faced UNLV in West Regional Semi-final action. The Runnin' Rebels would crush five other Tourney opponents by an average of 22 points per game. Duke would take a 103-73 thrashing in the eventual Championship Game. Against State, an errant Cardinal lob pass as time expired allowed the Rebs to escape 69-67. The greatest season in Ball State basketball history had come to a heroic end.

Additonal BSU marks of distinction from the 1989-'90 season include: being the first repeat winners of the eleven-year-old MAC Tournament; scoring back-to-back 20-victory seasons for the first time in school history; becoming the first MAC school to win NCAA Tourney games in successive season; compiling a two-year, 55-10 record—second best in the nation—and graduating all nine of the 1989-'90 seniors.

Whether or not Coach Hunsaker will be able to continue his successes is, of course, not certain at this writing. Chandler Thompson's 20-point 9.3 rebound averages would seem to indicate that MAC foes will be forced to wait at least one more season before enjoying any consistent revenge.

The dedication of a brand new 12,000 seat arena and the continuation of the spectacular moves of Thompson and others like him might even convince Muncie hoop fanatics that Central's game is not the only game in town.

Hometown boy makes good: Muncie Central's Chandler Thompson helped lead Ball State to the top of the college basketball world. Courtesy Ball State University.

The Unofficial History of the Indiana Pacers

It was a cold February night in 1967. Snowflakes were swirling around street lamps, but flakier things are happening inside the Lafayette Country Club. A franchise with no charter was about to enter a basketball league that didn't exist.

The American Basketball Association, born in Hollywoodland and later embalmed at the bank, was about to hurtle itself at an unsuspecting—and mostly uncaring—nation. The league wanted a franchise in Indianapolis. And there was so much interest in the Hoosier capital that two hardy adventurers had hit Lafayette in search of start-up money.

But let's jump back a bit. Constantine Seratin, one of many fringe characters destined to surface, then float away on a carpet of red, white and blue laughing gas, wanted to start a league called the American Basketball Association. And he had an unusual concept: all revenues would be shared. Players would be signed to league contracts. Salaries would be modest; players would make additional money from product endorsements supplied by Seratin's New York sports promotion company.

Seratin was peddling his dream cross-country when he contacted Chuck Barnes in Indianapolis. Chuck was president of Sports Headliners, a successful management company that handled most of the top auto racing drivers and later represented football star O.J. Simpson. Chuck's knowledge of professional basketball ended at the pit gate. But he was a born promoter with an appetite for the unusual.

Barnes was in Los Angeles on other business when the ABA conducted what was billed as an organizational meeting. Barnes attended and reported back that it was the wildest, silliest most totally unrealistic thing he'd ever seen. In other words, some of us in Indianapolis had to get in; it was too much fun to miss.

New people and new cities were represented at every session. People kept running out to the pay phones—evidently to find out if their backers at home could afford the room rent for an extra day.

Seratin, the George Washington of the league, was dismissed. The new leader was a man named Gardiner, who incidentally was long gone before the league opened for business.

It cost $6,000 to take a look at the ABA. A pittance. Pocket change for high rollers. And not so incidentally $6,000 more than Barnes, Tinkham, DeVoe or Bob Collins, the principals in this operation at that time, could produce.

So, let's rejoin the crowd on that cold evening in Lafayette. The occasion was Lyn Treece's annual wild game dinner. At one table were Treece, Joe Bannon and Dick Ebershoff, all of Lafayette and Ronnie Woodard, Indianapolis, Barnes and myself.

Barnes, between laughs, told of his visit to the new basketball wonderland. The idea appealed to their sense of humor more than their business instincts. Still they thought it was a capital idea. Little did they realize how much capital they'd expend before they bailed out.

The ABA was holding what it hoped would be its final organizational meeting at New York the following morning. And fate played a hand. Bannon was due there at the same time.

The group, plus DeVoe, covered the entry fee. So Bannon and Barnes, who was dying to see what exotic, new mystery guests would show, took off and arrived just in time to put down the money and join whatever it was they got themselves into.

The final meeting was even more frantic than the others. A fellow named Mark Bimstein, acting as commisioner, kept calling me and mentioning names of NBA stars who had been signed to secret contracts. I quickly got into the spirit and assured him we would get Oscar Robertson. I also said we wouldn't join the club unless Louisville received a franchise.

A phone call later the request was granted. But, by that time the situation was so chaotic Snow White and the Seven Dwarfs would have been considered a viable franchise.

The new league was supposed to have ten franchises. But nobody really could be sure for a while. This was because several promoters paid their entry fees, then took off trying to sell them.

(continued on next page)

Bob Collins Sports Profile

The league flew with the grace of a wounded albatross and the direction of a drunken fish in a whirlpool. The first thing the new entrepreneurs said was they would not try to sign NBA players; the first thing they did was go after them.

Additional investors were found here and Bannon, board chairman of Purdue National Bank, was named president. The new owners committed for $35,000 and ended up spending much more.

The new team was named the Pacers and an effort was made to sign Robertson, Terry Dischinger and Dick and Tom Van Arsdale. None of the four was interested, but Oscar offered a splendid bit of advice. Said he, "Get Roger Brown."

From start to finish, the ABA was a mess—an accident, that kept happening over and over. It ran through commissioners like popcorn—once operating for a while without one. Franchises constantly seemed to be moving, disappearing or changing owners. Many investors were dilettantes who wanted toys they couldn't afford.

It was a strange little league—perhaps more to be pitied than scorned. But most of the memories were happy ones. The ABA had the red, white and blue basketball and the three-point play. And it had charm. It still isn't unusual to hear people around here, say, "You know, I miss that crazy old league."

Some gyms were creaky and leaky. It's on record that several games were postponed by rain. One night in Miami shooters had to allow for windage, because due to the humidity all doors were open and gale force winds swept through the arena. Players in Pittsburgh and Dallas amused themselves before games by counting the number of spectators.

And the league certainly will be remembered for its wonderful "flakes." For a while the Pacers displayed Reggie Harding, whose reputation for sniffing the flowers of life was so well documented that he was paid by the game. Reggie was a seven-footer with a two-foot Afro. When he stood under the basket his hair nearly touched the net.

One of the more memorable characters was the intensely competitive Wendell Ladner, who ended his career with more stitches than a baseball. Wendell had a propensity for running into walls, plus knocking over humans and sundry stationary objects. Once he ran through plate glass. After shooting while on his knees, he uttered the classic line, "Well, I was open."

I'll never forget the riotous moment when Bobby Leonard threw a basketball rack at the officials. Play stopped. Spectators sat in stunned silence. The only sound was ka-whump, ka-whump, ka-whump as basketballs bounced all over the old Coliseum at the Indiana State Fairgrounds.

Through it all—the downs and further downs—the Pacers were the ABA's only semi-stable franchise. They were a contender nearly every season and usually led the ABA in attendance.

The owners were stretched tight, but met the payroll. And somebody in the organization always would go that extra step. When the team needed a big man, Treece signed a personal note for the 100 grand that got Mel Daniels.

Bill Eason, who joined the group later, poured several million into the operation and never complained.

The ABA finally began signing top talent. But it turned out to be the gun with which it would inflict the fatal wound. Salaries climbed out of sight.

The Coliseum, which held just over 9,100 for basketball, was too small. Expenses reached the point where the owners could lose money on a sellout. So, the Pacers pulled a successful bluff that, ironicaly, began the final slide for the original owners. They put out a smokescreen that they were shopping for land to build their own arena and waited to see what ran under it.

From the beginning, the city administration wanted the franchise downtown. Thus began the negotiations which led to building Market Square Arena—a beautiful facility with a 17,287 capacity.

Once again the owners had grandiose plans—a hockey franchise to go with basketball and a management contract for the arena. On the surface everything was lovely; the first game was played in MSA, Sept. 28, 1974 before a capacity crowd. Behind the scenes, though, the situation was grim. There was no money to implement the wonderful schemes.

(continued)

Bob Collins Sports Profile

Mel Daniels

The Rajah

Billy Knight

Slick

Courtesy Indiana Pacer

Mac

1990 NBA All-Star Reggie Miller

Clark Kellogg

The pie was sliced into small, uneconomical pieces. Once again the Pacers were tenants—with a team they couldn't afford and a lease they couldn't handle. The era of revolving door ownership was about to begin.

The grand little league had only a year to go. When it expired, only seven teams were dribbling the red, white and blue basketball. Three, Indianapolis, Denver and San Antonio, were absorbed by the NBA—and hit with some debilitating restrictions. They paid $3 million for what in their financial position was a dubious privilege of joining the club. They then were crushed by a second haymaker—no television money, worth something like $900,000 for a year to each team, for three years.

The only people who made money on the Pacers were photographers—doing portraits of new players and investors. It was joked that names should be printed on the office doors in pencil.

The Pacers couldn't meet George McGinnis' salary demands; he went to Philadelphia. Dan Roundfield became a free agent. The Pacers passed.

The cruelest blow landed when we had first shot at Larry Bird and couldn't even make a bid.

Leonard took the added duties of general manager. His wife Nancy took over as assistant. They poured their hearts and most of their waking hours into the team—sometimes, it seemed, keeping the doors open with will power.

In desperation, they became beggars. The sad story was written in headlines: "Business Throws Life Preserver to Pacers; Payroll Fulfilled." "New investors for Pacers set?" "Pacers Paid; Wagon Hitched to Telethon."

In June, 1977, the Leonards set a goal of 8,000 season tickets. The revenue was needed for a fairly good reason—to stay alive.

The community responded. Businesses, labor organizations, clubs and many individuals bought tickets. A telethon was held to take the drive over the top.

(continued on next page)

Bob Collins Sports Profile

The city went on an emotional high when Nancy stepped in front of the cameras and announced in a choked voice, "8,028."

Looking at it from another direction, though, it was a low point. Where do you go after you've borrowed from an entire city? They'd won a reprieve, but they'd put a Band-Aid on a leper.

On May 3, 1979, the team was sold to Californian Sam Nassi. Jerry Buss, owner of the Los Angeles Lakers, bought the MSA management contract. The team now was Indiana in name only.

Fans were skeptical. Nassi's relationship with the media, tenuous at first, deteriorated into guerrilla warfare. Both sides were searching for ambushes in every statement or story. Nassi made some big promises—then took them home to Hollywood.

Bobby and Nancy left. Nassi hired Jack McKinney as coach, a positive move.

But the front office operation was one day a Byzantine corridor, the next a Mac Sennett comedy. People with titles came and left almost before they were introduced. Finally came the veiled threats: if we don't get more aid and/or paying customers, we may be forced to move.

Indianapolis attorney Bob Salyers was named acting general manager. He was handed a sick horse and no cart.

Salyers soon discovered he was presiding over the city's longest running death watch. Demise, if not around the corner, was somewhere down the street.

He hardly had what could be called a mandate. Here was a young lawyer (oh, no, not another lawyer!) working part-time with a franchise most believed would leave, anyway.

The Californians told him to sell. But, even a person with the slightest knowledge of finance knows it's more than a little difficult to sell what can't be given away.

It was like walking through the looking glass—back to the beginning. The people who cared and wanted a team here were light in the wallet. People who could handle the transaction yawned. Worse still, fans were turned off. Attendance at MSA slipped to meetings of relatives and old friends.

Salyers went into battle armed only with an open-faced sincerity and an unflappable—some said insane—belief he could succeed in an arena littered with the carcasses of the failed.

The grimmer the news became, the harder he worked. And slowly he began picking up the right kind of friends. The media believed him. That's a big stride. Mayor Hudnut threw the prestige of his office into the fight. Attorney Ted Boehm and Jim Morris of influential Lilly Endowment kept trying to keep alive the slim hopes for local ownership.

And through it all was one constant, Herb and Mel Simon. The Simons figured they needed a professional basketball team every bit as much as they needed a brother named Simple. But, they agreed to put their prestige, to say nothing of money, as in m-o-n-e-y, behind any group that wished to grab a bucket and start bailing.

Several times it appeared the Pacers wouldn't complete the 1982-83 season. It reached a point where the franchise was going to leave or fold. There didn't seem to be any viable alternatives.

Finally, literally, at the eleventh hour, a deal was struck. It was the Simons or nobody. So, Herb and Mel bought the team. Lilly Endowment purchased the MSA contract and turned it over to the Capital Improvements Board.

The $6,000 franchise went for something like $11 million.

It was a great day for Indianapolis fans. But, I still felt a bittersweet tug. It almost was exactly the deal the original owners couldn't quite put together.

Bob Collins Sports Profile

Though an Indiana Pacer is yet to be inducted into the Naismith Hall of Fame, the franchise does claim many great moments and many outstanding ballplayers as part of its proud history. Memorable Hoosier hoopstars such as George McGinnis, Billy Keller, Don Buse, Rick Mount, Ron Bonham and Jimmy Rayl are profiled elsewhere in this volume. There are many more names guaranteed to put smiles on the faces of long-time Pacer rooters.

In addition to Jimmy, "The Splendid Splinter" Rayl, Coach Larry Staverman's first Pacer starting five boasted two of the top talents in team history—Freddie Lewis and Roger "The Rajah" Brown. (Reggie Harding was the Pacers' first center and Ollie Darden complemented Brown at forward.)

As a Brooklyn high schooler, The Rajah had developed a one-on-one rivalry with Connie Hawkins that still has some New Yorkers shaking their heads today. As a freshman at the University of Dayton, Brown led the Flyer frosh to a 36-4 record. His future in top-flight American basketball seemed secure.

There seems to be a nasty trend in this volume—pleasant stories turn ugly. Roger Brown's name was peripherally associated with a second major point-shaving scandal that rocked college basketball in 1961. The only link to Brown was that his name and phone number were found on a ledger containing the names of several of the gamblers involved in the scandal. Brown was never arrested, let alone charged with a crime.

Brown was forced to leave Dayton and along with Hawkins, Doug Moe, Tony Jackson, and several others, was banned from the NBA for life.

Instead of going into a long rationalization about why inner-city kids—courted by unprincipled coaches, fawned over by adoring fans and pampered by parasitic boosters—get involved with gamblers, it's a pleasure to report this story has a happy ending. Roger Brown has redeemed his good name many times over. No player is closer to the hearts of true Pacers fans than The Rajah.

Denied six season of major competition, in 1967 Brown became the first player signed to an Indiana Pacer contract. A member of the starting lineup for all nine Pacer ABA seasons, the captain averaged 18.0 PPG in 559 games for a 10,058 point career total, (not including 2,118 playoff points). In addition to his "Did you see that?" "I didn't see that!" "Did you see that!?" moves to the hoop, Brown distributed 2,214 assists.

The Rajah's 14 of 14 two-point shooting record against Denver in '69 and 5 for 6 three-point night against Florida in '70 remain Pacer standards. Brown was an All-ABA First Teamer in 1968, '70 and '71 and led Indiana to 1970, '72 and '73 ABA Championships.

Banned from the NBA for life, Roger Brown retired from basketball in 1975—the year before the Pacers joined the Big Time.

But Roger Brown was home in Indianapolis. He had developed an interest in the issues and political concerns of his adopted hometown. During his playing career, he was elected to serve as a member of the Indianapolis City-County Council.

In 1988 Roger Brown, George McGinnis and Mel Daniels became the first players to have their jerseys retired by the Indiana Pacers. The Rajah had come a long way from the trials and tribulations he endured as a naive kid from Brooklyn.

Freddie Lewis found a much smoother path to stardom. Fritz Lewis averaged 22.7 PPG during his senior season at Arizona State before spending 1966-'67 as Oscar Robertson's backup with the Cincinnati Royals.

Lewis jumped at the opportunity to become a starter with the brand new Indiana Pacers in '67-'68. During seven seasons with Indiana, and two with Memphis/St. Louis, Fritz scored 11,660 points for a 17.0 career average. He was a four-time ABA All-Star, and started for each of the Pacers' three ABA Champions. In 1972 Fritz was named ABA Finals MVP for leading the Pacers to a four-games-to-three victory over the Kentucky Colonels of Dan Issel, Artis Gilmore and Southport's Louie Dampier.

In 1976 Freddie Lewis returned to Indianapolis from his two-year stint with Memphis/St. Louis to play with the now NBA Pacers. His 32 NBA games in 1967 and his 32 in 1977 were separated by nine years and a lot of great memories for Pacer fans.

6'9" center Mel Daniels was a third member of the septet that laid the foundation for the Pacers' ABA dynasty. Following his 1967 All-America season at the University of New Mexico, Daniels averaged 22.2 PPG for the Minnesota Muskies and was named ABA Rookie of the Year.

Prior to the start of the '68-'69 season the Pacers received Daniels in a trade, and the nucleus of the Championship Team was set. Daniels was voted All-ABA in 1969 and '71. The big guy's 7,622 Pacer rebounds for a 15.9 career boarding average remain club records.

Daniels finished his nine-season career with a year in Memphis, followed by eleven games with the NBA's (NJ) Nets in 1976. His career numbers include 11,739 points and 9,494 rebounds.

From 1978-'82 Mel Daniels served as an assistant coach with the Indiana State University Sycamores. His tutelage of the ISU big men is credited with hastening the development of the Sycamores' 6'9" forward—Larry Bird.

Additional Pacer stalwarts of the dynasty era have been previously profiled. George McGinnis is often mentioned in the same sentence with Os-

That's Gotta Be Worth At Least Four, Maybe Five!

Pacer Jerry Harkness played in only 86 professional basketball games, but in one of them he left a record that still stands today. On November 13, 1967, "Hark" hit the longest shot in pro basketball history.

In 1963 the 6'2" forward had led Loyola of Chicago to a 29-2 record with 21.4 PPG average. His 14 NCAA Championship Game points had helped offset Ron Bonham's 22 as the "Ramblers" downed Cincinnati 60-58 for the title. A five-game stint with the NY Knicks in 1963-'64 was the sum total of Harkness' pro ball experience until the Pacers brought him on board for the ABA's inaugural campaign in 1967-'68.

Early in the season the Pacers were visiting player/coach Cliff Hagan's Dallas Chaparrals (San Antonio Spurs). The Chaps scored to forge ahead by two when Harkness, who had entered the game moments earlier for an injured Freddie Lewis—took an inbounds pass with two seconds remaining.

"I was near the baseline and the sideline and I just heaved the ball with all I had the length of the court," Harkness remembers. "The buzzer went off, and then it hit the backboard and went right in the basket." Everyone was stunned. The fans stopped screaming, and we all thought the game was going into overtime," Hark recalls. "It must have been five seconds before we realized that the basket was a three-point goal and that we had won."

The distance? 88 feet!

Jerry Harkness chose to remain in Indianapolis rather than return to his native New York City following his season and a half with the Pacers. Hark has become a familiar presence in the Indy sporting community as an occasional Pacer commentator and as an announcer for WTTV-TV, WIBC-AM and WTLC-AM among others.

car Robertson and Larry Bird—nothing more need be said.

Bobby Leonard brought the same fire and refusal to lose to the Pacer head coaching position in 1968 that he had used to drive IU to the '53 NCAA crown as a player. Slick guided the Pacers to a 529-446 record over twelve season (387-260 in the ABA), a 69-47 playoff mark and ABA Championships in 1970, '72 and '73. Brown, Lewis, Daniels and Purdue's Billy Keller suited up for all three Champions while McGinnis anchored the latter two. More important than his record is the fact that Bobby Leonard held the franchise together through all the difficult times in the ABA and for the first four precarious seasons in the NBA. The talent was there for the Pacers to use, but Slick supplied the Pacers' heart.

The last name necessary to complete our septet might not be quite as widely recognized, but the 6'9" center/forward's undeniable talent provided the final cog in the Pacer machine.

Bob Netolicky came to Indianapolis in 1967 from Drake University. He averaged 16.3 PPG and 11.4 rebounds win a spot on the '67-'68 ABA All-Rookie squad. "Neto" was an ABA All-Star from 1968 through 1971 and All-ABA in 1970. He was a member of the Pacers '70 and '72 Champs, but missed out on the '73 title due to a one-year stint with the Dallas Chaparrals (San Antonio Spurs).

Neto returned to Indy in 1974 and played out his career in 1975-'76. He registered 5,518 career rebounds and averaged 16.0 points a game for a 9,876-point career total.

One final remembrance of Bob Netolicky. According to *Who's Who in Basketball*, "Neto is widely regarded as one of the game's off-court swingers." In Indianapolis?

Pacer talent abounded during the glory years. Darnell "Dr. Dunk" Hillman averaged 7.1 PPG as a rookie for the Pacers '72 Champions and 9.6 for Indy's '73 league kings. In nine campaigns with the Pacers, Nets, Nuggets, Kings and Warriors, Dr. D. scored 6,666 points grabbed 5,187 boards and is credited with 666 blocked shots.

In addition to his thunderous slams, Dr. D. is best remembered for a world-class afro that brushed the net when the 6'9" center passed under the hoop.

Don Buse arrived from Evansville College in time to chip in 5.4 PPG as a rookie for the '73 Champs and went on to the sterling career described earlier.

As an All-American from Pitt, Billy Knight was a 1974 first round pick of the NBA's LA Lakers. Knight chose to go with the ABA's Pacers instead. His 17.1 PPG rookie average placed Knight on the 1975 All-Rookie Team. His 28.1 PPG in '75-'76 trailed only Julius Erving in the ABA and earned Knight a position on the league's final All-Star Team.

Billy demonstrated the depth of the Laker loss when in 1976-77 his 26.6 PPG average trailed only Pistol Pete Marvich during the Pacers' initial NBA season. Knight's scoring prowess in '76-'77 enabled him to join Don Buse as the two became the Pacers' first NBA All-Stars.

During eleven ABA/NBA seasons with Indiana, Buffalo, Boston and Kansas City, Billy Knight scored 13,514 points, grabbed 4,259 rebounds and handed out 1,782 assists. His 608 Pacer games, 4,218 Pacer 2-point field goals and 10,780 Pacer points all remained club records.

Since his retirement following the 1985 season, Knight has remained in Indianapolis to serve as the Pacers' representative at various community functions.

The Pacers' entry into the NBA in 1976-'77 and the All-Star designations of Buse and Knight that season marked the end of an era and the beginning of a long, painful slide into desperation. During the course of the next twelve seasons coaches Leonard, McKinney, Irvine, Ramsay, Daniels and Versace would combine for a 386-598 record. The 1980-'81 season—the one campaign above the 50% mark in this era (44-38) culminated with the '76ers bouncing the Pacers out of the First Round Playoffs 124-108 and 96-85.

In addition to the Dantleys, Buses and Knights, a number of other outstanding players passed through Indianapolis during this period. Unfortunately, whether due to free agency, horrendous trades, fire sales, injuries or other Acts of God, most of their stays were brief.

Dave Robisch spent two and one-half of his twelve ABA/NBA seasons in Indy. In 1977 "Robo" was packaged with Adrian Dantley for the Lakers' James Edwards and Earl Tatum. Tatum lasted barely two years in the league. Edwards averaged 15.8 PPG during four seasons in the Blue and Gold before playing out his contract and signing with Cleveland in 1981. James currently wears one World Championship ring on each hand courtesy of his labors in the Detroit Piston lane.

Danny Roundfield scored 2,247 points in three seasons as a Pacer before playing out his contract and signing with Atlanta in 1978. "Rounds" went on to score another 9,000 points, win 1980 All-Star recognition and gain NBA All-Defensive honors every season between 1980-'84 inclusive for. . . someone else.

Alex English signed as a Veteran Free Agent WITH the Pacers in 1978. Milwaukee used their first round draft pick compensation to claim Sydney Moncrief. English scored about 2,000 points in his two Indiana seasons before Sam Nassi and Jerry Buss—hoping to boost lagging attendance by bringing in the hometown hero—shipped him and a Number One pick to Denver for an aging George McGinnis. Big George scored about 2,000 points in his three-year return engagement. Alex English has scored about three zillion.

To date English has scored over 25,000 points, led the league in scoring in 1983 (28.4) has been a member of ten playoff teams and appeared in nine All-Star Games. Thanks, Sam.

In 1978 Clark Kellogg's 50 points in the Ohio AAA State Championship Game broke the twenty-three-year-old record set by Jerry Lucas. Kellogg went on to a career at Ohio State that culminated in his being named Big 10 MVP in 1982.

The Pacers' first round pick in the '82 draft (#8 overall) was one of only four NBA players to average 20 points (20.1) and 10 rebounds (10.6) per game in '82-'83. The 6'7", 227 pound forward finished second to Terry Cummings in the season's Rookie of the Year balloting.

Kellogg was well on his way to becoming one of the game's dominant inside players—scoring 4,918 points and hauling 2,482 boards in three and one-half seasons—when chronic knee problems forced a tragic end to his career late in the '86-'87 season.

With all of the unsavory characters and unhappy endings one is forced to deal with in chronicling sports history, it's a pleasure when an author can report on the good guys who cope in spite of bad breaks. An honorary head coach with the Indiana Special Olympics, Clark Kellogg has served as a commentator on Pacer broadcasts and as regional announcer for Big 10 telecasts since his forced retirement. He remains a visible, active, contributing member of Indiana's sports community.

The career of Steve Stipanovich closely parallels that of Clark Kellog. A 1979 Consensus Prep All-American, "Stipo" took St. Louis De Smet High School to a 32-0 record and a second consecutive Missour 4 A title by averaging 25 points and 12.7 rebounds during his senior season.

In 1983 Stipo overcame an accidentally self-inflicted gunshot wound to garner Consensus and Academic All-America honors. He was named Collegiate Player of the Year for 1983 by UPI and CBS-TV.

The Number Two player taken in the '83 draft—behind Ralph Sampson—the 7'0", 250 pound center averaged 12.0 points and 7.0 rebounds per game to win a spot on the NBA All-Rookie Team. Through 1987-'88 Stipo had career averages of 13.2 points and 7.8 rebounds per contest.

Early in the '88-'89 pre-season a seemingly minor pain in the kneecap worsened into a chronic disability. A full year of frustrating treatments and rehabilitation culminated with the annoucement of his retirement prior to the '89-'90 season.

Stipo can regularly be spotted in the vicinity of the Pacer bench cheering on his former teammates. How much more fun it would be to see the big guy still taking his slower, clumsier opponents to the hole for a slam, or pulling up for a soft 17-footer. . . .

The absence of two more former Indiana Pacers from the current roster, men with impeccable credentials, may say more about the current positive direction of the franchise than provide additonal examples of the club's hopelessness.

In return for thirty-two-year-old Herb Williams' 14.6 points and 7.7 rebounds per game—not to mention an all too frequent lackadaisical attitude—Pacer General Manager Donnie Walsh acquired twenty-seven-year-old forward Detlef Schrempf and a 1990 second round draft pick. A member of West Germany's 1984 Olympic Team (along with former IU center and current NBA player Uwe Blab), "Det" has shown a remarka-

---

They also serve who sit wringing their hands at the sidelines . . .

Somebody has to manage. And in this day and age that somebody better be savvy about promotions, good with ticket projections, able to arrange one hundred details a day that keep the teams and multi-million dollar facilities moving—in short a man for all reasons in the front office.

Donnie Walsh, the Pacers' president, has known the courts all his working life. But not all of them were polished wood—he comes from experience in both basketball and the law. Walsh has had a lifelong love affair with basketball; he played distinguished ball for four years at the University of North Carolina. After graduation he served as assistant head coach at the University of South Carolina 1965–1976 before joining his friend and fellow UNC guard Coach Larry Brown with the Denver Nuggets' coaching staff. After serving as the team's assistant coach, in 1979 he became head coach for the Nuggets, a post he held for two years. Meanwhile, Walsh had attended the North Carolina Law School and passed the bar in 1977, about the time the Nuggets called him. Walsh had three years in private business before joining the Pacers as George Irvine's assistant coach in the summer of 1984. Walsh was named Pacers' General Manager in 1986 and President of the Indiana Pacers Basketball Corporation, which not only runs the Pacers but directs the management of Market Square Arena, in 1989.

"The Pacers built themselves a fine reputation in Indiana basketball early on," Walsh says. "We're in the midst of a determined reorganization and building phase with a lot of parts to it. Reorganizing isn't always easy, but we're in for the long haul. The goal is there—building a World Championship team—and we're fairly single-minded about getting there."

ble versatility in two Pacer seasons—playing both forward positions, center and even two-guard. The 6'10", 214-pounder from Leverkusen scores at about a 12-point clip, pulls down about six boards a game and—in a refreshing change for Pacer fans—doesn't take anything stupid from anyone, no matter who. Det finished runner-up in the battle for the NBA's 1990 "Sixth Man" award.

Wayman Tisdale was a three-time college All-American, the NCAA's Number Two all-time scorer and an 1984 Olympic Gold Medalist when the Pacers made him the second selection—behind Patrick Ewing—in the 1985 NBA draft.

In three and one-half seasons in Indianapolis "Tis" scored nearly 5,000 points and grabbed over 1,200 rebounds. His likeable personality also made him a fan favorite. Unfortunately, with Tis on the floor you need a minimum of two basketballs—one for Tis and one for everybody else. Four days after engineering the Williams/Schrempf deal, Walsh announced the trade of Wayman Tisdale and a second round draft choice to Sacramento for Randy Wittman and LaSalle Thompson.

During the course of two Pacer seasons, Wittman has demonstrated the same steady hand and the same Hoosier jump-shot fans of Indianapolis Ben Davis High School and Indiana University came to know and love.

In 1982 LaSalle Thompson III led the nation in rebounding, averaging 13.5 boards per game for the University of Texas. Thompson's presence has provided the Pacers with a 6'10", 253 pound rebounding fool who, in another refreshing change for Pacer fans, doesn't take nothin' stupid from nobody.

Maybe Donnie has put together a team for himself. With the Number Four pick in the '86 draft, Walsh made a locally unpopular move in selecting Auburn All-American Chuck Conners "The Rifleman" Person. The 6'8" 225-pound forward vindicated Walsh's judgment by averaging 18.8 points to outdistance Ron Harper and Brad Daugherty for 1987 Rookie of the Year honors. Person's 19 point career average attests to his position as one of the NBA's most consistent offensive weapons. His designation as team captain attests to his (still developing) maturity.

Vern Fleming catches a lot of flak for not being the quickest point guard in the NBA, or the best outside shooter—6-56 (10.7%) from three-point range through 1989. But Bob Knight must have seen something when he tabbed the 6'5", 195 pound University of Georgia guard for the 1984 Olympic Gold Medal Team. Fleming's nearly 14 points and 6 assists per game over six Pacer seasons would seem to suggest that the criticism is vastly overblown.

Walsh went way out on a short limb again in 1988 when he made Dutchman Rik Smits the Number Two (behind Danny Manning) pick of the NBA draft. The 7'4" 250 pound (at the time) Smits had averaged 18.2 PPG as a collegian, but his alma mater Marist College hardly qualifies as the cradle of NBA centers. His inconsistent rookie season produced 11.7 points and 6.1 rebounds per game—good enough for All-Rookie honors, but hardly worthy of a Number Two pick.

With only a half-dozen or so years of experience in organized basketball, Rik Smits can do nothing but improve. The numbers were somewhat better in '89-90, but the big guy still lets himself be bullied and he commits too many silly fouls. The recent report that he has added twenty-three pounds of muscle to his enormous frame should send shudders throughout the NBA.

The final Pacer to be profiled may, in the end, turn out to be the finest Pacer of them all. Reggie Miller is pure gold. The 3,500 points in three seasons, the 1990 All-Star designation, the 30 foot bombs, the NBA 3-point contest runner-up finish are great. The work with the kids, the anti-drug messages, the easy accessibility to the press and public alike are even greater, and hold promise for the future.

The Indiana Pacers was the first sports franchise to start the citizens of Indiana believing that Indianapolis could be something more than a race track in the middle of a cornfield—could indeed be a Major League City. It started with a bunch of good ole boys and $6,000. It started in a cow barn at the State Fair. Everything else has come since. Market Square Arena, the NBA, the Hoosier Dome, the Colts, the Pan-Am Games and all the rest—it's unlikely any of them would have found their way to Indianapolis to date without the foundation laid by the American Basketball Association's Indiana Pacers.

Once—not really so very long ago—no other sports franchise in America carried itself any prouder. Perhaps that day is soon to return.

I.U. Football Closes in on Northwestern

The Indiana University football program that entered the Modern Era of sports was not to be confused with the University of Michigan or Notre Dame or Texas. The IU gridiron program suffered even by comparison to Northwestern or Kentucky.

In the eighteen seasons between Bo McMillin and 1967, the Hoosiers compiled a 1-1-16 record against Purdue squads great and ghastly. A 3-6 Boiler team finished the '48 season with a 39-0 triumph over Indiana. The '66 Rose Bowl Boilers thumped the Hoosiers 51-6. The 1960 and '61 Michigan State Spartans combined to drub IU 70-0. In 1960 Minnesota blanked IU 42-0 and in '65 the Northwestern Wildcats shut out IU 20-0.

With an overall conference record by 1967 of 77-174, Indiana University lagged behind every other school in the history of the Big 10, including the University of Chicago, which had dropped from the Conference in 1939. IU was the eleventh best team in the Big 10. To add insult to injury, the Hoosiers began the 1960s on probation for—you won't believe it—recruiting violations. What could they have been thinking?

There was an occasional outstanding individual.

Offensive tackle Bob Skoronski graduated from IU in 1955 and was a member of the '56 College All-Star Team. In 1956, and following military service in 1957 and '58 Skoronski was the left tackle for Vince Lombardi's Green Bay Packers until 1969. He opened holes for Starr, Taylor, Hornung, et al in the 1960, '61, '62, '65, '66 and '67 NFL Championship Games. The Pack prevailed in all but the '60 contest.

Earl Faison was a 6'5" 263 pound All-American defensive end in 1960. Faison played six seasons with San Diego and Miami in the AFL. Marv Woodson was a darting halfback for the '63 Hoosiers—until the Steelers turned him into a defensive back. Between 1964-'69 Woodson intercepted 18 passes while roaming the Pittsburgh and New Orleans secondaries.

The best Hoosier footballer of the mid '60's was fullback Tom Nowatzke of LaPorte. From 1963-64 Nowatzke rushed for 1,438 yards and 22 touchdowns. He was named to the All-Big 10 Team in '63 and '64. The Number One draft choice of the Detroit Lions, Nowatzke spent nine seasons with Detroit, Baltimore and Houston. He carried the ball for 1,249 career yards and 13 touchdowns. A favored target of John Unitas, Nowatzke also snared 100 passes for 605 yards and four touchdowns.

The Hoosier fullback's professional highlight came in the 1971 Super Bowl. Nowatzke's two-yard plunge provided the margin of difference in the Colt's 16-13 victory over the Dallas Cowboys.

Faison, Woodson, Skoronski and Nowatzke aside, IU posted a less than intimidating 14-50-1 record between 1960-66. This magestic legacy explains why 1967 was such a giddy season—a glorious season. It was a Rose Bowl season. Coach John Pont—Mr. Pont to his players—had arrived in Bloomington in 1965 with an immaculate pedigree. Born in Canton, Ohio, Coach Pont had played at Miami (Ohio) first under Woody Hayes and later in his final season, Ara Parseghian. Pont set eight Miami offensive records, served as a Parseghian assistant for four seasons and at the age of twenty-nine, succeeded his mentor at Miami when the future Fighting Irish icon moved to Northwestern in 1956.

Coach Pont was a no-nonsense disciplinarian who demanded excellence and expected to win regardless of the circumstances. He may have had some second thoughts about tilting at windmills when his first two Hoosier editions combined for a 3-16-1 slate. It seemed business as usual in the hills of southern Indiana.

But 1967 was a special season; it was a Rose Bowl season. Three sophomores and a veteran on offense: Harry Gonso, Jade Butcher, Phil Isenbarger and Gary Cassells, along with three vets on defense, Doug Crusan, Ken Kaczmarek and Jim Sniadecki, didn't know the Hoosiers were expected to finish last—would finish last—had to finish last. The "Cardiac Kids" won seven games by a touchdown or less. And it only *seemed* like every one of them was on the last play of the game.

The Hoosiers opened the '67 season with a deflected fourth-down pass that resulted in an IU TD and a 12-10 victory over Kentucky. The arthritic toe of the Hoosier place-kicker didn't prevent the Cream and Crimson from defeating Kansas 18-15—a last ditch field goal by a substitute kicker did the trick.

John Isenbarger is one of the greatest running backs in IU history. He is also the flakiest punter in Big 10 history. Failed improvisational fake-punts against Iowa and Michigan nearly cost the Hoosiers both games. The IU punter's explanation, "I don't know why I do these things," elicited this advice from a relative, "Dear John. Please punt for Pont. Mother."

John Isenbarger nearly turned the Cardiac Kids into the Cardiac Arrests during the '67 Rose Bowl year. Courtesy Indiana University Sports.

A season ending, 19-14 thriller over the Boilermakers put the Hoosiers in a three-way tie for the Big 10 crown with Purdue and Minnesota. The Cream and Crimson's 9-1 overall record earned the Rose Bowl ticket.

O.J. Simpson's two TD jaunts and a smothering Southern Cal defense put a 14-3 end to The Season, but no outcome could have ruined the memories for Hoosier faithful: the joyous trek to California made by a trainload of gray-haired alumni boosters, 10,000 fans jammed into the IU fieldhouse to watch road games on closed circuit TV, Harry Gonso scrambling right, scrambling left, scrambling right, scrambling left—"Butcher's open in the end-zone ... Touchdown!" John Pont voted NCAA Coach of the Year. Yeah, it really happened. It was a glorious year. It was a Rose Bowl year.

As one would expect, the '67 team left its mark on the IU record book. Gonso's 3,376 career passing yards, 32 TD tosses and 4,448 total yards, all set IU standards, as did Isenbarger's 1,217 rushing yards in 1967 and 2,465 career yards. Jade Butcher's 30 career touchdowns, 180 points and 116 receptions also set Cream and Crimson marks. Isenbarger and Cassells were named All-Americans in 1967, while Butcher joined Isenbarger on the '69 honors team.

As a group, the '67 squad didn't put up huge professional numbers. Isenbarger and Snidecki spent four and five seasons respectively with the 49ers—the former as a sometimes flanker, the latter as a semi-regular linebacker.

IU fullback Terry Cole split four years with Pittsburgh and Miami. Cole had the low-profile role of backup to Larry Csonka in the 1971 Super Bowl. Terry's Hoosier and Dolphin Teammate Doug Crusan enjoyed the lengthiest and most prestigious NFL career of the all the Rose Bowl Hoosiers. Miami moved Crusan to the left tackle spot where he stayed from 1968-1974. During that period, he opened Super Bowl holes for Csonka and his mate Jim Kiick in three consecu-

Harry Gonso, keystone of the Rose Bowl Hoosiers. Courtesy Indiana University Sports.

tive seasons. There is no report of Dolphin QB former Purdue All-American Bob Griese expressing any qualms about the protection offered by his Hoosier blocker. Miami went 36-5-1 from '71-73 and captured the '72 and '73 Super Bowls.

The 1967 season was not a harbinger of great things to come in Bloomington. Whether it was due to Mr. Pont's autocratic manner, or whether it was just a sign of the times, a boycott conducted by black players decimated the team in 1969. Always a fragile creature at best, the IU football program crumbled. The 1967 National Coach of the Year was fired following the '72 season with an IU record of 31-40-1.

Coach Pont's firing brought on a decade known to IU football fans as the "Lost Years." In 1973 Lee Corso moved up Highway 65 from that legendary football powerhouse, the University of Louisville, to take the reins in Bloomington. Corso had done his best to breathe life into the moribund Cardinal program, including riding an elephant onto the field—and he had in fact achieved some success.

Coach Corso didn't arrive at IU on an elephant, but he did bring his first team into Memorial Stadium on an English double-decker bus. The Fighting Illini weren't impressed and promptly thumped the Hoosiers 28-14. Throughout ten seasons Coach Corso was a media mega-hit. He hired the NCAA's first female assistant. He was a regular ready quote for *Sports Illustrated*. "I've attended one-hundred-fifty banquets this winter and have been served fried chicken all one-hundred and fifty times. I don't get a haircut any more. I get plucked," he said. Corso stalked the sidelines like a chipmunk on amphetamines. He cajoled. He promoted. He elevated the Hoosier football program to new heights of visibility.

As a football coach, however, Lee Corso was a great carnival barker. There were some great moments. The Hoosiers' 38-37 come-from-behind victory over Marc Wilson and Brigham Young in the '79 Holiday Bowl was IU's second Bowl appearance ever and one of the great Bowl games of all time.

There were some fine players. Carl Barzilauskas was an All-Big 10 defensive tackle who went on to six seasons with the Jets and Packers. Joe Norman received substantial All-America support in 1978 before putting in five campaigns with the Seahawks. Babe Laufenberg completed 361 of his 616 IU passes for 4,156 yards and 19 TDs prior to his eight seasons in the NFL. But as a whole, the decade was a wash at best.

"Barzo's" season with coach Corso produced a 2-9 record. In 1978 the Corso hype managed to get IU on big-time TV as the ABC Game of the week. Joe Norman was everywhere and he was named Defensive Player of the Game. Unfortunately, none of his teammates were anywhere. Nebraska's Cornhuskers squeaked to a 69-17 victory—IU's worst shellacking since 1925. The Babe became the answer to an immortal trivia question in 1987 when he became eligible for an NFL pension without actually playing a down of regular season professional football. Laufenberg was signed and released eight times between 1983 and 1988, before he was allowed to throw a pass for San Diego in 1988.

Tired of the gimmickry, the 41-68 record and reportedly nervous about unspecified lapses in recruiting and academic standards, the IU heirarchy fired Coach Corso following the '82 season. Like any good PR man, Lee landed on his feet. You can catch him at half-time of ESPN's NCAA games downgrading Anthony Thompson and exchanging intellectualisms with something called a Beano Cook.

Coach Sam Wyche blew through Bloomington in 1983. He changed the Hoosiers' uniforms to something resembling USFL rejects, showed signs of being the offensive genius everyone alleged he was and caught the gravy train to Cincinnati.

In '84 Coach Bill Mallory tried to pick up the wreckage and got flattened with an 0-11 greeting. But it appears this time around the IU movers and shakers may have gotten it right. There's no more beautiful sight than the hills of southern Indiana in the fall, viewed from high atop Memorial Stadium. Over the past five seasons there's actually been some beauty down in Memorial Stadium as well.

A 6-5 record in 1986 brought an All-America Bowl bid. And though a 27-13 loss to Florida State wasn't the perfect ending, the new attitude was obvious.

1987 marked the season that IU claimed collegiate football respectability. A 31-10 demolition of Ohio State followed by a 14-10 defeat of Michigan allowed the '87 Hoosiers to become the first IU squad in the school's 103-year football history to defeat both schools in the same season. A 35-14 crushing of Purdue capped off the season.

An 8-3 record in '87 took the Hoosiers to a Peach Bowl date with Tennessee where the Cream and Crimson accredited themselves well before falling to the Vols 27-22.

By 1988 Coach Mallory had brought IU all the way back to national football prominence. In the thick of the Rose Bowl race until the tenth game of the season, the Hoosiers downed Kentucky 36-15, humiliated Ohio State 41-7 and crushed Purdue in a record-setting 52-7 rout on the way to a 7-3-1 regular season mark. A 34-10 thrashing of South Carolina in the Liberty Bowl pushed that slate to 8-3-1. The Hoosiers gave the Gamecocks just 153 total yards while racking up a Liberty record 575 themselves. Game MVP Dave Schnell threw for 378 yards and two TDs. Flanker Rob Turner caught five pases for 181 yards, including an 88-yard TD—the third longest pass play in IU history. And Anthony Thompson's 140-yard, two TD effort gave him a share of the Big 10 single-season record with 26.

Many of the twenty-five seniors were fifth-year men from Coach Mallory's first recruiting class. From 0-11 to record setting Bowl victors, they will be remembered for laying the foundation of any IU football successes yet to come.

Outstanding teams are composed of outstanding players, and a number of recent Hoosiers have gone on to the NFL.

1987 defensive captain Van Waiters was a third round draft choice of the Cleveland Browns. At this writing, the linebacker was still patrolling Cleveland's notorious "Dog Pound."

From 1984-'87 flanker Ernie Jones re-wrote most of the IU receiving records. The 5'11", 186-pound burner from Elkhart holds Hoosier marks for career receptions (133), season receptions (66), career reception yardage (2,361), season yardage (1,265) and season TD receptions (13). A seventh round selection of the Phoenix Cardinals in 1988, Jones has grabbed nearly 50 NFL passes for close to 1,000 yards in two professional seasons to date.

Pete Stoyanovich came to Bloomington to join Jerry Yegley's soccer dynasty and departed four years later as the leading field-goal kicker in IU history. Stoyanovich holds IU records for career PATs (107), season PATs (45), game PATs (7, shared), and season field goals (17). Until Scott Bonnell's 55-yarder against Michigan in 1988, Stoyanovich's 53-yarder against Kentucky in 1988 was matched only by Stoyanovich's 53-yarder against Michigan in '89. A third round pick of the Miami Dolphins, Stoyanovich's flawless rookie performance suggests that he may be the NFL's place-kicker of the future.

"A.T.!" "A.T.!" "A.T.!"

From 1986 through 1989 IU put together a 27-19-1 record and appeared in three Bowls. Throughout this period, a 6', 209 pounder from Terre Haute manned the Hoosier tailback position. Anthony Thompson not only carried the ball 1,133 times (an IU record), he carried the entire Indiana University football program out of its traditional lethargy into the national limelight. A casual perusal of A.T.'s collegiate career reveals:

* *NCAA career TD leader, (Bowl games not included) 65*
* *NCAA career scoring record, (Bowl games not included) 394*
* *NCAA single-game rushing record, 377 yards VS Wisconsin, 1989*
* *1989 Walter Camp Player of the Year*
* *1989 AFCA "Coaches Choice" Player of the Year*
* *1989 Maxwell Award winner*
* *1989 Heisman Trophy Runner-up*
* *1989 Chicago Tribune Big 10 MVP—only the third two-time winner in the 66-year history of the award*
* *1989 Consensus All-Big 10 and All-America*
* *1989 AP Big 10 MVP*
* *28 games over 100 yards rushing—15 over 150 yards*
* *5,299 career rushing yards in all games, ranks second in Big 10 history*
* *68 TDs and 412 points in all games—Big 10 records*
* *4,965 rushing yards excluding bowl games ranks fifth on the NCAA all-time list*
* *Scored three or more TDs in one game twelve times in IU career*
* *In addition to the above numbers which are all school records, holds IU records for TDs in one game (5 VS Northwestern) and rushes in one game (52 VS Wisconsin).*
* *Led nation with 14.0 points per game in 1989*
* *Led nation with 163.0 rushing yards per game in 1989.*

To say that such accomplishments couldn't have come to a nicer guy sounds trite, but you'll have a hard time finding someone to dispute the point. Criticized for being too slow and/or too small, A.T. simply outworked everyone else in the nation. And while not as painfully shy as when he arrived in God's Country, he remains a modest, self-effacing man who credits his success to God and strong upbringing.

Phoenix got a steal on the second round. You'll be able to hear the echoes all the way to Terre Haute. A.T! A.T.! A.T.!

Boiler Football—Rags to Riches, to Rags to Riches, to Rags...

The story of the Purdue Boilermaker football program in the Modern Era actually begins in 1956. Co-Captains Len Dawson and Lamar Lundy put in a 3-4-2 campaign that left their career marks at 14-10-4.

A slender, quiet, Academic All-American, Dawson led by example. Lenny tossed four TDs in his first varsity appearance and followed that with four more in a 27-14 upset of Notre Dame. Providing nearly all the offense for three marginal Boiler teams, Dawson led the Big 10 in passing every varsity season and set Purdue marks for attempts (452) completions (243) and yards (3,325).

Richmond High grad Lamar Lundy—like any self respecting Hoosier athlete—had been an Indiana High School Basketball All-Star. Lundy cocaptained the 1956 Boiler basketball squad, and as a 6'7", 245 pound end patrolled both sides of the Boiler line of scrimmage with a vengeance.

After appearing in the 1957 College All-Star Game, Len Dawson and Lamar Lundy embarked on two of the finer professional football careers of the Modern Era.

Lenny Dawson's eighteen years, primarily with the Kansas City Chiefs of the AFL/AFC did as much to elevate the American Football League to parity with the NFL as any factor short of Joe Namath's Super Bowl heroics. Dawson completed 2,136 of the 3,741 professional passes he attempted, an amazing 57.1% career accuracy rate. Dawson's tosses went for 28,711 yards and 239 touchdowns. He led the AFL/AFC in passing five times, completion percentage seven times, TDs four times and yards per attempt four times. He ranks fourteenth in NFL career yardage, seventh in TDs, tenth in yards per attempt, etc. etc. Oh yes, he ran the ball 294 times for 1,293 yards and nine touchdowns.

After sitting on the Cleveland Brown bench for six seasons, Dawson rejoined his old Boilermaker quarterback coach Hank Stram in Dallas. Together they led the "Texans" of the fledgling American Football League to a 20-17 victory over the Houston Oilers for the AFL's third league crown. Dawson was named AFL MVP for his efforts.

In 1962 AFL teams occasionally found more people on the field than in the stands. In 1963 the Texans abandoned Dallas to the NFL's Cowboys and became the Kansas City Chiefs. Things soon began to click.

Lenny Dawson is most fondly remembered in many minds for the classic duels he, Hank Stram and the Chiefs had with Daryle Lamonica, Al Davis and the evil Oakland Raiders. Patience sports fans—Notre Dame's Lamonica and Gary's Stram will be covered soon. For now, let's give Lenny Dawson his due.

In 1966 All-Pro Len Dawson tossed 16 completions in 24 attempts for 227 yards and two TD's as Kansas City crushed Jack Kemp and the Buffalo Bills 31-7 to become the AFL's representative in the 1967 Super Bowl I. Though the mighty Packers of Green Bay proceeded to demolish KC 35-10, Dawson was 16 for 27 for 211 yards, and the Chief's lone touchdown. The road to NFL/AFL equality was well begun. Lamomica and the Raiders knocked Dawson and his Chiefs from their lofty perch in 1967, but Kansas City's revenge was to be sweet. On January 4, 1970, KC knocked off the Raiders 17-7 in the Oakland Coliseum and won the right to become the American Football League's last Super Bowl representative. (In 1971 the Baltimore Colts would become the American Football Conference's first Super Bowl representative.)

In Super Bowl IV, January 11, 1970, Lenny Dawson completed 12 of 17 (70.6%) for 142 yards and a TD while Jan Stenerud booted three field goals a two extra points. The Chiefs downed the Vikes 23-7 for the AFL's second consecutive Super Bowl victory. League parity was at hand.

Lenny Dawson's career slowly wound down over the course of the next five seasons, but his place in history was secure. Len joined names like Csonka, Green, and Upshaw in the NFL Hall of Fame's Class of '87.

Lamar Lundy labored in the trenches of professional football, so his efforts weren't as visible as those of Lenny Dawson. Lundy did, however, make a dramatic impact—literally as well as figuratively—on the NFL throughout the 1960s. Lundy came to the LA Rams at the end of the era of one-platoon football. Though he is better known for his defensive prowess, Lundy grabbed 35 career receptions for 584 yards and six touchdowns as a Ram tight end.

Scoring touchdowns soon gave way to dismembering quarterbacks full time. Deacon Jones joined Lundy in the Rams' defensive line in 1961. Rookie Merlin Olson impressed in 1963—the same year Rosie Grier came over from the Giants. By 1964 the "Fearsome Foursome" were "winning attention for their speed and violence." The dominating presence of the Fearsome Foursome, coupled with the passing of Roman Gabriel, carried the recently mediocre franchise to ever improving seasons. Only the great Green Bay Packers kept coach George Allen's Rams from representing the NFL in Super Bowl II. LA finished a combined 23-55-4 during the first six seasons of the 1960s and 40-13-3 during the last four 60's campaigns. The turnaround can be traced directly to the awesome domination of the Fearsome Foursome. LA led the team defense rushing stats from 1965 through 1968.

By 1970 Lamar Laundy was thirty-five, and the combination of age and chronic physical problems forced his retirement. Lundy went on to coach the defensive line of the San Diego Chargers, while the Rams became one of the dominant teams of the 1970s. The Fearsome Foursome gave way to the Purple People Eaters and the Steel Curtain, but their legend would remain.

So what does all of this wonderful football greatness have to do with the Purdue gridiron program of 1956? Very little. With the departure of Dawson and Lundy it appeared the Boilers were primed to continue the pattern of an occasional outstanding player playing for an incessantly mediocre team in the style that had become familiar since 1943. But there was something different about 1956. 1956 was the first Boilermaker season for head coach Kenneth "Jack" Mollenkopf.

Jack Mollenkopf, the man behind the glory years in West Lafayette. Courtesy Purdue University Athletic Department.

In 1947 Boiler head coach Stu Holcomb tapped the top football man at Toledo Waite High School as his defensive coach. Jack Mollenkopf apprenticed in that position for nine seasons, until Holcomb resigned to become the athletic director at Northwestern.

Mollenkopf was a workaholic. An outspoken and profane man, he worked hard to keep a "peel the paint off the wall" temper under control. In public he projected a relaxed jovial "I can sell refrigerators to Eskimos" persona. But Jack Mollenkopf was a driven man, and he bled Old Gold and Black. He drove those around him hard, and he drove the Boilermakers to an 84-39-9 record over fourteen seasons. His final five Purdue teams combined to forge a 32-10-1 mark with a Rose Bowl crown for icing.

Renowned for his reputation for developing linemen, Mollenkopf produced three Consensus All-American tackles at Purdue almost immediately. Gene Selawski anchored both lines for the 6-1-1 '58 team, while Jerry Beabout did the same for the '60 squad. Don Brumm wreaked havoc from his tackle position on the '62 Boilermakers before embarking on a fine ten-year career with St. Louis and Philadelphia in the NFL.

Don Brumm's teammate defensive back Ron Meyer won the 1962 Noble Kizer Award for academic excellence. Meyer was also named First-Team Academic All-Big Ten. Ron would show up in Indianapolis a couple of decades later as an employee of one Bob Irsay.

The greatest era in Purdue University football began the day Bob Griese walked onto the Ross-Ade stadium playing field in 1964. When he walked off that field three years later (taking with him a stadium record 51-6 thrashing of IU) the two-time All-American had led the Boilermakers to a 22-8-1 record and their first Rose Bowl appearance. His career scoring (189), career pass attempts (609), and career completions (348), career efficiency (.597%) and career passing yards (4,402) all established Purdue standards. The Boilers' place-kicker for three seasons Griese still ranks first in team career PAT attempts with 86.

Make no mistake, Bob Griese was no one-man team. During his tenure, defensive end Harold Wells, defensive tackle Jerry Shay, offensive tackle Karl Singer and defensive back John Charles were all named Consensus All-Americans. Jim Beirne caught 138 of Griese's tosses for 1,795 yards and 17 touchdowns. Yet another Consensus All-American, Beirne caught 142 passes from 2,011 yards and 11 TDs as a nine-year tight end/split end for Houston and San Diego in the AFL/AFC.

The golden moment came in the 1967 Rose Bowl. 4,000 Purdue fans and alumni, including astronauts Gus Grissom, Gene Cernan, Roger Chafee and Neil Armstrong, made the trip to Pasadena and cheered the Boilermakers to a 14-13 squeaker over the Trojans of Southern Cal. Griese completed 10 of 18 passes for 139 yards, directed both touchdown drives and kicked both extra points. Sophomore running-back Perry Williams scored both TDs and defensive back George Catavolos secured the victory, when he intercepted USC's two-point conversion try in the end zone with 2:28 left on the clock. John Charles was voted the game's MVP for his dominating defensive play.

Bob Griese departed West Lafayette as a somewhat embittered Heisman Trophy Runner-up to the University of Florida's Steve Spurrier. Revenge is as sweet as it is ironic. Spurrier went on to a something less than journeyman professional career, while Griese achieved one of the most successful NFL careers of the Modern Age. During his thirteen-year stay with the Miami Dolphins, the kid from Evansville completed 1,926 of his 3,429 attempts (56.2%) for 25,092 yards and 192 TDs. Those numbers currently rank 26th, 28th, 22nd, 24th and 20th, respectively, in the all-time NFL standings. Griese was the Number-One-rated QB in the AFC in 1971 and 1977, voted All-Pro in 1970, '71 and '77 and was voted NFL Player of the Year in 1971. Between 1971-'73 Griese led Don Shula's Dolphins to a 36-5-1 record and three consecutive Super Bowl appearances, losing to the Cowboys 24-3 before downing the Colts 21-0 and the Redskins 14-7. Griese's Super Bowl career completion percentage of 63.4% (26-41) ranks behind only two other Super Bowl quarterbacks, both with Hoosier roots—Joe Montana and Len Dawson. Bob Griese made it to the Hall of Fame in 1990. Steve Spurrier is still waiting.

A sophomore defensive back for the Rose Bowl Boilermakers picked up a Nick Eddy fumble at Notre Dame and returned it 95 yards for a TD in his second varsity game. The soph intercepted six passes in '66, returning them for a Purdue career record of 166 yards. He also carried the ball 12 times from scrimmage for 101 yard, averaged 26.1 on kickoff returns and was three for three passing with two touchdowns.

Coach Mollenkopf moved his dynamic corner back to halfback full time in 1967, and Leroy

George Catavolos, savior of the '67 Rose Bowl victory. Courtesy Purdue University Athletic Department.

Keyes became the most dominant runner in Purdue history. During consecutive 8-2 seasons coaching the Boiler offensive was a relatively simple chore. "Leroy left and Leroy right," said Coach Mollenkopf. "Leroy was my team," he later recalled.

The 6'3" halfback exuded charisma on the Ross-Ade turf. Head high, knees pumping, arms swinging, running over or around people, Lee-Roy electrified the crowd. In '67 he scored four touchdowns against Iowa—two rushing and two receiving—and followed up with 225 yards rushing and three TDs against Illinois. In the '68 Bucket Game Keyes rushed for 140 yards, caught six passes for 149 yards and scored four TDs as the Boilers came from 11 down in the fourth quarter to drop the Hoosiers, 38-35.

For his career Leroy Keyes set Boilermaker records for points (222), touchdowns (37) average per rush (5.97) and rushing yardage in three seasons (2,090). The first three marks still stand as does his 6.61 average per carry set in 1967. Keyes single-season scoring (114) and TDs (19) along with single-game standards in receiving yardage (184) and rushing (225), established targets for future Boilers to attack. Keyes also grabbed 80 passes for 1,204 yards, completed 12 of 22 passes for 187 yards and six TDs, traveled nearly 300 yards with kickoffs, kicked off for the

Boilers' special teams, sold popcorn and parked cars.

Leroy Keyes was a unanimous All-American in 1967 and '68. In the former year, he finished behind only Gary Beban and O.J. Simpson in the Heisman balloting. In the latter campaign he trailed only O.J. in the Heisman vote.

The marriage of nagging injuries (during his senior season, Keyes had fluid drained from his right knee twice a week) and horrendous teams conspired to frustrate Keyes NFL career. Immortal Eagle coaches Jerry Williams and Ed Khayat returned Leroy to the defensive side of the line of scrimmage. The Eagles went 12-25-1 during the Williams/Khayat experimentations. Leroy was limited to 569 total yards and three touchdowns in five seasons with the Eagles and Chiefs. He also intercepted eight passes as an Eagle corner back.

Leroy Keyes' running mate at Purdue fared pretty well. Sophomore Perry Williams, 689 yards rushing in '66 led the Rose Bowl Boilers. The 6'2", 220 pound fullback's 494 career carries for 2,003 punishing yards still rank fourth and fifth respectively on the all-time Purdue charts. During six seasons as a reserve fullback for the Packers and Bears, Williams racked up 832 total yards and two scores. Unfortunately for the outstanding Boiler back, the name Perry Williams will always be synonymous with glory in the hearts of myriads of football fans from that Other School in Bloomington because of one memorable moment in his career.

With 6:27 left in the '67 Bucket Game, the Hoosiers led 19-14, but the Boilers were on the Cream and Crimson one. Mike Phipps handed the pigskin to Perry Williams, for the certain score, but Hoosier Ken Kaczmarek shot a gap. According to radio announcer Don Fisher "Phipps hands to Williams, Williams is hit! Williams fumbles! IU recovers! The Hoosiers have the ball!" Mike Baughman fell on the miscue. It was a glorious day in Bloomington, a glorious season. It was a Rose Bowl season.

Speaking of Mike Phipps, the prep All-American from Columbus recovered from the '67 Bucket devastation to do right for himself. Before he was through, the Boiler strongarm had passed Bob Griese in nearly every offensive catagory and set twenty-four Purdue and/or Big 10 records. Phipps' three Boilermaker teams combined for a 24-6 slate and three top three league finishes.

Included among the plethora of Big 10 records Mike Phipps set are career pass attempts (733) career total offensive (5,883), game total offense (424 yards VS Jim Plunkett and Stanford), completed passes career (375), TD passes season (23), and TD passes career (37). Phipps was an Academic All-American in 1968 and in 1969 he finished second to Oklahoma's Steve Owens in the Heisman vote.

Chants of "Lee-Roy!" rocked Ross-Ade Stadium in the 1960s. Courtesy Purdue University Athletic Department.

Sir Robert

He was slightly built; in street clothes he appeared almost fragile. He resembled a choir boy who had grown slightly taller than the other kids in his class. And the scouting report was hardly encouraging to a school noted for its splendid quarterbacks. It read something like this: "Is not a good passer; can't throw long and is not consistent. But he's a football player. He'll make the team—probably as a defensive back."

That was in 1963 when the lad was playing quarterback for Evansville Rex Mundi High School. Exactly ten years later, Don Shula, coach of the Miami Dolphins, did not equivocate in his book *The Winning Edge*.

Don called Bob Griese a "great quarterback," adding, "He takes what the defense gives us. If it's a run, Bob goes with the run. If it's a pass, Bob can throw with the best. He's not interested in personal statistics. He's interested in winning. That's why he has been a winner so often."

Purdue fans got a delightful preview of things to come in the opening game of the 1964 season. Griese scored all the points—two touchdowns, two extra points and a field goal—in a 17-0 victory over Ohio University.

Griese was unflappable under fire and had a rare—for collegiate players—talent for reading defenses. He made up for the lack of steam in his pitching arm with a quick release and pin-point accuracy. And he was a great clock-saver. He could—and often did—pick a defense to pieces in the closing minutes of a game.

His greatest performance, undoubtedly, was against Notre Dame in the second game of his junior season. Robert completed 19 of 22 passes (an .864 percentage that still stands as a Boilermaker record) for 284 yards and took the Purdues 54 yards in four plays in the closing minutes for a 25-21 triumph over the Number One-ranked Irish.

His feats of derring-do that afternoon caused one writer to exclaim, "The last guy who did any better was David when he went one-on-one against Goliath."

The biggest comeback Sir Robert engineered at Purdue arrived October 29, 1966, against Illinois at Ross-Ade Stadium. With the Rose Bowl on the line, Griese was having a bad day. The young man who rarely threw an interception had five passes picked off by the Illini. The fifth resulted in a touchdown which gave Illinois a 21-10 lead with 15 minutes to play.

Griese, treating the clock like pure gold, worked the sideline like a pro. He got one touchdown back, then passed for two points: 21-18.

Purdue got the ball again at their own 35 with 3:30 left in the game. Robert used up two minutes in moving his team to the Illinois 32.

Then something went wrong. A busted play. It seemed like every Illinois lineman had a least two shots at Griese as he scrambled from one sideline to the other. Finally, he unloaded a perfect pass to Jim Finley in the end zone. Final score: Purdue 25-Illinois 21.

Bob Collins Sports Profile

The Columbus Rifle

During a spring practice session in 1967, Leroy Keyes, Purdue's great running back, sidled up to a sophomore quarterback. The conversation:

Keyes: I hear you might be our quarterback next season.
The soph: I hope so.
Keyes: Can you throw the ball?
The soph: Go down and I'll throw you one.

So Leroy took off. He ran thirty yards and paused. The soph waved him on. Another fifteen, same thing. Another ten, another wave. Finally when big Leroy was turning into a micro-dot on the field, the soph let it go. A perfect pass. At that moment the entire squad decided the press clippings that had preceded Mike Phipps were a long way from fiction.

Phipps possessed the kind of quarterbacking credentials coaches dream about. He was big (6-3, 203). And he could throw a ball out of the stadium. He was a punishing runner, a fine blocker. And he loved to hit. He was handsome, modest almost to a fault and coachable. He was the sort who always got the girl at the end of the movie.

In his sophomore and junior seasons he teamed with Keyes, fullback Perry Williams and receiver Jim Bierne to form the most exciting and explosive offense in Purdue history. During the Phipps years the Purdues could score on any play and from any place in the field. Purdue scored 291 points in both 1967 and 1968 and 354 in 1969.

Phipps was the third Purdue star in four years (Griese and Keyes preceded him) to be named Most Valuable Player in the Big 10. But he lost the race for the Heisman Trophy to Steve Owens of Oklahoma in the closest balloting in the history of the award.

Phipps also is the only quarterback in collegiate history to engineer victories over Notre Dame three years in a row.

However, his most memorable game was October 4, 1969, before a record crowd of 68,179 in Ross-Ade Stadium. At the time Phipps and Stanford's Jim Plunkett were the two most celebrated college quarterbacks in the nation, and they gave the fans a show they did not soon forget.

Plunkett had a sensational afternoon, completing 27 of 47 passes for four touchdowns. But Mike topped him with 23 of 44 for 499 yards and five TDs. On top of that, Phipps turned in what has to be the greatest fourth quarter passing show in collegiate history. With Purdue trailing by two touchdowns, he completed all of his thirteen passes for a mind-bending 233 yards and a pair of six-pointers. He then passed for the two points that won it, 36-35.

Phipps threw many sensational strikes for Purdue, but the one that still has fans shaking their heads was unloosed in the 1968 Indiana game, when, just before he ran out of football field on the east sideline Mike, on the dead run and off the wrong foot—let it fly—to Keyes on the two-yard line. Keyes caught the ball shoulder high and stepped into the end zone. The ball had travelled 58 yards in the air!

Bob Collins Sports Profile

Mike Phipps' NFL career was as long as it was bumpy. The First Round pick of the Cleveland Browns, the "Columbus Rifle" spent twelve seasons with Cleveland and Chicago. He fired the ball 1,799 times, completing 886 for 10,506 yards and 55 TDs. He also lugged the ball 254 times for 1,278 yards and an additional 13 scores. While those numbers would seem to add up to an outstanding professional career, Mike Phipps had more than his share of hills to climb. Phipps joined the AFC's Central Division about the same time as a few guys named Bradshaw, Green, Lambert, Harris and Russell. While the Browns were usually contenders, they never made it over the top. Phipps was eventually traded to Chicago, where Bear fans were in the midst of making hamburger out of a series of QBs. Michael also suffered two drawbacks typical of big strong arm quarterbacks—decreasing mobility and the belief you can fire the ball into a gap no matter how small. Phipps' 108 intercepts against 55 TDs helps explain much of the disdain eminating from Soldier Field. Still, all in all Mike Phipps can rightly be called one of the best—one of Indiana's best, one of Purdue's best, of the Big 10's best, and one of Cleveland's . . . average ones.

One more from the glory years. Tim Foley.

Timmy was a prototypical corner—smart (1968 Academic All America), quick and a headhunter. Foley intercepted five passes in 1969 and nine during his three Boilermaker seasons. He was named a Consensus All-American in 1969. The Boiller CB had the common experience of any great defensive back—nobody threw at him. As a professional Foley enjoyed a consummate career. An eleven-year cornerstone of the Miami Dolphins secondary, he played on the great Griese, Csonka, Warfield teams of '71, '72 and '73. Foley was also a member of the 1979 AFC Pro Bowl Team. During his NFL career he returned 22 interceptions for 96 yards, blocked two kicks for two touchdowns, scored a safety and recovered seven fumbles.

Jack Mollenkopf stepped down following the 1969 season to spend his last five years in retirment at West Lafayette. 1969 marked the close of a decade and the close of the greatest era in Purdue Boilermaker history.

A Changing of the Guard

1970 signaled the dawn of a new decade and a return to old Boiler habits—great players, lousy teams.

Bob DeMoss, first of the great Purdue quarterbacks, moved up from his offensive coaching position to succeed Mollenkopf. Granted that there was no Phipps, or Keyes or Foley or Bierne or Griese in West Lafayette for the first time in six seasons, but the '70 fall to 4-6 from '66-'69's 33-8 set off alarm bells in Boiler Country. Following 3-7 and 6-5 campaigns, DeMoss offered his resignation to athletic director George King. After twenty-eight seasons and 263 games as Boiler quarterback, muse to Bob Griese and Mike Phipps and finally head coach, Bob DeMoss departed the Purdue football program to take an administrative position. The shining light of DeMoss' three seasons was the passing of Gary Danielson, the running of Otis Armstrong and the hitting of Dave Butz.

Danielson's career at Purdue pretty much sums up the early '70s for the Boilers. The second best day of the QB's college career came in the 1971 Bucket Game. Danielson hit 15-24 for 264 yards and three touchdown as Purdue scored 31 points. The 3-8 Hoosiers tallied 38. Danielson currently ranks tenth among Boilermakers career total offense leaders with 2,950 yards.

Gary Danielson must have learned something from his frustrating years at Purdue, for in 11 NFL seasons he earned the reputation as one of the league's most persistent players. Despite being unwanted out of college and suffering two broken ankles and a broken wrist, he hung around less than scintillating teams at Detroit and Cleveland long enough to complete 1,105 of his 1,932 passes (57.2%) for 13,764 yards and 82 touchdowns. Danielson retired following the '88 season and can likely look forward to a lengthy coaching career if he so desires.

Otis Armstrong didn't have the charisma of a Leroy Keyes, but the kid from Chicago's southside ghettos was hard-nosed and tireless. The 5'11" halfback still holds Purdue marks for career rushes (670), season rushes (243), season rushing yards (1,361 and in second place 1,009), career rushing yards (3,315) and game rushing yards (276 and in second 233). In the final game of his final season Armstrong needed 173 yards to break the Big 10 mark Wisconsin's Alan Ameche needed four seasons to set. Armstrong's 276 yard, three touchdown shredding of the IU defense set a new league standard that would await the onslaught of Archie Griffin.

The quite Chicagoan comported himself quite nicely throughout eight seasons with the Denver

Broncos. Armstrong carried the ball 1,023 times for 4,453 yards and 25 touchdowns and caught 131 passes for 1,302 yards and an additional seven scores. Otis also returned 37 kickoffs for 879 yards a fine 23.8 average. He played in the 1974, '75 and '76 Pro Bowls and carried seven times for 27 yards in the Orange Crush's 27-10 loss to Dallas in Super Bowl XII.

Dave Butz is the nephew of former Secretary of Agriculture Earl Butz which alone may have been enough to make David one of the meanest defensive linemen in the history of American football. As a collegian Dave Butz captained the 1972 Boilermakers and won Consensus All-American honors. Butz was also named the 1972 Michigan Coaches Association Player of the Year.

The number five player taken in the '73 NFL draft (by St. Louis), the 6'7", 295 pound tackle evolved into one of the most feared hitters in the game. During sixteen seasons and 216 games in the trenches with St. Louis and Washington Butz recovered seven fumbles; intercepted two passes; played in the 1983 Pro Bowl and played in the 1982, '83, '86 and '87 NFC Championship Games. Dave Butz was a starting tackle on Redskin teams that lost Super Bowl XVIII to the Raiders 38-9 and won Super Bowls XVII 27-17 and XXII 42-10 over Miami and Denver respectively.

Any opposing running back looking to avoid Boilermaker Dave Butz probably ran into the arms of middle guard Greg Bingham. Bingham was named All-Big 10 in 1971 and '72 and received substantial All American support. During twelve seasons as a linebacker for the Houston Oilers' Bingham intercepted 21 passes for 279 yards and pounced on 14 fumbles for 59 yards and one touchdown. The former Boiler was a starting middle linebacker for great Oiler teams in 1978 and '79 that just weren't able to get over the hump against even greater Steeler teams in the AFC Championship Games.

A footnote to the Bob DeMoss years is provided by a stylish flanker named Darryl Stingley. As the principle target of Gary Danielson, Stingley had enjoyed a fine if not record setting Boilermaker career. Following his 1972 senior season in which he led the Boilers with 23 catches for 286 yards, Stingley was a member of most of the major collegiate All-Star teams. As a favored target of Jim Plunkett and Steve Grogan, between 1973-77 the former Boilermaker provided the New England Patriots with one of the AFC's most versatile offensive weapons. His 28 career rushes for 244 yards (8.7) and two TDs and 110 receptions for 1,883 yards (17.1) and 14 scores attest to that fact.

Darryl Stingley was entering his most productive professional years when he ran a crossing pattern against the Raiders during the 1978 preseason. A clean vicious hit from Jack Tatum put Stingley in a wheelchair for life.

Darryl Stingley was a thing of beauty. He would glide downfield with long, graceful strides. The comparisons are made often. The Lynn Swans and the Darryl Stingleys are the Baryshnikovs of the gridiron. Sometimes football can be a really stupid sport.

Anyway, things went from bad to worse in four Boilermaker seasons under former All-Big Tenner Alex Agase. The Purdues went 18-25-1 from 1973-'76. The only team the Boilers were able to handle consistently resided in Bloomington, and when the Black and Gold dropped the '76 Bucket Game at home 20-14, Coach Agase was history.

Three names that do stand out from the Agase era are Larry Burton, Mike Pruitt, and Ken Novak.

Wide receiver Burton grabbed 53 tosses for 973 yards and seven TDs in 1973 and '74 combined. He was elected a Consensus All-American and an Academic All-Big 10 in '74. Burton was a real burner who placed fourth in the 1972 Olympic 200-meters. Unfortunately, there was no Griese or Phipps to get him the ball in '73 or '74. As a professional Burton had the misfortune of playing for even worse teams. In five seasons with New Orleans and San Diego the flashy flanker caught 44 passes for 804 yards (18.4) and 7 TDs.

1975 Co-Captain defensive tackle Ken Novak was a Consensus All-American his senior season. The 6'7", 268 pounder's NFL career was cut short after three seasons with the Colts and Browns when an internal injury forced him from the game in 1979.

You would think that most of the Boilermaker excitement of the Agase years would have been provided by yet another flashy running back from Chicago. But though Mike Pruitt did carry the ball 217 times in 1975, a tailback named Scott Dierking was coach Agase's offensive weapon of choice. The Jets would eventually turn the 5'10" 215-pound Dierking into a reasonable facsimile of a fullback. Dierking gained 3,943 yards and scored 23 touchdowns during eight seasons in New York and Tampa.

Mike Pruitt meanwhile blossomed into one of the premier fullbacks in the NFL. The Browns saw enough in the 6'0", 235 pound bruiser to make him the number seven pick in the 1976 draft. During eleven seasons with Cleveland, Buffalo and Kansas City Pruitt carried the ball 1,846 times for 7,378 yards and 51 TDs. He also grabbed 270 passes for 1,860 yards and five more scores. Throw in 12 kickoff returns for another 237 yards and you have the 1979 and '80 NFC Pro Bowl fullback. Mike Pruitt trails only Jim Brown on Cleveland's all-time rushing/receiving charts.

In 1976 nobody in West Lafayette could spot the difference between a Scott Dierking and a Mike Pruitt, so Jim Young was brought in in 1977 to test his powers of observation. It only took two seasons for coach Young to resurrect the glories of Boilermaker football. During his five seasons at the helm, Young's Boilers cruised to a 38-19-1 mark. The Black and Gold dumped Georgia Tech 41-21 in the '78 Peach Bowl, Tennessee 27-22 in the '79 Bluebonnet Bowl and Missouri 28-25 in the '80 Liberty Bowl. And the All-Americans just kept coming.

The pipeline to Chicago stayed wide open when defensive end Keena Turner came down Route 65 to West Lafayette in 1976. Turner was All-Big 10 in 1978 when he set a Boiler single-season record by causing five fumbles. No sane man ran at Turner in '79, but he was named All-

---

Boiler Bombers
The 1980s marked the return of the legendary Purdue quarterback.

Purdue Career Records

	Pass Attempts	Completions	Yards	TDS
1977-80 Mark Herrmann	1,309 (1st)	772 (1st)	9,946 (1st)	71 (1st)
1980-83 Scott Campbell	1,060 (2nd)	609 (2nd)	7,636 (2nd)	45 (2nd)
1980-85 Jim Everett	965 (3rd)	572 (3rd)	7,411 (3rd)	43 (3rd)

Carmel's Mark Herrmann was a 1980 Consensus All-American and set nine NCAA passing records. Herrmann led the Boilers to three of the school's four post-season Bowl victories. He finished fourth behind George Rogers, Hugh Green and Herschel Walker in the 1980 Heisman balloting. Scott Campbell holds the Boiler single-game passing yardage mark (516) set with a 31 for 52 day against Ohio State in 1981. Jim Everett weighs in with a 497 yard day (35-55 VS Ohio State in 1985) and a 464-yard effort (27-47 VS Illinois in 1985.) Everett's 285-450 for 3,651 yards and 23 TDs in '85 are all current Boiler standards.

NFL Results (to date)

	Pass Attempts	Completions	Yards	TD's
Herrmann	512	303	3,636	15
Campbell	378	188	2,456	16
Everett	966	543	7,046	49

Mark Herrmann's NFL Career has been a mixed performance at best. Traded with Chris Hinton to the Baltimore Colts for John Elway, Herrmann has been with five clubs during his nine-year professional career. Though he has completed 59.2% of his pro passes, he has thrown twice as many interceptions as TDs. His problems would seem to stem from playing with marginal teams for much of his career, being overly in love with a strong right arm and having two extended stays out of play with a broken collarbone and with a broken thumb.

Scott Campbell has had a somewhat surprising six-year career with the Steelers and Falcons. His pro stats would be more impressive had he not been forced to sit out the entire 1988 season with a knee injury.

Jim Everett of the LA Rams has developed into one of the finest young quarterbacks in the NFL. His 31 TD passes in 1988 led the league. Taking into consideration the fact that Indianapolis and Buffalo traded LA every draft choice between 1988 and Armageddon in the Dickerson/Bennett trade, it's a foregone conclusion that it's only a matter of time before Jim Everett leads the Rams to their first Super Bowl victory.

Big 10 anyway.

At 6'3", 219 pounds, Turner was moved to linebacker by his professional employers, the San Francisco 49ers. Over the last eleven seasons he became a defensive mainstay on one of the most dominating teams in NFL history. To date Turner has recovered nine fumbles for 65 yards and a TD and intercepted ten passes for 92 yards. Turner has played in the 1984 Pro Bowl and the 1981, '83, '84, '88 and '89 NFC Championship games. His four Super Bowl rings are from the 1981, '84, '88 and '89 seasons.

In 1980 Dave Young became the first tight end in NCAA history to lead the nation in pass-receiving. The Consensus All-American and Academic All-Big 10 grabbed 70 passes for 959 yards to bring his Boilermaker career totals to 180 catches for 2,316 yards and 27 TDs.

Perhaps it was the quality of his QBs, perhaps it was some other factor, (the fact that the Giants were forced to place him on the non-football injury list for three weeks due to a weight problem provides a clue) but whatever the reason, Young was limited to 19 catches for 213 yards and three scores in four seasons with the Giants and Colts.

Believe it or not, winning records don't always assure harmonious relationships in athletics. Jim Young departed West Lafayette for West Point following the 1982 season, amid criticisms of his administrative practices.

Coach Leon Burtnett—an outstanding offensive mind and a poor recruiter—took over in 1982. Despite enjoying the luxury of playing Jim Young recruits Scott Campbell and Jim Everett for four seasons, Burtnett's five Boiler squads combined to forge a 21-34-1 mark. Coach Burtnett seems to have recently settled into the position for which he seems well suited—offensive coach of the Indianapolis Colts.

Rodney Carter made a pretty good Campbell/Everett target between '82-'85. His 81 career receptions remain a Boiler mark. The 13 grabs he had against Michigan State on October 26, 1985, would be a school record, except for the 15 he made against Ohio State the week before. Purdue lost both games.

Carter has continued to excel as a Steeler running back who specializes in pass-catching.

In addition to Campbell and Everett, Rod Woodson ranks as a Boilermaker superstar of the Burtnett era (we'll get to Jeff George in another context). Playing at corner, Woodson currently holds Boilermaker records in career interceptions (71), interception return yardage (276), career kickoff returns (71), (Purdue gave up lots of TDs during Woodson's tenure), career combined return yardage (2,014), career solo tackles (320), career opponents' fumbles recovered (7) and other assorted marks.

Woodson salvaged something of Purdue's 3-8 season in '86 by playing defense, rushing for over 100 yards and a TD and returning punts and kick-offs in the Boilers 17-15 Bucket victory over Bowl bound IU. He couldn't, however, salvage Coach Burtnett's job. The burner from Fort Wayne Snider, however, was named a Consensus All-American following the '86 campaign.

Drafted by the Steelers with the number ten pick in the '87 NFL draft, Woodson has had a fine career on the field and an erratic experience off the field.

Heading into the 1990 season he has intercepted eight passes, recovered six fumbles, returned over 150 punts and kickoffs and scored two TDs. He has also spent two months on the Steelers' reserve/unsigned list and has had an occasional run-in with the local constables. What's next?

The Purdue Boilermakers enter the 1990s with more than their share of question marks. Coach Fred Akers took over the Boiler program in '87 after an extremely successful and equally stormy tenure with the University of Texas Longhorns. Though Coach Akers posted an 86-31-2 mark at Austin, his last three UT editions combined for a 20-14-1 mark. Longhorn coaches who go 20-14-1 over three seasons can smell the distinct odor of boiling tar and chickens. It took Darrell Royal an entire decade to lose 14 games.

The wisdom of hiring a coach with a reputation as a running coach (see Jeff George below) at the "Cradle of Quarterbacks" and questions as to Aker's abilities as a recruiter are still open.

Though Purdue struggled to a truly awful 10-22-1 record in Coach Aker's first three Boilermaker campaigns, the Black and Gold have just recently shown signs of revival. Freshman Eric Hunter took over the Boilers' starting quarterback duties in the eighth game of the '89 season. His three TD passes in the final six minutes against Michigan State, followed by his four scoring strikes against Michigan (the first time the Wolves had ever surrendered four aerial scores in one game) had Boiler Backers reminiscing about the good old days. When the Boilermakers dropped IU to capture the Bucket and ruin Hoosier hopes for a fourth consecutive winning season and a fourth consecutive Bowl bid, the clouds seemed to part above West Lafayette.

Prep All-American Mark Herrmann of the Carmel Greyhounds. Of all the quarterbacks in Purdue history, he remains atop of the Boiler charts. Courtesy Purdue University Athletic Department.

The Slumbering Giant Awakens

Setting out to summarize the history of Notre Dame football during the Modern Era is more than a little daunting. The first thing the researcher does is to visit the Notre Dame Football Wing in the reference pavilion of Central Library in Indianapolis. The Notre Dame Football Librarian will ask if you wish to study Fighting Irish games, coaches, All-Americans, National Champions, Heisman Winners, miracles, near miracles or out-and-out Acts of God.

After declaring certain allegiances, passing certain tests and undergoing the proper reference checks, you may be admitted to the vault where the Notre Dame Football Books are kept. If you are so chosen, it is here that the task begins.

Gus Dorias, Knute Rockne, George Gipp, the Four Horsemen, Frank Leahy, Moose Krause, Angelo Bertelli, John Lujack, Leon Hart and John Lattner hover about your shoulders—just a reminder. The story of the Fighting Irish in the Modern Era begins where any other school in America would be delighted to stop.

Strangely enough, we begin our story in a year Notre Dame finished 2-8. In 1956 ND defeated IU 20-6 and North Carolina 21-14. The Irish also lost to Purdue 28-14, Michigan State 47-14, Oklahoma 40-0 and Iowa 48-8 among other debacles. In spite of being a part of this unique experience, Irish quarterback Paul Hornung was voted ND's fifth Heisman Trophy winner. A bit later we'll deal with the issue of whether registering a pulse is the primary requisite for any Notre Dame back who wishes to be considered for the Heisman.

Team record aside, Paul Hornung was a most deserving Heisman candidate. One of the greatest "triple-threat" backs of all time, Hornung did play for two outstanding Irish teams. A 27-14 loss at home to Purdue in 1954 was the lone defeat in a 24-1-1 four season Irish run. Hornung accounted for 354 yards in total offense in a 42-20 loss to USC in 1955. The Louisvillian's 70-yard interception return for a TD during his sophomore season of 1954 contributed to the 42-13 rout of North Carolina. Hornung's 78-yard pass to Jim Morse against the Trojans in '55 and his 95-yard kickoff return against USC in '56 still rank high on the Fighting Irish all-time charts. He also handled all of ND's kicking chores during his stay in South Bend. Coach Frank Leahy, who retired in 1953, said of Hornung, "He was like a mower going through grass."

Paul Hornung was the original Golden Boy of Notre Dame. Courtesy Notre Dame Sports.

Hornung was drafted by the Green Bay Packers in 1957 and a truly legendary career was born. Throughout the 1960s Hornung was the most dramatic player on the most dominant team in American professional football history—the first dynasty of the Modern Era.

From 1957 through 1966—excluding 1963—the converted halfback rushed for 3,711 yards and 50 TDs. He caught 130 passes for 1,480 yards and another 12 scores. Hornung also completed 24 passes for 383 yards and five TDs, booted 190 of 194 PATs and 66 of 140 field goal attempts. He was the NFL's leading scorer in 1959 (94 points) and in 1960 he set the league record with 176 points. In a 1961 game against the Baltimore Colts, Hornung scored three TDs, kicked six PATs and booted three field goals.

Those thirty-three points still rank third on the NFL single-game charts.

Hornung was voted All-Pro in 1960 and '61 and played on the Packers' NFL Champions in 1961, '65 and '66. His nineteen points in the '61 title game fueled The Pack's 37-0 demolition of the New York Giants and earned Hornung the game's MVP honors. In 1986 Paul Hornung joined his Packer backfield mates Bart Starr and Jim Taylor in the Hall of Fame.

Hornung likely would have made the shrine sooner if not for certain personality "quirks." In the great Fighting Irish tradition of George Gipp, Paul Hornung was a fun guy. With long, blond, naturally curly locks and a deep southern drawl, this ND QB had a reputation for getting to know cheerleaders and others of the gentle sex up close and personal. Even that most legendary of all disciplinarians, Packer boss Vince Lombardi forgave more than a few game-day hangovers because "Hornung smells that goal line."

One habit Coach Lombardi had no power to forgive was Hornung's inclination to gamble. In 1963 Hornung and the great Gary defenseman Alex "Mongo" Karras were suspended for a season by NFL Commissioner Pete Rozelle for gambling. No charges of betting on their own games were ever leveled against Hornung or Karras. There is however, a well-founded historical abhorrence of mixing athletics and professional gamblers, which justifiably operated in their cases.

Hornung couldn't have been much of a true gambler, though. He retired prior to the '67 season rather than join the New Orleans Saints, who selected him in the NFL expansion draft.

Montford Stickles (the author disclaims any responsibility for what parents do to their children when they go to select names) is another great Irish player who suffered with marginal ND teams. The 1958 All-American end saw his team go 6-4. His '59 Consensus All-America year was even worse. A 5-5 mark included a 28-7 drubbing at the hands of Purdue and a 19-0 shutout at Michigan State.

Make no mistake, "Monty" Stickles did have his great moments at ND. Turned down by West Point due to a failed eye exam, Stickles gained a measure of justification; with the first field goal of his career at Notre Dame, Monty provided the winning margin against Army 23-21 in 1957. A 7-0 victory over Oklahoma that same season broke the Sooners' 47-game winning streak.

The first draft pick of the San Francisco 49ers in the 1960 NFL draft, Stickles caught 222 passes for 3,199 yards and 16 touchdowns during nine seasons as a tight end for San Francisco and New Orleans.

Two more legendary Notre Dame football names captained miserable ND teams during this downswing in Irish football fortunes. Myron Pottios' '60 squad was humiliated 51-19 at home by Purdue's Boilermakers in the second game of the season and stumbled to a 2-8 mark. Nick Buoniconti's '61 version of the Blue and Gold gained a 22-20 revenge at Ross-Ade, but lost to Northwestern and Duke and finished 5-5. (Remember that Northwestern loss—its importance becomes clear shortly.) Despite their team's futility, Pottios was an All-American guard in 1960 and Buoniconti kept the honor at the same postion in '61.

Both these nice Catholic boys went on to terrific professional careers splattering people all over the gridiron. Moved to linebacker, "Mike" Pottios roamed the NFL for twelve seasons—it would have been thirteen if a broken arm hadn't stopped him in 1962. Pottios intercepted twelve passes for 224 yards during his years with the Steelers, Rams and Redskins. He was elected to the Pro Bowl in 1963, '64 and '65—three seasons in which Pittsburgh went a total of 14-25-3.

In 1973 Myron Pottios was the starting middle linebacker on the Washington Redskin team that fell to Miami 14-7 in Super Bowl VII. In 1973 Nick Buoniconti was the starting middle linebacker on the Miami Dolphin team that felled Washington 14-7 in Super Bowl VII.

The '73 Super Bowl was just one highlight in Buoniconti's sure-fire Hall of Fame career. In fifteen seasons with the Patriots and Dolphins, "Skip" intercepted 32 passes for over 300 yards and a TD. He also recorded one safety. A practicing attorney during his football career, the ND Academic All-American led the Dolphins in tackles in 1969, '70, '71, '72 and '73, and was an All Pro 1964-'67. The defensive heart of the great Miami Dolphin teams, Buoniconti was a member of Miami's '72 Super Bowl Team as well as the Dolphins '73 and '74 World Champions.

Daryle Lamonica led the Irish to a 12-18 mark in his three varsity seasons at South Bend. Lamonica's final ND game was a 25-0 shutout at the hands of USC in 1962. You have to look pretty hard to find the name Lamonica among the names of Irish QBs in the Notre Dame record books. Pro scouts were so impressed with his collegiate exploits that the AFL's Buffalo Bills snapped him up on the 24th round of the '63 draft. The Bills figured he'd make a decent punter, and his biggest rookie impact was the fifty-two punts for 2,070 yards (40.6).

Satisfied with the efforts of QB and future presidential candidate Jack Kemp, in 1967 the Bills traded Lamonica, Glenn Bass and two draft choices to Oakland for future Raider coach Tom Flores, Art Powell and a draft selection. Thus were the humble beginnings of one of the top quarterback careers in pro football history.

During his twelve-year career, Lamonica fired 1,288 completions in 2,601 attempts (49.5%) for 19,154 yards and 164 TDs—all of them seemingly to Freddie Biletnikoff. The 6'3", 215 pound QB also carried the ball 166 times for 640 yards and 14 scores. In his first season with Oakland, Lamonica elbowed George Blanda aside and immediately became the AFL's Number One rated QB. His 30 TD passes in '67 established a new AFL mark, and he soon established a new league standard for fewest passes intercepted on 1,000 or more attempts, with 58. Lamonica played for three AFL Champions, Buffalo in '64 and '65 and Oakland in '67; was AFL Player of the Year in '67 and '69 and played in every AFL Title Game between 1964-1969.

In 1968's Super Bowl II, Lamonica completed 15 of 34 passes for 208 yards and two TDs. The fact is, though, Daryle didn't have any more luck against the Packers than his nemesis—former Boiler QB Len Dawson—had had in Super Bowl I. The Raiders went down 33-14.

Speaking of Lenny Dawson and his Kansas City team, who could ever forget those epic Raider-Chief battles of the late '60s and early 70s? John Madden ranting and Hoosier Hank Stram fretting; Buck Buchanan's cheap shot and Ben Davidson's killer mustache; Jim Otto's double-zero and Curley Culp's earthquake hits; and all the while Boilermaker Len Dawson and Fighting Irishman Daryle Lamonica continuing along their ways, cool as ice. No one better exemplified the confident swagger of the Oakland Raiders than did Daryle Lamonica.

The Era of Ara

Remember the 1961 loss to Northwestern mentioned a few paragraphs back? It was part of a trend. The Wildcats dumped ND 30-24 in '59, 7-6 in '60, 12-10 in '61 and in the ultimate humiliation 35-6 in 1962. Notre Damers—always sensitive about their intellectual reputation—had the good sense not to schedule NU in 1963. In 1964 they went one better hiring their tormentor, Wildcat head coach Ara Parseghian.

Ara Parseghian's lineage reads like it descended from the Line of David. A halfback on Miami of Ohio's 1947 Sun Bowl team, Parseghian also played for the Great Lakes Naval Training Station and briefly with the Cleveland Browns. The immortal Paul Brown was his coach with GLNTS and with the Browns.

After a season assisting Woody Hayes at his alma mater, Parseghian took the head position at Miami—"The Cradle of Coaches." Following a 39-6-1 record at the Oxford, Ohio school between '51 and '55, Coach Parseghian took the reins at Evanston and proceeded to torture the Irish.

In 1964 Ara Parseghian moved to South Bend, and Lord, did he proceed to shake down the thunder! In 1963, the season before his arrival, the Irish stumbled to an increasingly familiar 2-7 mark. It likely would have been 2-8 if the November 23 game at Iowa hadn't been cancelled due to the assassination of President Kennedy. In Coach Parseghian's inaugural season the Irish stormed to a 9-1 slate. Purdue fell 34-15. UCLA was crushed 24-0. Michigan State heard the echoes of past glory 34-7. Only a 20-17 fall at Southern Cal in the last game of the season prevented a perfect slate. Notre Dame was back!

A capsulation of the Ara Parseghian reign at ND is a recitation of the bulk of the great moments in collegiate football during the 1960s and '70s. Names like Lynch, Page, Thiesmann and Bleier are conjured. Parseghian's 100th coaching victory, 51-0 over USC, clinched the 1966 National Title. The 10-10 tie with Duffy Daugherty, Bubba Smith and Michigan State the week before may be the most famous collegiate game of all time.

On New Year's Day, 1970, the Irish faced Texas in the Cotton Bowl. It was ND's first Bowl appearance since a bunch of guys on horseback had run rough-shod over Stanford in the '25 Rose Bowl. (The absence was by choice. Something about Bowl games interfering with academics, if you can believe that.) The Irish's return to Bowl competition began on a sour note as they fell to the Longhorns 21-17.

On New Year's Day, 1971, the Irish faced Texas in the Cotton Bowl. The 24-11 ND victory snapped UT's longest-in-the-nation winning streak at 30.

This could go on to great length; the teams of this era had a flair for the dramatic. The 24-22 win

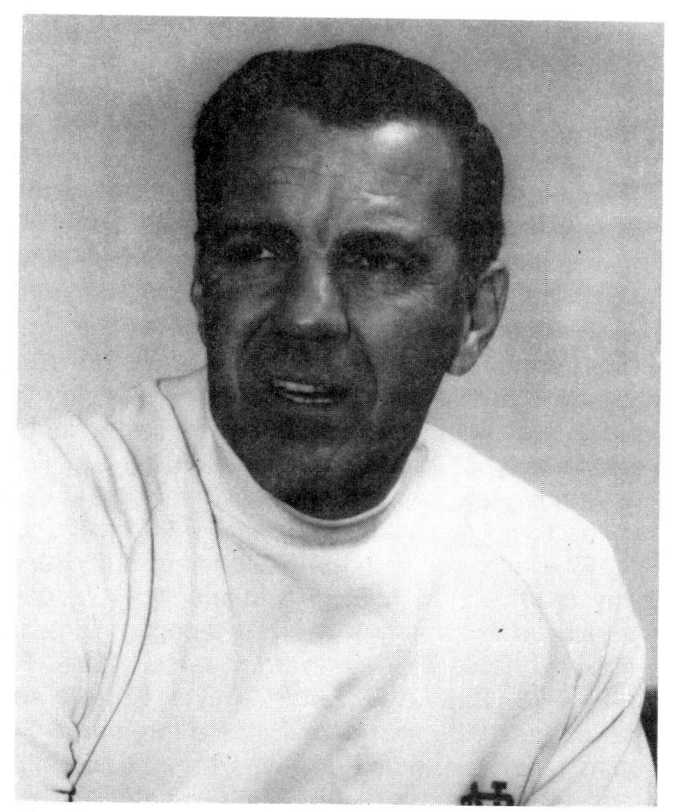

Ara Parseghian. Courtesy Notre Dame Sports.

at Miami in '67. The 28-21, 37-22, and 28-14 losses to Purdue in 67, '68 and '69. And the 48-0 revenge in 1970. The 21-21 tie with USC in '68. The horror of watching Anthony Davis destroy the fine '72 season by leading USC to a 45-23 December victory—and the added humiliation of crumbling 40-6 to Nebraska's Cornhuskers in the Orange Bowl. The glory of downing Alabama 24-23 in the '74 Sugar Bowl to lock up Coach Parseghian's second National Title. The 13-11 conquest of Bear Bryant's Crimson Tide in the '75 Orange Bowl that added fitting punctuation to the close of Ara Parseghian's coaching career. All these moments and hundreds in between.

With no more worlds to conquer, at the age of fifty-one, Ara Parseghian retired to the comforts of a network broadcast booth following the '74 season. His overall record of 160-56-6 included an 85-15-4 tenure at ND. His ten Irish teams all finished in the Top Ten in both wire service polls, racked up 31 shutouts and outscored all opponents 3,551-1,237.

So what about this guy Ara anyway? How many opposing players did he punch out? How many headsets did he slam down on the playing field? How many pieces of furniture did he hurl? How many articles of clothing did he rip off and fling to the ground while obscenely berating the officials? None. None. None. And none.

Ara Parseghian is an intense competitor and a perfectionist. He is also a thoughtful, urbane, articulate sportsman. Ara Parseghian—King of College Football, meet John Wooden—King of College Basketball. You gentlemen have done the Hoosier State proud.

Now, about this business of having a pulse, playing for Notre Dame and being considered a Heisman candidate. That current CFL laborer Tony Rice and the immortal Tom Clements leap to mind. Actually Tony and Tom are as much a part of a hallowed Irish tradition as is Rockne or Gipp or Parseghian—complete a pass, score a touchdown, be mentioned for the Heisman. Let's try out this name. John Huarte. A minute ago we made all those new friends saying all those nice things about Ara, and now the hounds are at the door. Well, let's take a look.

Prior to his senior season in 1964 Huarte, by his own admission was known to the Irish coaches as "Hey, you." He was a fifth string quarterback who had a hard time getting the equipment manager to give him a uniform. The quiet, insecure kid from Anaheim was lost under the shadow of the Golden Dome.

In '64 John Huarte set NCAA records in passing yards per attempt (10.1), yards per completion (18.1) ranked second in total offense per play (8.5 yards), completed 91 and 74 yard TDs against Pitt and Navy respectively, led Ara Parseghian's first Irish team to a 9-1 mark, and was named MVP of the College All-Star Game. There was no way John Huarte couldn't have been named the 1964 Heisman Trophy winner—unless he had been playing in West Lafayette or Bloomington or some other community the coastal press never heard of.

The question is: Did the player make the team or did the team make the player? All-American Jack Snow at end couldn't have hurt. Neither did the fact that the Irish defense gave up two or fewer TDs in every game save the 20-17 loss to USC. Neither did the 42-50-4 combined record of the 1964 opposition. Throw out Purdue's 6-3 and USC's 7-3 and the other eight losing records total a 29-44-4 mediocrity—not exactly stiff opposition.

So John Huarte went on to a fantastic pro career and proved all his doubters wrong, right? Huarte was selected on the second round of the '65 AFL draft by the Jets. A Heisman winner on the second round? He spent the season on the taxi squad and was traded to the Pats in '66. New England released him and he spent 1967 on the Eagles' taxi squad. The Eagles traded Huarte to the Vikes who relased him. Kansas City signed the former trophy winner and placed him on the long, sad bench. The quarterback-starved Bears purchased Huarte in 1972, but soon released him. Huarte completed 19 of 48 AFL/NFL passes (39.6%) for 230 yards, one TD and five intercepts.

John had a great year in '64; he played on a fine team. But the spotlight of historical perspective is cruel; real justice might have sent the Heisman to the the 1964 winner of the Knute Rockne Memorial Trophy for Lineman of the Year, Dick Butkus of Illinois or to '64 All-American "Broadway" Joe Namath of Alabama. Thank goodness Steve Spurrier and Gary Beban would be along soon.

P.S. In eleven seasons with the LA Rams, Jack Snow caught 340 passes for 6,012 yards and 45 touchdowns. Snow was Roman Gabriel's primary receiver from 1969 through 1972.

Hair-splitting aside, the ND All-Americans kept coming. Linebacker Jim Lynch anchored the '66 National Champs' defensive corps as team captain and as the winner of the Maxwell Award.

Taken by the KC Chiefs with the second pick in the '67 AFL draft, Lynch teamed with Willie Lanier and Bobby Bell to form one of pro football's most imposing linebacking corps. The trio provided more than ample support for the Len Dawson-led Super Bowl IV Champions. In eleven seasons with KC, Lynch grabbed 17 interceptions and scored one TD. He was also a member of the 1969 All-AFL squad.

Jim Lynch had plenty of Fighting Irish company on the 1966 All-America team. The ten All-Americans, including four Consensus picks, from that unit may mark the '66 Notre Damers as the greatest collegiate football team of all time. Lynch was one of the finest defensemen in collegiate history, surely, but he was only the second best defender on the '66 Irish squad. 6'4", 247 pound defensive end Alan Page was a major reason ND surrendered but 38 points in ten games. Shutout victims included Oklahoma (38-0), Pitt (40-0), and USC (51-0).

Bored with terrorizing his NCAA foes, Page became the Minnesota Vikings' first-round choice in 1967. During his fifteen-year, 186-game career with the Vikes and Bears, Page was named All-Pro eight times. He recovered 20 fumbles, intercepted two passes, scored two TDs, and in 1971, the year in which he became the first defensive player in NFL history to be named league MVP, he tied the NFL record for most safeties caused in a single-season with two.

Moved to tackle, Page joined with Gary Larsen, Jim Marshall and Carl Eller to form the feared "Purple Gang" that led the Vikes to Super Bowls IV, VIII, IX and XI. Unfortunately for Page and his teammates, others with Hoosier roots, Dawson, Lamonica, Griese, Buoniconti and Bleier—conspired to make Minnesota the most consistently frustrated Super Bowl participant in NFL history—a fact that does not detract from Alan Page's greatness.

Now a practicing attorney and union organizer, Page was elected to the Hall of Fame in his hometown of Canton, Ohio in 1988.

Running back Nick Eddy provided a great deal of the fire-power for the '66 Irish. Eddy racked up 2,737 total yards in three seasons at South Bend. He scored 23 touchdowns and one two-point conversion. Nick made a 91-yard reception against Pitt and hauled in a 74-yarder versus Navy. He had a 96-yard kickoff return against Purdue and an 85-yard return against Pitt. He threw in a 77-yard jaunt at Duke. Eddy was the '66 ND MVP and finished third behind Spurrier and Griese in the Heisman battle.

Nick Eddy's NFL career was severely hampered by a series of knee injuries that wiped out his '67 rookie season and the '71 campaign. In four years with the Lions the former Irish great was limited to 760 total yards and 5 TDs.

Guard Tom Regner opened crater-size holes for Nick Eddy, protected a rather well known Irish QB by the name of Terry Hanratty and was the fourth Consensus All-American on the '66 Fighting Irish. Regner moved on to a six-year career with the Houston Oilers.

A legendary Fighting Irish passing combo debuted in 1966. Hanratty to Seymour would get more than a little monotonous for ND foes over the course of three seasons. Hanratty would toss 304 completions in 540 attempts (55.3%) for 4,152 yards and nearly 30 TDs. Seymour nabbed 138 of those throws for 2,113 yards and 16 scores. When Paul Seymour graduated in '68, his name ranked second, third and fifth on ND's all-time single-season receiving chart.

Notre Dame outscored all opponents 1,075-332 during the Hanratty/Seymour era, finished 24-4-2 and ranked first, fifth and fifth in three seasons. Paul Seymour was a three-time All-American, while Terry Hanratty finished third in the '68 Heisman derby, behind O.J. and Leroy Keyes.

Hanratty and Seymour followed similar, uneven paths in the NFL. In three disappointing seasons with the Bears, Seymour caught 21 passes for 385 yards and five TDs. Chicago QBs Jack Concannon and Virgil Carter can rightly shoulder some of the blame for such a mediocre performance. It was much simpler to hand the pigskin to the relentless efforts of Sayers, Bull and Piccolo than it was to find a 6'4" moving target.

Hanratty's eight seasons with Pittsburgh and Tampa were a bit more eccentric. Locked in a perennial battle with Terry Bradshaw and Joe Gilliam for the right to take Ray Mansfield's snaps, Hanratty was eventually shipped to the Bucs while Bradshaw collected four Super Bowl rings.

The former Irish All-American principally watched Super Bowls IX and X from the Steeler bench. Hanratty completed 165 of 431 NFL passes (38.3%) for 2,510 yards, 24 TDs and 35 interceptions.

"The Rat" really deserved a better fate. At least he has the satisfaction of knowing he did his level best to continue the hallowed tradition of the Gipper and Paul Hornung—Hanratty's social adventures would take up a page or two more than his academic exploits.

Speaking of the Steelers, though a reserve running back on the '66 Irish National Champions did become the '67 team captain, he never made it to All-America status. He nearly never made it to his twenty-fourth birthday.

After an 8-3 senior season (including a 28-31 setback at Purdue and a 36-3 victory over Georgia Tech that marked ND's 500th win), Rocky Bleier was taken by Pittsburgh on the sixteenth round. A nondescript rookie season was followed by a year of military service.

Then in 1970 a Viet Cong shell not only nearly ended Bleier's football career, it nearly cost him his life. Rocky spent the entire '70 season recovering from his wounds.

Bleier returned to the Steelers in '72, but struggled. In 1973, six years out of college, his NFL stats read 18 carries for 70 yards and no TDs. During the seven seasons that followed, the name Rocky Bleier became synomymous with the words perseverance and courage, as he teamed with Franco Harris to produce one of the most prolific running back tandems in NFL history.

A crunching blocker for Franco, Bleier carried the ball 923 times himself for 3,864 yards and 22 touchdowns. He also grabbed 115 passes for over 1,300 yards and another TD. Bleier played in the 1972, '74, '75, '76, '78 and '79 AFC Championship Games.

The Steeler dynasty was originally built on the

Viet Nam vet and Franco Harris' main man—Rocky Bleier. Courtesy Notre Dame Sports.

relentless battering of Harris and Bleier. Rocky earned his four Super Bowl rings with 44 carries for 144 yards. He also snared three Bradshaw passes for 18 Super Bowl yards and a TD.

It's extremely unlikely that this Notre Dame alumnus will ever join Harris, Bradshaw, Greene, Ham, Blount, Lambert and those Steelers yet to be enshrined at Canton. It's also questionable as to whether these men would have reached the heights they achieved without the indomitable spirit of Rocky Bleier.

As is expected at Notre Dame, the Hanratty-Seymour-Bleier era was quickly replaced by the Theismann (rhymes with Heisman) McCoy-Di Nardo, etc. era.

Joe Theismann came out of Hanratty's shadow in 1969 to lead the Irish to a 17-2-1 mark over two seasons. His 155 completions in 268 attempts for 2,429 yards and 16 TDs achieved in 1970 all remain Irish standards, as is his career 57.8% completion rate (290 of 509). ND's 38-28 loss to USC in the final game of the '70 season undoubtedly cost the Irish yet another National Championship. But Theismann's 526 passing yards in that contest will likely remain a Notre Dame standard for some time. Theismann finished runnerup to Jim Plunkett in the 1970 Heisman vote.

Following graduation Theismann was taken by

Joe Theismann—rhymes with Heisman—but he didn't win it anyway. Courtesy Notre Dame Sports.

Miami on the fourth round. Being an ND grad, Joe had the good sense not to challenge Bob Griese for the Dolphins' top QB spot. Besides, Toronto is a magnificent city, so three years laboring for the Argonauts couldn't have been that unpleasant. In 1974 Miami traded Theismann's rights to George Allen's Redskins for a first-round pick, and another Notre Dame/NFL legend was born.

During his twelve seasons in Washington, Theismann completed 2,044 of his 3,602 passes (56.7%) for 25,206 yards and 160 touchdowns. His Pro Bowl seasons in 1982 and '83 seasons led the Skins to Super Bowls XVII and XVIII. Theismann's 15 for 23 (65.3) for 143 yards and two TDs backed up John Riggins' MVP effort as Washington downed Miami 27-17 in Super Bowl XVII. His 16-35 (45.7%) for 243 yards, no TDs and two interceptions, partially explains the 38-9 drubbing the Skins absorbed in Super Bowl VIII at the hands of the Raiders.

Quarterback Joe Theismann also returned 17 NFL punts for 162 yards and rushed 330 times for 1,700 yards and 15 scores.

On Monday night, November 18, 1985, Joe would have been well advised to go down quickly and easily. As it was, Lawrence Taylor put him down hard—really hard. It was a glorious way to go out. They carried Theismann from the field on his shield. Fans put down their potato chips and drinks long enough to gape again and again in fatal fascination at the slow motion replays of Theismann's agonizing compound fracture. Well, at least today we don't throw Christians to lions after the gladiators have us warmed up. Perhaps Major Taylor was right in those early days of Indiana sports history when he said people crave violence in sports.

We don't need to worry about Theismann. His easy enthusiasm has put him in good stead with the networks since that fall evening. And remember, his diploma says "Granted by the University of Notre Dame."

Joe Theismann was hardly a one-man team at ND. 1970 team captain, guard Larry DiNardo made several All-America teams in 1969 and 1970. His '69 teammate defensive tackle Mike McCoy was an All-American that season before moving on to ten campaigns in the trenches at Green Bay, Oakland, New York (Giants) and Detroit. The 6'5", 275 pounder recovered 15 fumbles for 41 yards and a TD, and intercepted one pass.

In the '77 AFC Championship Game Jack Tatum met Rob Lytle in mid-air. The resultant loose ball was scooped up by Mike McCoy, who headed for the Bronco end zone. Amazingly, the referees whistled the play dead and Denver's Jon Keyworth scored from the one on the next play. The blown call culminated in a 20-17 Raider defeat and a Bronco Super Bowl trip.

Dave Casper, McCoy's Raider teammate on that '77 AFC Championship Game team, did his best to put Oakland in Super Bowl XII by snaring five Ken Stabler passes for 71 yards and two fourth-quarter TDs.

But then, by 1977, Dave Casper was an old hand at last minute heroics. His 30-yard reception of a Tom Clements pass in the final minutes of the 1973 Sugar Bowl got the Irish out of the shadow of their own end zone. ND downed the Crimson Tide of Alabama 24-23 to finish 11-0 and captured the 1973 National Championship. Tri-captain Dave Casper joined defensive back Mike Townsend on several '73 All-America Teams.

Casper graduated to eleven seasons with Oakland, Houston and Minnesota. He caught 378 passes for 5,216 yards and 52 TDs. A Big Game receiver, the 6'4", 235 pound tight end played in all AFC Championship games following seasons '74 through '77. His four receptions for 70 yards and a TD led the Raiders to a 32-14 demolition of the Vikings in Super Bowl XI. Casper was an NFL Pro Bowler in 1976, 1977, 1978, 1979 and 1980.

Bob Thomas did all right for himself too. During twelve seasons with the Bears, Lions, Chargers and Giants, the former Irish place-kicker booted 303 extra points and 151 field goals. His post-season experience was limited to kicking-off to start the 1984 NFC Championship Game, as the 'Niners skunked the Bears 23-zip.

Tom Clements finished fourth in the 1974 Heisman balloting and was never seen or heard from on the sports scene again.

End of an Era

By the end of the 1974 season, Ara Parseghian had climbed all his football mountains. His "retirement" to other pursuits ushered in one of the most tumultuous periods in Notre Dame football history.

It's impossible to follow a legend. In 1972 Dan Devine led Green Bay to a 10-4 mark and the Packers' first divisional title since the Glory Years. But Dan wasn't Vince. His four Green Bay teams combined to struggle to a 25-28-4 mark. So those "Packer Backers"—the greatest of all football fans (though not known for their subtlety)—shot his dog. Not one to learn his lessons easily, Devine decided to see how he would fare replacing Ara in South Bend.

Despite going 50-15-1 in six Irish campaigns and capturing the 1977 National Championship, Danny Boy nearly got run out of town on a rail. A moody loner, Devine faced a threatened player revolt in his first season. Chicago area sportswriters, accustomed to the comfortable and articulate Parseghian, vilified Devine to the point of dismissing his Championship as a victory for Parseghian's holdovers. Numerous articles in the South Bend and Chicago papers complained incessantly that Ara wouldn't have lost anywhere near fifteen games in six seasons with all that talent. When you try to join the ranks of the Rocknes, Leahys and Parseghians, you have to be prepared to pay the price that may be demanded.

Make no mistake, there was great talent in South Bend between 1975 and 1980. Tight end Ken MacAfee was named to several All-American teams in 1975 and 1976. In 1977 he was named to the Consensus Team. His 54 catches for 797 yards and 6 TDs that season place him third on the Irish single-season reception list. Limited by a gimpy knee, and with a dental career as an alternative, MacAfee left the 49ers after two seasons, 46 receptions, 471 yards and 5 TDs.

Ken MacAfee was a fine tight end, and the man pitching to him was a right fair hurler too. During MacAfee's senior season, Joe Montana went 99 for 189 for 1,604 yards and 11 touchdowns. Montana returned in 1978 without MacAfee and tossed 141 completions in 260 attempts for 2,010 yards and 10 scores (Number Three on the ND single-season passing chart). Montana's ice-water-in-the-veins leadership drove the Irish to a 34-10 record and the 1977 National Championship during his four seasons as the Blue and Gold signal caller.

Strangely enough, Montana received little Heisman mention, and wasn't even voted an All-American. He lasted until the third round (pick number 82) in the '79 NFL draft. Fortunately for San Francisco, Montana has blossomed into the greatest quarterback in NFL history.

Joe Montana had several Irish teammates, in addition to Ken MacAfee, who were more highly regarded as pro prospects than he.

Defensive end Ross Browner of the Ross, Jim, Joey, Keith Browner family spent 1976 and 1977 picking the remains of opposing quarterbacks out of his teeth. A Consensus All-American in 1976, Ross added the 1977 Lombardi and Maxwell Trophies to his 1976 Outland Award. Browner captained the 1977 Irish National Champions and finished a remarkable sixth in that season's Heisman vote.

Selected by Cincinnati with the eighth pick of the '78 draft, Browner spent ten seasons with the Bengals and Packers. He recovered twelve fumbles, intercepted a pass and registered one safety. Browner's career was interrupted by a brief but useful suspension for violating the NFL's drug policy in 1983, and by a 1985 flirtation with the USFL. He was the starting right tackle—intent on destroying Joe Montana—on the Bengal team that fell to the 'Niners 26-21 in Super Bowl XVI.

Linebacker Bob Golic was a co-captain, with Jerome Heavens and Joe Montana, on the 9-3 '78 Fighting Irish team that defeated Houston 35-34 in the Cotton Bowl for the school's 600th vic-

To date **Joe Montana** *has:*
* *Established NFL records for highest completion percentage, career (63.23%) and most consecutive 300-yard games, season (5), 1982.*
* *Been named an NFC Pro Bowler in 1981, 1983, 1984, 1985, 1987 and 1989.*
* *Led the 'Niners to the NFC Championship Game in 1981, 1983, 1984, 1988 and 1989.*
* *Led San Francisco to Super Bowl Championships following the 1981, 1984, 1988 and 1989 seasons.*
* *Completed over 2,500 passes (6th), for over 30,000 yards (11th) and nearly 220 touchdowns (9th).*
* *Tied or established at least nine current Super Bowl records.*
* *Been named Super Bowl MVP twice.*

Joe Montana has been at the heart of two dynasties—Notre Dame football and the San Francisco 49ers. Courtesy Notre Dame Sports.

If Joe Montana never goes anywhere near a football for the rest of his life, he's already made it to Canton and immortality.

tory. He was named to various All-America teams following the '77 championship season, and was a Consensus choice in 1978.

Taken by New Orleans with the 52nd pick in the '79 NFL draft, the 6'2", 260 pound lineman has labored eleven seasons with the Saints, Browns, and Raiders. Despite spending much of two season on injured reserve with a shoulder separation and a broken arm, Golic has enjoyed an oustanding professional career. He was named to the AFC Pro Bowl Team in 1985, '86 and '87 and was a defensive stalwart on the '86 Browns who fell 23-20 to Denver in the match for the right to face the Giants in Super Bowl XXI.

Cleveland likely would have represented the AFC in Super Bowl XXII had Golic not broken his arm in the final game of the regular season. The Golic-less Browns fell to the Broncos again 38-33 in the AFC Championship Game.

Two other Golic/Browner/Montana/MacAfee teammates from the '77 champs achieved sterling collegiate careers, but faded in the NFL. Both had deep Hoosier roots.

Muncie North's Luther Bradley won All-America honors as a cornerback in 1976 and '77 and became Detroit's Number One pick in the '78 NFL draft. Playing for simply horrendous Lion teams that went 26-38 during his stay, Bradley intercepted nine passes in four seasons. The 6'2", 195 pound defensive back jumped to the USFL in 1983. When that league went belly-up after the '85 season, Bradley went with it.

A second Indiana High School All-Star enjoyed a brilliant late '70's career with the Fighting Irish—Richmond's Vagus Ferguson. In 1978 his 219 yards on 18 carries against Navy established a Notre Dame single-game rushing record. The 6'1", 194 pound sprinter broke his own mark two weeks later with 255 yards on 30 carries against Georgia Tech. That effort still stands as a ND record.

During the course of his 1979 senior season, Tri-Captain Ferguson established the Notre Dame standard for points in a single season by scoring 17 touchdowns for 102 points. The 3,472 yards he compiled in 673 career carries (5.2) remain an ND record. Ferguson was named a Consensus All-American following the '79 season. Drafted in the first round by New England, Ferguson's NFL career fell far short of his cousin Lamar's Lundy's record. During four seasons with the Pats, Oilers and Browns, Ferguson was limited to 1,411 total yards and five TDs. He put in one final nondescript season with the USFL's Chicago Blitz and retired from pro football.

Despite Vagus Ferguson's heroics, the '79 Irish team finished 7-4 and the hounds were hard at Dan Devine's door. The '80 team started the season 9-0-1, including victories over Purdue, Michigan, Miami and Alabama. You would think that that performance would be sufficient to quiet the most demanding critic. But a 20-3 setback at USC to end the regular season, and a 17-10 fall to Georgia in the Sugar Bowl started the baying all over again.

Coach Devine, who had announced his planned resignation early in the season, departed South Bend with a heartfelt blast. "I'm not going to say 'sayonara' because that means ' 'till we meet again.' There are a number of guys here I don't care if I ever meet again."

In 1981 the most rabid Fighting Irish fans and the most unyielding of the ND press got what they deserved. Gerry Faust may be the greatest high school football coach in history. In eighteen season at Cincinnati Moeller, his teams went 174-17-2. Moeller was practically a Notre Dame farm team. Coach Faust was also a friendly, aggressive, charismatic speaker. As the new head coach of the 1981 Fighting Irish, Gerry Faust was also in way over his head.

Five miserable seasons under Faust produced a 30-26-1 record. The 26 defeats stand as an ignominious Notre Dame coaching record. The Faust regime produced three losses to Purdue, four losses to Air Force, a 13-13 tie with the Oregon Ducks, two 5-6 seasons and—in his final game—a 58-7 embarrassment at Miami on national TV. The 6-5 '83 team struggled by Boston College 19-18 in the Liberty Bowl, while the '84 squad dropped the Aloha Bowl 27-20 to the about-to-be-disbanded SMU Mustangs.

Following the '85 season, Coach Faust escaped to Akron, where he is currently much more comfortable as the head coach of the University of Akron Zips.

There were, as always, great moments and great players in South Bend during the Gerry Faust era. Linebacker Bob Crable was named to most All-America teams following Dan Devine's final season. As team captain, he was a Consensus choice after Gerry Faust's inaugural campaign.

Although he was selected by the Jets with the 23rd pick of the '82 draft, a bad knee destroyed Crable's professional career. During six seasons with New York, the Cincinnati Moeller grad spent four stints on the injured reserve or physically unable to perform lists. Crable was forced from the game following the '87 season.

In 1982, former Muncie North All-State safety Dave Duerson co-captained the Irish to a 6-4-1 improvement and was named to several All-America teams.

Duerson was selected by the Chicago Bears on the third round of the '83 NFL draft and has put together a sterling professional career since. Duerson—cousin of former Muncie Central and Houson Rocket guard Allen Leavell—has stolen nearly 20 interceptions to date, returned 15 punts or kickoffs for 222 yards, and recovered four fumbles. The 6'1", 210 pound hitter was an NFC Pro Bowler following the 1985, '86, '87 and '88 seasons and played in the NFC Championship Game following the '84, '85 and '88 campaigns. Duerson was the starting strong safety on the Bear team that demolished New England 46-10 in Super Bowl XX.

Notre Dame made another small improvement to 7-5 in 1983 under the senior co-captaincy of Hoosiers Blair Kiel and Stacey Toran.

As a *Parade Magazine* All-American quarterback from Columbus East, Blair Kiel was the object of an intense recruiting war between Notre Dame and IU. Notre Dame won. And, while he has struggled somewhat since leaving Columbus, Kiel hasn't been as awful as most IU loyalists will claim. Though he doesn't show at the top of many ND record charts, the 96-yard TD Kiel threw to Joe Howard in the '81 35-3 victory over Georgia Tech remains atop the Fighting Irish record books.

To date, Blair Kiel has put in five inconsequential NFL seasons as a quarterback/punter with Tampa, Indianapolis and Green Bay.

Stacey Toran immortalized himself in the

hearts of Hoosier Hysteria fanatics when his record 57-footer at the buzzer downed Marion 71-69 and put Indianapolis Broad Ripple into the 1980 State Championship Game. Toran's 15 points helped lead the Rockets to a 73-66 conquest of New Albany for the title.

Toran, however, chose to pursue his talent for football at ND. After receiving his degree, Toran spent six seasons at safety for the LA Raiders. He intercepted six passes for two touchdowns prior to his untimely death in an automobile accident.

Though Kiel and Toran were the captains of the '83 Fighting Irish, Allen Pinkett was the unchallenged star. The 5'9", 195 pound fireplug ranks at or near the top of every ND rushing chart. The 108 points he scored in 1984 rank second to the 110 he scored in 1983. Pinkett's 189 yards against Penn State, 197 against Air Force and 219 VS Penn State are all ND Top Ten efforts, and his 3,031 career rushing total ranks second only to Vagus Ferguson. Pinkett was voted to numerous All-America squads in 1983 and '85.

As a professional, Pinkett has had the misfortune of laboring for the running-back-loaded Houston Oilers. Nevertheless, despite sharing duties with the likes of Mike Rozier and Lorenzo White, Pinkett has racked up over 2,500 total yards and 15 TDs as an Oiler tailback/kick returner. His 106 rushing/receiving yards and one TD led Houston to a 24-23 victory over Cleveland in the 1988 AFC Wildcard Playoff Game.

Mark Bavaro provided the final greatness of the Gerry Faust era. The principal beneficiary of the Blair Kiel/Gerry Faust school of passing offense, the 6'4", 245 pound tight end led the Irish in receiving in 1983 and was named to several All-America Teams in '84.

Taken by the Giants in the fourth round of the '85 draft, Bavaro has developed into one of the NFL's premier tight ends. To date, he has caught over 250 passes for over 3,500 yards and nearly 25 TDs. Bavaro was named to the NFC Pro Bowl Team following the 1986 and '87 seasons. His four catches for 51 yards and a touchdown helped the Giants down Denver 39-20 in Super Bowl XXI and landed Bavaro on the cover of *Sports Illustrated*.

Tim Brown, 1988 Heisman Trophy winner.   *Courtesy Notre Dame Sports.*

Lou Holtz, the man who reawakened the echoes. Courtesy Notre Dame sports.

In 1984 the University of Minnesota hadn't had a winning season in five years. Within two seasons Lou Holtz had completely rebuilt the program and the Golden Gophers received an invitation to face Clemson in the Independence Bowl.

In 1986 Fighting Irish fanatics were looking for a miracle worker and the former Kent State linebacker appeared to be just the Saint for the job.

There were no miracles in 1986. Quarterback Steve Beurlein had a non-descript season that gave little hint of the respectable LA Raider career that would soon begin. ND floundered to a 5-6 mark.

What there was in South Bend in '86 was a junior flanker/kick returner named Tim Brown. A ninty-five yard kickoff return VS Air Force, 184 receiving yards against Navy, an 84-yard TD reception against SMU, a 96-yard kick-off return against LSU and a 59-yard punt return against USC helped earn Brown Consensus All-America honors and provided a preview of 1987.

Though the Irish stumbled to three consecutive losses to close out the '87 season—including a 35-10 setback to Texas A&M in the Cotton Bowl—Tim Brown's 846 yards on 39 receptions for 3 TDs and his 57 punt/KOR for 857 yards and 3 TDs were more than enough to make him ND's seventh Heisman Trophy winner.

The Irish finished 17th in the final 1987 AP Poll—their first Top Twenty finish since 1980. But skeptics questioned whether 1988 would witness a dramatic collapse with the loss of Tim Brown to the NFL.

Brown, by the way, was taken by the Raiders with the Number Six pick. He broke into the NFL with 43 receptions good for 725 yards and five TDs. His 41 kickoff returns for 1,098 yards (26.8) and one TD all led the league and earned the rookie 1988 Pro Bowl honors as a special teamer.

Notre Dame recovered from Brown's graduation. On October 15, 1988 Number One Miami went for two with forty-five seconds remaining. They failed. Final score ND 31-Miami 30. The no-class 58-7 drubbing Hurricane coach Jimmy Johnson laid on Gerry Faust's last team was avenged.

During the course of the season the Fighting Irish also overcame Number Four Michigan 19-17, Number Seven USC 27-10 and—in the Fiesta Bowl—Number Three West Virginia. Oh yeah, they squeezed by Purdue 52-7 and Rice 54-11.

The National Championship was the school's eleventh. QB Tony Rice was named team MVP. His 75 yards rushing, 213 yards passing and two scores earned Rice Fiesta Bowl offensive MVP honors, an unprecedented third *Sports Illustrated* cover and grossly overblown support for the 1989 Heisman Trophy.

All-America honors went to linebacker Michael Stonebreaker, offensive tackle Andy Heck and defensive end Frank Stams. Coach Holtz picked up Consensus Coach of the Year accolades.

In 1988 Freshman Raghib Ismail led the nation with 12 kickoff returns for 433 yards (36.08) and two touchdowns. In 1989 "Rocket" Ismail returned two kickoffs for TDs against Michigan's Wolverines alone. He also chipped in with a TD punt return against the Air Force Academy.

A 27-10 setback at Number One Miami was the only thing that prevented the 12-1 Irish from successfully defending their '88 crown. A 21-6 victory over Colorado in the Orange Bowl ruined the Buffalos shot at a National Championship and placed ND Number Two in most polls.

With the return of Rocket Ismail, Michael Stonebreaker, tailback Ricky Waters and a cast of thousands; the Fighting Irish enter the 1990 collegiate football season as the odds-on favorite for a twelfth National Championship. The natural laws of an ordered universe remain intact.

The *Indianapolis* Colts

If you look to the centerfield wall in Candlestick Park, you'll find the names Bresnahan, Hubbell, Mathewson, McGraw and Ott. Even though these Hall of Famers had nothing to do with the San Francisco Giants, probably never even visited the Bay City, you'll find them alongside the names of Mays and McCovey.

Walter O'Malley broke about a million hearts when he jerked the Dodgers out of Flatbush and eventually dropped them in the middle of Chavez Ravine. No athletic team ever received more fanatical support from their loyalists than "Da Bums" received from the Brooklynites. In 1957 the Brooklyn Dodgers were synonymous with American sports history. In 1958 they ceased to exist. As the LA Dodgers have become one of America's most successful athletic franchises on the field, and draw about three million paying customers every year, you don't hear many folks second-guessing O'Malley's long-ago decision.

When Laker fans talk about their legendary centers, Chamberlain and Jabbar come quickly to mind. But true Laker fans will remind you that the franchise employed the first great professional center. Even though George Mikan left the Lakers two years before the Lakers left Minneapolis he remains part of the Laker tradition.

So what's all this nonsense about returning the Indianapolis Colts' name, colors and team logo to Baltimore? The fact is that following the 1990 season, the Colts will already have played more than 20% of their NFL games as an Indianapolis franchise, and Baltimore didn't receive the team by Divine Right at any rate. The history of the club calling itself the Colts goes back a long way. It began after World War II, when, the initial Colts' franchise proved to be a false start.

When the Miami Seahawks of the short-lived, post-war NFL challenger, the All-American Football Conference, ran aground, the franchise shifted to Baltimore. The renamed Baltimore Colts were by unanimous call the most pathetic franchise in the AAFC.

Coach Cecil Isbell could count on quarterback Y.A. Tittle to connect with former IU All-American Billy Hillenbrand on a regular basis, but little else. Even though the Colts amassed a miserable 10-29-1 record between 1947-'49, they were strong enough financially to become one of three AAFC teams—along with the Browns and 49ers—to merge with the NFL in 1950.

The change in leagues didn't result in an improvement in the record. Counting pre-season games, the Colts finished 1-18 in 1950. Attendance evaporated and owner Abe Watner sold the club back to the league at the end of the season. The NFL disbanded the franchise and disbursed the players throughout the league.

In 1952 NFL Coach Jimmy Phelan's Dallas Texans went 1-11. George Taliafero's 1,111 total yards and four TDs did little to help. Neither did Frank Tripuka's 91-186 for 809 passing yards and three touchdowns. The former NY Yank franchise abandoned the cavernous Cotton Bowl in mid-season to become a "road team." Hershey, PA served as a practice site. In 1953 Baltimore football fans snapped up 15,000 season tickets and the NFL agreed to the Dallas Texans' becoming the Baltimore Colts.

Though the team finished a marginal 3-9, general manager Carroll Rosenbloom's Colts nearly led the league in attendance with a 28,000 per-game average. The Colts were back for good.

From this point on there can be no denying that the Baltimore Colts represent a glorious NFL tradition. When Richmond native Weeb Ewbank took over the head coaching duties in 1954, he was only able to lead the Colts to a 3-9 mark. By 1958, behind names like Unitas, Ameche, Moore, Berry, Thurston, Marchetti, Parker, Donovan and Lipscomb, Coach Ewbank had the Colts at the top of the NFL.

Many football purists insist that the 1958 NFL Championship Game between the Colts and Giants is the greatest game every played. Unitas hit Moore for sixty yards on the game's first drive, but the Giants' Sam Huff blocked Steve Myhra's 27-yard field goal attempt. New York's Frank Gifford swept 38 yards on an end-around to set up Pat Summerall's 36-yard field goal.

A Gifford fumble then set the stage for Ameche's plunge from the two. A 15-yard strike from Unitas to Berry followed a second Gifford fumble. Myhra's conversion made it Colts 14, Giants 3.

Triplett went over from the one in the third and Sumerall's kick made it 14-10. Gifford snared a 15-yard Conerly bullet to begin the fourth and the Giants forged ahead 17-14 when Summerall nailed the PAT. With seven seconds remaining in regulation, Unitas maneuvered the ball to the New Yorkers' 13. Myhra's boot made it 17-17. Sudden Death at Yankee Stadium! The Giants received, but neither Gifford nor Rote could break free. The Colts held. Thirteen plays later, including a 33-yard bomb from Unitas to Berry, Ameche went over from the one. Colts 23—Giants 17.

If this recitation didn't give you goose bumps, put the book down and go read *Little Women*. It's been nearly three dozen names since we last really needed a given name, and you recognized every single player mentioned, from a game played over thirty years ago. There is no greater legacy than the one left by the Baltimore Colts.

The '58 season was the beginning of Colt greatness. The legends came in order: Matte, Coach Shula, Bubba, Curtis, Hendricks, Nowatzke, Mitchell, Jones and the rest. Big games crowd the history books. The Colts returned to swamp the Giants 31-16 in the 1959 NFL Championship. The '64 Colts swept to a 12-2 mark before falling 27-0 to Brown, Groza, Warfield and Collins in the title game. If the '58 Championship Game isn't the most famous pro football game of all time, then Super Bowl III, played a decade later, surely is. Behind the arm of Broadway Joe Namath, Weeb Ewbank's Jets pulled the upset of the ages—downing the Colts 16-7 and finalizing the AFL/NFL merger in the process.

The Colts lived down the humiliation and returned to edge the Cowboys 16-13 in Super Bowl V. Baltimore was trailing 13-6 in the fourth quarter when IU's Tom Nowatzke smashed across from the two. Rookie place-kicker Jim O'Brien's 32-yard three-pointer as time expired gave the Colts the title. A 21-0 loss to Bob Griese's Miami machine in the 1971 AFC Championship Game prevented the Colts from defending their title in Super Bowl VI.

Perhaps the Colts' long journey into purgatory began when Robert Irsay acquired the team in 1972. The folks in Baltimore will say "no ifs, ands, buts or perhapses about it." But then, what do they know? On July 26, 1972, Irsay traded his recently acquired LA Rams' franchise to Carroll Rosenbloom for Rosenbloom's Colts. Irsay had purchased the Colts with the fortune he had amassed through a Chicago-based heating and air conditioning business.

Whether or not Irsay should take the blame for the Colts' trip to hell in a handbasket is a matter for acrimonious debate. The franchise did capture three straight AFC Eastern Division titles under Irsay's watch, after all (1974, '75, '76).

Many things went askew in Baltimore. A long, bitter salary holdout culminated with Lydell Mitchell's being shipped to San Diego in 1978. Bert Jones suffered the chronic separated shoulder that would eventually end his career, and a suspect defense collapsed entirely. The Colts slumped to a humiliating 5-11 in '78.

As with Jones' shoulder, the team's woes became chronic. Public bickering erupted between Jones and Irsay, between Irsay and Coach Marchibroda, and between Jones and the over-inflated ego of running back Curtis Dickey. The state of Maryland refused to fund badly needed improvements at ramshackle Municipal Stadium, and Irsay responded with constant threats to move the team.

The club struggled to a 26-60-1 mark between 1978-83, and fans began staying away in droves. Though the '80 squad finished 7-9, those supposedly great, loyal, never-say-die fans in Baltimore showed up 16,941 strong to boo the "Dolts" in the season's final game. This "stick with our boys through thick and thin" attitude came after three mediocre seasons that followed on the heels of three straight Division Crowns.

When 1983's first pick, John Elway of Stanford, flatly refused to sign with the Colts, the ultimate schism between team and fans was opened. Though Baltimore received Mark Herrmann, future All-Pro tackle Chris Hinton and two first round draft choices for Elway, Colt fanatics were understandably livid.

In 1983 a 7-9 Colt team was last in NFL attendance. The franchise broke 40,000 only twice and drew less than 30,000 in both of their final two home games. As the introduction to this "Modern Era" section said, professional football cannot be mistaken for a game—it is Big Business. No league, city or fan can claim a franchise by Divine Right. On a cold, blustery March night in 1984 Bob Irsay backed the Mayflower vans up to Baltimore Colt headquarters and moved his team to Indianapolis.

The rest—as they say so tritely—is history. In truth, the jury is still out on the Indianapolis Colts. Jim Irsay continues to affirm his obsession to create a world-class club, but the team has been mediocre at best during six campaigns on the Hoosier Dome Astro Turf. Despite this fact, the team averaged 58,456 spectators in 1989 and never fell below the 55,500 mark in any one game.

Robert Irsay has kept a low profile since moving to Indy. He surfaces periodically to rattle the saber over issues when he wants to, but most of his appearances have been confined to the good-citizen contributions he makes around the state.

Son Jim Irsay has been left to run the club as the team's general manager. And while some—many? most?—may question Jimmy's penchant for trading bushels of draft picks for the questionable rewards to be reaped from the likes of Eric Dickerson, Fredd Young and Jeff George, you've got to give the young man credit for intestinal fortitude.

At any rate, the Colts are in Indianapolis to stay. The blue and white will remain in Indy. The horseshoe will remain in Indy. The team name will remain in Indianapolis.

Unless... unless the NBA would consent to moving Isiah Thomas, Bill Laimbeer, the Bad Boys and their consecutive World Championships back to the Fort Wayne Coliseum. Then maybe we could strike a deal. Otherwise... Johnny Unitas, lighten up.

Not all of the outstanding players in Colt history claim Baltimore loyalties. A growing number of fine football names came after the team received the designation, "Indianapolis Colts." The most dramatic personality to play for the Indianapolis Colts is one Eric Demitric Dickerson. A product of Sealy, Texas (population 4,418) and Sealy High School, the youthful Dickerson was named *Parade Magazine* High School Back of the Year in 1978. Playing for Coach Ron Meyer at SMU, Dickerson amassed 4,450 collegiate rushing yards on 790 carries (5.6 YPC) to break Earl Campbell's Southwest Conference record for yards and carries. His 48 career TDs tied Doak Walker's SMU career points mark at 288. Dickerson finished third in the 1982 Heisman race. As a professional, Eric Dickerson has received just about every honor and broken nearly every rushing record available.

He was the first pick of the LA Rams in the '83 draft, and his "short list" of accomplishments includes:
* NFL rookie rushing record, 1,808 yards on 390 carries for 18 TDs
* Ram rookie scoring record 120 points
* 1983 Rookie of the Year
* 1983 *Sports Illustrated* Player of the Year
* Surpassed O.J. Simpson's NFL single-season mark by rushing for 2,105 yards in 1984
* 12 100-yard games in '84 broke NFL single-season mark shared by Simpson and Earl Campbell
* Set NFL record in 1984 for most total yards from scrimmage (2,244)
* 1984 Consensus NFL Player of the Year
* Set NFL Playoff record with 248 yards on 34 carries in Rams' 20-0 defeat of Cowboys in 1985 NFC Playoffs.

There's more:

Eric Dickerson, one of the great running backs in the history of the NFL. Courtesy Indianapolis Colts.

* 1986 AP NFL Offensive Player of the Year
* 1987, Became third back in Colts' history to post a 1,000-yard rushing season (Mitchell three times, Dickey once) when he gained 1,011 yards in eight games.
* Captured fourth NFL rushing title with 1,659 yards on 388 attempts in 1988, tied with Steve Van Buren and O.J. Simpson for second-most titles behind Jim Brown's eight.
* Yards and attempts in 1988 established Colt franchise standards.
* 3,961 rushing yards as a Colt, ranks Dickerson Number Five on all-time Colt list.
* Only player in NFL history with seven consecutive 1,000-yard seasons.
* 58 100-yard games—tied with Jim Brown for second-most in NFL history.
* Pro Bowl 1983, '84, '85, '86, '87, '88 and 1989.
* All Pro First Team 1983, '84, '85, '86, '87, and 1988.
* 11,226 rushing yards is 11 shy of O.J. Simpson's sixth place NFL standing.

If Eric Dickerson wants to become the greatest running back in football history, Eric Dickerson will become the greatest running back in football history.

The increasingly boring question became, "What DOES Eric want?" After listening to incessant complaining about being unappreciated in LA, the Rams were all too happy to exchange Dickerson for half of two years' worth of NFL drafts.

After coming to Indy, Eric Dickerson has performed admirably on the field. When healthy, he dominated the league. He took a battering—which is what professional football players do for a living. Dickerson served as the NFL spokesman for the "Just Say No" campaign and lent his time and name to a variety of worthy social causes.

Dickerson also developed a serious liability—the tendency to whine publicly about his life as a football player. It was difficult for the average farmer, policeman, coal miner or steel worker in Indiana to take Eric Dickerson seriously when he complained about having to work nine, or even ten months a year or to hear that he was wracked with aches and pains.

Indianapolis Colt fans loved to watch Eric Dickerson work. There is nothing more beautiful than watching the thoroughbred slashing his way into the open field. No painting, ballet, or work of art; not Payton or Jordan in flight has ever been prettier. Many fans, though wondered if he was worth all the heartache.

Eric Dickerson has had one major complaint with the Colts. In an offensive line beset with question marks, Chris Hinton was a constant. In 1989 he was the best offensive lineman in the NFL. If there's a doubt, ask a Bruce Smith or a Michael Dean Perry. They can be found still flat on their backs—put there and kept there by a crunching Chris Hinton block.

To get a true picture of how good Chris Hinton is, you have to know he was a Collegiate All-American despite playing for the Northwestern Mildcats. Hinton came to Northwestern as a 218 pound tight end with 4.8 40 speed. He came to Indianapolis as a 272 pound lineman with 4.8 40 speed. Bulking up to 300 has cost him a tenth or two.

Hinton was the undeniable talent offered by Denver that clinched the John Elway deal. During his seven seasons with the Colts, Chris opened gaping holes and was named to the AFC Pro Bowl six times.

In '89 he was the best. In '90 he was packaged with Andre Rison and a first-round pick and shipped to Atlanta for the rights to QB Jeff George.

Hinton's trenchmate Ray Donaldson remains a Colt, and the Pro Bowl center is really going to have to anchor the line now. At this writing, the University of Georgia All-American had appeared in 149 Colt games and had started in every non-strike game since 1981. One of four remaining holdovers from the Baltimore Colts (along with Donnell Thompson, Rohn Stark and Pat Beach) the old man of the Colts (32) has been the AFC's Pro Bowl Center since 1986.

Bill Brooks has been another constant in the Indianapolis Colts' offense. Despite 228 collegiate receptions for 3,579 yards and 32 TDs, Brooks hasn't always received a great deal of media attention.

Coming out of Boston University and lacking blazing speed, Brooks lasted until the fourth round of the '86 draft. His 65 rookie catches (including an 84-yard TD at San Francisco) for 1,131 yards and eight scores, earned Billy All-Rookie Team honors and designation as the NFL Players Association Offensive Rookie of the Year. With the sweetest hands you've ever seen and a fearless style over the middle, Brooks is ninth in Colts' career receptions (233) and sixth in career yardage (3,639).

Bill Brooks and Andre Rison formed one of the AFC's deadliest pass-catching duos in 1989. With Rison now a Falcon, Brooks will be forced to carry an increased load while counting on constant double coverage.

Two other offensive stalwarts of the Indianapolis Colt years have been Albert Bentley and Pat Beach. Bentley came to the Colts from the Miami Hurricanes 1984 National Champions in the '84 supplemental draft. His seven-yard TD run against Nebraska boosted the 'Canes to a 31-30 Orange Bowl victory and clinched the title.

In five seasons with the Colts, Bentley has shown himself to be the club's most versatile offensive weapon. In the strike-torn 1987 season his 1,578 all-purpose yards (631 rushing, 447 receiving, 500 KOR) trailed only Herschel Walker in the NFL. Bentley's career 6,352 all-purpose yards and 21 career TDs would seem to evidence a promising future in pro ball. Surely he should not remain forever the Colts' "forgotten man." Give the ball to Bentley.

Through 1989 Washington State alumnus Pat Beach had nabbed 138 passes for 1,308 yards and eleven TDs since joining the Colts in Baltimore in 1982. The 6'4", 252 pound tight end has also laid some lovely hits on persistent linebackers and unsuspecting corner backs. Besides—

he's the best thing to happen to morning drive-time radio since... well, you pick.

On special teams the Indianapolis Colts can boast a number of the NFL's very best. Rohn Stark was named the All-Pro punter in 1983 and has performed in three Pro Bowls. The Florida Stater has won three NFL punting titles, one short of matching Sammy Baugh and Jerrel Wilson for the most in league history. Stark's 44.1 yards-per-kick career average ranks fifth in NFL history.

Western Carolina's Dean Biasucci connected on 21 of 27 field goal attempts and 31 of 32 PATs in 1989. Signed by the Colts as a free agent in 1986, after being waived by the Falcons, Biasucci is the most accurate place kicker in Colt history (.741, 86–116 FGs), and his 391 points already rank fifth on the Colts' all-time list. A budding Shakespearean, the 6',189 pound Biasucci has connected on 52 of his last 56 field goal attempts inside 45 yards and booted a 55-yarder against Denver in 1989.

Clarence Verdin has provided more than a little excitement as a kick returner. His 23 punt returns for 296 yards (12.9) and a TD was second best in the NFL in 1989. Moreover, career receptions of 82, 54, 48, 42 and 34 yards and a 59-yard end-around against Miami have provided additional sparks. And, the 5'9", 170 pound Southwestern Louisiana burner's "Verdance" is the hottest celebration strut in the NFL. If only Verdin didn't have the nasty ability to make Colts fans all over Indiana mutter "nice hands, Clarence," at least once a game.

Speaking of special teamers—Fredd Young was a perennial kamikaze Pro Bowler for Seattle between 1984–1987. But it is as an inside linebacker that the 6'1", 235 pound New Mexico State product will have to make his impact, if the 1988 trade that sent '89 and '90 first round picks to the Seahawks is to be justified. Young's 122 tackles, two sacks and two interceptions in 1989 was a better record than average, but that was *two* Number One picks the Colts gave up. Not one, but two.

Perhaps Indianapolis Colts fans have come to expect too much from their linebackers. No matter how awful the Colts got—and they got pretty awful—the linebacking corp remained excellent. Players like Barry Krause, Cliff Odom and Johnny Cooks always put in a solid day's work; USC's Duane Bickett was the pick of the bunch.

The 6'5", 251 pound USC Trojan introduced himself to Indiana when he was named Southern Cal's Defensive Player of the Week following a 1983 loss to Notre Dame. The 1985 All-American and three-time Pac-Ten All-Academic selection was the fifth player selected in the '85 draft. Bickett justified the Colts admiration with 141 rookie tackles and a team high six sacks, which earned him AP Defensive Rookie of the Year honors.

Despite back and hamstring problems, Bickett has registered 624 tackles, 31.5 sacks and seven interceptions at this writing. He has caused or recovered an assortment of fumbles as the Colts Number One defenseman for the past five seasons. Duane Bickett's efforts were rewarded with a 1987 selection to the AFC Pro Bowl Team.

The eighteenth selection in the 1981 draft, 6'4", 280 pound defensive end Donnell Thompson has been a ten-year constant on the Colt line. Entering the '90 season, Thompson is the leading active Colt tackler, registering 811 stops, including 31 sacks and nine fumbles caused or recovered, in 120 games.

Thompson's counterpart at right defensive end, 6'7", 301 pound Jon Hand, was the fourth selection in the 1986 draft. A Consensus All-American out of Alabama, Hand has slowly developed into the defensive force the Colts anticipated. In 1989 Hand totaled 85 tackles, four forced fumbles and two fumbles recovered.

Additional past or current Indianapolis Colts who have distinguished themselves on the NFL gridiron include: nose tackle Harvey Armstrong, linebacker Chip Banks, receiver Matt Bouza, offensive lineman Kevin "The Creature" Call, cornerback Eugene Daniel, safety Nesby Glasgow, offensive lineman Ron Solt, and offensive lineman Ben Utt. Two young linebackers who appear to have bright futures in pro football are O'Brien Alston and Jeff Herrod.

Quarterback Jack Trudeau may have put together the most frustrating career in the NFL over the past four seasons. The 47th player taken in the 1986 NFL draft, Trudeau holds University of Illinois records for career pass attempts (1,151), completions (737), yards (8,146) and TDs (51). He completed 64% of his career passes at Illinois and set an NCAA record by throwing 215 consecutive passes without an interception.

Four games into his rookie season, Trudeau was forced into the starting lineup due to a shoulder injury suffered by veteran QB Gary Hogeboom. Though his 204-417 and 2,225 yards established club rookie records and ranked third best on all-time NFL rookie charts, the lame Colts stumbled to a 0-11 records during his rookie tenure.

The fact that new coach Ron Meyer felt compelled to bring Hogey back with three games remaining couldn't have done much for Trudeau's confidence. The fact that Hogey finished off the season 3-0 was great for the team but didn't do much for Trudeau's reputation.

A season-long unresolved competition with Hogeboom in '87, a season-ending knee injury in 1988 and an early-season back seat to Chris Chandler in '89 add up to four seasons of uncertainty and frustration.

Despite this history, Jack Trudeau's 536 of 1,042 for 6,187 yards and 29 TDs rank him as the fourth most productive Colt quarterback in franchise history heading into the 1990 season. The fact that Jack persevered with a broken finger on his left hand, split third and fourth fingers on his pitching hand, and a concussion that required hospitalization during the course of the '89 season, earned the current Carmel resident a great deal of respect in several football quarters.

At this writing Trudeau is locked in battle with Jeff George for the Colts starting quarterback position. It appears to be a battle that he is pre-ordained to lose eventually.

Evidence that Trudeau appears destined for a backup role is found in the fact that no pro team pays anyone $2 million a year to sit on the bench. The Colts probably didn't sign their first year signalcaller to the largest rookie contract in history and the fourth highest QB contract currently in force—to have him wearing a headset and carrying a clipboard. If the Indianapolis Colts have a future, his name is Jeffrey Scott George.

Jeff George's pedigree is flawless, but the particulars of his experience to date tend to make one wince.

As a three-year starter at Indianapolis Warren Central High School, he led the school to a 36-2 record and state titles in 1984 and '85. His 8,126 passing yards and 94 TDs rank third on the all-time national prep charts. In 1985 he was named a *USA Today,* Gatorade, Washington Press Club and National High School Coaches Association Prep Player of the Year nominee. George also amassed 1,002 career points for the Warrior basketball team and hit .456 while playing three seasons at shortstop.

A freshman starter at Purdue before transferring to Illinois, George's collegiate numbers read 596-1,016 for 6,406 yards and 35 TDs. In 1989 he led the Illini to scores in ten of twelve two-minute drives, threw five TDs against IU, achieved three consecutive 300-yard passing games and was a Consensus All-Big 10 choice.

That's the good news. On the not so hopeful side—George threw four TDs while at Purdue

Jim Irsay, Jeff George—"The Future", and Coach Ron Meyer—Indianapolis Star *Photo by John Warner.*

Key Dates in Indianapolis Colt History

March 30, 1984
The equipment, records and some front office personnel of the Baltimore Colts, arrive in Indianapolis and the franchise is renamed the Indianapolis Colts.

April 18, 1984
Indianapolis Colts tickets are offered for sale. 143,000 season tickets requests are received within two weeks.

September 10, 1984
The Indianapolis Colts play their first regular season game losing 24-13 to the New York Jets at the Hoosier Dome.

December 1, 1986
Former Purdue Boilermaker Ron Meyer is named head coach. Over the franchise's first two-and-a-half seasons in Indiana, the Colts had compiled a 9-36 record under coaches Kush, Hunter, and Dowhower. The team stood 0-13 at Meyer's appointment, but would finish 3-13. Coach Meyer had led the Colts to a 29-21 mark at this writing.

October 31, 1987
In one of the biggest trades in NFL history, the Colts obtain running back Eric Dickerson from the LA Rams. Indianapolis sends the rights to linebacker Cornelius Bennett to Buffalo while LA receives the Colts' first and second round picks in the '88 draft, the Colts second pick in the '89 draft, running back Owen Gill, Buffalo's first pick in the '88 draft, the Bills' first and second picks in the '89 draft, and running back Greg Bell.

December 20, 1987
Eric Dickerson becomes the quickest back to reach 8,000 yards beating Jim Brown to the plateau 74 games to 80 games.

December 27, 1987
Dickerson rushes 33 times for 196 yards—second highest in Colt history. The Colts clinch the AFC Eastern Division title with a 24-6 thrashing of Tampa Bay before a sold-out Hoosier Dome throng.

January 9, 1988
Pat Beach and Eric Dickerson receive TD passes from Jack Trudeau as the Colts forge a 14-14 half-time tie before 78,586 fans at Cleveland Stadium for the AFC First Round Playoffs. Albert Bentley crashes across from the one in the fourth quarter, but the Colts fade to a 38-21 defeat.

October 31, 1988
The Colts lead the Broncos 45-10 at half-time and go on to down Denver 55-23 in the first Monday Night Game played in Indianapolis. Eric Dickerson rushes for a club record—four touchdowns during the Halloween Night blast.

April 20, 1990
The Colts complete a trade with Atlanta which yields the first pick of the 1990 draft. Jeff George of Indianapolis Warren Central High School and Purdue/Illinois fame is selected with the pick. All Pro offensive lineman Chris Hinton, promising receiver Andre Rison and the Colts first pick in the 1991 NFL draft are shipped to the Falcons. Colt fans hold their breath.

and 15 interceptions. Granted that his Boiler teammates were less than awe inspiring, but the sight of an injured Big 10 quarterback leaving the field in a golf cart with mama alongside to stroke his forehead had fans around the league snickering in their post-game brews.

Add that to the QB's hasty departure from West Lafayette following the hiring of Fred Akers and his short flirtation with the Univerisity of Miami (the presence of Hurricane quarterback Steve Walsh allegedly had little influence on George's decision to forego a fling with the Sunshine State) and you have to be wary of the strong-arm's intangibles.

It's possible that Jeff George will be one of the biggest busts in NFL history—in which case the Indianapolis Colts will rapidly sink back into the depths from which they have so recently emerged. It's also possible that Jeff George will be the combination John Elway/Dan Marino some are saying he is, so go the Colts. With few upcoming draft choices and lots of holes to fill, Jeff George represents the future well being of the Indy franchise.

Indianapolis Colt owner Robert Irsay. Courtesy the Indianapolis Colts.

Former Purdue Boilermaker, Coach Ron Meyer of the Indianapolis Colts. Courtesy the Indianapolis Colts.

Little Big Men

Hoosier Hall of Famer Wilbur Charles Ewbank. Courtesy Pro Football Hall of Fame.

Both are built close to the ground. Native Hoosiers, they reached the top of their profession and won Super Bowl Championships. But there all similarity ends.

Weeb Ewbank of Richmond is a shaggy, soft-spoken grandfatherly type. A fundamentalist and a hard worker, he was always over-shadowed by the great stars who performed for him.

Gary's Henry Stram is ebullient and elegant, impeccably attired from the top of his expensive toupee to his elevated heels. A restless innovator who enjoys the limelight, he was as much a media star as any of his players. Yet both seemed to be trodding a path to the Hall of Fame.

In *The Golden Age of Pro Football,* Mickey Herskowitz wrote of Ewbank: "With patience and a fine instinct for what Norman Mailer called 'the talent in the room,' Weeb Ewbank re-created the (Baltimore) Colts. He did not strike people as an exciting presence. He scolded players, but never bullied them. With his clipboard and whistle and portly shape, he often reminded you of the kindly counselor at Camp Runamuck. Yet no coach ever won more Olympian games than Weeb Ewbank: with the Baltimore Colts in 1958, The Game of the Ages; and against them in 1969, the victory Joe Namath 'guaranteed,' Weeb Eubank coached the winning team both times, a trick that could have gotten most coaches elected Caesar. But Weeb never put on airs. His nature was benign..."

Weeb starred in three sports at Richmond High School and at Miami of Ohio. After two years of high school coaching, he returned to Miami and was on the athletic staff for 13 years until he joined the United States Navy in 1943.

It was at Great Lakes Naval Training Station that he began his association with Paul Brown as an assistant coach. Following his discharge, Ewbank coached basketball for one year at Brown University, then took the job of rebuilding the football program at Washington University at St. Louis, which had been discontinued during World War II. His first team went 5-5, his second 9-1.

Ewbank rejoined Paul Brown at Cleveland in 1949 and remained with the great teacher until January, 1954, when he was appointed coach of the Baltimore Colts. That team had been a disaster and they had three more losing seasons before Weeb turned the program around. The turn-around was aided considerably by the fact that Weeb always read every letter he received. He pulled one out of the pile; it was from a fan in Pittsburgh imploring the Colts to give a tryout to a young sandlot quarterback. Since Weeb was hardly knee deep in first-rate quarterbacks, he gave the kid a shot. He made the team. Boy, did he ever make the team! The kid's name was Johnny Unitas.

The Colts barely missed a share of the Western Division title in 1957, then placed NFL titles back to back in 1958-59. Their 1958 overtime victory over the New York Giants—the first overtime game in NFL history—has been called "The greatest football game ever played." The Colts came back for a second straight title in 1959, whipping the Giants 31-16, but Weeb's fortunes ebbed after that. His next three teams compiled a lackluster 21-19 record, and he was dismissed after the 1962 season.

The American Football League came into existence during Ewbank's tenure at Baltimore, and the struggling New York franchise brought Weeb out of retirement to begin yet another rebuilding job.

Show Biz whiz Sonny Werblin bought the failing Jets from Harry Wismer and hired Weeb. The

Bob Collins Sports Profile

dollar war between the two leagues was red-hot, and happy college stars were walking out of pro football front offices with satchels full of money.

Werblin wanted to do something spectacular. After losing his first draft choice, Tom Nowatzke of IU, to the Detroit Lions, he got the rights to Alabama's Joe Namath. He then sent a cannon shot through the world of pro football by announcing that he had landed Namath—the tab was generally believed to be a three-year contract that reached $400,000. The cocky, talented Namath became an instant celebrity in New York, and Weeb immediately went to work on building a team around him.

The Jets won the American League title in 1968 and headed for Miami to meet the fearsome Baltimore Colts in Super Bowl III. By then Namath had become the most controversial man in football. Brilliant on the field, he went his own way usually following a trail of bright lights after the game. Half of the football world wanted him to perform wonders, while the other half wanted him to get his block knocked off. Namath enraged the proud Colts in Miami by saying often, usually at swinging late-night spots, that the Jets were a cinch; he would guarantee a victory. Though Namath did not play an outstanding game, the Jets won, 16-7. The AFL had instant respectability, Weeb Ewbank had another championship.

Although Gary's Henry Stram reached the top of the pro football world at an earlier age than Ewbank, his route was more varied. He was an assistant coach at Purdue, Southern Methodist, Notre Dame and Miami before landing his first head coaching position—with Dallas of the newly formed American Football League.

Stram had been an outstanding football and baseball performer for Lew Wallace High School in Gary—making all-state as a halfback and pitching a no-hit game for the baseball team. He won seven letters at Purdue in 1942, '46 and '47 and was voted the Big 10 Medal, which goes to the athlete who best combines athletics with academics.

Upon graduation he joined Stu Holcomb's staff and soon began displaying his talents as an innovator. Purdue quarterback Dale Samuels was only 5'9". Tall opposing linemen were making it difficult to pass merely by rising up in front of him. So Stram devised a "moving pocket," in which Samuels and his blockers sprinted away from traffic, and the quarterback got a clear view of the passing lanes. Thus, Samuels became the first roll-out quarterback.

As a college assistant, Stram was credited with the development of four All-American quarterbacks, Samuels and Len Dawson at Purdue, George Izo at Notre Dame and Fran Curci at Miami. In pro football, Stram introduced the "stack defense" and the "tight-end I" offensive alignment.

A fast-talking, wise-cracking extrovert, who makes friends wherever he goes and is much in demand as a speaker, Hank first caught the attention of Lamar Hunt when Stram was an assistant at Southern Methodist. When Hunt formed the Dallas Texans in the new American Football League, Stram was his first choice for coach.

One of Hank's early moves was to acquire Len Dawson, his old student at Purdue. Lennie had been suffering through a lackluster career in the NFL, but he quickly established himself as one of the premier play-callers in the AFL.

Together, Stram and Dawson took the team to three AFL titles (1962, '66, '69) and two Super Bowl appearances. Kansas City lost to Green Bay, 35-10, in the first Super Bowl after trailing only 14-10 at the half. But with Dawson playing superbly, the Chiefs came back to wipe out Minnesota, 23-7, in Super Bowl IV.

Although he had only three losing seasons in fifteen years with Dallas-Kansas City, Stram was released after the 1974 season.

He spent 1975 in the broadcast booth for CBS and quickly established himself as a budding television star. But the lure of the sidelines was too great and he returned in 1976 to coach the New Orleans Saints.

Stram ranks tenth on the all-time list of pro football coaching victories with 131. Ironically, the man he passed—in 1976—to move into tenth was the retired Ewbank. Weeb has 130. Retired again in 1978, Hank Stram has spent the past several seasons in the broadcast booth. Weeb Ewbank was elected to the Pro Football Hall of Fame in 1978.

Bob Collins Sports Profile

Alex "Mongo" Karras.   *Courtesy University of Iowa Athletic Department*

Of course, not all Hoosier football greats of the Modern Era earned their highest laurels while in Indiana.

East Chicago's Ray Wietecha served as Vince Lombardi's line coach from 1962-'68 and collected Super Bowl rings in 1967 and '68. Wietecha later spent three seasons coaching the LA Rams offensive line.

The 6'1", 225-pound center/linebacker came by his coaching position honestly. An All-Big 10 lineman with Northwestern's 1949 Rose Bowl Team, Wietecha spent ten seasons in the NY Giant trenches. A five-time All-Pro, he played for the Giants' 1956 World Champions and for the '58 and '61 NFL Runners-up.

The greatest Hoosier-bred defensive lineman to come down the pike so far grew up working in the Gary steel mills. Alex Karras was a three-time all-stater at Gary Emerson. In 1957, as a senior at the University of Iowa, he was named the recipient of the Outland Trophy awarded to college football's premier lineman. The first pick of the Detroit Lions in the '58 draft, Karras spent twelve seasons terrorizing opposing linemen, running-backs, quarterbacks and anyone else who came within an arm's length. Despite playing for consistently mediocre teams, he was named the NFC's All-Pro tackle four times. The brother of NFL linemen Ted (Steelers) and Lou (Redskins) Karras, Alex recorded four career interceptions and a safety.

Famous for his ferocious quarterback sacks, the former steelworker was more infamous for his irreverent ways. Nicknamed "Tippy Toes" by Lion QB and constant drinking buddy Bobby Lane, the 6'2", 255 pound Karras occasionally had difficulty controlling his social exuberance. On April 4, 1963, it caught up with him. When informed that Commissioner Pete Rozelle had suspended him and Notre Dame alumnus Paul Hornug indefinitely for betting on NFL games, Karras exploded "Everyone in Gary bets on sporting events. I shouldn't be shelved for doing what I was reared to do."

Reinstated on March 16, 1964, Alex Karras went on his merry way. In 1971 he turned down an offer from the Washington Redskins with a curt "Why should I want to go with Washington?

Former Indianapolis Cathedral High School star Mark Clayton. *Courtesy University of Louisville*

I've played with a loser all my life." The following season the Redskins dropped Super Bowl VII 14-7 to Bob Griese and Nick Buoniconti's Miami Dolphins.

Football fans too young to remember Alex Karras joyously careening about the gridiron surely will recognize him as a superbly talented performer in other arenas. An impressive film debut in "Paper Lion" led to his classic character "Mongo" in Mel Brooks' "Blazing Saddles." Additional credits include starring roles in the film "Victor-Victoria," the TV movie "Babe: The Story of Mildred Didrikson Zaharias"; the TV series "Webster," a stint on ABC's "Monday Night Football" and authorship of the book *"Even Big Guys Cry."*

Alex Karras—yet another Hoosier original.

In recent years former Hoosier high schoolers have continued to impact the NFL. Mark Clayton graduated from Indianapolis Cathedral High School in 1978 before attending the University of Louisville. Approaching his eighth season with the Miami Dolphins, Clayton has made nearly 400 catches for close to 6,500 yards and 60 TDs. Teaming with Mark Duper and Dan Marino, the four-time Pro Bowler gave Miami the most explosive NFL passing attack of the 1980s.

The 223rd pick of the 1983 draft, Clayton led the league with 18 touchdown receptions in 1984 and 14 in 1988. His four receptions for 95 yards and a TD led the Dolphins to a 45-38 rout of the Steelers in the 1984 AFC Championship Game. He followed that performance with a six-reception, 92-yard effort in Miami's 38-16 loss to San Francisco in Super Bowl XIX. Clayton also contributed three receptions good for 41 yards in Miami's 31-14 setback against New England for the 1985 AFC Championship.

Indianapolis North Central's Lars Tate signed with the University of Georgia as a highly recruited prep All-American. Following an all SEC collegiate career, Tate was selected by Tampa Bay with the 53rd pick in the 1988 NFL draft. To date, the bruising 6'2", 215 pound fullback has hammered the ball over 250 times for over 1,000 yards and 12 TDs.

One more to keep your eye on. Indianapolis Cathedral's Moe Gardner began the 1990 season as the odds-on favorite for the Outland Trophy, playing nose tackle for the University of Illinois.

Ya Still Can't Beat Fun at the Old Ball Park

The Modern Era of sports history has seen a relative decline in the popularity of baseball. Relative in the sense that the sport is no longer the unquestioned, unchallenged National Pastime. Professional football and increasingly, professional basketball, are now on a par with professional baseball in terms of media coverage and fan support. Intercollegiate football and basketball have replaced minor league baseball as the principle spectator sports in large portions of the country. Whereas in the heyday of minor league baseball there were over 1,000 teams in North America at any given time—Texas alone had nearly 100 teams during the 1920s and '30s—today there are fewer than 170 bush league ball clubs nationwide.

In addition to losing athletes to football and basketball, the minors lost to television as well. During the 1930s, '40s and '50s if a Hoosier had electricity and he had a radio, he might be able to tune in a Reds game, or the Cubs, or on particularly clear evenings the Pirates and Cards. He could sit by the radio listening through the static to great men far away or he could attend a game in his hometown Fort Wayne, Evansville, Indianapolis, Terre Haute, Richmond, South Bend, Muncie, Kokomo, Michigan City, Lafayette or Vincennes and watch Big League stars of the future. By the mid 1960s most Indiana fans could catch at least one Major League game a week on television. Today almost any baseball junky can watch a game a day on the tube—and three or four on the weekend. Former loyalists who kept countless bush league clubs afloat have become couch potatoes.

This is not to imply that baseball is a dying sport. Not at all. Major League teams drew over 30,000,000 paying customers last year, attesting to the game's vitality. The point made is that baseball is no longer the only game in town.

At the beginning of the Modern Age short-lived Midwest League (Class A) teams in Kokomo, Lafayette and Michigan City folded their tents never to reappear. More distressing to baseball traditionalists—and any true baseball fan is a traditionalist—was the collapse of minor league franchises in Terre Haute and Evansville.

In one incarnation or another, by one name or another, the Terre Haute Hottentots had fielded a team more or less continuously since 1902. Playing principally in the Class AA Three-I League (Illinois-Iowa-Indiana) and the AA Central League the Totts had seen a load of talent pass through Terre Haute.

The Hotentotts suspended operations in 1956, and were never able to restructure as the Three-I League collapsed in 1961.

The Evansville Triplets were an even more stable minor league franchise. Except for a few Depression and war years the Trips had fielded Central or Three-I teams since 1903. The demise of the Three-I took the Trips with it.

Evansville, however, was well established as a great baseball town, and in 1970 the Detroit Tigers established their principle farm club in the Ohio River community. The Pocket City joined Indianapolis, Omaha and Iowa (Des Moines) in the Eastern Division of the Class AAA American Association. The Tigers stayed in Evansville for fourteen seasons—until they moved the franchise to the larger city of Nashville, Tennessee in 1985.

The Triplets had some memorable moments during those fourteen years. Former Brave catcher Del Crandall managed the team in 1971, and in '72 he led them to the American Association pennant. Former Tiger third baseman Fred Hatfield managed the Trips to a second pennant in 1975. Current Pittsburgh Pirate manager Jim Leyland handled the team from 1979 through 1981. The Trips won a third Association title in Leyland's maiden season. Mark "The Bird" Fidrych, Ron LeFlore, Lance Parrish, Jack Morris, Kokomo's Tom and Pat Underwood, Tom Brookens, Bob Melvin and Glenn Wilson are a few of the Major Leaguers who spent significant time with the Evansville Triplets between 1970 and 1984.

A pleasant sporting development can be found in the recent resurrection of minor league baseball in the city of South Bend. The Northern Indiana community had fielded a Central League team at least as early as 1903 but had been without professional baseball since 1932—until the South Bend White Sox came to town. Since 1988 the Midwest League (Class A) farm team of the Chicago White Sox has been entertaining fans at Stanley Coveleski Stadium in downtown South Bend.

Hall of Famer Stan Coveleski spent the last fifty years of his life in South Bend. As a notorious spitballer, Stan won 214 games with Washington and Cleveland and put together a 2.84 lifetime ERA. In the '20 Series, Coveleski hurled three complete game victories in Cleveland's sweep of Brooklyn. Perhaps future legendary baseball doctors are perfecting their craft in the South Bend stadium that today bears the master's name.

The Indianapolis Indians; A Minor League Dynasty

The Indianapolis Indians Baseball Club has been in continuous operation since 1887. A charter member of the American Association (1902) they have enjoyed consistent success at the box office and on the field.

Highlights of Indian history in the Modern Era include:

1962: Beginning a six year affiliation with the Chicago White Sox, the Indians finish 89-58 and regular season American Association (A.A.) Champions. Former White Sox shortstop and Hall of Famer **Luke Appling** *is named A.A. Manager of the Year. Tribe pitcher* **Herb Score**, *attempting a comeback from the line-drive he took in the face in 1957, goes 10-7.*

1963-1968: The American Association suspends play for the first time since 1901. The Indians join the International League (1963) then the Pacific Coast League ('64-'68). The Tribe downs Atlanta for the '63 International League Pennant. Indianapolis third baseman **Don Buford** *is voted 1963 Minor League MVP.*

1968: The Tribe joins the Cincinnati organization and begins a sixteen-year relationship as principle developer of Big Red Machine talent. **Don Zimmer** *manages Indianapolis to a 66-78 record—twenty-seven games back of Warren Spahn's Tulsa squad.* **Hal McRae** *is named Tribe MVP.*

1969: The American Association is resurrected, and Indianapolis rejoins the league. Heavy financial losses result in a front office shake-up and the "personality conflict" resignation of club president **Ownie Bush**. *Victory Field is renamed Bush Stadium. The Reds pass over Double A Manager* **Sparky Anderson** *and name St. Louis Cardinals Coach* **Vern Rapp** *manager. Tribe outfielder* **Bernie Carbo** *is named Amer. Assoc. MVP.*

1974: **Vern Rapp** *is named American Association Manager of the Year for guiding the Indians to their second A.A. Eastern Division crown in four years. Tom Spencer, the season's team MVP is not destined to become as well known as three of the previous four Tribe MVPs:* **Ross Grimsley**, **Pedro Borbon** *and* **Ken Griffey**.

1982: Manager **George Scherger's** *Indians defeat Western Division Champion Omaha four games to two to capture the Tribe's first American Association Championship since 1956. Tribe outfielder* **Gary Redus** *hits .333 and leads the Association with 54 stolen bases. Fellow Indian outfielder* **Nick Esasky** *belts 27 round-trippers.*

1986: In the third year of their present affiliation with the Montreal Expos, the Indians capture the first of a Class AAA record four consecutive League Championships. **Billy Moore's** *bottom of the ninth, two-out, two-strike single off* **Rob Dibble** *scores* **Tom Romano** *and* **Casey Candeale** *for a 5-4 victory.* **Joe Sparks** *is named Minor League Manager of the Year.*

1987: The year of the "rabbit ball" sees the Tribe's **Pascual Perez** *lead the American Association with a 3.79 ERA.* **Joe Sparks** *claims his second consecutive American Association Manager of the Year Award as the Indians defeat Denver four games to one in the Championship Series.*

Indians Through the Ages

Tommy Agee, 1965
Joaquin Andujar, 1973-'74
Bo Belinsky, 1970
Kurt Bevacqua 1970-'71
Pedro Borbon, 1970-'71
"Three-fingers" Brown, 1919 *
Tim Burke, 1984
Owen J. Bush, 1908
Johnny Callison, 1958-'59
Norm Cash, 1958
Rocky Colavito, 1954-'55
Dave Concepcion, 1969
Buck Crouse, 1930
Mike Cuellar, 1961
Eric Davis, 1983
Dave DeBusschere, 1964-'65
John Dopson, 1985-'86
Dan Driessen, 1973
Rawley Eastwick, 1973-'75
Lee Elia, 1965-'67
Hod Eller, 1924
Jumbo Elliott, 1935
Kerby Farrell, 1944

Fat Freddie Fitzsimmons, 1922-'25
Tom Foley, 1981-'82
John Franco, 1983
Bob Friend, 1950
Andres Galarraga, 1985
Dick Grapenthin, 1984-'85
Gabby Harnett, 1942 *
Joe Hesketh, 1984
Oral Hildebrand, 1930-'31, '42
Jay Howell, 1979-'80
Harmon Killebrew, 1958 *
Ray Knight, 1973-'76
Jeff Lahti, 1981
Nap Lajoie, 1918 *
Bill Landrum, 1983
Charlie Leibrant, 1978-'79, '81
Al Lopez, 1948
Roger Maris, 1956
Rube Marquard, 1908 *
Gene Mauch, 1947
Eddie Milner, 1979-'81
Ed Montague, 1931
Russ Nixon, 1956

Ron Oester, 1977-'79
Claude Osteen, 1961
Wally Post, 1953
Eddie Roush, 1914 *
Amos "Thunderbolt" Rusie, 1889 *
Reb Russell, 1926-'29
Nelson Santovenia, 1985-'86
Dan Shatzeder, 1985
Herb Score, 1952-'54 and '62-'63
Razor Shines, 1984-'87
Frank Sigafoos, 1931-'34
Sebi Sisti, 1946
Mario Soto, 1977-'79
Champ Summers, 1978
Jay Tibbs, 1987
Dizzy Trout, 1935-'36
Bob Uecker, 1960
Pat Underwood, 1983
Johnny VanderMeer, 1940
Dallas Williams, 1982-'83 and '85-'87
Herm Winningham, 1985-'86
Joel Youngblood, 1973-'75
Pat Zachary, 1975-'75

et cetera
* = Member, Cooperstown Hall of Fame

1990 INDIANAPOLIS INDIANS—front row: (l to r) Houston, Castro, Mack, Paredes, Green, Bullock, Beltre, Marchok, Neely; second row: Schumacher, Johnson, Hodge, Kerrigan, Rivera, Cucjen, Marquez, Steels, Burleson; third row: Galvez, Chambers, Rojas, Thompson, Anderson, Gakeler, Dixon, Farmer, Davins, Fireovid; top row: Schneider, Doehrman, Clay, Braun, Goff, Lowry, Mohorcic, Spinosa, Schumacher, Madden.

MAX SCHUMACHER

One reason sports heroes achieve spectacularly on the playing fields is that there are also other kinds of sports heroes—less spectacular—in the offices back of the stands making it all possible.

Max Schumacher IS the Indianapolis Indians in several very specific ways. His thirty-three years with the A.A. club in a variety of management capacities has been one of the factors for the Indians' preeminent minor league success. He's now general manager. "I have always loved baseball," Shumacher says. "I can still remember the records of the Shortridge teams I played for—14-5 and 18-4."

Shumacher completed Butler, served in the army and then went to work for the Indians in '57. He met his wife in the ticket cage; she is a baseball enthusiast too, and their children grew up at Bush Stadium. "But I sat them behind the screen for safety and never let them run around bothering people. I am a firm believer in manners at sporting events."

Son Bruce is also involved in Indians' management as Director of Special Projects. "In this operation everybody does everything," Schumacher says. "I supervise the maintenance, smooth the way when the team is rained out, negotiate, drum up publicity. I talk to the Park Board to be sure the arrangements we have for the stadium are OK. I've sold tickets and taken care of the hot dogs in my time, too." Persistence and continuity are what it takes to make a minor league franchise work. "There were tough years—in '62 the American Association folded. We stuck it out and played in the Pacific Coast League, flying coast to coast. Finally the A.A. was resurrected."

"Minor league work has its rewards and frustrations. There is no big name recognition for the fans to hang on to and our players come through the league—up or out of baseball." There are many satisfactions, though—the club has its loyal advocates and many Hoosiers grew up as Indians rooters, with the whole family involved.

"300,000 people a year now are coming out to see the team," Schumacher continues, "and with all the special nights we sponsor and the degree of community and corporate support, it's pretty satisfying. I've had some tempting offers to move up myself, but Indianapolis—and Bush Stadium—are my home."

Hoosier State Scores with Baseball Greats

As has been the case since the earliest days of organized baseball, the Hoosier State has provided the Major Leagues with many of the finest players and many of the most intriguing personalities of the Modern Era. Robert Bartmess Friend of Lafayette had the misfortune of being one of the National League's top pitchers on one of Major League Baseball's worst teams. After one full year in the minors—split between Waco and Indianapolis—Friend was called up to the Pittsburgh Pirates in midseason, 1951.

From '51 through '65 he won 191 games for the Bucs. His 230 losses, however, rank tenth on the all time Major League futility list. With such hallowed names as Joe Garagiola, Woody Main, Johnny Lindell and the immortal Eddie Pellagrini the Bucs went 145-317 from 1952 through '54. In 1955 Bob earned the distinction of becoming the first player in National League history to lead the League in ERA while pitching for a last place team (2.83). In 1958 Friend's stablemate Harvey Haddix fired a no-hitter for eleven innings only to lose on a single in the twelfth. Friend lost 19 games to lead the NL in two different seasons.

But Bob Friend was a fine pitcher—an outstanding pitcher. If he had started with the Yankees in 1951 instead of finishing with them in 1966, he might be in the Hall of Fame today. In addition to leading the NL in ERA in '55, he was the league's top starter in 1956, '57 and '58, led in innings pitched in '56 and '57 and in victories in 1958 (22).

The Hoosier hurler's long wait for a team commensurate with his abilities finally came to an end during the Modern Age of sports. By 1960 the Pirates had acquired a few respectable athletes—guys with exotic names like Mazeroski, Clemente, "Smokey" and Elroy. The Bucs swept to a 95-59 record and into the World Series against the Yankees.

The '60 Series was one for the ages. The Bronx Bombers scored 55 runs and Whitey Ford tossed two shutouts. But Bill Mazeroski slammed a ninth-inning Ralph Terry offering over the left field ivy at Forbes Field in the seventh game and the Bucs claimed the World Championship.

The reward for which Bob Friend labored so long and so thanklessly had finally been delivered. Robert, unfortunately, had the unpleasant experience of witnessing the abilities of Mantle, Maris, Berra, Skowron, Richardson, Kubek, and company up close and personal. His contribution to the affair was an 0-2 slate with a 13.50 ERA in six innings pitched.

The humbling World Series performance didn't detract from Friend's reputation as one of baseball's finest pitchers. The winner of the '56 and '60 All-Star games and the loser of the '58 Mid-Summer Classic, Friend was named 1962 and '63 NL All-Star representative. In those seasons he won 18 games with a 3.04 ERA and 17 games with a sterling 2.34 ERA respectively.

In 1966 Bob Friend finally found himself pitching for NY baseball clubs. Unfortunately, he split the season with the ninth place Mets and the now lowly tenth place Yanks. Finding the territory all too familiar, Friend retired at the end of the season.

The most colorful Hoosier to bemuse the baseball powers-that-be since Judge Kenesaw Mountain Landis was born in Ensley, Alabama in 1918. But in 1934 Charles Oscar Finley moved to Gary, Indiana and in 1936 "Charley" Finley graduated from Horace Mann High School. A restless, aggressive sort from day one, Finley worked the brutal shifts demanded by Gary steel mills and still found time and energy to organize and play first base for the semi-pro Gary Merchants of the Indiana-Michigan Industrial Baseball League.

World War II found Charley working at a defense plant in LaPorte. He took a liking to the place and purchased a local 300-acre farm which was to grow into a 1,280-acre estate. Finley's presence and influence may explain why LaPorte has become the unquestioned hotbed of Indiana high school baseball over the past three decades.

After spending nearly three years in a Crown Point hospital recuperating from tuberculosis, Finley began his own insurance company in 1949 to market a group liability policy he had developed during his convalescence. The resulting $40-odd million gross provided the basis for launching Charley Finley into one of the most turbulent roller-coaster careers in American sports history. In December of 1960, Finley acquired 52% of the Kansas City Athletics for the paltry sum of $1.975 million. He moved the club to Oakland in '68, and began building one of baseball's most powerful and engaging dynasties.

With the possible exception of Bill Veeck, Charley Finley has been baseball's premier innovator. Start with Reggie Jackson, Sal Bando, Bert Campenaris, Rollie Fingers, Vida Blue, Blue Moon Odom, Catfish Hunter, Joe Rudi and Ken Holtzman. Put ' em in handlebar moustaches and

Charley O. Finley—Father of the designated hitter. Courtesy Baseball Hall of Fame.

green and gold double-knit uniforms with "matching" white kangaroo shoes. Play your home games on a field with pink florescent foul poles. Hire a shepherd and his flock of sheep to keep the infield grass cropped. Turn the left field foul area into a picnic grounds and institute an annual "Hot Pants Night"—what have you got? The best team in baseball AND the most controversial team in baseball. A natural born PR man's fantasy.

In 1964 Finley was one of the first baseball men to suggest that World Series games be played at night to increase the audience. He was roundly booed by the sport's multitude of traditionalists. But, night World Series baseball wasn't nearly as sacreligious as say, the designated hitter. In 1972 Charley Finley's Oakland "A"'s won the first World Series game played at night. They would win several more. The A's were American League West Champs from 1971 to 1975 and World Champions in 1972, '73 and '74.

Charley Finley, however, was neither completely successful in his athletic endeavors or universally respected throughout the American sporting community. His Memphis Tams of the American Basketball Association went 24-60 in 1972-'73, lost half a million dollars and folded. He had a similar experience with the California Seals of the NHL.

The more publicized trials and tribulations of Charley Finley involved his ongoing feuds with his players and with the then Commissioner of Baseball, Bowie Kuhn. In 1972 Kuhn fined Finley $2,500 for violating the Major League prohibition against offering player performance bonuses during the World Series. The following season Finley absorbed a $7,000 levy for coercing Mike Andrews into signing a false medical disability report. Finley had become enraged when Andrews made three errors in one World Series game and was trying to replace the veteran infielder on the A's roster with Manny Trillio. Kuhn had already ruled against the move prior to the three-error game and subsequently meted out the fine as punishment for the shabby ruse.

Finley's most profound and long-lasting impact on baseball resulted from his 1974 failure to observe a deferred payment clause in Catfish Hunter's contract. An arbitration panel consequently ruled Hunter a free agent, and the era of athletic free agency was born. Perhaps future historians may mark this event as the true beginning of the Modern Era in American sports.

Charley O. responded to the loss of Catfish Hunter to the NY Yankees by attempting to sell Reggie Jackson, Vida Blue and Bert Campenaris for cash. Finley maintained that he was attempting to get some value for the inevitable free agents before they jumped ship. Commissioner Kuhn vetoed the fire sale; the three in question did in fact abandon the A's and a long franchise slide into mediocrity began—a slide that would not be reversed prior to Finley's sale of the club in 1982.

Opinions on Finley as a businessman and as a person varied wildly. Former A's coach Vern Hoscheit proclaimed Charley "the fairest man I've ever worked for in baseball."

In Reggie Jackson, Charley Finley found a man who could match him ability for ability, ambition for ambition and ego for ego. RJ on CF: "I told Dave Duncan that Finley treated his black players like niggers. Dave told me not to worry or feel hurt. He said Charley treats his white players like niggers too." A man famous for his pride, "Mr. October" nonetheless acquiesced to work for Finley long enough to collect three World Series rings and several million dollars.

Wells Twombly of the *New York Times* summed up the complexities of Charley Finley as well as anyone can.

"Never has there been anyone in baseball to match Charles O. Finley. He is capable of great generosity and great parsimony. He is at once earthy and capable of the grand gesture. He does not like to be corrected, defied or challenged. He loves the game of baseball with an overriding passion, and yet there is hardly anyone in it he hasn't offended."

Charles Oscar Finley—from the steel mills of Gary to the bright lights of Gotham City, yet another Hoosier original.

Meanwhile, Back on the Diamond

Paul W. Splittorff, Jr. set an American League mark in 1982 that he would probably just as well forget. Splittorff started 28 games for the Kansas City Royals in '82 and failed to complete any of them. Like Bob Friend, however, this Evansville native was one of Major League Baseball's premier hurlers throughout much of his long career.

Splittorff went 20-11 in 1973, 19-13 in 1978 and his .727 winning percentage (16-6) led the AL in 1977. Paul went to the mound a total of six times for the Royals in the 1973, '77, '78, and '80 American League Championship Series (ALCS) and compiled an outstanding 2-0 record with a 2.68 ALCS ERA. The Royals of the late '70s, however, were annual bridesmaids to the Yankees, and Splittorff's World Series' experience was limited to one ineffectual outing in the 1980 Royals' Series loss to the Philadelphia Phillies. Paul finished his sixteen-year Major League career in 1984 with 166 lifetime victories.

Ron Reed of LaPorte is a contemporary of Paul Splittorff's, and he enjoyed similar baseball success. A true Hoosier through and through, Reed left the heart of Hoosier baseball country in 1961 to attend the University of Notre Dame on a basketball scholarship. He was drafted by the Detroit Pistons on the third round of the 1965 NBA draft, and from '65 through '67 averaged 8.1 points and 6.5 rebounds a game as a forward for the Motor City franchise.

Probably because he was from LaPorte, Reed was torn between his love of basketball and his obsession with baseball. In 1966 baseball won out. During an eighteen-year career with the Braves, Cardinals, Phillies and White Sox, Reed threw 2,476 innings in 751 games. He lodged 146 victories against 140 defeats and tossed in 103 saves for good measure.

Reed tied a National League record for fewest home runs in a season (250 or more innings pitched), when he served up only five gopher balls in 1975. His All-Star experience was as memorable as it was limited. In 1968 Ron relieved Tom Seaver and retired the only two All-Star batters he ever faced, as the National League posted the Classic's single 1-0 victory.

Reed's National League Championship Series (NLCS) and World Series experience is considerably more extensive. A member of the Hank Aaron-led Atlanta Braves and the powerhouse Schmidt-Luzinski-Bowa-and, later, Rose Philadelphia Phils, Reed pitched in the 1969, '76, '77, '78, '80 and '83 NLCS. The six participations place Reed in a tie for first in number of Championship Series pitched. Appearing principally in relief, his NLCS slate reads 0-2 in thirteen games.

The Phillies were successful in the 1980 and '83 NLCS and in five World Series appearances, Reed served as Tug McGraw's principle setup man—logging a shining 1.69 Series ERA. The Phils split the two Series defeating Kansas City (and Paul Splittorff) in 1980 and losing to Baltimore (which still had Tim Stoddard on the roster though he did not pitch) in '83.

Ron Reed set out to be just another run-of-the-mill Hoosier basketball superstar and ended up as one of Indiana's finest contributions to the American Pastime.

Speaking of basketball superstars—don't ever challenge Tommy John to a game of one-on-one. Howard Sharpe is the winningest coach in Indiana high school basketball history, and in 1961 the best player on Sharpe's Terre Haute Gerstmeyer "Black Cats" was a senior named Thomas Edward John. Following graduation the 6'3" forward intended to enroll at his hometown Indiana State Teacher's College as a basketball/baseball player. The Cleveland Indians disrupted all intentions by selecting him in the '61 Major League draft. A promising basketball career was thus ended, and a likely Hall of Fame baseball career was thus launched.

During a Major League record, twenty-six years on the mound with the Indians, White Sox, Dodgers, Yankees and Angels between 1963-1989, Tommy John won 288 games with a lifetime ERA of 3.34. He fired 4,702.3 innings in 760 outings, posted 46 shutouts and K'ed 2,245 batters. John tied for the American League lead in shutouts with five in 1966 and six in 1976. He led the AL with six blanks in 1980. The owner of a wicked curve ball, John also led the AL with 17 wild pitches in 1970 and tied a league record by beaning four batters in one nine-inning game

Miracle man Tommy John of the Yankees. Courtesy Baseball Hall of Fame.

(1968). The three errors he committed in the fourth inning of a 1988 game also tied him with numerous other AL pitchers for the league record in that memorable single-inning category.

Tommy John was a member of the 1968, '79 and '80 American and 1978 National League All-Star squads. In seven League Championship Series appearances over five seasons, he compiled a 4-1 record with a magnificent 2.08 ERA for the Dodgers, Angels and Yankees. He shares Championship Series records for most games won (4), consecutive games won (4) and most wild pitches (2). John shares NLCS records for most complete games in total Series (2) and most hit batsmen in one Series (2). He also holds Championship records for most wild pitches total Series(4) one Series (3) and game (3). If you weren't nervous hitting against Tommy John, you'd probably already taken too many beanings without a helmet.

John's World Series experience is both unique and bizarre. In 1977 and '78, he pitched for Dodger teams that lost the Series to the Yanks. In

1981 he threw for a Yankee team that finished second to—you guessed it—the LA Dodgers. The Terre Haute hurler was in no way responsible for this strange turn of events. In six World Series appearances he won two games and lost one while compiling a fine 2.67 Series ERA.

If John's career had ended in 1975 it would have been a proud run. If he had retired in 1989 after twenty-six injury-free seasons, this would have been a magnificent showing. But an injury did occur, and the pitcher's recovery from that setback makes the Tommy John story one of the most phenomenal in American sports history.

In 1975 a tendon in John's left arm—his pitching arm—popped. It appeared the hurler's career was over; that is, until a doctor persuaded John to undergo an experimental operation. A tendon from the pitcher's right arm was removed and transplanted into the left arm. There was little certainty that the arm would ever again be fully functional—let alone fit to pitch in the Major Leagues.

After a year of constant, strenuous rehabilitation, Tommy John returned to the Los Angeles Dodgers. On the surface the 10-10 record wasn't stupendous, but it was in reality a miracle. It earned John the 1976 Major League Comeback Player of the Year Award. The 20-7 record the following season was inconceivable. John pitched in five League Championship Series, three World Series and three All-Star games AFTER undergoing what is now commonly referred to as the "Tommy John Operation."

No other facet of sport has undergone more revolutionary change over the past twenty years than has the field of sports medicine. Tommy John's name will forever be associated with a most fortuitous development in this promising field.

South Bend shortstop Dickie Thon is a second outstanding Hoosier baseball player who nearly had his career ended by injury. Thon's tragic accident also endangered his life.

In 1984 Dickie Thon was the premier shortstop in the National League. Playing for Houston he led the NL in triples with 10 in 1982. In 1983, he came into his own. His 18 game-winning RBIs led the NL as did his 533 assists. He hit 20 home runs, drove in 79 runners and stole 34 bases while batting .286—prodigious numbers for a slick-fielding shortstop. Thon went one for three in the 1983 All-Star Game. At the age of twenty-five, his potential seemed limitless.

Then in the fifth game of the 1984 season a Mike Torrez fastball caught the Hoosier athlete

The pride of the Pocket City, Don Mattingly. Courtesy Baseball Hall of Fame.

square in the left eye. Thon's season was over. After several weeks of concern, baseball fans were relieved to learn that the Astro shortstop would not lose sight in the injured eye, but it appeared his career had ended.

It's easy to overstate the benefits of sport. Competition does teach perseverance and fortitude in the face of adversity, but Dickie Thon is likely to have persevered regardless of his avocation. After five years of blurred vision, uncertainty and periodic minor league rehabilitation, Thon is back at the top of his profession. In 1989 the Philly shortstop hit .271 with 15 homers and 60 RBIs. His .972 fielding average was the best of his career.

Dickie Thon may never be an All-Star again. He'll never reach the Hall of Fame. But he is a survivor, and he is a shortstop in the Big Show.

One current Hoosier Major Leaguer who's a shoe-in for the Hall of Fame is Donald Arthur Mattingly of Evansville. Despite the Looney Tune experience of playing eight seasons in Yankee Stadium for George Steinbrenner, Don Mattingly has become the most consistent hitter in the American League.

Since being called up from Columbus (Ohio) at the end of the 1982 season, the Yankee first baseman has set Major League records for most home runs in seven consecutive games (9) and eight consecutive games (10). His six grand slams in 1987 is also a Major League record. Mattingly also shares Major League records for most doubles in an inning (2), most sacrifice flies in one game (3) and most put-outs by a first baseman in a nine-inning game (22).

Mattingly holds American League records for most at-bats by a lefthander in one season (677) and most consecutive games with one or more extra base hits (10).

In one or more seasons, Mattingly has led the American League in RBIs, total bases, slugging percentage, doubles, game winning RBIs, sacrifice flies, hits, batting average, fielding percentage and put-outs. He has slugged more than 30 homers three times, driven in 100 or more runs five times and hit over .300 in six seasons—including .343 in 1984 and .352 in 1986. This kind of thing goes on to great length, but you get the picture. He was named American League MVP in 1984, '85 and '86 and *Sporting News* Player of the Year in 1985. He has been the American League All-Star first baseman since 1984. He surpassed 1,400 hits, 170 home runs and 750 RBIs—all of this before he was 30.

Now that Steinbrenner can't sell him to the Taiyo Whales for one hundred pounds of sushi, Don Mattingly will take his place at Cooperstown alongside the other Bronx Bombers: Ruth, Gehrig, Dimaggio, Mantle . . . .

A Rookie of the Year Named Kittie?

A second Hoosier power-hitter to make it to the Majors in 1982 is former White Sox outfielder Ron Kittle of Gary. In fact, in 1983 there was a great deal of debate about which Indianan could look forward to a finer career, Kittle or Mattingly. Kittle had led the Eastern and Pacific Coast Leagues with 90 home runs and 247 RBIs over the 1981 and '82 seasons combined. After a cup a coffee with Chicago in '82, he joined the Sox full time at the beginning of the 1983 season. With 35 homers and 100 RBIs to his credit, the '83 Rookie of the Year balloting was a mere formality.

The ensuing years haven't been quite as kind to "Kittie." The modern athlete's bugaboo—recurring knee problems—has become a familiar part of his routine. Two disability rehab assignments to the minors and a year as a designated hitter have limited the 1983 AL All-Star's overall effectiveness. Save the tears, though. Back in the White Sox outfield after stops in Cleveland and Yankee Stadium, Kittle hit a career best .302 in '89. With 156 career homers and 407 RBI's Ron appears to be in the middle of a fine Big League career. His 1990 mid-season trade to the Orioles prevented him from making an on-going contribution to the Pale Hose surprising run for the pennant in their final season at ancient Comiskey Park.

"Now playing first base—Walleeee Johnson." *Courtesy Indiana State University.*

Coach Bob Warn and the Sycamores

The baseball portion of this book would be incomplete without some mention of the success Coach Bob Warn has had with the Indiana State University Sycamores. Since 1976, Coach Warn has led ISU to nearly 600 victories and six NCAA Tournament appearances. In 1986 the Sycamores advanced to the College World Series (final round of eight) before falling to perennial collegiate powerhouses Florida State and Oklahoma State.

One of the few baseball schools north of the Mason-Dixon Line, Indiana State can point to over forty former players who have signed professional contracts since 1977. Among those alumni are Major Leaguers Dick Grapenthin (P/W.Sox), Zane Smith (P/Expos), Brian Dorsett (C/Yankees) and Wallace Johnson (1B/Expos).

Wally Johnson of Gary was also a fan favorite on the Indianapolis Indians' 1986 American Association Champions. "And now . . . batting third . . . first baseman . . . Waaaleee Johnson!" Playing behind another former Indian (Andres Galarraga) at Montreal, Johnson hasn't had a great deal of opportunity at first base with the Expos. He did, however, turn himself into one of the most dependable pinch-hitters in the National League—a difficult, valuable and much appreciated role on any Major League team.

It can be expected that the Indiana State Sycamores of Coach Bob Warn will continue to dominate Midwestern collegiate baseball while providing talented college graduates for the Major Leagues.

The Greatest Single-Day Sporting Event in the World

The Indianapolis "500" entered the Modern Era of American sports history with a roar and a crash. The roar came from Jim Rathman's Ken-Paul Offy. His 138.767 MPH winning average in 1960 set a new track record. The $369,150 total prize money also set a new "500" standard. The crash—a horrible one—emanated from the collapse of a homemade scaffold that sent 125 spectators sprawling into the infield grass. Two Race fans were killed and forty were injured in the disaster.

The 1960s were historic years for the Indianapolis "500." The event enjoyed its most dramatic growth to that time during this tumultuous decade of communes and Vietnam protests. Record speeds, record purses and record crowds became yearly expectations.

During the early portion of the decade, the changing of the guard that had begun during the '50s accelerated. A.J. Foyt captured his first Indianapolis "500" in 1961 with a record 139.130 MPH average speed. In what would become an unfortunate trend, A.J.'s victory was marred by a tragic crash. One of the "500"'s most popular drivers, Monrovia's "Tony" Bettenhausen, flipped his racer during a practice run. The twenty-eighth time Bettenhausen had been upside-down in a moving Indy car was his last. Tony was 1961's only fatality, but the name Bettenhausen would remain one of the "500"'s most familiar. Eldest son Gary has been a perennial contender since the late '60s. Tony's youngest son and namesake Tony, Jr., has been a Speedway regular since 1981. Indy car racing has its own royal bloodlines.

Foyt's 1964 victory—his second at Indy—was also overshadowed by a historic calamity. An estimated 300,000 fans crowded the IMS in hopes of witnessing the fastest "500" ever. On turn four of lap two, a seven car pile-up sent a roiling cloud of black smoke billowing hundreds of feet into the air. Drivers Dave MacDonald and Eddie Sachs were burned alive in front of thousands of horrified Race fans—many of whom vowed never to return.

Eddie Sachs was probably the most popular driver to ever compete at Indy. Dubbed "The Clown Prince of Auto Racing," Sachs was known to fans and drivers alike for his good-natured wise cracks and gentle practical jokes.

The horror of and revulsion toward Sach's death culminated in one of the "500"'s most significant reforms. During the summer of '64, USAC and IMS management mandated that gasoline be replaced by less volatile, more stable, cooler burning alcohol as the fuel for all Indy cars. This directive remains in effect today.

As the switch to alcohol fuel exemplified, the 1960s were years of innovation and technical advancements. Owner Andy Granatelli's STP Oil Treatment Special seemed like a sure bet in 1967. Piloted by '63 champ Parnelli Jones, the revolutionary turbine-powered car led for 171 laps. A "silent-running" and bizzarely-shaped vehicle, the turbo was variously dubbed the "Silent Screamer," the "Wooshmobile" and the "Pregnant Porpoise." Parnelli had a fifty-second lead on A.J. Foyt less than ten miles from the checkered flag when a six-dollar ball bearing failed in

---

Sid Collins "The Voice of the '500'" broadcast this eulogy of Eddie Sachs to millions of radio listeners

Some men try to conquer life in a number of ways—these days of our outer space attempts—some men try to conquer the universe—race car drivers are courageous men who try to conquer life and death and they calculate their risks ... A race driver who leaves this earth mentally when he straps himself into the cockpit—to try for what to him—is the biggest conquest he can make—is aware of the odds and Eddie Sachs played the odds. He was serious and frivolous. He was fun. He was a wonderful gentle man. He took much needling and he gave much needling ... We are all speeding toward death at the rate of sixty minutes every hour—the only difference is—we don't know how to speed faster and Eddie Sachs did. And so since death has a thousand or more doors—Eddie Sachs exits this earth in a race car—knowing Eddie—I assume that's the way he would have wanted it ...

At the age of thirty-seven, Eddie Sachs left a widow and two small children. The Race resumed one hour and forty-three minutes after the crash.

A.J. Foyt positions himself to take the lead in '61. Indy "500" Photos.

the drive line, forcing the STP Special from The Race. A.J. picked his way through a five-car, last lap pile-up and crossed the finish line at 50 MPH for his third Indy victory. His average speed was a bit faster—151.207 MPH—for a new track record.

Improvements in IMS amenities also continued throughout the decade, as ever increasing throngs of Race fans demanded ever increasing facilities to accommodate them. The additional bleachers Tony Hulman added in 1968 brought permanent seating capacity to 204,000. That number, of course, took no note of the throngs that jammed the "Snake Pit" and other infamous infield haunts. Race Day attendance invariably topped the 300,000 mark by decade's end.

Everyone associated with the Indy "500" eagerly looked to the 1970s as a decade of promise. As all should have anticipated, the '70s were to be years of victory and glory, but also tragedy at the Indianapolis Motor Speedway.

The 1970s got off to a blazing start when Al Unser, Sr. captured the '70 pole with a record 170.221 MPH. "Big Al" went on to lead 190 of the 200 laps to capture his first Indy crown. Unser's $271,697 cut of the "500"'s first million dollar purse ($1,000,002.22) was more than double the total purse offered in Tony Hulman's first year of Speedway ownership. The $1,000,000 purse would essentially hold steady throughout the decade.

As Race Day approached in 1973, most Hoosiers, perhaps, had begun to take the "500" for granted. Indy had been an annual event for most of the six previous decades, and the days of horrendous body counts seemed to be memories from the distant past. The '73 Indy "500" brought the Hoosier State back to reality. The "500" was a spectacle—an awesome display of technical acumen—and it still retained the power to kill.

Driver Art Pollard became the year's first fatality when his racer flipped upside-down in the second turn during qualifications. On Race Day Number One, Salt Walther and Jerry Grant bumped at the green flag, setting off a twelve-car pile-up. Walther slammed into the outside wall, spewing flaming fuel and debris into the crowd. Thirteen Race fans required medical attention. A persistent rain soon halted The Race and aborted an attempted start the following day.

Wednesday, May 30—Race Day Number Three—proved to be the worst day of all. Driver Swede Savage slammed the fourth turn's inside wall and was fatally injured in the resultant fiery crash. Armando Teran, a crewman for driver Graham McRae, was struck and killed by an emergency vehicle speeding the wrong way through the pits attempting to rush to the Swede Savage crash site.

A torrential downpour after 332.5 miles finally—mercifully—forced the cancellation of the remaining 67 laps. Gordon Johncock was declared the winner while sitting in the pits under the red flag. The three-day race was the longest in Indianapolis history and the deadliest since 1937.

Nine years later Gordie Johncock would capture his second "500" defeating Rick Mears by 0.16 of a second in the closest Indy finish in history. But in 1973 the "Old Brickyard" reminded everyone again what a deadly serious game the Indianapolis "500" can be.

1977. What a great year it was for racing. '77 was the year for firsts. Pole-sitting Tom Sneva became the first to turn a 200 MPH qualifying lap-

188

The voice of the Indianapolis "500," Sid Collins. Indy "500 Photos."

A 1939 graduate of Indianapolis Shortridge High School, Sid Collins did as much to popularize and internationalize the Indianapolis "500" as any single person. He began his radio career at WKMO (WIOS) Kokomo in 1946. In 1948 he became the Race's south turn announcer for WIBC Indianapolis. When live lap-by-lap "500" coverage began in 1952, Collins was named Chief Announcer for WIBC, the Indianapolis Motor Speedway Network's flagship station.

Collins was well respected for the tedious research he conducted in preparation for the four hour broadcast. His extensive card file on drivers, mechanics, cars and minute history provided colorful coverage as The Race unfolded or during times of rain or cleanup delay. His tireless promotion and colorful reportage led to the expansion of the IMS Network from twenty-six stations in 1952 to 1,200 US stations, the Armed Forces Radio Network and numerous foreign translating stations by 1976. Over 100,000,000 listeners world-wide were familiar with Collin's stirring admonition, "Stay tuned for the Greatest Spectacle in Racing!"

Sid Collins was a twelve-time winner of the Indianapolis Press Club award for Sportscasting and a nine-time winner of the American Auto Racing Writers and Broadcasters award for best National Auto Racing Broadcast.

The year 1977 perhaps more than any other epitomized the agony and the ecstasy that is the Indianapolis "500." Sid Collins, the admired "Voice of the '500'" had become despondent over his long, painful, losing battle with Lou Gehrig's disease. On May 2—barely a week prior to qualifications—Collins ended his ordeal through suicide.

hitting 200.535. Janet Guthrie bacame the first woman to drive in the "500"—qualifying 26th and finishing 29th. Guthrie would return to Indy in 1978 and 1979—finishing ninth in '78. And, A.J. Foyt finished first to become the first four-time winner at Indy when he pushed his Gilmore Foyt to a scorching 161.331 MPH average speed.

What a great year for racing, but what a sad year for race fans. On October 27, at the age of seventy-six, Tony Hulman passed away. During three decades of IMS ownership Hulman had developed a reputation as a modest, quiet, almost shy man. An unpolished public speaker given to punctuating his speech with numerous "ahs" and "ums," he projected a folksy, humorous, Midwestern image that greatly enhanced the Speedway's popularity.

Tony and his self-described "band of yokels"— Wilbur Shaw, Leo Marshall, J.R. Cloutier and J.L. Quinn—took the IMS from a ramshackle ruin on the verge of abandonment and transformed it into the home of the world's largest single-day sporting event. In the last year of Hulman's ownership the Speedway drew over 500,000 fans during the month of May. A record purse of over $1.1 million dollars was awarded in 1977.

Former Democratic National Chairman and Indianapolis banker Frank E. McKinney, Sr. summarized Hulman's contribution in this way:

I see Tony Hulman as the very essence of the spirit that has made Indiana great. His broad horizons encompass every facet of worthwhile activity and affect every citizen of the Hoosier State. Tony Hulman is at the same time a product and a stalwart builder of our Indiana heritage.

1977 was a great year for racing, but there's been something missing ever since.

Give Us Your Tires, Your Porsches, Your Huddled Drivers Yearning to Breathe Fees

Indy Car racing is a sport for those residing in the fastest of all fast lanes. Pausing only briefly to note the passing of Tony Hulman and Sid Collins, the Indianapolis Motor Speedway and the Indianapolis "500" roared into the 1980s. The decade witnessed a literal explosion in the growth and popularity of The Race.

Relative newcomers like Rick Mears, Danny Sullivan and Bobby Rahal came to dominate Indy. Mears' Pennzoil Cosworth clocked a winning 163.612 MPH average in 1984 to erase Mark Donohue's twelve-year-old mark. Rahal's 170.722 obliterated Mears' record a scant two years later. "Rocket Rick's 223.855 MPH qualifying record, set in 1989, lasted all of one year.

Old familiar names cropped up at the Speedway every year throughout the '80s, but in many cases they belonged to second and even third generation Indy Car drivers. Al Unser, Jr., Tony Bettenhausen, Jr., Billy Vukovich III, and cousins Michael, John, and Jeff Andretti are but a few of the top drivers who came to Indy during the '80s to carry-on racing's royal bloodlines.

A phenomenon of the 1980s was the proliferation of foreign drivers as leading contenders at Indy. Not since the early French domination of Jules Goux, Rene Thomas and Dario Resta has the Old Brickyard seen such an invasion of mighty foreigners. As live international television broadcasts have joined with the IMS Radio Network to bring The Race into the homes of even more millions world-wide, victory in the "500" has become a prize sought by athletes from around the globe.

A short list of foreign-born drivers who have contended at Indy during the '80s would include at least: Roberto Guerrero, Josele Garza, Raul Boesel, Teo Fabi, Jim Crawford and Derek Daley. 1989 Co-Rookies of the Year John Jones and Bernard Jordain are Canadian and Mexican citizens respectively. '89 Champion Emerson Fittipaldi hails from Sao Paulo, Brazil. Perhaps IMS Chief Steward Tom Binford should consider rechristening the Brickyard the Indianapolis International Motor Speedway.

Though Fittipaldi's record 225.301 captured the '90 pole and stamped him as the Race favorite, it was the "500" performance of Dutchman Arie Luyendyk that had long time Race fans mumbling to themselves weeks later.

Luyendyk's 185.981 MPH average Race speed obliterated Bobby Rahal's four-year-old record by an incomprehensible 15 MPH. The Race was over in 2 hours, 41 minutes, 18.404 seconds. Race fans barely had time for a second piece of chicken, let alone a second six-pack.

Major renovations continued at the IMS throughout the '80s. In 1984 31,000 permanent seats were added. Recent construction has pushed reserve seating capacity over the 1/4 million mark. Along with the infield hordes, yearly Race Day attendance is estimated to top the 400,000 mark. Nearly 1,000,000 Race fans visit the track every May for practice, qualifications, sun-bathing, beer-drinking, Kentucky Fried

To the Winner Goes the Prize...

No statistic better exemplifies the tremendous growth of the Indianapolis "500" during the 1980s than does the meteoric rise in the Total Prize Money Awarded annually.

Year	Amount	Year	Amount
1980	$1,503,225	1986	4,001,450
1981	1,605,375	1987	4,490,375
1982	2,067,575	1988	5,025,400
1983	2,411,450	1989	5,723,725
1984	2,795,899	1990	6,325,803
1985	3,271,025		

The $1,090,940 won by Arie Luyendyk in 1990 was more than twenty times the entire $50,000 purse offered annually during the earliest years of the "500." Gary Bettenhausen collected $101,903 for completing no laps and finishing 33rd in 1989—$13,000 less than the Total Purse offered by Tony Hulman in 1946.

Chicken-eating, girl-watching (and boy-watching) and—oh yes—to witness "The Greatest Spectacle in Racing." There are corporate suites costing tens of thousands of dollars to reserve and appoint. On the other hand, you can rent a patch of infield grass for fifteen bucks. Some Race Fans arrive in Lear Jets. Some buy $100 clunkers to be abandoned on the infield. The Indianapolis "500" has become part of the culture. The Race is part of what America is.

A few things can be guaranteed as the years go along. Veteran sportscaster Tom Carnegie will shout "Heeeess On It!"—followed two minutes later by "Aaaannd it's a New Track Record!." A.J. Foyt will mutter "This is Jus' Ridikulus." Disc-jockies will make rude jokes about Linda Vaughn. Someone will command "Gentlemen Start Your Engines!" And "The Greatest Spectacle in Racing" will be on again.

Brownsburg, Indiana's Pancho Carter. Indy "500" Photos.

Still More "500" Facts

1965: Scotsman Jimmy Clark becomes the first to break the 150 MPH average Race speed barrier when his rear-engine Lotas-Ford clocks a 150.686. Rookie-of-the-Year Mario Andretti finishes a strong third. Fellow rookies Gordon Johncock and Al Unser, Sr. finish fifth and ninth respectively.

1969: Hard luck driver and crowd favorite Mario Andretti wins his only Indy "500" when he pilots owner Andy Granatelli's STP Oil Treatment Special to victory with a record 156.867 MPH average.

1971: The Dodge pace car driven by Indianapolis car dealer Eldon Palmer spins out of control in the pit area and slams into a photographers stand injuring twenty-two. All future pace cars are to be driven by professional drivers. Al Unser Sr. wins his second consecutive race—one of six Indy "500s" won by the Unser brothers, Al and Bobby.

1979: The Championship Auto Racing Team (CART) is formed in response to dissatisfaction over USAC's running of the "500." It takes a court order to allow CART drivers Al and Bobby Unser, Johnny Rutherford, Danny Ongais, Gordon Johncock, Steve Krisiloff and Wally Dallenbach the right to qualify. A second court mandates an extra day of quals in response to confusion over turbo-charger specifications. "Rocket Rick" Mears captures his first "500" — averaging 150.899 MPH.

1980: Starting on the pole, "Lone Star J.R." Johnny Rutherford becomes the sixth driver in "500" history to take a third trip to Victory Lane. Tom Sneva comes from thirty-third to finish runner-up for the third time.

1981: Bobby Unser takes the checkered flag on May 24th. On May 25th USAC declares Mario Andretti the victor after penalizing Unser a lap for passing on the yellow. Five months later, on October 8th, a USAC Board of Appeals reinstates Unser's victory by a 2-1 vote. At the age of forty-seven, Unser is the seventh three-time winner and is the oldest driver to ever capture Indy.

1986: In a record setting Indy "500" Bobby Rahal drives his Budweiser Truesports March to a blazing 170.722 MPH average speed. Over a dozen Race speed records are set in '86 including averages for 10, 25, 200, 400 and 500 miles.

1989: In one of the most exciting Indy "500s" in history, Emerson Fittipaldi outduels Al Unser, Jr. in a dash to the Finish Line. Racing side-by-side, Emmo and Little Al bump in turn three on the last lap. Unser spins and slams the outer wall. Emmo picks his way through the resulting chaos and glides the final mile to Victory Lane.

The Indianapolis Motor Speedway covers 559 acres and features a two-and-a-half-mile oval track. Each year fans leave approximately 1,300 cubic yards of litter on Race Day. Many of the over 6,000 people employed at the IMS during the month of May are charged with cleaning up this mess.

Over the course of the past three decades the opportunities for participating in a myriad of competitive sports have skyrocketed. The following photo gallery provides a brief introduction to the vast host of Hoosiers who have contributed to the development of an American sports culture.

**GALLERY
OF GREATS**

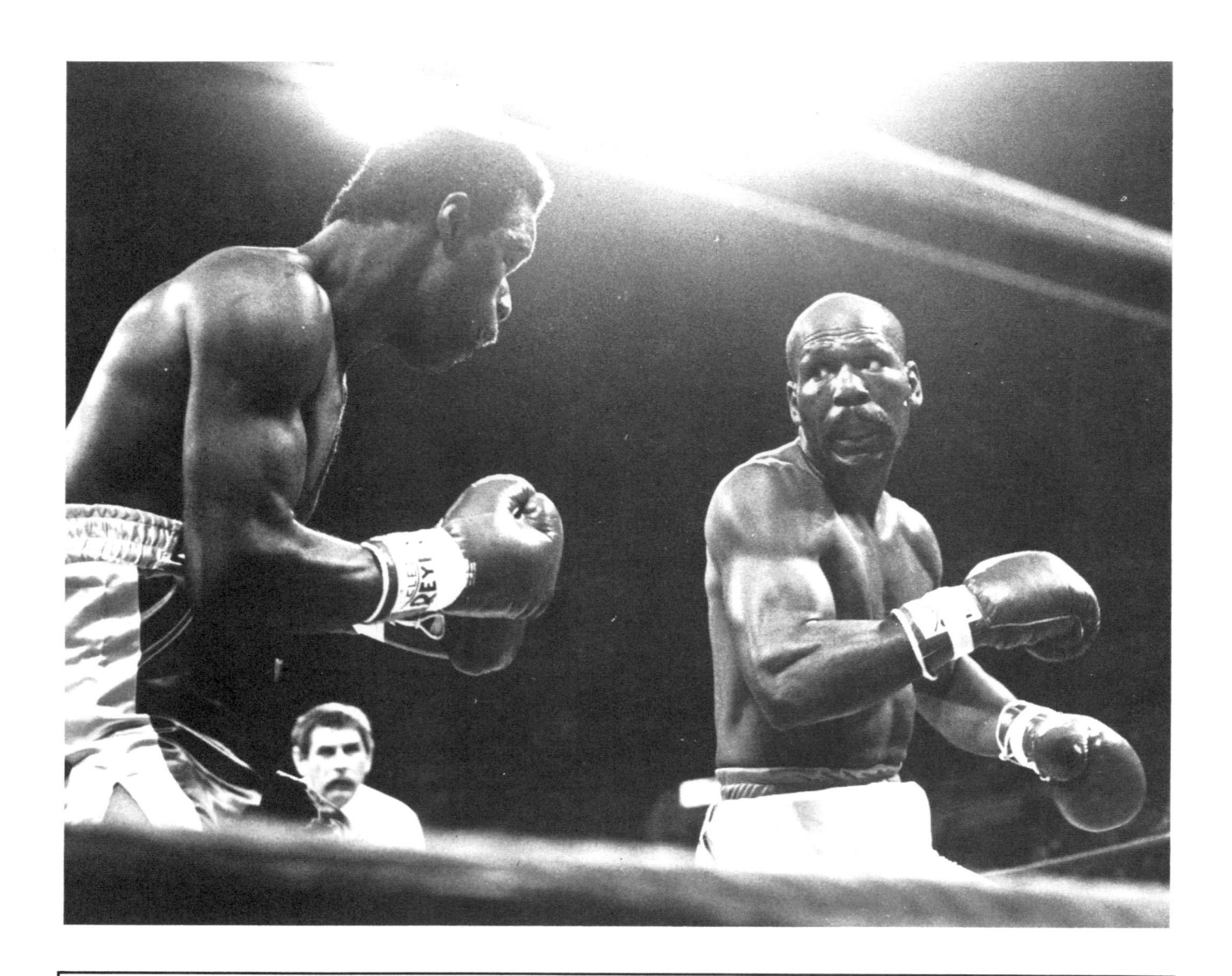

As a junior at Indianapolis Crispus Attucks High School, Marvin Johnson captured the 1970 National Golden Gloves Middleweight Championship. Two years later, at the age of eighteen, Johnson won the Middleweight Bronze Medal at the Munich Olympics.

In 1978 Marvin Johnson knocked out Matte Parlov to win the World Boxing Council (WBC) Light Heavyweight Crown. The Indy native followed his triumph with a '79 decision over Victor Galendez for the World Boxing Association (WBA) title. Johnson soon lost both of his belts, but regained the WBA title with a 1986 TKO of Leslie Stewart at Indianapolis' Market Square Arena. The victory over Stewart enabled Johnson to become the first light heavyweight in history to gain three world titles. After losing a 1987 re-match to Stewart, Marvin Johnson retired from professional prize-fighting. He has remained a prominent figure in the Indianapolis community as a deputy for the Marion County Sheriff's Department. Courtesy Marvin Johnson.

Junior welterweight Harold Brazier of South Bend is another Hoosier boxing great of the Modern Era. 70-10-1 at this writing, Brazier has won 51 of his last 54 rounds on the judges' scorecards. Defeated in his two attempts at the World Jr. Welterweight Title, he has nonetheless earned the nickname "ESPN's Darling" for his action-packed and highly rated bouts on that sports channel's "Top Rank Boxing."

Bill "Honeyboy" Brown, Champ Chaney and Thomas Sarge Johnson (l to r) coached the 1972 Indiana Golden Gloves Team to a national runner-up finish. Honeyboy was the Southern Welterweight Champion during the 1930s; he has handled numerous contenders including Stormin' Norman Goins and Ernie Terrell and has served as chairman of the Indiana Jr. Olympics boxing program for over twenty years.

Champ Chaney reached the Number Three World Heavyweight Contender position during the 1940s. He trained a number of the past decade's top fighters, including Marvin Johnson and former Light-heavyweight Champ J.B. Williamson. Chaney has been coach of the Indy Police Athletic League (PAL) boxing team since 1969.

Sarge Johnson was the premier American amateur boxing coach of the 1970s. At the request of the US State Department, Sarge spent 1974 in Indonesia setting up that nation's national boxing team. In 1976 Johnson was the head coach of the US Olympic Boxing Team that stunned the world by unveiling future World Champions like Ray Leonard and the Spinks brothers. He was slated to coach the '80 Olympic Team prior to the American boycott of the Moscow Games.

In 1981 the US National Boxing Team, including Head Coach Sarge Johnson, were killed in a place crash en route to Poland for an exhibition match. Courtesy Bill Brown.

Photo Courtesy IU Sports

Winner of the 1981 Hermann Trophy—awarded annually to the top American collegiate soccer player, Armando Betancourt went on to an outstanding professional career in the Major Indoor Soccer League (MISL.)

Since Coach Jerry Yeagley's Hoosiers gained varsity status in 1973, IU has compiled a 293-50-23 record (371-75-30 since Yeagley took over the IU Soccer Club in 1963).

The Hoosiers have captured three NCAA Championships (1982, '83 and '88) and finished Runner-up five times. Jerry Yeagley's program has produced over 30 All-Americans, including Collegiate Players of the Year Angelo DiBernardo (1978), Armando Betancourt (1981) and Ken Snow (1988).

At this writing the Hoosiers had contested over 60 varsity games against Big 10 competition and had never lost a game—never. IU's 46-game overall unbeaten streak (1983-'84) remains an NCAA record. The Cream and Crimson outscored all opposition 145-35 during this run.

IU may be facing increasingly stiff in-state competition in the immediate future. The Hoosiers have recently dropped contests to both the University of Evansville and the University of Notre Dame.

Mark Spitz—perhaps the greatest swimmer of all time—graduated from Indiana University in 1972. Spitz won the Gold in the 800 and 400 freestyle relays and a Bronze in the 100 butterfly and 100 freestyle at the '68 Olympics, but it was at the '72 Munich Games that he became a legend. Not only did the IU swimmer gain seven Gold Medals at Munich (100 and 200 butterfly, 100 and 200 freestyle, 400 and 800 freestyle relay and 400 medley relay) he also set a new World Record in the Finals of each race he contested.

The object of intense media promotion in the wake of his accomplishments, Spitz' celebrity was short-lived. At this writing he—like Kurt Thomas—was considering a comeback at the 1992 Summer Olympics.

During the 1960s and 70s the Indiana University swimming and diving teams of coaches James "Doc" Counsilman and Hobie Billingsley achieved one of the most dominant dynasties in the history of American sports. IU was the Big 10 Swimming and Diving Champion from 1961-1980. From 1968-'73 the Hoosiers captured an unprecedented six consecutive NCAA Championships. IU has finished in the NCAA Top 10 nineteen times. The Hoosiers captured over 90% of their duel meets between 1958-1989.

Coach Billingsley led the 1968 US Women's Olympic Diving Team as well as the 1972 Men's Team. He has also coached two or more individual Olympic divers at three different Games. His latest protege and IU's most recent NCAA Champion—Mark Lenzi—will likely be one of America's top diving prospects at the '92 games.

Coach Counsilman is simply the most important name in the history of American swimming. In addition to the above-mentioned accomplishments, he has coached five US/AAU Team Champions, coached the '64 and '76 US Men's Olympic individual champions, been named US Swimming Coach of the Year thirteen times, served as president of the American Swimming Coaches Association, authored six books on swimming and designed the top competition pool in the world—the Indiana University Natatorium at Indianapolis.

In 1965 Kenneth "Tug" Williams, then president of the US Olympic Committee, offered this opinion: "Of all the universities in the United States, I don't think any have produced as many Olympic Champions as has Indiana University."

Additional IU Olympians from the Counsilman/Billingsley era include:

1960

Mike Troy (IU and Indianapolis—200 butterfly and 800 free relay, both Gold and World Records. (Troy also carried the American flag at the '60 closing ceremonies.)

1964

Kevin Berry—200 free Gold
Chet "The Jet" Jestremski—200 breaststroke Bronze
Bob Loh—400 meter freestyle
Fred Schmidt—400 medley relay Gold, 200 butterfly Bronze
Larry Schulhof—400 freestyle relay
Tom Trethewey—200 breastroke
Bob Windle—1,500 free Gold
Kathy Ellis (IU and Indianapolis) 100 butterfly Bronze, 100 freestyle Bronze, 400 freestyle relay Gold, 400 medley relay Gold
Terri Stickles—400 free Bronze
Louis Rivera—10-meter platform diving
Kenny Sitzberger—3-meter springboard Gold
Tom Dinsley—3-meter springboard
Lesley Bush—10-meter platform Gold

1968

Charlie Hickcox—200 and 400 individual medley and 400 medley relay Gold, 100 backstroke Silver
John Kinsella—1,500 freestyle Silver ('72, 800 freestyle relay Gold)
Don McKenzie—100 breaststroke and 400 medley relay Gold
James Henry—springboard Bronze
Win Young—platform Bronze
Gary Hall—400 individual medley Silver ('72, 200 butterfly Silver, '76 100 butterfly Bronze)

1972

Gary Conelly—800 freestyle relay Gold
Rich Early—platform diving
John Murphy—400 freestyle relay Gold, 100 backstroke Bronze
Cynthia Potter—springboard ('76 springboard Bronze, '80 springboard)
Fred Tyler—800 freestyle relay Gold
Mike Stamm—100 backstroke Silver

1976

Jim Montgomery—100 freestyle, 800 freestyle relay and 400 medley relay Gold; 200 freestyle Bronze (l to r) Doc Counsilman with IU swimmers Bill Barton and Frank McKinney, Jr. One of the greatest swimmers of his era, Indianapolis' McKinney set the World Record for the 200-meter backstroke in 1955, won the 100-meter backstroke Bronze at the '56 Olympics and captured the 100-backstroke Silver and a share of the 400-medley relay Gold at the '60 Games.

Additional Indiana athletes who have competed in the Olympics since 1960 and not mentioned elsewhere in this volume include:

1960
Lee Calhoun, Gary—110 high hurdles Gold (also '56 220 h.h. Gold)
George Breen, Indianapolis—1,500 freestyle Bronze (also '56 800 freestyle relay Silver, 400 and 1,500 freestyle Bronze.)
Willie May, IU—110 meter high hurdles Silver
Jim Hill, Portland—small bore rifle Silver

1968
Sharon Wichman, Ft. Wayne—200 breastroke Gold, 100 breaststroke Bronze

1976
Anita DeFranz, Indianapolis—Eight with Coxwain Bronze; Matt Vogel, Ft. Wayne—100 butterfly and 400 medley relay Gold; Rick Wolhuter, Notre Dame—800 meter run Bronze

1984
Sunder Nix, IU—1,600 meter run relay Gold
Connie Young, Indianapolis—women's match sprint bike racing ('88 match sprint Bronze and three-time World Match Sprint Champion.)
Rick McKinney, Muncie—Archery Silver in 1984 and 1988

IU Diving Coach Hobie Billingsley   IU Swimming and Soccer Photos Courtesy IU Sports

Fuzzy Zoeller.	Photo credit Jeff McBride, PGA Tour.

In 1970 Fuzzy Zoeller was a forward on the New Albany High School basketball team. By 1974 he was a PGA touring pro. In 1979 he reached the pinnacle of the golfing world when he defeated Ed Snead and Tom Watson to capture the first sudden-death playoff in The Masters' fabled history.

In 1984 Fuzzy's US Open playoff victory over Greg Norman (65-75) set records for the biggest playoff winning margin in Open history and the lowest playoff round in a Major PGA Championship.

One of pro golf's all-time fan favorites, "The Fuz" claimed $255,000 in the '85 "Skins Game" and $370,000 in the '86 Skins. The 1979 Andy Williams San Diego Open; '81 Colonial; '83 Heritage; '85 Bay Hill Classic; '86 Heritage, AT&T Pebble Beach Pro-Am and Anheiser Busch Classic and the 1987 Merrill Lynch Shootout are numbered among Zoeller's tournament victories. Fuzzy has also been a three-time member of the American team in the annual US-Great Britain Ryder Cup Series.

Begun as the Bloomington (Indiana) Classic in 1976, the renamed Mayflower Classic became one of the top stops on the Ladies Professional Golf Association (LPGA) circuit. Moved to Harbour Trees in Noblesville in 1977, then to the Tournament's eventual home at CCI in 1981 the Mayflower was televised to a national audience from 1980 through 1988.

Most of the great names in women's golf, including Judy Rankin, Jane Blalock, Hollis Stacy, Amy Alcott, Sally Little and Sandra Palmer are found on the list of Mayflower champions.

Citing increased costs and a diminished public relations return, Mayflower Transit Inc. suspended sponsorship of the Tournament following the '88 competition. The Mayflower Classic had grown to the fourth largest LPGA event prior to its suspension. Courtesy Mayflower, Inc.

1988 Mayflower Classic victor Terry Jo Meyers tees off on the Fifth Hole of the Country Club of Indianapolis (CCI). Meyers won $60,000 out of a $400,000 Tournament purse. An estimated 40,000 fans attended the '88 Classic.

Joe Campbell and Coach Sam Voinoff   *Photo from Mentor Magazine*

Joe Campbell of Anderson won the 1951 and 1953 Indiana High School Golf Championships. He has won 11 Indiana Junior, Amateur, Senior or Open titles to date. Campbell cocaptained the 1956-'57 Purdue basketball team with Lamar Lundy and won the 1956 and '57 Big 10 Individual Golf Championships. He was NCAA Champion in 1955.

The 1959 PGA Rookie of the Year, Campbell counts the 1961 Beaumont Open, '62 Baton Rouge Open and 1966 Tucson Open among his PGA victories. Additionally, Campbell played for the 1956 Americas Cup Team and for the 1957 Walker Cup Team.

Campbell has served as the Purdue University Golf coach since 1975. He led the Boilers to the 1981 Big 10 crown in that capacity. During the past few years, Joe has been an occasional participant on the PGA Seniors Tour.

When Boris Becker (pictured) defeated Peter Lundgren for the 1990 GTE Hardcourt Championship, he was carrying on a tradition that began in Indianapolis in 1924. That was the first year that the US Clay Court Championships were held in Indy. The Capitol City has been a tennis hotbed ever since.

From the mid-1920s until 1968, the Western Championships were alternated annually between Indianapolis' Woodstock Country Club and the Town Club in Milwaukee.

In 1966 US Tennis Association (USTA) sanctioning chairman, Stan Malless of Indianapolis, had the permanent home of the US Clay Courts shifted from Chicago to Milwaukee. When a fire destroyed the Town Club in 1968, Malless moved the Clay Courts to Woodstock. The tournament was contested there until 1974, when matches were played at the Indianapolis Racquet Club. In 1979 the Clay Courts took up residence at the brand new Indianapolis Sports Center.

Courtesy GTE Hardcourts

Indy inherited a magnificent Clay Court legacy. Legends like Big Bill Tilden, Bobby Riggs, Pancho Gonzales, Arthur Ashe, Maureen Connolly, and Nancy Richey are numbered among the former Champions.

The parade of greats continued for the nineteen years the Clay Court Championships made Indianapolis their home. Jimmy Connors reigned in 1974, '76, '78 and '79. Ivan Lendl was the '85 Champ and the Number One rated player of 1987, Mats Wilander, captured the final Indianapolis version of the US Clay Court Championships.

Despite this litany of legends, the women often dominated Indy fan and media attention. Billy Jean King was the victor in '71. Chris Evert captivated the Hoosier crowd and the Clay Court title from 1972-1975 and in '79 and '80. Steffi Graf's '86 crown presaged the greatness to come.

By 1988 fewer and fewer Americans were playing Clay Court tennis. Though most of the world's courts are clay, Americans increasingly preferred the power game of hard courts over the finesse of the game played on clay. The tennis courts at the Indianapolis Sports Center were paved in 1988. The US Clay Courts moved to South Carolina and Indianapolis inaugurated the first GTE Hardcourt Championships.

Though the GTE Hardcourts are for some inexplicable reason—and against the wishes of Stan Malless—a men's only event, the move to the fast surface has been a smashing success. Boris Becker captured the '88 Indy event, while John McEnroe picked up the winners check in '89. An Indianapolis record 79,840 fans attended the week long event in 1990. Hundreds of thousands more watched two days of coverage on ESPN. Becker's second Hardcourt Championship brought him $140,000 out of a $1 million total purse.

As the last major tournament prior to the US Open, the Hardcourts are increasingly viewed as the principle tune-up for that Grand Slam event.

Richard Anthony "Dick" Weber graduated from Indianapolis Tech High School in 1948. The victor in over 25 Professional Bowlers Association (PBA) tournaments, Weber was named American Bowler of the Year in 1961 and '63. In September, 1965, Weber became the first pro bowler history to roll three "perfect games" in a single tournament, when he accomplished the feat at the Houston PBA Open. He has rolled over twenty 300's to date. A charter member of the PBA (1958), Dick Weber served as the Association's president in 1970—the same year he was elected to the American Bowling Congress Hall of Fame. Bowling Photos courtesy Bowling Hall of Fame,

Pat Striebeck Dryer of Greenwood was an outstanding female bowler in the 1940s and '50s. Her 201 average was the best mark of the 1949-'50 Women's International Bowling Congress (WIBC) season. Her 183.78 average over thirty-five years of WIBC competition is the top lifetime mark in Indiana and fifth best nationally.

The winner of 25 Indiana State singles, doubles, and team championships, Dryer was a member of the 1951 Hickman Oldsmobile Whirl-A-Ways' WIBC National Champions. Patty Dryer is one of five Hoosier members of the WIBC Hall of Fame. Others include Anita Rump of Fort Wayne, Sally Twyford of Nashville and Pearl Switzer of South Bend.

Franklin Central High School's Mike Aulby made an impressive debut on the Professional Bowlers Association (PBA) tour. The 1979 PBA Rookie of the Year captured his first professional championship with a victory in the '79 PBA National Tournament—one of pro bowling's most prestigious annual events. Aulby has gone on to win 19 PBA titles, including the 1985 National, the '89 US Open and the '89 American Bowling Congress (ABC) Masters. The Hoosier kegler was named the PBA and US Bowling Writers Association (USBWA) Player of the Year in 1985. He repeated as the USBWA MVP in '89.

Courtesy Indianapolis Ice

While the sport of hockey doesn't have the Hoosier heritage of basketball, two Indiana cities do boast a long and zealous relationship with the game.

The Indianapolis Capitols were founded in 1939 as the top farm team for the NHL's Detroit Red Wings. The Caps won the American Hockey League Western Division in '39 and the league's Calder Cup trophy in 1942 and '50. Prior to their demise in the mid-50s, the Caps trained such future NHL stars as Terry Sawchuck, Glen Hall and Johnny Wilson.

In 1963 Indianapolis entered a team in the Central League in affiliation with the Red Wings. The team was 1-4-1 when an explosion at the State Fairgrounds Coliseum killed several people during a performance of the Ice Capades. Finding themselves without a place to play, the Hoosier franchise moved to Cincinnati.

In 1974 the short lived Indianapolis Racers of the short lived World Hockey Association enjoyed the distinction of being the first professional hockey team to employ the services of one Wayne Gretzky. It took about two weeks for people to realize The Great One was ready for the NHL.

The Indianapolis Checkers competed in the International Hockey League (IHL) from 1979 through 1986. After a two-year hiatus Indy returned to the IHL wars as the Indianapolis Ice. A recent affiliation with the Chicago Blackhawks appears to have established the Ice as the most stable hockey franchise in Indy since the 1940s.

Founded in 1952, the Fort Wayne Komets are one of the oldest continuously operating professional hockey teams in America. The K's have captured five International Hockey League (IHL) regular season championships and three IHL Turner Cup Series.

Komet alumni include: John Ferguson, who spent eight seasons with Montreal before becoming coach and general manager of the Rangers; longtime Blackhawk goalie Murray Bannerman; '84 Olympic goalie Daryl Jensen; Pittsburgh and Quebec head coach Mark Boileau; Alain Chervier, who has coached a number of NHL clubs; and Connie Madigan, who became the oldest rookie in NHL history when he broke in with the St. Louis Blues at the age of thrity-eight.

Bruce Baumgartner of Indiana State University won the 1982 NCAA Heavyweight Wrestling Championship with a 4-2 decision over Steve Williams of Oklahoma. An All-American in 1980, '81 and '82 the 6'2", 265 pound grappler compiled a collegiate record of 134 wins (with 70 pins) against 12 losses.

In 1984 "Big Bruce" was the top amateur wrestler in the world.

He proved this fact by capturing the Freestyle Super-Heavyweight Gold at the LA Olympics. Baumgartner continues to be one of the top international competitors, as evidenced by his Silver Medal awarded at the 1988 Olympics in Seoul, Korea. Courtesy Indiana State University.

Indiana State University Sycamore Kurt Thomas won the NCAA All-Around Championship in 1977 and '79. The inventor of the dramatic "Thomas Flair," he was named the American Gymnastics Federation Male Gymnast of the Year from 1977 through 1980. Thomas was the All-Around Runner-up at the 1978 World Cup—the same year he was a Sullivan Award finalist. His Olympic career was curtailed by the US boycott of the 1980 Moscow Olympics.

ISU Coach Roger Council's Sycamores captured nearly 75% of the matches they contested between 1963 and the mid-1980s. His three dozen All-Americans included fifteen Individual National Champions. Coach Council was a six-time NCAA Mideast Coach of the Year and would have led the US Gymnastics Team at the '80 Olympics. His Sycamores hosted the 33rd NCAA Gymnastics Championship in 1975, competed in six of seven NCAA Finals between 1972-'79 and captured the 1977 NCAA National Championship. Courtesy Indiana State University.

Courtesy Ball State University Sports

Since 1964 the Ball State University Volleyball team has compiled a 610-187-6 record under the leadership of Coach Don Shondell. The Cardinals have won or shared 16 Midwest Intercollegiate Volleyball Association (MIVA) titles and earned a berth in 11 NCAA Championships. BSU has finished third in the nation six times and fourth five times. BSU and UCLA are the only two teams to make the NCAA Voleyball Final Four in five consecutive seasons.

Coach Shondell has been named MIVA Coach of the Year six times. He has served as chairman of the NCAA Volleyball Committee, president of the US Volleyball Association (USVBA) and as the USVBA representative to the US Olympic Committee.

Ball State alumni who have achieved All-America and/or Olympic stature include Jerre McNamara, Tom Beerman, Mick Haley, Lee Killian, Rick Niemi, Steve Arnett, Scott Nelson, Dave Shakel, Chris Cooper, Chris Beerman, Stephan Stamato and Brian Begor.

When the Cardinals host the 1992 NCAA Final Four it will mark the fourth time that Muncie has been the home for the NCAA Volleyball Championships (1972, '76 and '80). Courtesy Ball State University.

An immediate challenge to the Cards' Midwest supremacy will come from the Mastadons of Indiana-Purdue Fort Wayne (IPFW). Coach Arnie Ball—a BSU grad himself—had IPFW ranked in the nation's Top 10 for most of last season. As they merge a strong recruiting class with an experienced nucelus of returning lettermen, the Mastadons appear to be a strong contender for a spot in the 1991 Final Four.

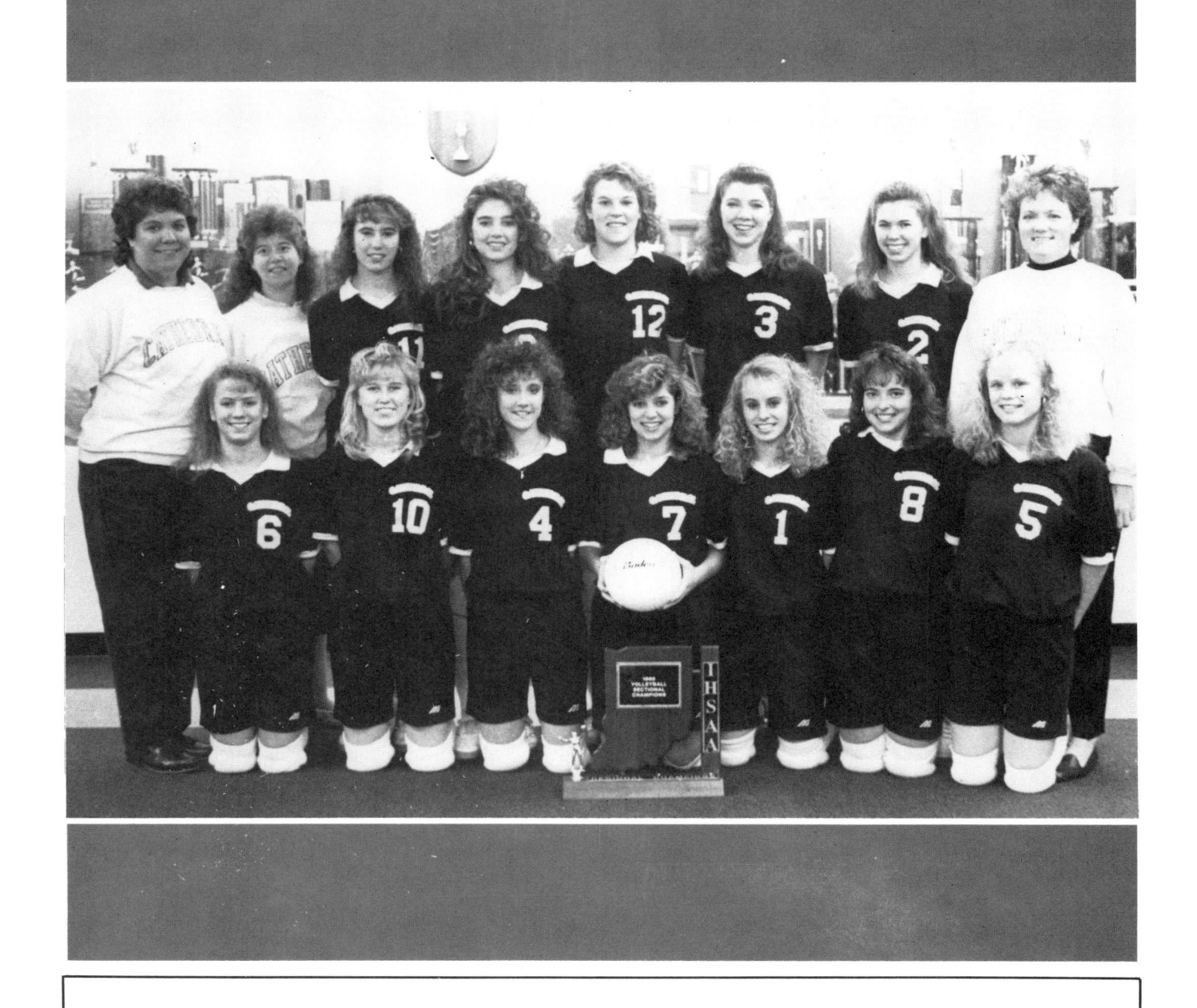

Indianapolis' Cathedral High School's strong athletic program is one of many in the state of Indiana which consistently turn out outstanding teams. Shown here is the '89 Volleyball Semistate Finalists (33-4). Back row, (l-r): Head Coach Denise Farrell, Assistant Coach Debbie Barrett, Kimberly Roberts, Kelly Kennedy, Leah Lentz, Amy Greer, Deborah Callaghan, Assistant Coach Jean Kesterson.

Front row, (l-r): Cathy Lekens, Stephannie Keefe, Kellyn Feeney, Mollie Peebles, Sheri Osterhaus, Cindy Stuart, Jackie Schaefer.

Today the Indiana High School Athletic Association (IHSAA) administers the competition of 390 member schools. In the 1989-'90 season nearly 150,000 athletes participated in nine boys and nine girls sports. IHSAA Championship Tournaments drew over two million paying fans.

E.C. Roosevelt 1947 Mythical State Champs (9-0)

Though an official IHSAA football championship wasn't awarded until 1973, mythical state champs were crowned according to wire service polls on conference championships. The city of East Chicago claimed nine such titles between 1937 and 1970.

The state of Indiana finally instituted a high school football playoff format in 1973—sixty-two years after the first Indiana Boys Basketball Tournament was contested. Hoosier schools were originally divided into three classes by student body size. In 1985 the 312 participating teams were regrouped into five classes according to school size.

Since moving the Finals to the Hoosier Dome in 1984, the Indiana High School Athletic Association (IHSAA) has seen a steady growth in the popularity of the playoffs. In 1987 a record 41,565 fans attended the five Championship games that were contested over a three-day period.

With a true Championship to shoot for, Hoosier high school football appears to be gaining a degree of parity with its neighboring states. Indiana's collegiate programs should prosper accordingly.

214

High School Football Photos Courtesy IHSAA

The Hobart Brickies have been the most consistently successful Indiana prep grid team of the past decade. After finishing a bridesmaid in 1979, '80, '82, '84 and '85, the Brickies trashed Jasper 31-0 (pictured) to capture the '87 4A crown. Hobart followed its long sought success with the '89 4A title. At this writing the Number One rated team in 4A at the start of the 1990 season is—Hobart High School.

Brett Law, shown here leading Sheridan High School to a 59-0 conquest of Bremen in the 1988 1A final, set a fistful of Indiana and US prep records. Law's 453 single-season and 952 career points are national standards. So are his 55 single-season rushing TDs, 114 career rushing TDs, 66 single-season total TDs and 141 career total TDs. Law's 6,854 career rushing yards established an Indiana prep standard.

The 5'10" tailback entered IU as a freshman in 1990. Bremen recovered from the '88 shellacking to capture the '89 1A championship. Coach Larry Wright's Sheridan Blackhawks have also taken the 1980, '84 and '87 Single-A titles.

Franklin Central's Flashes, pictured chasing down Northwood 19-13 for the 1980 2A title is the only school to date to win three consecutive Indiana high school crowns (1980, '81 and '82). Since moving up to Class 4A in 1984, the Flashes have finished Runner-up three times.

Since the split to five divisions in 1985, Indianapolis area schools have captured every 5A title (Warren Central in '85, Carmel in '86 and '89, and Ben Davis in '87 and '88).

The Bippus High School Class of '42 boasted nine graduates. It's a safe bet that when Chris Schenkel graduated from Purdue University three years later, he found himself in a somewhat larger student body.

One of the most experienced announcers in the history of American sportscasting, Schenkel has been named National Sportscaster of the Year three times, been nominated for four Emmys and won the Peabody Award for anchoring ABC-TV's coverage of the 1968 Summer Olympics in Mexico City. The Hoosier broadcaster has served as the chief announcer for ABC's Wide World of Sports, The ABC Pro-Bowlers Tour, The NBA on CBS, Major League Championship Baseball, NCAA football coverage, the NFL's NY Giants, horseracing's Triple Crown, most major golf tournaments and several heavyweight championship fights. For six years Schenkel called five or six fights every Monday night—fifty-two weeks a year on TV's "Monday Night Fights."

Cutting back on his hectic schedule, Chris Schenkel today resides on the shores of Lake Tippecanoe, near the bustling metropolis of Leesburg, Indiana.

Since Purdue has supplied American sports fans with one of their favorite announcers, is it any surprise that IU would feel compelled to do the same?

Armada, Michigan's Dick Enberg received his MA from Indiana in 1959 and his Ph.D. in Health Science in 1962. In '59 Enberg called football and basketball play-by-play on IU's first radio sports network. As a play-by-play man for the UCLA Bruin basketball dynasty of the 1960s, Enberg was a three-time California Sportscaster of the Year. He has also called games for the California Angels and—with Merlin Olsen—NFL Football for NBC. The chemistry generated by the team of Dick Enberg, Billy Packer and Al McGuire did much to elevate the popularity of NCAA basketball coverage in the early '80s.

IU's Dick Enberg has been voted National Sportscaster of the Year four times by his colleagues.

The dean of Indiana sportscasters, Tom Carnegie has been the chief announcer of the Indianapolis Motor Speedway public address system since 1946. His distinctive, "He's on it!" often followed closely by, "And it's a new track record" are as familiar as a Mario Andretti breakdown to any fan who's attended one of the last forty-four Indy "500" qualifications.

A former sports director for WOWO-WGL, Fort Wayne; WIRE, Indianapolis and WRTV, Indianapolis, Carnegie broadcast over 250 Big 10 football and basketball games during his forty-three years at those stations.

Between 1953-1976 Carnegie teamed with Tony Hinkle to announce the Indiana High School Boys Basketball Tournament on state-wide television. That service won him a role playing himself in the Academy Award nominated motion picture "Hoosiers." Courtesy Indy "500" Photos.

Between 1941 and 1946 WOWO and WKJG announcer Hilliard Gates called every game the Ft. Wayne Pistons ever played. In 1950 as an announcer for the Mutual Broadcasting System, Gates did the play-by-play for the first NBA All-Star game. The Summit City sportscaster also served as an announcer for NBC Radio's coverage of the 1967 and '68 Rose Bowl Games. Gates has been vice president and general manager of WKJG-TV Ft. Wayne since 1962.

Opening Ceremonies, 1987 Pan Am Games. Courtesy Indiana Sports Corporation.

Athletic competition at all levels has become Big Business. And no city in the world demonstrates that fact better than does Indianapolis.

Chartered in 1980, the Indiana Sports Corporation (ISC) is a private not-for-profit organization that represents Indianapolis in the national and international sports marketplace. The organization recruits, coordinates and markets major amateur and professional sporting events for Central Indiana.

Due in part to the efforts of the ISC, Indianapolis has hosted over two hundred national and international sporting events since 1980. Nearly 3.5 million people have attended events in Indy such as the 1987 Pan-Am Games, the 1982 National Sports Festival, the 1988 Olympic Trials for swimming and diving, and track and field, and various NCAA, national and world championships.

Additional events supervised by the ISC include the annual awarding of the Indianapolis-based AAU's Sullivan Award, the annual Circle City Classic, which pits top black university football teams against one another and the annual Larry Bird Pro All-Star Scholarship Classic.

Each year the ISC hosts the Finals of the White River Park State Games (WRSPG) in downtown Indianapolis. More than 25,000 Hoosier amateur athletes begin the competition in nineteen sports at eight regionals statewide. Begun in 1983, the WRSPG is one of the nation's largest state competitions.

The economic impact of such competitions is staggering. Indy's state-of-the art sports facilities are valued at more than $150 million. The Pan-Am Games are estimated to have generated $175 million statewide. Another study estimates that amateur sports as a resident business in Indianapolis generates $30 million annually.

With a full slate of NCAA, national and International events already booked into the 21st century, it's a safe bet that the one-time "India-No-Place" will retain its newly won moniker—"The Amateur Sports Capital of America"—for a long time to come.

US Gymnastic Competition Awards, 1987. Photos Courtesy Indiana Sports Corporation

The Major Taylor Velodrome in Indianapolis honors a timeless Hoosier sports hero in the way he would wish to be remembered—in the midst of the competition.

INDIANAPOLIS

Greg Lougainis, 1988 Olympic Trials, IU Natatorium, Indianapolis. Courtesy Indiana Sports Corporation.

PART ONE INDEX

Adams, Charles "Babe", 6, 8
Adios, 17
Aldridge, Vic "The Hoosier Schoolmaster", 6

Billy Direct, 17
Brown, Mordecai Peter Centennial "Three Fingers", 7
Bush, John T., 5

Carey, Tom, 5
Cobb, Ty, 18
Corbett, Jim, 10
Crandall, Arnold, 9
Crandall, James "Doc", 9
Crandall, Karl, 9

Dan Patch, 17
DePalma, Ralph, 16
Dillon, Jack, 9
Dorias, Gus, 21, 24

Eggleston, Edward, 6
Eller, "Hod", 6
Em-Roes, 24
Ewry, Ray C. "Jumping Deak", 18

Feeney, Al, 21
Fisher, Carl G., 14, 16
Fitzsimmons, Fredrick "Fat Freddie", 6
Ford, Henry, 10

Gilmore, James, 6
Good Times, 17
Goux, Jules, 16
Griese, Bob, 1
Griffith, D.W., 10

Hargrave, Eugene "Bubbles", 6
Hargrave, William "Pinky", 6
Harroun, Ray, 14

Johnson, Marvin, 1

Knight, Bob, 1

Lambert, Ward "Piggy", 4
Leibold, "Nemo", 6
Lennon, Jim, 5
Lightbody, James "Deerfoot", 18

Maher, Peter, 10
Mann, Henry T., 19
Matthews, Bobby, 4, 5

McDermott, Joe, 5
McHenry, Myron, 17
Messner, Dan A., 17

Nehf, Art, 7
Newby, A.C., 14

Oldfield, Barney, 16
Orth, Al "The Curveless Wonder", 6

Patchen, Joe, 17
Price, Ernest, 9

Rambling Willie, 17
Resta, Dario, 16
Rickenbacker, Eddie, 15
Rickey, Branch, 7
Robertson, Oscar, 1
Robinson, Jackie, 7
Rockne, Knute, 1, 21, 24
Rudolph, Wilma, 1
Rusie, Amos "The Hoosier Thunderbolt", 8
Russell, Ewell "Reb", 6

Savage, Marion Willis, 17
Selby, Norman "Kid McCoy", 10
Sennett, Mack, 10
Sharkey, Tom, 10
Shaw, Wilbur, 1
Sinclair, Harry, 6
Spitz, Mark, 1
Stagg, Amos Alonzo, 18
Star's Pride, 17
Stonebraker, Homer, 22, 24
Street, Gabby, 7
Summers, "Kickapoo", 6

"Take Me Out To The Ball Game", 4
Taylor, Charles "Bud" "The Blond Terror of Terre Haute", 9
Taylor, Marshall "Major", 12, 13
Thomas, Rene, 15
Thompson, Sam "Big Sam", 8
Thompson, Will, 11

Wabash College, 19, 22
Wadena "Plowboys", 9
Wallace, Lew, 11
Williams, Fred "Cy", 9
Wooden, John, 1
Worthy Boy, 17

Zeider, "Bunions", 6
Zelica, 17
Zoeller, Fuzzy, 1

PART TWO INDEX

Aaron, Hank, 31
Abrams, Georgie, 76
Adkins, Roger, 51
Agase, Alex, 66
Aguirre, Mark, 45
Akron Firestones, 45
Aldridge, Vic, 29
Alexander, Betsy, 80
Alford, Steve, 44
Allen, Phog, 43
Allison, Moody, 32
Anderson, "Nub", 32
Andres, Ernie, 52, 53
"Armstrong, Curley", 43, 44, 54, 55
Atha, Dick, 51

Baird, Frank, 47
Baker, Mary, 36
Barker, Cliff, 54
Barnes, John, 32
Barnhorst, Leo, 54
Barton, Brenda, 80
Barton, Linda, 80
Beard, Ralph, 54, 61
Bell, Cool Papa, 32
Bell, Greg, 78
Bellamy, Walt, 44
Benson, Kent, 55
Beretta, Fred, 42
Bergere, Cliff, 84
Berra, Yogi, 39
Bertelli, Angelo, 72
Bird, Larry, 50
Bonham, Ron, 57
Borgman, Bernhardt "Benny", 49
Boryla, Vince, 45
Boudreau, Lou, 52
Bowers, Sally, 80
Brian, Frankie, 54
Brink, Wilbur, 82
Bryant, Hallie, 57
Bush, Owen J. "Ownie", 29, 30
Butler, Sol, 73
Butkovich, Tony, 66

Calhoun, Phyliss, 80
Camp, Ann, 80
Campanella, Roy, 32
Campbell, Milt, 78
Carnarius, Maximillian (Max Carey), 30, 36, 37
Carnera, Primo, 76
Carr, Austin, 48
Carter, Duane, 84
Carter, Pancho, 84

Case, Everett, *41, 62*
Cerdan, Marcel, *76*
Charleston, Benny, *33*
Charleston, Oscar, *32, 35*
Clair, Bill, *33*
Collins, Sid, *84*
Cottey, Bud, *76*
Cottom, Norm, *42*
Counsilman, Doc, *81*
Cox, Tracey, *75*
Craft, Ray, *47, 57*
Crocker, Lucy, *81*
Crowe, George, *62*
Crowley, Jimmy, *67*
Cunningham, Mary Frances, *80*

Dahlback, Carl, *65*
Darling, Lonnie, *52*
Davis, Floyd, *86*
Davis-Grossfield, Muriel, *81*
Dawson, Lenny, *66*
Dean, Everett, *41, 43, 78*
Deckard, Tommy, *78*
Dees, Archie, *44*
DeMoss, Bob, *67*
Dempsey, Jack, *26*
DePaolo, Peter, *85*
Dietz, Bob, *47*
Dimancheff, Babe, *66*
Donahue, Sheila, *80*
Doyle, Jimmy, *47*
Dro, Bob, *43, 44*
Duvall, John L., *57*

Edwards, Leroy "Cowboy", *45, 61*
Elliott, E.C., *64*
English, Alex, *54*
Erskine, Carl, *38*

Farley, Dick, *44*
Feeney, Sharon, *80*
Fisher, Carl, *82*
Ford, Henry, *74*
Fort Wayne Daisies, The, *37*
Foster, Rube, *33*
Four Horseman, The, *70*
Foust, Larry, *55*
Fowler, Bud, *32*
Foyt, A.J., *84, 85*
Frick, Ford, *27-29*
Fuqua, Ivan, *78*
Furillo, Carl, *39*

Gardner, William "Wee Willie", *58*
Garrett, Bill, *62*
Gibson, Josh, *32*
Gilbert, Bob, *51*

Gipp, George, *67, 70, 71*
Grange, Red, *25*
Grant, Chet, *35*
Graziano, Rocky, *76*
Gresham, Walter Q., *25*
Groza, Alex, *54, 63*
Guzek, Ted, *47*

Halas, George, *49, 63*
Hanks, Sam, *84*
Hanzlik, Bill, *55*
Hargis, John, *55*
Harmon, Tom, *74*
Harris, Bob, *55*
Hart, Leon, *72*
Hawkins, Tom, *45*
Hayes, Anna, *80*
Hayes, E.C. "Billy", *78*
Heisman Trophy, *72*
Herman, William Jennings "Billy", *30*
Hildebrand, Oral, *47*
Hinkle, Paul D. "Tony", *47, 48*
Hodges, Gil, *38, 39*
Hornsby, Rogers, *31*
Huffman, Marv, *43*
Huffman, Vern, *44*
Hulman, Anton "Tony", *83*

Jabbar, Kareem, *56*
Jackson, "Shoeless Joe", *26*
Jackson, Ed, *57*
Jackson, Jimmy, *84*
Jeannette, Buddy, *52*
Jewell, Bob, *57*
Jochum, Betsy, *36*
Johnson, Boag, *54, 55*
Johnson, Judy, *32*
Jones, "Wah Wah", *63*
Jungclaus, Barbara, *80*

Kautsky, Frank, *52*
Kennedy, J. Walter, *45*
Kern, Jim, *51*
Kerris, Jack, *55*
Kiser, Noble, *64*
Klein, Chuck, *30*
Klier, Leo "Crystal", *45*
Klueh, Duane, *50, 51, 54*
Krause, W. "Moose", *44*

Laimbeer, Bill, *55*
Lamotta, Jake "The Raging Bull", *77*
Landis, Kenesaw Mountain, Judge, *26-28, 30*
Larsen, Don, *39*
Lash, Don, *78*
Lattner, Johnny, *67, 72*

Layden, Elmer, *67*
Leahy, Frank, *67, 72*
Leonard, Bobby "Slick", *44*
Lieb, Tom, *78*
Lombardi, Vince, *72*
Long, John, *55*
Longfellow, John, *56*
Lovellette, Clyde, *62, 63*
Lowery, Emmett, *42*
Lucas, Jerry, *46*
Lujack, Johnny, *72*
Lundy, Lamar, *67*
Lynch, Betty, *80*

Mahon, Elizabeth, *36*
Mantle, Mickey, *38, 39*
Manuel, Kay, *80*
Marchino, Mary Ann, *80*
Marshall, Penny, *37*
Martin, Orval, *79*
McCracken, Branch, *41-43, 49, 78*
McCreary, Jay, *43*
McDermott, Bobby, *52*
McGannon, Tom, *65*
McGinnis, George, *48*
McGraw, John, *35*
McIntyre, Larry, *62*
McKinney, Frank E., *29, 81*
McMillin, Alvin "Bo", *64*
McNulty, Carl, *43*
Mendenhall, Murray, *53, 54*
Menke, Bill, *43*
Menke, Bob, *43*
Merriweather, Willie, *58*
Meyer, Louis, *46*
Meyer, Ray, *45, 85*
Mikan, George, *53, 54*
Miller, Charles, *65*
Miller, Don, *67*
Mitchell, Clarence, *29*
Mitchell, Dave, *30, 39*
Mitchell, Sheddrick, *58*
Moir, John, *45*
Moll, Gail, *80*
Moll, Patricia, *80*
Mollenkopf, Jack, *66*
Montross, Eric, *48*
Moore, Doxie, *54*
Morrison, Ann, *81*
Moss, Ann, *80, 81*
Moss, Paul, *65*
Mullen-Brey, Betty, *80, 81*
Murphy, Charles "Stretch", *40, 41*
Murry, Cliff, *51*

Naismith, James Dr., *61*
Newcombe, Don, *32*

Nickolson, John, *78*
Nowak, Paul, *45*

O'Brien, Pat, *70*
O'Brien, Ralph "Buckshot", *47*
O'Connor, Pat, *85*
O'Shea, Kevin, *45*
Oldham, John, *55*
Oliphant, Elmer, *65*
Overton, John, *32*
Owens, Bill, *32-34*
Owens, Jesse, *26, 28*

Page, Harlan O. "Pat", *46, 47*
Page, Rube, *32*
Paige, Satchel, *32, 33*
Parsons, Johnnie, *84*
Patton, Stanford, *58*
Pence, Carol, *80*
Phelan, Jimmy, *64, 65*
Phillips, Herman, *77*
Pihos, Pete "Big Dog", *64*
Plump, Bobby, *47, 48, 57, 58*
Podres, Johnny, *38*
Pollard, Fredrick, "Fritz", *73*
Pollard, Lataunya, *48*
Pollock, Syd, *32*
Purvis, Duane, *53, 65, 79*
Ravensburg, Bob, *64*
Ray, George, *33*
Rayl, Jimmy, *62, 67*
Reagan, Ronald, *70*
Ribicoff, Abe, *46*
Rickenbacker, Eddie, *82*
Rickey, Branch, *32*
Roberts, Judy, *79, 81*
Robertson, Bailey, *57*
Robertson, Oscar "Big O", *47, 48, 57, 61*
Robinson, Jackie, *35, 39*
Robson, George, *84*
Rockefeller, John D., *26*
Roosevelt, Teddy, *26*
Root, Charlie, *26*
Rosazza, Joan Ann, *80*
Rose, Mauri, *84, 85*
Rosen, Max, *49*
Roush, Eddie, *28*
Ruddick, Sandy, *81*
Rupp, Adolph, *54, 62*
Ruth, Babe, *26, 28*
Ruttman, Troy, *85*
Rzeszewski, "Leaping Lenny", *51*

Sandback, Kenneth, *77*
Saperstien, Abe, *58*
Schaefer, Herm, *43*
Schaefer, Susan, *80*

Schaus, Fred, *46, 54*
Schayes, Dolph, *53, 54*
Schlundt, Don, *44, 45*
Scott, Bill, *47*
Sears, Ray, *77*
Sexson, Joe, *43*
Shaw, Wilbur, *83, 85*
Shelbourne, John, *73*
Shelton, Jim, *84*
Shepherd, Billy, *48*
Shipp, Charley, *53*
Siwak, Joe, *77*
Sleight, Elmer "Red", *65*
Smith, Earl, *31*
Smith, Jimmy, *28*
South Bend Blue Sox, *37*
Stagg, Amos Alonzo, *74*
Steinbeck, John, *59*
Steiner, Jerry, *47*
Stephenson, D.C., *53*
Stonebraker, Homer, *49*
Storer, Sue, *81*
Stuhldreher, Harry, *67*
Stunyo, Jeanne, *80*

Taliaferro, George, *64*
Tanabe, Richard, *81*
Taylor, Ben, *31*
Taylor, C.I., *31*
Taylor, Jackie, *76*
Taylor, Jim, *32*
Thomas, Isiah, *55*
Tolbert, Ray, *56*
Traynor, Pie, *29*
Trester, Arthur L., *52*
Tripucka, Kelly, *55*
Trout, Paul "Dizzy", *31*
Truex, Max, *79*
Truitt, Mel, *78*
Tunney, Gene, *76*
Turner, Betsey, *80*

Unser, Jerry, *84*

Vallee, Rudy, *83*
Vandivier, Robert P. "Fuzzy", *40, 47*
Vukovich, Bill, *85*

Walker, Jimmy, *68*
Walton, Luke, *84*
Wambsganss, Bill, *30*
Waner, Lloyd, *29*
Waner, Paul, *29*
Ward, Roger, *84*
Warren, Judi, *48*
Weismuller, Johnny "Tarzan", *77*
Welch, Ralph "Pest", *65*
Wells, Clifford, *52*

Wiggins, Chuck "The Hoosier Playboy", *76*
Williams, "Inky", *73*
Williams, Ted, *29*
Wilt, Fred, *78*
Wolsey, Bill, *81*
Wood, Marvin, *40, 42, 56*
Wooden, John, *41, 42, 48, 50, 51, 53*

Yardley, George, *54*
Young, Jewell, *41*

Zaleski, Anthony Florian, *75*
Zollner, Fred, *52*

PART THREE INDEX

Abernethy, Tom, *94, 103*
Agee, Tommy, *178*
Akers, Fred, *150*
Alcindor, Lew "Abdul Jabbar, Kareem", *94, 99, 103, 107, 109*
Alcott, Amy, *Gallery*
Alford, Steve, *105*
Allen, George, *142*
Allen, Lucius, *99*
Ameche, Alan, *164*
Anderson, Eric, *104*
Anderson, Sparky, *177*
Andretti, John, *190*
Andretti, Mario, *192*
Andretti, Michael, *190*
Andujar, Joaquin, *178*
Appling, Luke, *177*
Armstrong, Neil, *142*
Arnett, Steve, *Gallery*
Arnzen, Bob, *111*
Ashe, Arthur, *Gallery*
Aulby, Mike, *Gallery*

Bailey, Damon, *97, 98, 103*
Bando, Sal, *180*
Banks, Chip, *168*
Baratto, John, *88*
Barlow, Ken, *115, 117*
Barnes, Chuck, *126*
Barnes, Roosevelt, *94*
Bass, Glen, *154*
Bates, Marv, *121*
Baugh, Sammy, *168*
Baughman, Mike, *144*
Baumgartner, Bruce, *Gallery*
Beabout, Jerry, *142*
Beach, Pat, *170*
Beban, Gary, *144*

Becker, Boris, *Gallery*
Beerman, Tom, *Gallery*
Begor, Briam, *Gallery*
Beirne, Jim, *142, 147*
Bell, Bobby, *156*
Bellamy, Walt, *99, 106*
Bellinsky, Bo, *178*
Benson, Kent, *94, 102, 103, 115*
Bently, Albert, *167*
Berry, Ray, *164*
Betancourt, Armando, *Gallery*
Bettenhausen, Gary, *187*
Bettenhausen, Tony, *187*
Bettenhausen, Tony, Jr., *187, 190*
Bevacqua, Kurt, *178*
Biasucci, Dean, *168*
Bickett, Duane, *168*
Billingsley, Hobie, *Gallery*
Binford, Tom, *190*
Bingham, Greg, *148*
Bird, Larry Joe, *94, 97, 108, 117-120, 132*
Blalock, Jane, *Gallery*
Bleier, Rocky, *157*
Boessel, Raul, *1901*
Bonham, Ron "The Muncie Mortar", *89, 90, 93, 130*
Borbon, Pedro, *177, 178*
Bouza, Matt, *168*
Bradley, Luther, *160*
Bradshaw, Terry, *157*
Brazier, Harold, *Gallery*
Breen, George, *Gallery*
Bridgeman, Ulysses, *93, 94*
Brokaw, Gary, *113, 114*
Brookens, Tom, *176*
Brooks, Bill, *167*
Brown, Bill "Honeyboy", *Gallery*
Brown, Roger, *92, 131*
Brown, Three Fingers, *178*
Brown, Tim, *163*
Browner, Keith, *159*
Browner, Ross, *159*
Brumm, Don, *142*
Buckner, Quinn, *102, 103, 121*
Buford, Don, *177*
Buoniconti, Nick, *153*
Burke, Tim, *178*
Burtnett, Leon, *150*
Burton, Larry, *147*
Buse, Don, *120, 121, 130, 133*
Bush, Ownie, *177, 178*
Buss, Jerry, *130*
Butcher, Jack, *136, 137*
Butts, Billy, *124*
Butz, Dave, *148*
Butz, Earl, *148*

Calhoun, Lee, *Gallery*
Call, Kevin, *168*
Callison, Johnny, *178*
Calloway, Rick, *105*
Campbell, Joe, *Gallery*
Campbell, Scott, *149, 150*
Candaele, Casey, *177*
Carbo Bernie, *177*
Carnegie, Tom, *191, Gallery*
Carr, Austin, *112-114, 117*
Carr, Kenny, *115*
Carroll, Joe Barry, *109, 111*
Carter, Rodney, *149*
Carter, Virgil, *157*
Cash, Norm, *178*
Casper, Dave, *158, 159*
Cassells, Gary, *136*
Catavolos, George, *143*
Chafee, Roger, *143*
Chaney, Calbert, *104*
Chaney, Champ, *Gallery*
Charles, John, *142*
Clark, Jimmy, *192*
Clay, Dwight, *113, 114*
Clements, Tom, *158, 159*
Cloutier, J.R., *190*
Colavito, Rocky, *178*
Cole, Terry, *137*
Collins, Sid, *187, 189*
Concepcion, Dave, *178*
Connolly, Maureen, *Gallery*
Connors, Jimmy, *Gallery*
Cook, Cheryl, *96*
Cooks, Johnny, *168*
Corso, Lee, *138, 139*
Council, Roger, *Gallery*
Counsilman, James "Doc", *Gallery*
Coveleski, Stanley, *176*
Crawford, Jim, *190*
Crews, Jim, *121*
Cross, Russell, *110*
Crouse, Buck, *178*
Crum, Denny, *94, 124*
Crusan, Doug, *136, 137*
Cuellar, Mike, *178*
Curci, Fran, *173*

Daley, Derek, *190*
Dallenbach, Wally, *190*
Daniel, Eugene, *168*
Daniels, Mel, *92, 131*
Danielson, Gary, *147, 148*
Dantley, Adrian, *113, 115, 117*
Darden, Oliver, *131*
Daugherty, Brad, *135*
Davis, Al, *141*
Davis, Eric, *178*

Dawson, Lenny, *141-143, 154, 173*
DeBusschere, Dave, *178*
DeFranz, Anita, *Gallery*
DeMoss, Bob, *147*
Devine, Dan, *159, 161*
Dibble, Rob, *177*
DiBernardo, Angelo, *Gallery*
Dickerson, Eric Demitric, *166, 167, 170*
Dickey, Curtis, *168*
Dierking, Scott, *148, 149*
DiNardo, Larry, *158*
Dischinger, Terry, *99, 106, 107*
Donaldson, Ray, *168*
Donohue, Mark, *190*
Dopson, John, *178*
Dorsett, Brian, *Gallery*
Downing, Steve, *92, 101*
Driessen, Dan, *178*
Duerson, Dave, *161*

Eastwick, Rawley, *178*
Eddy, Nick, *156*
Edmonson, Keith, *110*
Edwards, James, *113, 115, 133*
Edwards, Jay, *93, 97, 98, 104*
Elia, Lee, *178*
Eller, Carl, *156*
Eller, Hod, *178*
Ellis, LaPhonso, *117*
Enberg, Dick, *Gallery*
Esasky, Nick, *177*
Evans, Oscar, *122*
Everett, Jim, *149, 150*
Evert, Chris, *Gallery*
Ewbank, Weeb, *172, 173*

Fabi, Teo, *190*
Faison, Earl, *136*
Farrell, Kerby, *178*
Faust, Gerry, *161, 162, 163*
Ferguson, Vagus, *160, 161, 162*
Feinstein, John "A Season on the Brink", *97*
Finley, Charles Oscar, *180, 181*
Finley, Jim, *144*
Fisher, Don, *143*
Fittipaldi, Emerson, *190, 194*
Fitzsimmons, Fat Freddie, *178*
Flynn, Mike, *94*
Foley, Tim, *147, 178*
Ford, Whitey, *180*
Foyt, A.J., *187-189, 191*
Franco, John, *178*
Friend, Robert Bartmess, *178, 180*
Fuller, Tony, *122*

226

Gabriel, Roman, *142*
Galarraga, Andres, *178*
Garrett, Dean, *105*
Garrett, John, *94*
Garza, Josele, *190*
Gates, Hilliard, *Gallery*
George, Jeff, *150, 167, 169*
Gilliam, Joe, *157*
Glasgow, Nesby, *168*
Godby, Linda, *96*
Goins, Norman, *Gallery*
Golic, Bob, *159, 160*
Gonso, Harry, *136-138*
Goodrich, Gail, *99*
Goux, Jules, *190*
Graf, Steffi, *Gallery*
Graham, Pat, *104*
Granatelli, Andy, *187*
Grant, Jerry, *188*
Grapenthin, Dick, *178*
Green, Bill, *97*
Green, Ricky, *121, 122*
Green, Steve, *94, 103*
Gretzky, Wayne, *Gallery*
Grier, Rosie, *141*
Griese, Bob, *138, 142-145, 158*
Griffey, Ken, *177*
Griffin, Archie, *147*
Grimsley, Ross, *177*
Grissom, Gus, *141*
Grogan, Steve, *147*
Guthrie, Janet, *190*

Haffner, Scott, *121*
Hall, Gary, *Gallery*
Hall, Ricky, *111*
Hall, Vicki, *96*
Hand, Jon, *168*
Hanratty, Terry, *156, 157*
Hanzlick, Bill, *115, 116*
Harding, Reggie, *131*
Harnett, Gabby, *178*
Heaton, Bob, *118*
Herrmann, Mark, *149*
Herrod, Jeff, *168*
Herskowitz, Mickey, *172*
Hesketh, Joe, *178*
Hickcox, Charlie, *Gallery*
Hicks, Scott, *116, 117*
Hildebrand, Oral, *178*
Hillenbrand, Billy, *164*
Hillman, Joe, *104*
Hinkle, Tony, *123*
Hinton, Chris, *167*
Hodges, Bill, *117*
Holcomb, Stu, *142*
Hornung, Paul, *152, 153, 157*
Howell, Jay, *178*
Hulman, Tony, *187, 188, 197*

Irsay, Bob, *142, 171*
Irsay, Jim, *171*
Irvine, George, *134*
Isbell, Cecil, *168*
Isenbarger, Phil, *136, 137*
Ismail, Raghel, *163*
Izo, George, *173*

Jackson, Reggie, *181*
John, Thomas Edward, *182, 183*
Johncock, Gordon, *188, 192*
Johnson, Wally, *186*
Jones, Bert, *167*
Jones, Lyndon, *97*
Jones, Parnelli, *187*
Jordain, Bernard, *190*
Jordan, Walter, *94, 109, 117*
Joyner, Butch, *100*

Kaczmarek, Ken, *136, 144*
Karras, Alex, *153, 174*
Keady, Gene, *97, 106, 110, 112*
Keller, Billy, *108, 130*
Kendrick, Frank, *94, 109*
Keyes, Leroy, *144, 146, 147, 156*
Khayat, Ed, *144*
Kidd, Curtis, *124*
Kiel, Blair, *161, 162*
Killebrew, Hermon, *178*
Killian, Lee, *Gallery*
King, Billy Jean, *Gallery*
King, George, *108, 147*
Kinsella, John, *Gallery*
Kitchel, Ted, *94, 104*
Kittle, Ron, *185*
Kline, Chanda, *95*
Knight, Bobby, *88, 92, 97-101, 104-106, 109, 113, 117, 122, 135*
Knight, Ray, *178*
Krause, Barry, *168*
Krisiloff, Steve, *192*
Kuhn, Bowie, *181*

Ladner, Wendell, *130*
Lahti, Jeff, *178*
Laimbeer, Bill, *115, 116*
Lajoie, Nap, *178*
Lambert, Ward, *100*
Lamonica, Daryl, *141, 153, 154, 156*
Landis, Kenesaw Mountain, *180*
Landrum, Bill, *178*
Larsen, Gary, *156*
Law, Brett, *Gallery*
Lazkowski, John, *103*
Leahy, Frank, *152*

LeFlore, Ron, *176*
Leibrant, Charlie, *178*
Lendl, Ivan, *Gallery*
Lenzi, Mark, *Gallery*
Leonard, Bobby "Slick', *92, 129, 130*
Leonard, Nancy, *129, 130*
Lewis, Freddie, *92, 131*
Lewis, Troy, *92, 131*
Lindell, Johnny, *112*
Little, Sally, *Gallery*
Loh, Bob, *Gallery*
Lopez, Al, *178*
Lundgren, Peter, *Gallery*
Lundy, Lamar, *141, 142*
Luyendyk, Arie, *190, 191*
Lynch, Jim, *156*

Macadoo Bob, *121, 122*
MacAfee, Ken, *159, 160*
MacDonald, Dave, *187*
Macy, Kyle, *94, 109*
Main, Woody, *180*
Malless, Stan, *Gallery*
Mallory, Bill, *139*
Maris, Roger, *178*
Marquard, Rube, *178*
Marshall, Jim, *156*
Mattingly, Don, *184, 185*
Mauch, Gene, *178*
May, Scott, *100, 103*
May, Willie, *Gallery*
McCoy, Mike, *158*
McCurdy, Paris, *124*
McCutchan, Ara, *120, 121*
McEnroe, John, *Gallery*
McGinnis, George F., *91, 92, 101, 108, 113, 117, 129-131, 133*
McGlocklin, Jon, *99*
McGuire, Al, *106, 117*
McKinney, Frank E. Sr., *190*
McKinney, Frank Jr., *Gallery*
McKinney, Jack, *130*
McMillin, Bo, *136*
McRae, Graham, *188*
McRae, Hal, *177*
Mears, Rick, *188, 190, 192*
Melvin, Bob, *176*
Metheny, Amy, *96*
Meyer, Ron, *142*
Meyers, Terry Jo, *Gallery*
Miller, Reggie, *108*
Milner, Eddie, *178*
Mitchell, Lydell, *168*
Molcdet, John, *93*
Mollenkopf, Kenneth "Jack", *114, 122, 143, 147*
Montague, Ed, *178*

Montana, Joe, *143, 159, 160*
Montross, Eric, *97*
Moore, Billy, *177*
Morris, Jack, *176*
Morris, Jim, *152*
Mount, Rick "The Rocket", *92, 106-108, 112, 113*

Nassi, Sam, *130*
Nicosan, Angus J., *96, 123*
Niemi, Rick, *Gallery*
Nix, Sunder, *Gallery*
Nixon, Russ, *178*
Novak, Gary, *113*
Novak, Ken, *148*
Nowatzke, Tom, *136, 173*

Oester, Ron, *178*
Ongais, Danny, *190*
Osteen, Claude, *178*

Page, Alan, *156*
Palmer, Eldon, *190*
Palmer, Sandra, *Gallery*
Palombizio, Dan, *110*
Parrish, Lance, *117*
Parseghian, Ara, *136, 154, 155*
Paxson, Jim, Jr., *117*
Paxson, Jim, Sr., *117*
Payton, Gary, *124, 167*
Perez, Pascual, *177*
Phelps, Richard "Digger", *113, 116, 117*
Phipps, Mike, *144, 146*
Pierce, Marion, *91*
Pinkett, Allen, *162*
Platt, Joe, *90*
Plump, Bobby, *92*
Pollard, Art, *188*
Pollard, LaTaunya, *94-96*
Pont, John, *136-138*
Post, Wally, *178*
Potter, Cynthia, *Gallery*
Pottios, Myron, *153*
Pruitt, Mike, *148, 159*

Radford, Wayne, *94*
Rahal, Bobby, *190, 192*
Rankin, Judy, *Gallery*
Rapp, Vern, *177*
Rathman, Jim, *187*
Rayl, Jimmy, *99, 130*
Redus, Gary, *177*
Reed, Ron, *182*
Rison, Andre, *167*
Rivers, David, *117*
Robertson, Bailey "Flap", *123*

Robertson, Oscar, *88, 89, 91, 92, 97, 99, 100, 111, 116, 124*
Robisch, Dave, *113*
Romano, Tom, *177*
Rose, Lee, *109, 110*
Ross, Joe, *117*
Ross, John, *117*
Roundfield, Dan, *133*
Roush, Eddie, *178*
Rudolph, Wilma, *89*
Rusie, Amos, *178*
Russell, Reb, *178*
Rutherford, Johnny, *192*

Sachs, Eddie, *187*
Samuels, Dale, *173*
Savage, Swede, *188*
Sawchuck, Terry, *Gallery*
Schaus, Fred, *108, 109*
Schellhase, Dave, *106, 107, 108*
Schenkel, Chris, *Gallery*
Scherger, George, *177*
Schumacher, Max, *179*
Score, Herb, *177, 178*
Selawski, Gene, *142*
Sexson, Joe, *123*
Seymour, Paul, *156*
Shaw, Wilbur, *190*
Shay, Jerry, *142*
Shepherd, Billy, *123*
Shepherd, Dave, *93*
Shines, Razor, *178*
Shondell, Don, *Gallery*
Shula, Don, *168*
Shumate, John, *113, 114*
Sichting, Jerry, *94, 109, 110*
Siegfried, Larry, *100*
Sigafoos, Frank, *178*
Simon, Herb, *130*
Simon, Mel, *130*
Singer, Karl, *142*
Sisti, Sebi, *178*
Sitzberger, Kenny, *Gallery*
Skiles, Scott, *97, 116*
Skoronski, Bob, *136*
Sloan, Jerry, *120*
Sloan, Norm, *94, 122*
Smith, Dean, *97, 100, 121*
Sneva, Tom, *188*
Sniadecki, Jim, *136, 137*
Sobers, Ricky, *121*
Solt, Ron, *168*
Soto, Mario, *178*
Soyez, Janice, *94, 95*
Sparks, Dan, *121*
Sparks, Joe, *177*
Spitz, Mark, *Gallery*
Splittorff, Paul W., Jr., *182*

Stack, Maria, *96*
Stacy, Hollis, *Gallery*
Stamato, Stephan, *Gallery*
Stamm, Mike, *Gallery*
Stams, Frank, *163*
Stark, Rohn, *168*
Staverman, Larry, *130*
Stephens, Everette, *113*
Stingley, Daryl, *148*
Stoddard, Tim, *94*
Stonebraker, Homer C., *91*
Stonebreaker, Michael, *163*
Stoyonovich, Pete, *139*
Stram, Hank, *141, 172, 173*
Streibeck, Pat, *Gallery*
Sullivan, Danny, *190*
Summers, Champ, *178*

Taylor, Fred, *88*
Teran, Armando, *188*
Theismann, Joe, *157, 158*
Thomas, Bob, *159*
Thomas, Darryl, *105*
Thomas, Isiah, *103, 104, 106, 117*
Thomas, Kurt, *Gallery*
Thomas, Rene, *190*
Thompson, Anthony, *139, 140*
Thompson, Chandler, *124, 125*
Thompson, Donnell, *167, 168*
Thon, Dickie, *184*
Tibbs, Jay, *178*
Tolbert, Ray, *94, 103*
Towe, Monte, *94*
Trgovich, Pete, *93, 94*
Tripucka, Kelly, *114-116*
Trout, Dizzy, *178*
Troy, Mike, *Gallery*
Trudeau, Jack, *169*
Turner, Bob, *139*
Turner, Keena, *149, 150*
Turner, Landon, *94, 103, 104*
Tyler, Fred, *Gallery*

Uecker, Bob, *178*
Underwood, Pat, *176, 178*
Underwood, Tom, *176*
Unitas, John, *172, 166*
Unser, Al, *188, 192*
Unser, Al, Jr., *190*
Unser, Bobby, *192*
Utt, Ben, *168*

VanArsdale, Dick, *90, 91, 99*
VanArsdale, Tom, *90, 91, 99*
Vandivier, Fuzzy, *93*
Vaughn, Linda, *191*
Verdin, Clarence, *169*
Vincent, Jay, *118*

228

Vogel, Matt, *Gallery*
Vukovich, Billy, III, *190*

Waiters, Van, *139*
Walls, Wayne, *109, 117*
Walsh, Donnie, *134-136*
Walther, Salt, *188*
Warn, Bob, *186*
Warren, Judi, *94*
Warren, Michael, *99*
Waters, Ricky, *163*
Watson, Lou, *99*
Weber, Richard Anthony "Dick", *Gallery*
Werblin, Sonny, *172*

Whitaker, Jodie, *96*
Wichman, Sharon, *Gallery*
Wilander, Mats, *Gallery*
Wilkerson, Bob, *94, 103*
Williams, Dallas, *178*
Williams, Perry, *144, 146*
Williamson, J.B., *Gallery*
Wilson, Glen, *176*
Windle, Bob, *Gallery*
Winningham, Herm, *178*
Wismer, Harry, *172*
Witte, Courtney, *122*
Wittman, Randy, *104, 942*
Wooden, John G., *91, 93, 94, 98, 99-101, 106, 120*

Woodson, Marv, *136*
Woodson, Mike, *94, 103*
Woodson, Rod, *150*
Woolridge, Orlando, *114-116*

Yeagley, Jerry, *139*
Young, Connie, *Gallery*
Young, Fred, *168*
Young, Jim, *148, 149*
Youngblood, Joel, *178*

Zachary, Pat, *178*
Zimmer, Don, *177*
Zoeller, Fuzzy, *Gallery*

Watermelon, watermelon
Pumpkin squash
Can we beat 'em
Yes, by gosh.

OOOOOOOH, WA WA
(Wabash College)

Heidey heidey heidy ho
Heidey heidey heidy hi
You can beat anybody,
But you can't beat us.

Heidey heidey heidey hey
Heidey heid heidey ho
We can beat anybody
That's the crazy song.

Crispus Attucks 1950s.

Felix, felix, meow, meow, meow
Short-ridge-High

(sung by girls leaning side to side)

Ride 'em in sand,
Ride 'em in lard
Tear 'em up, Bosse,
Tear 'em up, hard.

Lean to the left, lean to the right
Stand up, sit down, fight, fight, fight.
(anytime)

Fight 'em, bite 'em
Give 'em plenty!
Yay, rah Class of 1920.
(Indiana University)

Hi-Ho! Hi-O!
Ricka Racka, Boomlacka, boomlacka
Sis! Boom! Bah!
Sullivan High School
Rah, rah, rah!

Hey, Bo, Let's Go
Hump stump flumpadiddle
Jig-toom, rig-toom,
Body-moddy Cairo Ee-ro, My-ro
Haw, saw, sisboom bah
Wheatland High School,
Rah, rah, rah!
(1918)

Horn and hoof! Horn and hoof!
Hold the floor and raise the roof!
Razzle! Dazzle! Zizzle! Zip!
Monroe City, Let 'er rip!
(1920s)

Give 'em the axe, the axe, the axe
Give 'em the axe harder
Right in the neck, the neck, the neck
Right in the neck, harder.
(1920s)

Gr-r-r-r-r-r Blood!
G-r-r-r-r-r Blood!
Hit that (opponent) line.
Smash it right--
Go it, Central
Fight! fight! fight!
(1920s)

In the land of milk and honey
In the central west
Stands a school of many virtures
Ranked among the best . . .

Shortridge High School song

In the land of mud and money
In the city dump
Stands a school of many vices
Ranked among the worst

*Broad Ripple High school
version of Shortridge song
(1930s)*